P9-BYB-665

LAW

A TREASURY OF ART AND LITERATURE

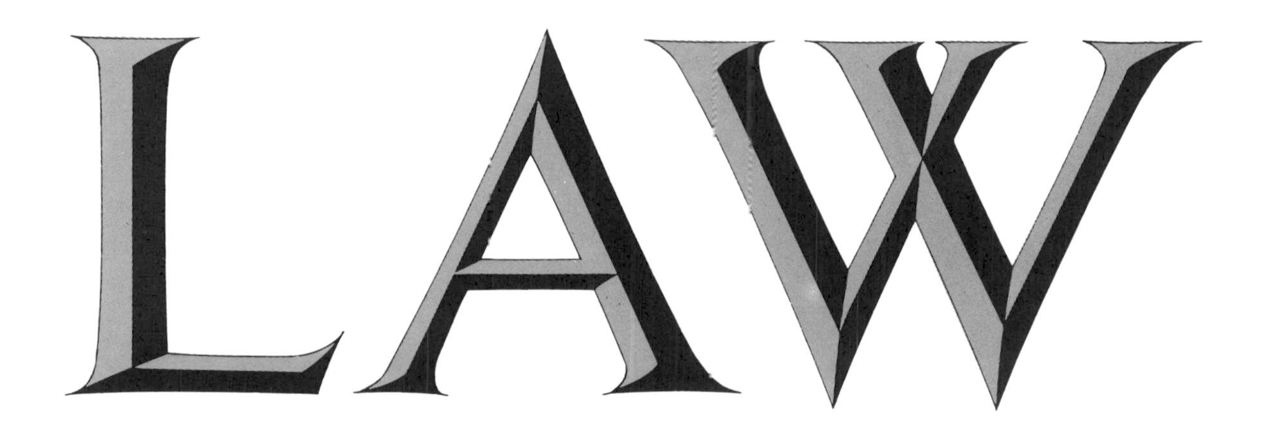

A TREASURY OF ART AND LITERATURE

Edited by Sara Robbins

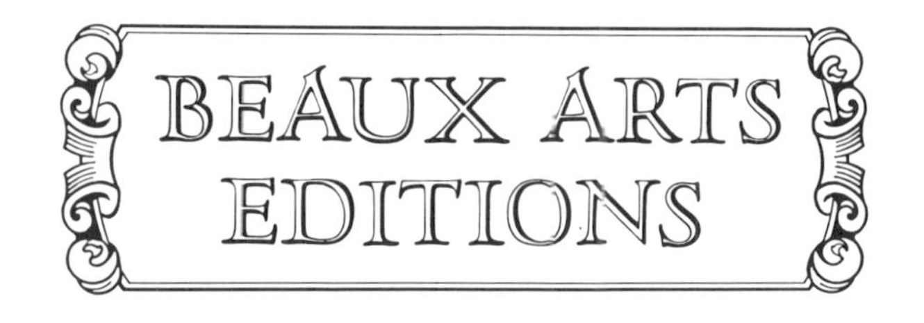

Design by Philip Grushkin
Photo research by PHOTOSEARCH, INC., New York
Typeset by A&S Graphics, Inc., Wantagh, New York
Editorial production by Harkavy Publishing Service, New York
Printed in China
ISBN 0-88363-300-0

ACKNOWLEDGMENTS

I take this opportunity to thank those individuals who have so graciously contributed their efforts to the production of this volume. My appreciation goes to Hugh Levin, the publisher, who provided the inspiration and guidance for the book, and Ellin Yassky Silberblatt for her support, patience, and management of the project. Thanks are also due to Deborah Bull and Linda Sykes of Photosearch, Inc., Whitney S. Bagnall of the Columbia University Law School Library, and Harkavy Publishing Service for their diligent efforts on behalf of this book.

I also want to express my deepest gratitude for the assistance and support provided by friends, family, and colleagues. No words can adequately express my appreciation of the generosity of Morris L. Cohen, Law Librarian and Professor of Law at Yale Law School, with both his time and his extensive knowledge of legal history materials. George Grossman, Law Librarian and Professor of Law at Northwestern University Law School, kindly loaned me the fruits of earlier efforts on his part in a similar endeavor. Bernice Loss, Curator of Art at Harvard Law School, and her able assistants provided invaluable guidance during my exploration of the Harvard Law School Art Collection, as did Michael Horn, Curator, and Barbara L. LaBorde, Assistant Curator, of the Hyder Collection at the University of Texas at Austin Law School. My sister, Kay R. Ehrenkrantz, and good friend, Elaine Lazorwitz Kokolis, both contributed extensive time and energy in assisting me in researching and preparing materials for the book; my secretary, Peggy Seddo Buono, and other members of my staff at the Brooklyn Law School Library helped when needed, without complaint. I also want to thank all who called to tell me about their favorite works, many of which are included in this volume.

SARA ROBBINS

CONTENTS

INTRODUCTION

As the title of this book suggests, we are less concerned here with the philosophy or history of law than we are with examining it as a signal artifact of human existence. The reason for its centrality to our experience is not hard to establish. Law, far more than art and literature, deals with the quotidian—the normally pedestrian, often mean, occasionally sublime, everyday practices of people. Thus we learn in great detail about societies, about our own and others', by looking—even if only cursorily—at the laws and legal procedures of each. Far from being a subject fit only for scholars and experts, law is universal, and as just a quick browse through these pages reveals, it is multifaceted, touching on almost every who, how, and wherefore of people's lives in society. As this book will show, the more things change, the more they remain in need of the law.

Law—"dry, dusty law" to its detractors—is bound to the concerns of all people on all levels—not just the upper crust, as so much of history, art, philosophy, and literature seems to be. We can read the ancient epics from cover to cover and come away with little or no idea of how people actually managed in those times. But is there anything that can convey quite so immediate a sense of past civilizations as reading their law codes? Here is the stuff of real life:

> If a man rented an ox and damaged its eye, he shall pay one half of [its] price. . . .
> If a man rented an ox and injured the flesh at the nose ring, he shall pay one third of [its] price. . . .
> If a man rented an ox and broke its horn, he shall pay one fourth of [its] price. . . .

Thus the ancient Sumerian Code of Lipit-Ishtar unwittingly gives us a peek into some real problems Sumerians faced about 2000 years before the birth of Christ. It is the code's specificity that throws the ancient world into such sharp relief. An ox damaged at the nose ring is deemed to be hurt more seriously than one with a broken horn. We could do well to imagine what future generations will make of our own welter of laws, ordinances, and trials. What *could* one make of our lawsuits, our tangled web of tax regulations, the seemingly endless stream of legislation? It's a little frightening and more than a little chastening to consider what our laws may reveal about us!

But if law opens a door into the attics and cellars of civilizations, it also affords a glimpse into their aspirations, and so we move into the chambers of literature and art in these pages, too. Simply put, law is a procedure (however crude or ultrasophisticated) for conflict management. If there were no conflicts, there would be no need for laws. But conflicts occur as certainly as the night follows the day, and conflict, too, is the wellspring of the *drama* upon which so much art and literature are founded. Because the nature of law involves conflict and people in crisis, artisans have found the law a particularly rich lode of ideas for their crafts. At the simplest level, from Tintoretto's *Susanna and the Elders* to last night's TV docudrama of a crusading attorney defending an abused woman, artists and writers have told stories of a basic human interest drawn from law. However, at another level, from Trumbull's *The Declaration of Independence* to Martin Luther King, Jr.'s greatest speeches, they have expressed in artistic creations some of humanity's highest ideals, such as liberty and justice for all.

Given that law commonly implies issues of the personal responsibility of citizens, of coercion, and of punishment, is it any wonder that artists have mined the law for its ability to call up ethical, moral, and practical questions and situations of peril, guilt, and retribution? Law deals with public and societal questions of conflict, but it just as surely involves personal questions of innocence and culpability. What does individual guilt mean? Or individual innocence, for that matter? Since Adam and Eve's expulsion from Eden the question has been asked, and it is still being asked—in law courts and in the human conscience.

The scope of the law's drama is especially evident in its most theatrical manifestation: the trial. In the following pages the reader will sample trials for heresy (Galileo), witchcraft (Joan of Arc), piracy (Captain Kidd), sedition (John Peter Zenger), murder (the slave Peter), pornography (U.S. vs. One Book Called *Ulysses*), and more. Fictional trials are here, too, dealing with mercy and justice (from Shakespeare's *The Merchant of Venice*) and what it means to be a man (from Benét's "The Devil and Daniel Webster"). We have illustrations of art prompted by legal themes ranging from Rubens' *The Judgment of Solomon* to Goya's "Inquisition Scene" to Warhol's *Red Disaster*. There is scarcely a human emotion that cannot be found in the annals of the law. To paraphrase Pogo, "We have met the law, and it is us!"

This volume does not, and could not, pretend to be comprehensive; it would require a series of volumes—enough to fill a library—to do that. Rather, it culls from different eras samples of what law meant in those periods and how artists of different ages depicted that meaning. Our aim is at once to amuse and, in the words of Agatha Christie's famous Belgian sleuth Hercule Poirot, "to stimulate the little gray cells." Dip anywhere into this book and you will find things to wonder at and to ponder over.

Societies create laws to keep chaos at bay. Where there is no law, there is only whim and force. Order, place, and degree are not fixed but rather depend on the say-so of the strongest. In Act I, scene iii, of *Troilus and Cressida,* Shakespeare has the character Ulysses depict what a world would be without law and order (which he calls "degree"):

> *Take but degree away, untune that string,*
> *And hark, what discord follows! Each thing meets*
> *In mere oppugnancy. The bounded waters*
> *Should lift their bosoms higher than the shores*
> *And make a sop of all this solid globe.*
> *Strength should be lord of imbecility,*
> *And the rude son should strike his father dead.*
> *Force should be right; or rather, right and wrong,*
> *Between whose endless jar justice resides,*
> *Should lose her names, and so should justice, too.*
> *Then everything includes itself in power,*
> *Power into will, will into appetite,*
> *And appetite, a universal wolf,*
> *So doubly seconded with will and power,*
> *Must make perforce a universal prey*
> *And last eat up himself.*

To keep that "universal wolf" from the door, societies create laws, and in so doing reveal their preoccupations, their vulnerabilities, fears, and hopes—in short, themselves. So linked to the concept of order is law that it is even used as a metaphor for the understood arrangement of things; we like to speak of "laws" in physics, chemistry, economics, and so on. The United States boasts that it is a nation "governed by laws, not men," which on the face of it seems preposterous. Yet we know instantly that it means we are governed by enunciated, publicly declared rules that are to be obeyed by all, even the powerful. Otherwise, government is by fiat, and scarcely anyone is safe.

Thus, by bitter experience, mankind has learned that liberty and security reside only where there is *mutual* constraint under a system of law. Not always liberating and protective, law has been used to oppress and to despoil. The harsh laws of the *ancien régime* in France or of Nazi Germany fashioned systems of an entirely different order from what we understand by "governed by laws."

Fortunately, laws *do* change, as societies change. Alter the values and the perceptions of a people, and their laws will follow suit. Today, for instance, an oppressive system of laws in eastern Europe and Russia that we long considered petrified has evaporated. Laws are not carved in stone but written on erasable bond. Bad law can be bettered. Legally sanctioned social injustices and inequities can be redressed. Mr. Dooley's observation, "Th' Supreme Court follows th' illection returns" is not just sardonic; it holds out the promise of hope, too. But, of course, things can go the other way; change is not always for the better. A society *in extremis* may jettison justice and decency for expediency and the quick fix. Panic makes a poor legislator, and desperation offers unreliable counsel.

Law, then, is nowhere near as firm and powerful as it seems, and even the best intentioned and most strictly written law code will not save a society bent on self-destruction. Change is a dicey business. Revolutions, often bloody, have been necessary to effect a change in the way a society thinks and hence a change in its laws. That the whole enterprise, in its mutability and utility, is fraught with danger, uncertainty, pathos, and comedy, is conveyed again and again in the readings selected for this book.

The selections begin at the ancient beginnings, providing excerpts from law codes of the early societies of Sumer and Babylonia. Note that both are codifications of laws which had already been in effect, presumably, for a long time. The Code of Lipit-Ishtar of Isin dates from around 1850 B.C., and the Code of Hammurabi from around 1780 B.C. The steles (upright, inscribed stone pillars) containing the codes are illustrated in the text. The head of the stele containing Hammurabi's code depicts the ruler receiving the law from the Babylonian sun god. A recurrent theme in law is that its authority stems from the divine.

Jewish law, as embodied in the Mosaic Code, dates from the thirteenth century B.C. Its influence on the development of Western civilization is noted—and supplemented by selected Old Testament stories that are part of our heritage. The stories of Cain and Abel, Solomon's judgment, and Susanna and the elders present legal problems of a keenly human sort and in a particularly philosophic mood. Here wisdom is especially prized, and the establishing of truth is emphasized rather than the meting out of punishment. The inherent drama of these stories has recommended them to people in later ages, far removed from the land of their origin. For example, the illustrations here include works by such later artists as Giotto, Michelangelo, Tintoretto, Rubens, and Doré.

Considerations of space permitted this volume to devote an all too brief span of pages to the vitally important Greco-Roman contribution to the development of Western law. By the seventh century B.C., it is believed, most of the Greek city-states possessed written law codes, attributed either to a ruler or to a commissioned compiler. The Athenian politician Drakon (also Draco or Dracon; fl. 621 B.C.) is famous as a law codifier, but all that remains of his work is the selection included here on involuntary homicide. From other references, such as Aristotle and Plutarch, we learn that Drakon's approach to law enforcement was hard-line in the extreme, with even trivial crimes punishable by death. Today we still apply the term "draconian" to especially harsh regulations. Another noted Greek lawgiver, Solon (c. 639–c. 559 B.C.) reformed the Athenian law system around 594 B.C.

The Greek city-states guarded their independence, making it impossible to have a unitary law system throughout the country, though many of the local codes shared common elements. As the selections from Protagoras, Plato, and Aristotle show, the Greeks had a speculative turn of mind and tended to concern themselves more with abstract questions of government and ethics that with nitty-gritty legislation. Their approach could be playful, as in Protagoras' conundrum, or deadly serious, as in Plato's account of Socrates' trial. The trial of Phryne, shown in an illustration, bears out the peculiarly unrigorous Greek approach to matters of law.

It was Rome, with its more down-to-earth sensibility, that put the law on a practically structured footing. (Romans were inclined to view themselves as *gravitas*, while they saw the Greeks as *levitas*.) From Augustus Caesar on, Roman law reflected the growth of the Roman Empire, which lasted until about 476 A.D. and encompassed, at its height, the entire Mediterranean, most of Western Europe including Britain, and Asia Minor. To order and organize this civilization, the Romans developed a systematic and comprehensive legal system whose impact is still felt in the modern world. Roman jurists studied, analyzed, discussed, and wrote about law as a serious intellectual discipline, and from these studies a new legal profession was created that concentrated on legal literature, thought, and education. The politician and philosopher Marcus Tullius Cicero (106–43 B.C.) whose orations against the conspirator Catiline (see illustration) are still studied today, exemplifies this Roman approach to law.

After the Western half of the Empire ended in A.D. 476, the Eastern Empire, centered in Constantinople, continued to develop Roman law. Justinian (who reigned A.D. 527 to 565), commissioned the collection, organization, and revision of the constitutions (the *Codex*) and the jurists' writings (the *Digest*). He also compiled a basic law manual for students (the *Institutes*). These efforts preserved much historical Roman law, which served as the basis for later legal systems throughout Europe. Not all the effects of law were so salubrious, though, as can be seen in the selection from Edward Gibbon, which, if not an example of out-and-out lawyer-bashing, certainly sounds a familiar note of dismay about over-lawyering.

The so-called Middle Ages saw Europe wracked by invasions and wars that divided it into numerous Germanic kingdoms, each possessing its own military and legal customs. As the kingdoms expanded and matured, Roman legal traditions were influenced by these tribal systems, to say the least. The *Fuero Juzgo*, illustrated in these pages, was a law code for both Visigoths and Romans, in which the territorial law of the Visigoth kingdom supplanted the personal law in Spain.

Clovis I (466–511) began as king of the Salian Franks, a Germanic tribe living along the lower and middle Rhine. By the time Clovis died, he had expanded Frankish rule to embrace almost all of Gaul (France) and southwest Germany. He united all the Frankish tribes, converted to Christianity, settled on Paris as the center of the kingdom, and had the warrior ways of the Franks written down and revised as the *lex Salica*.

In England, things were different. The Germanic Anglo-Saxons, who overcame the earlier Romanized Celts of the island, chose to preserve their own language and customary law and eliminated most of the Roman tradition that still existed. Over time, Anglo-Saxon kings compiled local customary laws into codes, promulgated them, and supplemented them from time to time by further royal enactments. These compilations come down to us as the purest statement of Germanic law as it existed then, for they were not influenced by Roman law, as were those of the Germanic tribes (like the Franks) on the Continent. After the Norman Conquest of 1066, William the Conquerer chose not to impose Norman law or other Roman-based law traditions on the Anglo-Saxons; rather, he opted for maintaining the existing laws. These he in fact strengthened, by erecting a more centralized and efficient government to carry them out. His concentration on a system of land tenure contributed to the development of common law in England, which assumed its basic characteristics during the reign of Henry II (1154–1189): Centralized courts of law had definite jurisdictional responsibilities; itinerant judges represented the King's justice throughout the country; a professional judiciary and bar had its beginnings; stronger procedures guided the administration of justice; trial by jury was instituted; and judicial decisions assumed growing importance as a source of law.

Magna Carta, to which King John was forced by his barons to fix his seal in 1215, fixed limitations on the king's power for the first time. The Inns of Court, another fascinating medieval creation, arose to serve the legal profession, especially in the training of lawyers, as legal doctrines, particularly in property, contract, and tort law, were becoming more refined and complicated.

On the Continent during this period, legal procedures, canon law, commercial and maritime law, and more, were developing as sophisticated and studiously written systems as the countries of Europe became more centralized. Fashioning their own bodies of law, societies such as that of the Saxons produced beautifully illuminated documents befitting their importance—our text illustrates the *Mirror of Saxony* as but one proud example.

The thirteenth century saw the rediscovery and revival of the law of Justinian, especially in Bologna, increasing the influence of Roman law on existing legal systems. The legal profession itself expanded in most continental countries, creating a large community of judges, scholars, lawyers, and educators. Germany, perceiving itself as the inheritor of the Roman Empire, aggressively adopted Roman law during the fifteenth century. France split into two regions, with the north relying mainly upon Germanic-based customary law and canon law, and the south upon Roman law. It would not have a unified legal system for the whole country until after the French Revolution.

Law engaged the talents of medieval artists. The Inquisition, which began around 1231 and lasted well into the 1800s, prompted numerous works; so did trials by combat and fire and medieval forms of punishment. The illustration of drawing and quartering particularly reminds us why "medieval" is sometimes used to connote a certain dark side of human capabilities.

The text at this point takes a quick detour for a look at legal systems in the East, which, like those of the West, arose generally from religion and custom. These systems' early origins have remained strongly influential. Eastern religions and philosophies (particularly Confucianism) stressed ethical behavior, or right conduct, and clearly enunciated rules of propriety for all social relationships. These rules were supplemented by written codes of penal law, in existence since at least the sixth century B.C.

The Confucian ideal of harmony between man and nature led to the concept that moral conduct consists in seeking harmony in situations of conflict. This in turn fostered an Asian preference for mediation and conciliation, rather than litigation, as a way for settling disputes. This approach continues in the East today, even after exposure to the very different focus of the Western law tradition.

The text selections include a piece on early Chinese law, one on Japanese law, and a statement by Mohandas K. Gandhi, on his conviction for sedition by the British Raj. Artistic renderings of legal subjects seem rare in the East, perhaps due to moral or social strictures on depicting rulers or ruling classes.

Modern legal history begins with the Renaissance. Roman law still formed the basis of most European legal systems, except in England. The Reformation, however, weakened the influence of the pope and altered the roles of canon law and the ecclesiastical courts. Moreover, the invention of printing and the rediscovery of classical learning and art stimulated new ways of thinking in many fields, including law. Liberalized thought explored concepts like natural right and consent of the governed that challenged the old bases of jurisprudence. Across Europe new national legal structures took on a remarkably similar shape. In contrast, the common-law system in England concentrated on the development of judge-made law, basing its legal practice on the concepts of precedent and *stare decisis*.

An entertaining assortment of comments on the law emerges from this period, as the text selections show. Lawyers are likely to catch it pretty heavily, especially in the William Cole excerpt, and they don't come off too well in *Hamlet*, either. (A loftier consideration of the legal profession can be found in the Francis Bacon essay.) Renditions of the characters in Shakespeare's *The Merchant of Venice* appear with the famous trial from that play and more recent reflections on its exemplification (or not) of good lawyering. The quintessential Galileo and the Lefebvre selections reflect not only how the new thinking of the Renaissance came into conflict with, and worked to change, established "truth," but also how the law figured in when questions of order—perceiving it, maintaining it, and so on—became no longer academic ones.

English common law underwent a sea change on the trip across the Atlantic as the New World was settled. Adapted to the special needs of the individual colonies, the law was improvised upon by each colony to suit its own particular situation. The age of Enlightenment notwithstanding, the law proved, in Salem, Massachusetts, that irrationality can be its driving force. Subsequent events in human history have demonstrated that the tragic witch trials—which hardly epitomized colonial America's exercise of the law—were no mere last-gasp of medieval darkness.

In the early days of the nation, there was a strong anti-lawyer campaign for the administration of justice without lawyers that led to legislation curtailing the activities of attorneys. In addition, there were few trained lawyers in the colonies and few books besides Blackstone's *Commentaries* from which to learn the complexities of the English legal system. As the eighteenth century progressed, more English legal materials were imported, more American lawyers were trained at the Inns of Court, and a more strict supervision of the colonies on the part of the English government was imposed. Nevertheless, the colonies continued to develop their own legal systems. They often refused to accept English laws—or laws from anywhere else, for that matter—unless they were specifically approved by their local governing bodies. They adapted whatever they borrowed to suit their less formal, less structured society. Of course, the American colonists developed a strong sense of independence, with a deep appreciation for the ideals of the rights of the individual, such as freedom of the press, speech, and assembly.

From the Declaration of Independence on, the American legal system was pretty much self-reliant in developing its own tradition. The selections in this section of the book give evidence of the "new dawn" approach of the American bar to law (see especially the excerpt from Erwin Surrency's article on the lawyers' role in the Revolution.) More mundane matters pertaining to the practice of law in eighteenth-century America are briefly touched on, too. That the excitement of the revolutionary era has fired the imagination of American artists, as one would expect, is amply illustrated.

France, America's ally in the Revolution, was the next setting for social upheaval. What of its legal traditions? During the sixteenth century, the customary laws in France had been officially compiled, with each province producing its own local code. These codes allowed for a distillation into a common customary law, and ultimately the *Coutume de Paris* was considered the standard French law by other countries. In the next two centuries, royal legislation was also systematized into new codes affecting major areas of the law. Jurists produced significant French legal treatises while continuing codification efforts, and much of their work survived, with modifications, to shape the law after the French Revolution swept away the absolutist monarchy. Codification of French law was undertaken again at the behest of Napoleon Bonaparte: the French Civil Code (1804), the Code of Civil Procedure (1806), the Commercial Code and the Criminal Procedure Code (1808), and the Penal Code (1811). The emperor is depicted gloriously with his code in the painting by J.B. Mauzaisse—appropriately, for the Napoleonic code, in its impact upon legal systems throughout the world, was probably his greatest legacy.

A great sweep of European history can only be suggested by the selections from this point. Some are pressed into service—pieces from Charles Dickens, Guy de Maupassant, Oscar Wilde, for instance—to hint at the literary works enriched by the drama of the law that lie, as it were, at the back of this treasury. (There are baubles, too, from W.S. Gilbert, Lewis Carroll, and other humorists.) Certain continuities have been indicated, on the other hand—as in the excerpts from Zola's *J'Accuse*, Willig's "The Bar in the Third Reich," and Jackson's "Summation of the Prosecution at Nuremburg." One highlight of the art works illustrating this sweep of European culture is four of Honoré Daumier's immortal cartoons on the law profession.

During the nineteenth century, the United States grew from a small, isolated, largely rural democracy to a mighty industrial republic with worldwide interests and commitments. That period of expansion provides a number of writings and pictures that show the advance of the law onto frontier America. On the forefront of this period of legal history is the Marshall Court, a landmark in the development of the Supreme Court, which is certainly America's unique gift to jurisprudence. Difficult issues faced our legal institutions and the nation—religious freedom, slavery, women's rights, and the rights of minorities. It's not to our discredit that many of these same questions are still under discussion today; they form, after all, the warp and woof of our social fabric, and generation after generation will have to ravel and unravel them, each in its own way.

Artists found much to depict in this period, ranging from portraits of great jurists of the American mainstream (Daniel Webster, Oliver Wendell Holmes, Jr.) to something more improvisatory but just as American (Matteson's *Justice's Court in the Backwoods*). Also of interest are works like Pippin's *John Brown Going to His Hanging*, and Schultze's *Dred Scott*, which deal with questions of crime and of justice that cut very deep during the nation's expansionary era.

The book winds up with numerous writings about lawyering, in most cases *by* lawyers, among them Clarence Darrow, Roscoe Pound, Benjamin Cardozo, Erle Stanley Gardner, Leon Jaworski, Melvin Belli, Louis Nizer, and Seymour Wishman. The big trials make the big stories, reflecting the influence of the mass media on modern society—and its interaction with the law. Such disparate cases as the Scopes trial, the Sacco and Vanzetti affair, and the trial of James Joyce's novel *Ulysses*. Additionally, modern fiction—including the movies—yields selections by Stephen Vincent Benét, Robert O'Neil Bristow, and George S. Kaufman and Morrie Ryskind (on behalf of the Marx brothers). In the clash of state power with the law we find, perhaps, the most significant emblem of our nation's aspirations as they survive in the crucible of twentieth-century life. Two heroes, Joseph Welch and Leon Jaworski, led the way to a reaffirmation of the rule of law in postwar affairs, but whether their victories are secure is a question we shall want to keep asking ourselves. There are legal horizons before us.

The volume's final piece, an excerpt from a recent novel by the estimable Louis Auchincloss (surely a personification of law and literature's conjoining), represents American modernity on the brink of post-modernity. Thus pointing to the mutability of human affairs with which this introductory essay began, this book tries to broaden our sense of the law away from the anecdotes of the court docket and toward the universal. Always in flux, the law could yet be safely said to have a future. It is an ongoing story in which all humanity plays a part. This treasury is but a brief sampling of that rich and vibrant "artifact" of the lives of all people throughout time.

ANCIENT BEGINNINGS

FROM THE CODE OF LIPIT-ISHTAR

. . . When Anu and Enlil had called Lipit-Ishtar—Lipit-Ishtar the wise shepherd whose name had been pronounced by Nunamnir—to the princeship of the land in order to establish justice in the land, to banish complaints, to turn back enmity and rebellion by force of arms, and to bring well-being to the Sumerians and Akkadians, then I, Lipit-Ishtar, the humble shepherd of Nippur, the stalwart farmer of Ur, who abandons not Eridu, the suitable lord of Erech, king of Isin, king of Sumer and Akkad, who am fit for the heart of Inanna, established justice in Sumer and Akkad in accordance with the word of Enlil.

★ ★ ★

If a man entered the orchard of (another) man and was seized there for stealing, he shall pay ten shekels of silver.

★ ★ ★

If a man cut down a tree in the garden of (another) man, he shall pay one half mina of silver.

★ ★ ★

If adjacent to the house of a man the bare ground of (another) man has been neglected and the owner of the house has said to the owner of the bare ground, "Because your ground has been neglected someone may break into my house: strengthen your house," and this agreement has been confirmed by him, the owner of the bare ground shall restore to the owner of the house any of his property that is lost.

★ ★ ★

If a man married a wife and she bore him children and those children are living, and a slave also bore children for her master (but) the father granted freedom to the slave and her children, the children of the slave shall not divide the estate with the children of their (former) master.

★ ★ ★

If a man's wife has not borne him children but a harlot (from) the public square has borne him children, he shall provide grain, oil and clothing for that harlot; the children which the harlot has borne him shall be his heirs, and as long as his wife lives the harlot shall not live in the house with the wife.

★ ★ ★

The identification in the 1930s of four tablet fragments from Nippur established Lipit-Ishtar, ruler of Isin from 1868 to 1857 B.C., as the earliest-known codifier of law and gave historians a long-awaited law code in the Sumerian language.

Code of Lipit-Ishtar: Reverse of Fragment C of Code Tablet. From Nippur, Iraq. c. 1860 B.C. Cuneiform tablet. 3⅛ × 4 × 1¼" (7.9 × 10.1 × 3.1 cm). The University Museum, University of Pennsylvania, Philadelphia.

If a man rented an ox and injured the flesh at the nose ring, he shall pay one third of (its) price.

* * *

If a man rented an ox and damaged its eye, he shall pay one half of (its) price.

* * *

If a man rented an ox and broke its horn, he shall pay one fourth of (its) price.

* * *

If a man rented an ox and damaged its tail, he shall pay one fourth of (its) price.

FROM THE CODE OF HAMMURABI

When the lofty Anu, king of the Anunnaki, and Enlil, lord of heaven and earth, who determines the destinies of the land, committed the rule of all mankind to Marduk, the first-born son of Ea, and made him great among the Igigi; when they pronounced the lofty name of Babylon, made it great among the quarters of the world and in its midst established for him an everlasting kingdom whose foundations were firm as heaven and earth—at that time Anu and Enlil named me, Hammurabi, the exalted prince, the worshiper of the gods, to cause righteousness to prevail in the land, to destroy the wicked and the evil, to prevent the strong from plundering the weak, to go forth like the sun over the black-headed race, to enlighten the land and to further the welfare of the people.

* * *

If a man accuse a man, and charge him with murder, but cannot convict him, the accuser shall be put to death.

* * *

Before the discovery of Lipit-Ishtar's code, the code of the Babylonian king Hammurabi (reigned c. 1792–1750 B.C.) was thought to be the first and most important codification of law. The later code, which was written in the Akkadian language, was discovered in Susa in 1901.

If a man charge a man with sorcery, but cannot convict him, he who is charged with sorcery shall go to the sacred river, and he shall throw himself into the river; if the river overcome him, his prosecutor shall take to himself his house. If the river show that man to be innocent and he come forth unharmed, he that charged him with sorcery shall be put to death. He who threw himself into the river shall take to himself the house of his accuser.

* * *

If a judge pronounce a judgment, render a decision, deliver a sealed verdict, and afterward reverse his judgment, they shall prosecute the judge for reversing the judgment which he has pronounced, and he shall pay twelve fold the damages which were (awarded) in said judgment; and publicly they shall expel him from his seat of judgment, and he shall not return, and with the judges in a case he shall not take his seat.

* * *

If a man steal ox or sheep, ass or pig, or boat—if it belonged to god or palace, he shall pay thirty fold; if it belonged to a common man, he shall restore tenfold. If the thief have nothing wherewith to pay, he shall be put to death.

* * *

If a man aid a male or a female slave of the palace, or a male or a female slave of a common man, to escape from the city, he shall be put to death.

* * *

If a fire break out in a man's house and a man who goes to extinguish it cast his eye on the household property of the owner of the house, and take the household property of the owner of the house, that man shall be thrown into the fire.

* * *

If a man owe a debt and Adad [the storm god] inundate the field or the flood carry the produce away, or, through lack of water, grain have not grown in the field, in that year he shall not make any return of grain to the creditor, he shall alter his contract-tablet and he need not pay the interest for that year.

* * *

If a man who is a tenant have paid the full amount of money for his rent for the year to the owner of the house, and he (the owner) say to him before "his days are full," "Vacate," the owner of the house, because he made the tenant move out of his house before "his days were full," shall lose the money which the tenant paid him.

* * *

If a man receive grain or silver from a merchant and do not have grain or silver to repay, but have personal property, whatever there is in his hand, when he brings it before witnesses, he shall give to the merchant. The merchant shall not refuse (it), he shall receive (it).

* * *

If the agent be careless and do not take a receipt for the money which he has given to the merchant, the money not receipted for shall not be placed to his account.

* * *

If a priestess or a nun who is not resident in a convent open a wineshop or enter a wineshop for a drink, they shall burn that woman.

* * *

If the wife of a man be taken in lying with another man, they shall bind them and throw them into the water. If the husband of the woman spare the life of his wife, the king shall spare the life of his servant.

★ ★ ★

If a woman hate her husband and say, "Thou shalt not have me," her past shall be inquired into for any deficiency of hers; and if she have been careful and be without past sin and her husband have been going out and greatly belittling her, that woman has no blame. She shall take her dowry and go to her father's house.

★ ★ ★

If a man, after (the death of) his father, lie in the bosom of his mother, they shall burn both of them.

★ ★ ★

If a man take a wife and she bear him children and that woman die, her father may not lay claim to her dowry. Her dowry belongs to her children.

★ ★ ★

If a man destroy the eye of another man, they shall destroy his eye.

★ ★ ★

If he break a man's bone, they shall break his bone.

★ ★ ★

If a man knock out a tooth of a man of his own rank, they shall knock out his tooth.

★ ★ ★

If he knock out a tooth of a common man, he shall pay one-third mana of silver.

★ ★ ★

If a man hire an ox and cause its death through neglect or abuse, he shall restore ox for ox to the owner of the ox.

★ ★ ★

If an ox when passing through the street gore a man and bring about his death, that case has no penalty.

Stele of Hammurabi, detail. From Susa, Iran. c. 1750 B.C. Basalt stele. Full height: approximately 88″ high (223.5 cm). Louvre, Paris.

David Werner Amram

FROM LEADING CASES IN THE BIBLE

"The Murder of Abel"

The record of the first murder case is found in the fourth chapter of Genesis. The history of the crime, its motive, the trial and sentence are all given in a few terse phrases, clearly enough to enable us, with little effort, to reconstruct the entire incident. The facts of the case are as follows: Cain and Abel were brothers; Cain was an agriculturist and Abel a herdsman. At a certain time each of them brought an offering unto the Lord; Cain's offering consisted of the fruits of the ground and Abel's offering of the firstlings of his flock and the fat thereof. For some reason not given, the Lord accepted the offering of Abel and turned from the offering of Cain, "and Cain was very wroth and his countenance fell." His anger appears to have turned against his brother, and although the Lord warned him against yielding to it, he bided his time and "it came to pass when they were in the field that Cain rose up against Abel his brother and slew him." This is the record of the case in all its simplicity; a crime, common enough at all times, committed under the influence of jealousy, hatred and anger.

The suggestion made in the case of Adam and Eve, that the popular imagination conceived the Deity administering justice in the manner of the patriarchal chieftain of that time applies to this case also. Here God cautioned the enraged Cain to govern his anger, lest it be translated into action, but Cain remained deaf to the voice of conscience and, taking advantage of the opportunity when he was alone with Abel in the field, killed him. The legend gives no reason why the offering of Abel was accepted and the offering of Cain refused, and assumes that there was no sufficient justification for the crime. But whatever may have been the reason for God's refusal of Cain's offering, it can hardly have any bearing on the legal aspect of the case. Comparative sociology and folklore suggest various reasons with which at present we are not concerned . . . .

The only witness to the crime was the blood of the murdered Abel, which, according to the primitive notion of the time, had a voice and cried out for vengeance, and was heard by God, who appears for the purpose of conducting an investigation. He summons Cain to appear before him and, as in Adam's case, immediately subjects him to a cross-examination. The only facts that could have been known were these, that Cain and Abel were seen going out to the field together and that Cain returned without his brother, of whom no trace was found except the blood stains in the field. Suspicion naturally fell upon Cain, who was brought before his judge, and addressed by one of those short incisive questions which are the delight of the Cadi and the admiration of the people, "Where is Abel thy brother?" When Adam was asked, "Hast thou eaten of the tree whereof I commanded thee that thou shouldest not eat?" he promptly confessed. When Cain was asked, "Where is Abel thy brother?" he answered, "I know not. Am I my brother's keeper?" This answer naturally strengthened the suspicion that he was the murderer. An innocent man accused of fratricide would hardly have given an answer like this, which not only breathed defiance and showed an unexpected and, therefore, highly significant heartlessness, but even alluded sarcastically to his dead brother's occupation as a keeper of sheep, whose duty it was to guard them from ravening wild animals. "Am I my brother's keeper?" asked Cain, sarcastically. "Is it my duty to look after him as he looks after his sheep?" Cain made no further attempt to defend himself, apparently relying on the fact than no witnesses could be produced against him, and that silence was his best

---

Perhaps the best-known homicide in western civilization is the case of fratricide set forth in the Book of Genesis, 4:1–16.

GUSTAVE DORÉ. *The Death of Abel.* From *La Saint Bible.* 1866. Engraving.

defense. But he forgot that he left a witness crying out against him in the field, and his denial of the crime is brushed aside in the next question put to him, "What hast thou done? The voice of thy brother's blood crieth unto me from the ground. . . ."

It can hardly be said that Cain was tried for his crime, because the method of examination was the merest rudiment of what subsequently became an orderly system of procedure in judicial investigation. As his guilt was assumed from the circumstances of the case and, beyond a bare denial, he made no attempt to defend himself, the sentence of the Court followed immediately. His punishment was not death, but exile.

The first statute on the subject of homicide is recorded in Genesis IX, 6, "Whoso sheddeth man's blood, by man shall his blood be shed." Cain feared death, saying, "every one that findeth me will slay me"; but this had no reference to lawful punishment for his crime, but to the fact that by being exiled he was outlawed and compelled to wander away from the settled habitations of men into the surrounding wilderness, where there was neither family, nor law, nor God to protect him. The sentence was pronounced in these words, "And now art thou cursed from the earth, which hath opened her mouth to receive thy brother's blood from thy hand. When thou tillest the ground it shall not henceforth yield unto thee her strength; a fugitive and a vagabond shalt thou be in the earth." After this sentence was pronounced Cain no longer denied the crime, but impliedly confessed, saying, "My punishment is greater than I can bear. Behold, thou hast driven me out this day from the face of the earth; and from thy face shall I be hid; and I shall be a fugitive and a vagabond in the earth; and it shall come to pass that every one that findeth me shall slay me." And the Lord said unto him, "Therefore, whosoever slayeth Cain vengeance shall be taken on him sevenfold." And the Lord set a mark upon Cain, lest any one finding him should kill him. And Cain went out from the presence of the Lord and dwelt in the land of Nod, on the east of Eden.

David Werner Amram

FROM LEADING CASES IN THE BIBLE

"The Judgment of Solomon"

The king was seated on the judgment seat in his great hall, when two women that were harlots entered and stood before him. The one woman said, "Oh, my lord, I and this woman dwell in one house and I gave birth to a child with her in the house, and on the third day that I was delivered this woman was delivered also, and we were together, no stranger was with us in the house, save we two alone. And the child of this woman died in the night for she overlaid it, and she arose at midnight and took my child from me and she laid it in her bosom, and her child, the dead one, she laid in my bosom. And when I arose in the morning to give suck to my child, behold, he was dead, but when I had considered it in the morning, behold, it was not my son which I did bear."

Then said the other woman, "Nay, for my son is the living one and thy son is the dead." And this one said, "Nay, for thy son is the dead one and my son is the living." Thus they spoke before the king.

Upon this state of facts the king was asked to render judgment—a test worthy of his wisdom. Here was the statement of one against the statement of the other, no witnesses being produced by either side, no husband, friend or relative to add to the weight of the testimony of either of the parties. The legend states the fact in such a manner as to preclude any judgment based upon ordinary methods of investigation, and requiring the exercise of extraordinary sagacity to discover the truth. It may be, that by cross-examination Solomon might have confounded the liar and brought out the truth, and it may be presumed that he was a cross-examiner *par excellence*, but this method would not have satisfied the exigencies of the legend. What would have delighted a lawyer would have bored a layman and legends do not spring up among lawyers. The popular imagination does not follow the intricacies of close reasoning, nor has it the patience to unravel painfully the thread of a fine spun argument. It delights in swift and sudden changes of situation and in a sensational cutting of the Gordian knot. In the popular mind, the great judge is he whose methods are direct, swift and striking.

The king having heard the statements of the women, fell a thinking about the case and repeated their words. This one says, "My son is the living and thy son the dead"; and that one says, "Nay, thy son is the dead and mine the living." Some Bible commentators find the clue to the judgment in the manner in which the women made these statements. The false woman, whose object was to retain possession of the living child, shows it in her eagerness to claim him, saying, "Mine is the living and thine the dead." It is the living child, the one she has in her possession, that she emphatically names first, whereas the true mother, who has the dead child thrust on her, says, "Nay, thine is the dead child and mine is the living." She desires to be rid of the dead child and regain possession of her own child. The value of this suggestion is left to psychologists; it could hardly have been the means of giving light in so difficult a case. But whether this was the clue or not, the king, after having repeated these words of the women, suddenly cried out, "Fetch me a sword."

His repetition of the pleas before proceeding to judgment is approved by the Talmudists, who made it a rule that the judge, before rendering judgment, must publicly state the case of both sides, very much in the manner in which a judge sums up to the jury. On the other hand, his abrupt call for a sword is severely condemned by some

---

The most famous legend surrounding the reign of King Solomon of Israel (973–933 B.C.) is told in the First Book of Kings, 3:16–28.

Talmudists as an act unworthy of a judge, who sought by illegal means to frighten the parties and who, had his sentence of judgment been carried out, might have caused the death of an innocent child. It must be remembered that the Talmudists who lived under a highly developed system of jurisprudence, which compelled judges to follow an orderly and well regulated system of procedure, could not countenance the capricious methods of an irresponsible judge, even though he were the king. Hence Rabbi Judah, a great master of the law, and the compiler of the great code known as the Mishnah, said, "If I had been present when he said, 'Fetch me a sword,' I would have put a rope around his neck, for if God had not been merciful and prompted the mother to give up her child rather than see it die, it would surely have been killed by him." Evidently the ancient methods of procedure found little favor in the eyes of Rabbi Judah. In fact the Talmudists were rather impatient of the primitive methods of the biblical law, even of the law of Moses, and they sought under the influence of more refined theories of law and procedure to modify the severity of the ancient Mosaic law, even going so far as to abrogate it entirely when it was found to be out of harmony with the conditions and requirements of a later stage of civilization.

When the king cried out "Fetch me a sword," he was probably eyeing the two women and noting the effect of his order. At this point, one might suppose that the false woman would have shown signs of terror and could easily, by a question or two, have been made to confess her fault. But, no, the legend is not satisfied with such proof of Solomon's wisdom; as yet there is no climax to the wrought up feelings of the popular mind. And now comes the climax in all its magnificence. Imagine the Eastern professional story teller telling this tale and gradually working up to the words, "Cut the living child in two, and give one-half to the one, and one-half to the other." The death of the child is to be the touchstone by which to discover the mother. Josephus, in his account of this scene, makes the king order both the living and dead child to be divided, so that absolute equity shall

GUSTAVE DORÉ. *Judgment of Solomon.* From *La Saint Bible.* 1866. Engraving.

be observed in the division. The story would have had a sad ending if the mother had fainted when the sword was produced, and the sentence had been carried out. However, the story teller will not leave us in the lurch. It is his purpose to show that Solomon was wise, and he may be safely trusted to get over the difficult places.

The king's threat had the desired effect, for the mother of the living child cried out, "Oh my lord, give her the living child and do not kill it," but the other woman said, "Let it be neither mine nor thine; divide it." Now what possessed the woman to make such a statement? What reason was there for her demand that the child should be killed? How lame and impotent a conclusion to her case, which, up to this time, she had conducted with so much pertinacity, boldness and skill. She had stolen the living child from its mother, presumably because she wanted it; she had resisted the mother's demands for it, presumably because she wanted to keep it; she had even compelled the mother to go before the king himself to get her child, and there in the royal presence she had thus far, under great stress, maintained her right of possession, and now at the very moment of her triumph, when the mother publicly relinquished her rights and acquiesced in her possession, she not only declines to take it, but insists upon its destruction. What can be the reason for such unreasonableness?

Let us suppose that after the mother had said, "Give her the living child but do not kill it," the false woman had said nothing. Solomon would have been compelled to give the child to the wrong woman and a good story would have been spoiled, because there would have been no way of determining whether the true mother or the false claimant was the one who said, "Give her the living child but do not kill it." This might as well have been said by the mother who was in terror lest her child be killed, as by the false woman who was seized with remorse at the last moment and prayed that the child might not be killed. Now the reason for the remarkable statement of the false woman appears. The legend had to add these words in order to make it clear to the popular mind that the woman who wanted to save the child was indeed the true mother, by contrasting with her words those of the false woman who was thus made base even to fiendishness. And thus the famous words of Solomon, "Fetch me a sword," are justified and virtue is triumphant, for the king said, "Give her the living child, and do not kill it; she is its mother."

Max I. Dimont

FROM JEWS, GOD AND HISTORY

On Mosaic Law

The Mosaic Code . . . was the first truly judicial, written code, and eclipsed previously known laws with its all-encompassing humanism, its passion for justice, its love of democracy. It also helped to establish a new Jewish character and directed Jewish thinking into new paths which tended to set the Jews further apart from their neighbors.

The ideological content of these Mosaic laws is of great interest. Here we find the Jewish concept of the state and philosophy of law. These laws were essentially divided

---

According to scholar Max Dimont, the ancient Hebrews were the first people to embody in their code of laws a passion for justice and a democratic spirit. Written by Moses, the code served as their legal system for over eight centuries. This excerpt is taken from Dimont's popular study published in 1962.

MICHELANGELO
(MICHELANGELO BUONARROTI).
Moses, detail. 1513–1516.
Marble.
Approximately 8′4″ high
(2m 54cm).
San Pietro in Vincoli, Rome.

into three categories: those dealing with man's relation to man, those dealing with man's relation to the state, and those dealing with man's relation to God.

The laws of Moses anticipate the statehood God promised the Israelites. Though at this juncture of their history the Jews are still nomads, the Code of Moses is not for a nomadic people. These laws of Moses are designed to safeguard a national entity, not merely the family unit, though individual rights are never subordinated to the needs of the state. The lofty framework of these laws permitted the emergence of a democratic form of government virile enough to last eight hundred years until the Prophets in turn renovated them. The American Constitution thus far has weathered less than two hundred years.

The Mosaic Code laid down the first principles for a separation of church and state, a concept not encountered again in world history until three thousand years later, during the Enlightenment in the eighteenth century of our era. In the Mosaic Code the civil authority was independent of the priesthood. Though it is true that the priesthood had the right to settle cases not specifically covered by Mosaic law (Deuteronomy 17:8–12), that did not place it above the civil government. The priesthood was charged with the responsibility of keeping this government within the framework of Mosaic law, just as the United States Supreme Court is not above the federal government but is, nevertheless, charged with the responsibility of keeping it within the framework of the Constitution. Moses also laid the foundation for another separation, which has since become indispensable to any democracy. He created an independent judiciary.

There is a curious resemblance between the philosophic outlook of American constitutional law and that of Mosaic law. The federal government has only the powers specifically granted to it by the Constitution. The individual states can do anything not specifically denied to them. In essence, the Mosaic law also established the principle that the Jews could do anything not specifically denied to them. Instead of saying "Do such and such a thing," the laws of Moses usually say "Don't do this or that." Even where the Mosaic law makes a positive statement, it is often either an amendment to a negative commandment or else hemmed in by a negative admonition, saying, in effect, "When you do this, then don't do that." The Ten Commandments, for instance, list only three *do's* but seven *don'ts*. The three positive commandments are: "I am the Lord thy God"; observe the Sabbath; and honor your parents. The seven *don'ts* leave little doubt as to what one is not supposed to do. By fencing in only the negative, Moses left an open field for positive action. This allowed the Jews great flexibility. As long as they did not do anything specifically prohibited, they could, like the individual American states, do anything they wanted to do. This type of thinking led Jewish philosophers into stating their maxims in negations.

We can see this gulf in thinking interestingly illustrated in a maxim attributed by Christians to Jesus and by Jews to Hillel, one of the great teachers of Judaism. According to the Christians, Jesus said, "*Do* unto others what you want others *to do* unto you." According to the Jews, Hillel, who lived 100 years before Jesus, said, "*Do not do* unto others want you *don't want* others to do unto you." There is a world of philosophic difference between these two expressions, and the reader is invited to ponder on them and reason out why he would prefer one to the other as applied to himself.

In reading these laws, formulated some three thousand years ago, one is amazed at their humanitarianism. One cannot help but wonder if the world would not be better off today if these laws, in the main, had been universally adopted.

FROM THE APOCRYPHA

"Susanna and the Elders"

There dwelt a man in Babylon, called Joacim: and he took a wife, whose name was Susanna, the daughter of Chelcias, a very fair woman, and one that feared the Lord. Her parents also were righteous, and taught their daughter according to the law of Moses.

Now Joacim was a great rich man, and had a fair garden joining unto his house: and to him resorted the Jews; because he was more honorable than all others.

The same year were appointed two of the ancients of the people to be judges, such as the Lord spoke of, that wickedness came from Babylon from ancient judges, who seemed to govern the people. These kept much at Joacim's house: and all that had any suits in law came unto them.

Now when the people departed away at noon, Susanna went into her husband's garden to walk. And the two elders saw her going in every day, and walking; so that their lust was inflamed toward her. And they perverted their own mind, and turned away their eyes, that they might not look unto heaven, nor remember just judgments.

And albeit they both were wounded with her love, yet durst not one show another his grief. For they were ashamed to declare their lust, that they desired to have to do with her. Yet they watched diligently from day to day to see her. And the one said to the other, "Let us now go home: for it is dinner time."

So when they were gone out, they parted the one from the other, and turning back

---

This tale from the apocryphal Addition to Daniel dates from the second century B.C., but the theme of false witnesses confounded is immemorial.

again they came to the same place; and after that they had asked one another the cause, they acknowledged their lust: then appointed they a time both together, when they might find her alone.

And it fell out, as they watched a fit time, she went in as before with two maids only, and she was desirous to wash herself in the garden: for it was hot. And there was nobody there save the two elders, that had hid themselves, and watched her.

Then she said to her maids, "Bring me oil and washing balls, and shut the garden doors, that I may wash me."

And they did as she bade them, and shut the garden doors, and went out themselves at privy doors to fetch the things that she had commanded them: but they saw not the elders, because they were hid.

Now when the maids were gone forth, the two elders rose up, and ran unto her, saying, "Behold, the garden doors are shut, that no man can see us, and we are in love with thee; therefore consent unto us, and lie with us. If thou wilt not, we will bear witness against thee, that a young man was with thee: and therefore thou didst send away thy maids from thee."

Then Susanna sighed, and said, "I am straitened on every side: for if I do this thing, it is death unto me: and if I do it not, I cannot escape your hands. It is better for me to fall into your hands, and not do it, than to sin in the sight of the Lord."

With that Susanna cried with a loud voice: and the two elders cried out against her. Then ran the one, and opened the garden door.

So when the servants of the house heard the cry in the garden, they rushed in at a privy door, to see what was done unto her. But when the elders had declared their matter, the servants were greatly ashamed: for there was never such a report made of Susanna.

And it came to pass the next day, when the people were assembled to her husband Joacim, the two elders came also full of mischievous imagination against Susanna to put her to death; and said before the people, "Send for Susanna, the daughter of Chelcias, Joacim's wife."

And so they sent. So she came with her father and mother, her children, and all her kindred. Now Susanna was a very delicate woman, and beauteous to behold. And these wicked men commanded to uncover her face (for she was covered), that they might be filled with her beauty. Therefore her friends and all that saw her wept.

Then the two elders stood up in the midst of the people, and laid their hands upon her head. And she weeping looked up toward heaven: for her heart trusted in the Lord. And the elders said, "As we walked in the garden alone, this woman came in with two maids, and shut the garden doors, and sent the maids away. Then a young man, who there was hid, came unto her, and lay with her. Then we that stood in a corner of the garden, seeing this wickedness, ran unto them. And when we saw them together, the man we could not hold: for he was stronger than we, and opened the door, and leaped out. But having taken this woman, we asked who the young man was, but she would not tell us: these things do we testify."

Then the assembly believed them, as those that were the elders and judges of the people: so they condemned her to death.

Then Susanna cried out with a loud voice, and said, "O everlasting God, that knowest the secrets, and knowest all things before they be: thou knowest that they have borne false witness against me, and, behold, I must die; whereas I never did such things as these men have maliciously invented against me."

And the Lord heard her voice.

Therefore when she was led to be put to death, the Lord raised up the holy spirit of a young youth, whose name was Daniel: who cried with a loud voice, "I am clear from the blood of this woman."

Then all the people turned them toward him, and said, "What mean these words that thou hast spoken?"

So he standing in the midst of them said, "Are ye such fools, ye sons of Israel, that without examination or knowledge of the truth ye have condemned a daughter of Israel?

Will of Uah, detail. c. 1800 B.C. Papyrus. Courtesy Petrie Museum of Egyptian Archaeology, University College London. *One of the earliest wills discovered, this is inscribed in Egyptian calligraphy.*

Return again to the place of judgment: for they have borne false witness against her."

Wherefore all the people turned again in haste, and the elders said unto him, "Come, sit down among us, and show it us, seeing God hath given thee the honor of an elder."

Then said Daniel unto them, "Put these two aside one far from another, and I will examine them."

So when they were put asunder one from another, he called one of them, and said unto him, "O thou that art waxed old in wickedness, now thy sins which thou hast committed aforetime are come to light: for thou hast pronounced false judgment, and hast condemned the innocent, and hast let the guilty go free; albeit the Lord saith, 'The innocent and righteous shalt thou not slay.' Now then, if thou hast seen her, tell me under what tree sawest thou them companying together?"

Who answered, "Under the mastic tree."

And Daniel said, "Very well; thou hast lied against thine own head; for even now the angel of God hath received the sentence of God to cut thee in two."

So he put him aside, and commanded to bring the other, and said unto him, "O thou seed of Chanaan, and not of Juda, beauty hath deceived thee, and lust hath perverted thine heart. Thus have ye dealt with the daughters of Israel, and they for fear companied with you: but the daughter of Juda would not abide your wickedness. Now therefore tell me under what tree didst thou take them companying together?"

Who answered, "Under a holm tree."

Then said Daniel unto him, "Well; thou hast also lied against thine own head: for the angel of God waiteth with the sword to cut thee in two, that he may destroy you."

With that all the assembly cried out with a loud voice, and praised God, who saveth them that trust in him. And they arose against the two elders, for Daniel had convicted them of false witness by their own mouth: and according to the law of Moses they did unto them in such sort as they maliciously intended to do to their neighbor: and they put them to death. Thus the innocent blood was saved the same day.

Therefore Chelcias and his wife praised God for their daughter Susanna, with Joacim her husband, and all the kindred, because there was no dishonesty found in her.

CLASSICAL FOUNDATIONS

FROM DRAKON'S LAW ON HOMICIDE

Even if a man not intentionally kills another, he is exiled. The basileis are to adjudge responsible for homicide either the actual killer or the planner; and the Ephetai are to judge the case. If there is a father or brother or sons, pardon is to be agreed to by all, or the one who opposes is to prevail; but if none of these survives, by those up to the degree of first cousin once removed and first cousin, if all are willing to agree to a pardon; the one who opposes is to prevail; but if not one of these survives, and if he killed unintentionally and the fifty-one, the Ephetai, decide he killed unintentionally, let ten phratry members admit him to the country and let the fifty-one choose these by rank. And let also those who killed previously be bound by this law. A proclamation is to be made against the killer in the agora by the victim's relatives as far as the degree of cousin's son and cousin. The prosecution is to be shared by the cousins and cousins' sons and by sons-in-law, fathers-in-law, and phratry members . . . is responsible for homicide . . . the fifty-one . . . is convicted of homicide. . . . If anyone kills the killer or is responsible for his death, as long as he stays away from the frontier markets, games, and Amphiktyonic sacrifices, he shall be liable to the same treatment as the one who kills an Athenian; and the Ephetai are to judge the case. It is allowed to kill or arrest killers, if they are caught in the territory . . . starting a fight . . . kills . . . and the Ephetai are to judge the case . . . is a free man, and if he defending himself straightway kills someone forcibly and unjustly plundering or seizing him, the victim shall die without the killer paying a penalty.

The harsh ("draconian") code of laws of Drakon (c. 621 B.C.), under which even a minor crime was a capital offense, stood in Athens until the humanizing revisions of Solon (c. 630–560 B.C.).

Artist unknown. *Solon*. c. First century. Marble. Museo Nazionale, Rome.

COLORPLATE 1

Maat, Goddess of Justice. Upper fragment of a bas-relief from the Tomb of Seti I, Nineteenth Dynasty. c. 1306–1290 B.C. White limestone. 29⅛ × 18½″ (74 × 47 cm). Archaeological Museum, Florence.

COLORPLATE 2

Moses Receives the Tables of the Law; Moses Presents Them to the People. From the Bible of Montier-Grandval. Mid-ninth century. Miniature on parchment. 16 × 11½" (40.6 × 29.2 cm). British Museum, London.

COLORPLATE 3

REMBRANDT (REMBRANDT HARMENSZ VAN RIJN). *Moses with the Tables of the Law*. 1659.
Oil on canvas. 65¾ × 53" (167 × 135 cm). Gemäldegalerie Staatliche Museen Preussischer Kulturbesitz, Berlin.

COLORPLATE 4

PETER PAUL RUBENS. *The Judgment of Solomon.*
1615–1617. Oil on canvas.
91¾ × 118⅞″ (233 × 302 cm).
Royal Museum of Fine Arts, Copenhagen.

MONS. IOSIAS COMTE DE RANSAV. MAR. DE FRANCE
MELA DORRE

COLORPLATE 5

GIOTTO (GIOTTO DI BONDONE). *Last Judgment.* 1304. Fresco. Cappella Scrovegni (Arena Chapel), Padua.

COLORPLATE 6

MICHELANGELO (MICHELANGELO BUONARROTI). *The Last Judgment.*
West wall of the Sistine Chapel. 1536–1541. Fresco. The Vatican, Rome.

COLORPLATE 7

TINTORETTO (JACOPO ROBUSI). *Susanna and the Elders*. c. 1555. Oil on canvas. 57¾ × 76¼″ (146.6 × 193.6 cm). Kunsthistorische Museum, Vienna.

COLORPLATE 8

JACQUES LOUIS DAVID. *The Death of Socrates*. 1787. Oil on canvas. 57 × 77½" (129.5 × 196.2 cm).
The Metropolitan Museum of Art, New York. Wolfe Fund, 1931. Catherine Lorillard Wolfe Collection.

COLORPLATES 9, 10

GERARD DAVID. *Judgment of Cambyses.* Two panels. 1498. Oil on panel. Each panel: 71¾ × 62¾″ (182 × 159.4 cm). Groeningemuseum, Bruges. *The panels of this Renaissance painting depict the seizing and flaying of Sisamnes, an untrustworthy judge of Cambyses II, king of Persia (reigned 529–522 B.C.), briefly recounted a generation later by the historian Herodotus. Herodotus tells of the many atrocities committed by Cambyses during the conquest of Egypt (525 B.C.), attributing them to madness. According to Darius I the Great, king of Persia from 521 to*

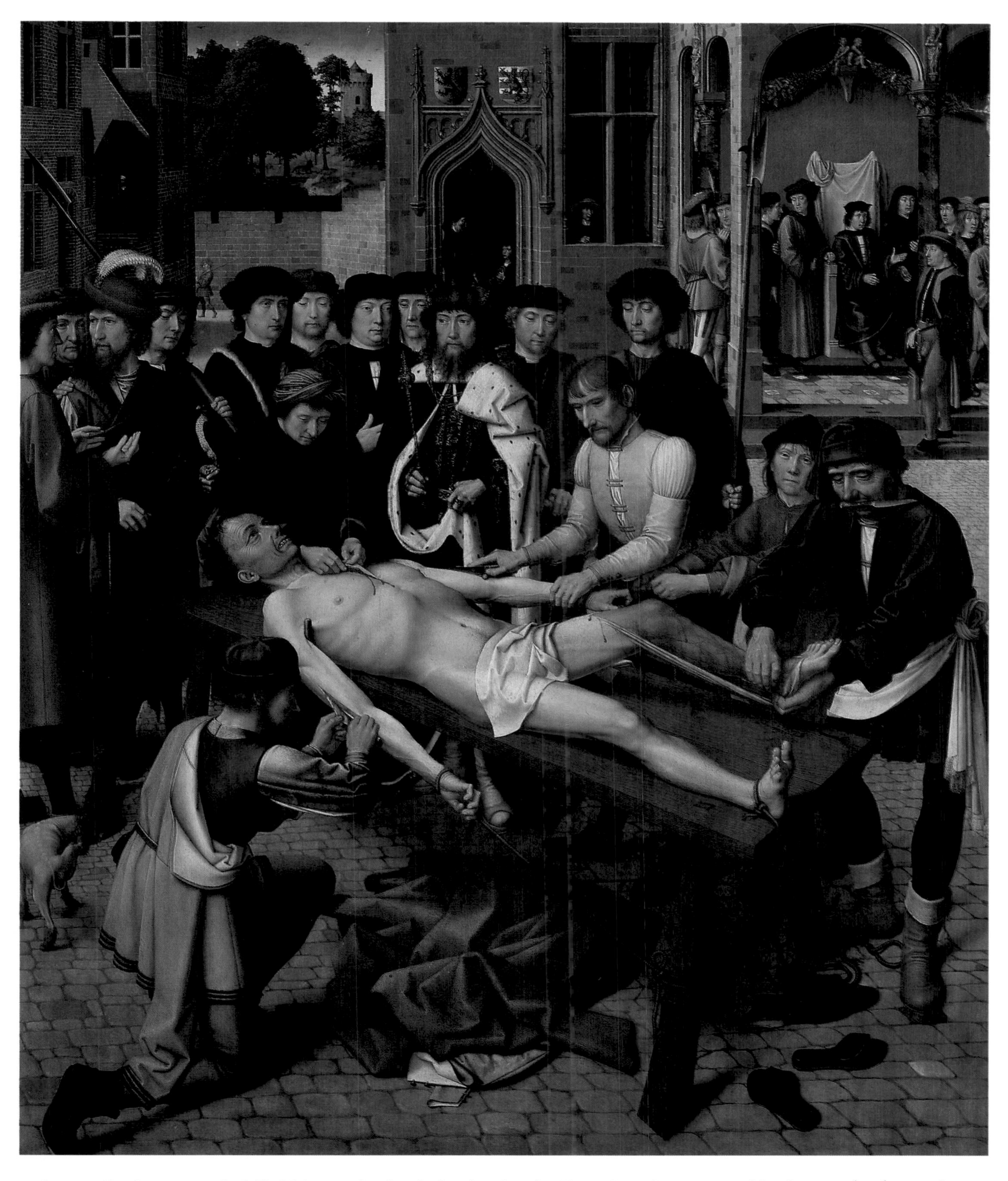

486 B.C., Cambyses secretly killed his own brother before leaving for Egypt in order to secure his place on the throne. In Herodotus, it is Cambyses' paranoid interpretation of a dream that drives him to fratricide.

The left panel shows a startled Sisamnes being arrested. In the upper left-hand corner, under the canopied doorway, Sisamnes accepts a bribe. The panel on the right shows him tied tightly to a wooden table, his red cloak crumpled beneath him, as he is flayed alive by four men. Standing nearby is a crowned figure, possibly Cambyses.

Characteristic of sixteenth-century European art, this painting has figures dressed anachronistically in Renaissance styles.

COLORPLATE 11

Justinian and His Court. c. 547. Mosaic. Basilica of San Vitale, Ravenna. *Justinian I (Flavius Petrus Sabbatius Justinianus, called Justinian the Great) was emperor from 527 to 565. During his reign, Roman law was preserved in the five books of the* Corpus Juris Civilis.

COLORPLATE 12

Bust of Cicero. First century. Marble. Uffizi, Florence. *Marcus Tullius Cicero (106–43 B.C.), lawyer, orator, philosopher, and champion of Republican principles, was quaestor in Sicily in 75 B.C. and consul of Rome in 63 B.C., at which time he stirringly denounced the treason of Catiline. An opponent to the Triumvirate that was formed after the assassination of Julius Caesar, Cicero was proscribed for his Philippics, an outspoken attack of Marc Antony, and killed.*

COLORPLATE 13

CESARE MACCARI. *Cicero Denouncing Catiline.* 1882–1888. Oil on canvas. Villa Madama, Rome. *Catiline (Lucius Sergius Catilina, c. 108–62 B.C.) was tried for plotting insurrection against the Roman Republic in 63 B.C. Cicero, serving as consul of Rome, spoke in the Senate against the traitor, declaiming,* "Quousque tandem abutere, Catilina, patientia nostra? O tempora! O mores!"*("How long, Catiline, will you abuse our patience? Oh, what times! Oh, what standards!") After his co-conspirators were executed, Catiline, at the head of an army, tried to enter Gaul in 62 B.C., but his forces were inadequate, and he was defeated and killed.*

COLORPLATE 14

JACQUES LOUIS DAVID. *Trial of Phryne.* Late eighteenth century. Oil on canvas. 57 × 78⅞″ (145 × 195 cm). Musées département aux de Loin-Atlantique, Musée Dobrée, Nantes. Ch. Hémon Collection. *Known for her beauty, Phryne, a Greek "woman of pleasure," was accused of profaning the Eleusinian mysteries and tried in 340 B.C. Her lover, the orator Hyperides, who represented her, sensing that the trial was not going well for Phryne, tore her clothes off her in front of the tribunal, imploring them to gaze upon her and have pity upon a priestess of Aphrodite. He won the trial.*

Protagoras

A Sophist's Problem

A law professor made a contract with a pupil on a contingent basis. The professor was not to be paid until his pupil won his first case as a lawyer. When the professor thought he had taught the pupil enough, he asked for his fee, but the pupil refused because he had not won his first case. The shrewd professor sued the pupil, since he thought he could not lose. If the professor won he would get a judgement against the pupil and thus get paid, whereas if he lost the pupil will have won his first case and the professor would be entitled to be paid, under the terms of the contract. At the trial, the pupil, in his first case ever, moved that there is a non-suit. The pupil explained that he could not lose because if he won the case he would not have to pay the professor, whereas if he lost he would not have won his first case and therefore would not have to pay, under the terms of the contract.

Who should win the lawsuit, and why?

"Man is the measure of all things": So posited the orator and philosopher Protagoras, the first of the Sophists of Athens in the fifth century, B.C. He also enjoyed posing legal conundrums like this famous (if hypothetical) stumper for his lawyerly pedagogues in the age of Pericles.

Plato

FROM CRITO

Socrates on His Death Sentence

Socrates: . . . Ought a man to do what he admits to be right, or ought he to betray the right?

Crito: He ought to do what he thinks right.

Socrates: But if this is true, what is the application? In leaving the prison against the will of the Athenians, do I wrong any? or rather do I not wrong those whom I ought least to wrong? Do I not desert the principles which were acknowledged by us to be just—what do you say?

Crito: I cannot tell, Socrates; for I do not know.

Socrates: Then consider the matter in this way: Imagine that I am about to play truant (you may call the proceeding by any name which you like), and the laws and the government come and interrogate me: "Tell us, Socrates," they say; "what are you about? are you not going by an act of yours to overturn us—the laws, and the whole state, as far as in you lies? Do you imagine that a state can subsist and not be overthrown, in which the decisions of law have no power, but are set aside and trampled upon by individuals?—What will be our answer, Crito, to these and the like words? Anyone, and especially a

---

Athens' gadfly Socrates (470?–399 B.C.) symbolized the ideal man for his student Plato (427?–347 B.C.). This excerpt is from one of the series of dialogues (including the Euthyphro, Apology, *and* Phaedo*) that deal with the trial and execution of Socrates.*

Artist unknown. *Plato*. c. First century. Marble. The Vatican Museum, Rome.

Artist unknown. *Aristotle*. Roman statue, after Greek original. c. First century. Marble. Galleria Spada, Rome.

rhetorician, will have a good deal to say on behalf of the law which requires a sentence to be carried out. He will argue that this law should not be set aside; and shall we reply, "Yes; but the state has injured us and given an unjust sentence." Suppose I say that?

Crito: Very good, Socrates.

Socrates: "And was that our agreement with you?" the law would answer; "or were you to abide by the sentence of the state?" And if I were to express my astonishment at their words, the law would probably add: "Answer, Socrates, instead of opening your eyes: you are in the habit of asking and answering questions. Tell us: What complaint have you to make against us which justifies you in attempting to destroy us and the state? In the first place did we not bring you into existence? Your father married your mother by our aid and begat you. Say whether you have any objection to urge against those of us who regulate marriage?" None, I should reply. "Or against those of us who after birth regulate the nurture and education of children, in which you also were trained? Were not the laws, which have the charge of education, right in commanding your father to train you in music and gymnastic?" Right, I should reply. "Well then, since you were brought into the world and nurtured and educated by us, can you deny in the first place that you are our child and slave, as your fathers were before you? And if this is true you are not on equal terms with us; nor can you think that you have a right to do to us what we are doing to you.

★ ★ ★

"Listen, then, Socrates, to us who have brought you up. Think not of life and children first, and of justice afterwards, but of justice first, that you may be justified before the princes of the world below. For neither will you nor any that belong to you be happier or holier or juster in this life, or happier in another, if you do as Crito bids. Now you depart in innocence, a sufferer and not a doer of evil; a victim, not of the laws, but of men. But if you go forth, returning evil for evil, and injury for injury, breaking the covenants and agreements which you have made with us, and wronging those whom you ought least of all to wrong, that is to say, yourself, your friends, your country, and us, we shall be angry with you while you live, and our brethren, the laws in the world below, will receive you as an enemy; for they will know that you have done your best to destroy us. Listen, then, to us and not to Crito."

This, dear Crito, is the voice which I seem to hear murmuring in my ears, like the sound of the flute in the ears of the mystic; that voice, I say, is humming in my ears, and prevents me from hearing any other. And I know that anything more which you may say will be vain. Yet speak, if you have anything to say.

Crito: I have nothing to say, Socrates.

Socrates: Leave me then, Crito, to fulfill the will of God, and to follow whither he leads.

Aristotle

FROM NICHOMACHEAN ETHICS

On Political Justice

Political Justice means justice as between free and (actually or proportionately) equal persons, living a common life for the purpose of satisfying their needs. Hence between people not free and equal political justice cannot exist, but only a sort of justice in a metaphorical sense. For justice can only exist between those whose mutual relations are regulated by law, and law exists among those between whom there is a possibility of injustice, for the administration of the law means the discrimination of what is just and what is unjust. Persons therefore between whom injustice can exist, can act unjustly towards each other (although unjust action does not necessarily involve injustice): to act unjustly meaning to assign oneself too large a share of things generally good and too small a share of things generally evil. This is why we do not permit a man to rule, but the law, because a man rules in his own interest, and becomes a tyrant; but the function of a ruler is to be the guardian of justice, and if of justice, then of equality. A just ruler seems to make nothing out of his office; for he does not allot to himself a larger share of things generally good, unless it be proportionate to his merits; so that he labours for others, which accounts for the saying mentioned above, that "Justice is the good of others." Consequently some recompense has to be given him, in the shape of honour and dignity. It is those whom such rewards do not satisfy who make themselves tyrants.

Although he studied under Plato at the Academy in Athens, the temperament and outlook of Aristotle (384–322 B.C.) were diametric to his teacher's. This selection is taken from Book V of the collection of his lectures.

Cicero

FROM LAWS

A Definition of Law

Cicero: Ever since we were children, Quintus, we have learned to call, "If one summon another to court," and other rules of the same kind, laws. But we must come to the true understanding of the matter, which is as follows: this and other commands and prohibitions of nations have the power to summon to righteousness and away from wrongdoing; but this power is not merely older than the existence of nations and States, it is coeval with that God who guards and rules heaven and earth. For the divine mind cannot exist without reason, and divine reason cannot but have this power to establish right and wrong. No written law commanded that a man should take his stand on a bridge alone, against the full force of the enemy, and order the bridge broken down behind him; yet we shall not for that reason suppose that the heroic Cocles was not obeying the law of bravery and following its decrees in doing so noble a deed. Even if there was no written law against rape at Rome in the reign of Lucius Tarquinius, we cannot say on that account that Sextus Tarquinius did not break that eternal Law by violating Lucretia, the daughter of Tricipitinus! For reason did exist, derived from the Nature of the universe, urging men to right conduct and diverting them from wrongdoing, and this reason did not first become Law when it was written down, but when it first came into existence; and it came into existence simultaneously with the divine mind. Wherefore the true and primal Law, applied to command and prohibition, is the right reason of supreme Jupiter.

Quintus: I agree with you, brother, that what is right and true is also eternal, and does not begin or end with written statutes.

Cicero: Therefore, just as that divine mind is the supreme Law, so, when [reason] is perfected in man, [that also is Law; and this perfected reason exists] in the mind of the wise man; but those rules which, in varying forms and for the need of the moment, have been formulated for the guidance of nations, bear the title of laws rather by favour than because they are really such. For every law which really deserves that name is truly praiseworthy, as they prove by approximately the following arguments. It is agreed, of course, that laws were invented for the safety of citizens, the preservation of States, and the tranquillity and happiness of human life, and that those who first put statutes of this kind in force convinced their people that it was their intention to write down and put into effect such rules as, once accepted and adopted, would make possible for them an honourable and happy life; and when such rules were drawn up and put in force, it is clear that men called them "laws." From this point of view it can be readily understood that those who formulated wicked and unjust statutes for nations, thereby breaking their promises and agreements, put into effect anything but "laws." It may thus be clear that in the very definition of the term "law" there inheres the idea and principle of choosing what is just and true. I ask you then, Quintus, according to the custom of the philosophers: if there is a certain thing, the lack of which in a State compels us to consider it no State at all, must we consider this thing a good?

Quintus: One of the greatest goods, certainly.

Cicero: And if a State lacks Law, must it for that reason be considered no State at all?

Quintus: It cannot be denied.

Marcus Tullius Cicero (106–43 B.C.), philosopher, orator, and statesman, was a courageous proponent of, and martyr for, republican principles. This excerpt is from Book II of his dialogue.

Cicero: Then Law must necessarily be considered one of the greatest goods.

Quintus: I agree with you entirely.

Cicero: What of the many deadly, the many pestilential statutes which nations put in force? These no more deserve to be called laws than the rules a band of robbers might pass in their assembly. For if ignorant and unskilful men have prescribed deadly poisons instead of healing drugs, these cannot possibly be called physicians' prescriptions; neither in a nation can a statute of any sort be called a law, even though the nation, in spite of its being a ruinous regulation, has accepted it. Therefore Law is the distinction between things just and unjust, made in agreement with that primal and most ancient of all things, Nature; and in conformity to Nature's standard are framed those human laws which inflict punishment upon the wicked but defend and protect the good.

Edward Gibbon

FROM THE DECLINE AND FALL OF THE ROMAN EMPIRE

On Lawyers and the Byzantine State

All the civil magistrates were drawn from the profession of the law. The celebrated Institutes of Justinian are addressed to the youth of his dominions who had devoted themselves to the study of Roman jurisprudence; and the sovereign condescends to animate their diligence by the assurance that their skill and ability would in time be rewarded by an adequate share in the government of the republic. The rudiments of this lucrative science were taught in all the considerable cities of the East and West; but the most famous school was that of Berytus, on the coast of Phoenicia, which flourished above three centuries from the time of Alexander Severus, the author perhaps of an institution so advantageous to his native country. After a regular course of education, which lasted five years, the students dispersed themselves through the provinces in search of fortune and honours; nor could they want an inexhaustible supply of business in a great empire already corrupted by the multiplicity of laws, of arts, and of vices. The court of the Praetorian praefect of the East could alone furnish employment for one hundred and fifty advocates, sixty-four of whom were distinguished by peculiar privileges, and two were annually chosen with a salary of sixty pounds of gold to defend the causes of the treasury. The first experiment was made of their judicial talents by appointing them to act occasionally as assessors to the magistrates; from thence they were often raised to preside in the tribunals before which they had pleaded. They obtained the government of a province; and, by the aid of merit, of reputation, or of favour, they ascended, by successive steps, to the *illustrious* dignities of the state. In the practice of the bar these men had considered reason as the instrument of dispute; they interpreted the laws according to the dictates of private interest; and the same pernicious habits might still adhere to their characters in the public administration of the state. The honour of a liberal profession has indeed been vindicated by ancient and modern advocates, who have filled the most important stations with pure integrity and consummate wisdom; but in the decline of Roman jurisprudence, the ordinary promotion of lawyers was pregnant with mischief and disgrace. The noble

---

Edward Gibbon (1737–1794), indisputably one of the greatest historians of the Enlightenment period, produced his masterpiece in six volumes, from 1776 to 1788. This excerpt is from the seventeenth chapter.

art, which had once been preserved as the sacred inheritance of the patricians, was fallen into the hands of freedmen and plebeians, who, with cunning rather than with skill, exercised a sordid and pernicious trade. Some of them procured admittance into families for the purpose of fomenting differences, of encouraging suits, and of preparing a harvest of gain for themselves or their brethren. Others, recluse in their chambers, maintained the gravity of legal professors, but furnishing a rich client with subtleties to confound the plainest truth, and with arguments to colour the most unjustifiable pretensions. The splendid and popular class was composed of the advocates, who filled the Forum with the sound of their turgid and loquacious rhetoric. Careless of fame and of justice, they are described for the most part as ignorant and rapacious guides, who conducted their clients through a maze of expense, of delay, and of disappointment; from whence, after a tedious series of years, they were at length dismissed, when their patience and fortune were almost exhausted.

Artist unknown. *Notaries*. Detail from a Roman frieze. c. First century. Marble. Ostia, Italy.

Justinian

FROM THE DIGEST OF ROMAN LAW

"Concerning Theft"

(GAIUS) There are two degrees of theft: manifest and nonmanifest.

* * *

(ULPIAN) A manifest thief is one whom the Greeks describe as "caught in the very act," that is, one who is caught with the stolen goods on him. It matters little who it is who actually catches him—whether it is the owner of the stolen goods, or anyone else. But it

---

Flavius Petrus Sabbatius Justinianus—Justinian the Great—was Byzantine emperor from A.D. 527 to 565. His Corpus Juris Civilis, *from which this excerpt is taken (Book 47, Title 2), collected previous imperial law; opinions of the jurists, including Gaius, Ulpian, and Pomponius; an outline of the law; and laws introduced by Justinian himself.*

may be asked whether a thief is only a manifest thief if he is caught in the very act of stealing or indeed whether it is good enough that he be apprehended just anywhere. The better view—and this was Julian's opinion—is that even if he is not caught in the place where he committed the theft, he is nevertheless a manifest thief if he is caught with the stolen thing on him before he has taken it to the place he intended.

* * *

(PAUL) "The place he intended to carry it to" is understood as "the place where he intended to stop that day with the stolen thing."

* * *

(ULPIAN) Therefore irrespective of whether he is caught in a public or in a private place, so long as he has not yet borne the thing to the place he was making for, the charge will be one of manifest theft if he is caught with the stolen thing on him: and that was the view of Cassius. But if he has got his loot home, even if he is caught with the stolen things in his possession, he is not a manifest thief.

* * *

(PAUL) It is a common question whether if someone takes a bushel out of a whole heap of corn, he commits theft of the heap or only of as much as he carried off. Ofilius says that he steals the whole heap. Consider the case of touching someone's ear. Trebatius says this seems to be a case of touching the whole person. Thence it follows that he who opens a cask and draws off a small quantity of wine seems to be a thief not only of what he takes but of the whole cask, though he will only be liable to pay damages for the amount he actually took. Take the case of a man who opens a chest which is too heavy to lift and handles everything inside and then goes away, but later comes back and carries off some item or other and is caught before reaching the place he was making for: in such a case he is both an "ordinary thief" and a red-handed (manifest) thief in respect of the same thing. And similarly a man who cuts corn and handles it during daylight is both an ordinary thief and also a red-handed thief in respect of that which he is caught carrying off during the following night. . . .

Again, if someone steals a bushel of corn from a whole shipload, is this theft of the whole cargo or just of the bushel? The problem can be considered more easily in respect of a full warehouse. Surely it is a bit hard to hold that this would be theft of the whole contents? But what then should be said of a cistern of wine, or of water—or what indeed of a ship carrying wine (and there are many ships whose holds are brimming with wine)? What shall we say of someone who draws off some of the wine? Would this be theft of the whole cargo? It is most likely that we would not go that far. There is no doubt though, if you put the case of jars in a storeroom and they are stolen, that that is not one theft of the whole store but of the individual jars, just as when a thief takes away one individual thing from among a number of movable things in a warehouse. . . .

If two or more men steal a piece of timber which no one of them could lift by himself, it must be said that they are all equally liable for the whole theft even though no one of them could handle or remove it alone, and this is indeed the law, for we cannot say that each one committed a part of the theft, but the whole thing was the act of them all and thus each man is individually liable for the theft. But although a man may be guilty of the theft of things which he did not himself carry away he will not be liable to make restitution, because the relevant action only lies for the things which a man has actually taken—and thus Pomponius writes.

* * *

(PAUL) He who aids and abets a theft is never himself a manifest thief; and therefore it can happen that the helper is liable for "ordinary" theft while the actual perpetrator, when caught, is liable as a manifest thief, albeit that they were both involved in the same theft.

* * *

(ULPIAN) A person who persuades a slave to run away is not a thief, nor does anyone who simply gives bad advice to someone else commit theft, any more than anyone who persuades another to throw himself off a cliff or to lay violent hands on himself. No action for theft lies for this sort of thing. But if one man persuades a slave to run away, so that his colleague may capture him, he who does the persuading will be liable for theft because theft was committed by his aid and advice. Pomponius writes more on this point—he says that he who did the persuading, although he would not at that time be liable for theft, does become liable as soon as the other party begins to appropriate the runaway, because this seems to be a proper case of a theft by his aid and advice.

Similarly, it seems right that anyone who helps another's son, slave or wife in committing theft should himself be liable for theft, even though such thieves are not themselves liable to a theft action. Again, Pomponius says, if a runaway slave takes goods with him he who advised him can also be sued on account of those goods too, because he gave advice to the handler himself. Sabinus says the same.

If two slaves encourage each other to run away and they both abscond together, neither of them can be a thief of the other.

What then if they both concealed each other—is it possible that they could then be thieves of each other? It can be said that each was a thief of the other to the extent that if other people stole them individually they would be liable if each gave counsel and advice to the other. By the same reasoning Sabinus says they would both be liable for any goods which the other took away with him.

★ ★ ★

(POMPONIUS) If my tame peacock strays from my house and you chase it until it dies, I can sue you in theft as soon as anyone takes possession of it.

★ ★ ★

(ULPIAN) It is true that if someone carries off or conceals someone else's slave who is a prostitute, this is not necessarily theft; for we must consider not only the act, but also its motive—and if the motive was lust, this is not theft. Accordingly even he who broke down a prostitute's door to gratify his desires and thereby let in thieves (acting independently, not in concert with him) who carried off her property is not guilty of theft. But would a man be liable under the Lex Fabia if he secretly harboured a harlot to satisfy his lusts? I do not think so, and I base this opinion on a case which actually happened. In this case he acts more basely than someone who steals, but this is balanced by the disgrace he brings on himself. At all events it is clear that he is not a thief.

★ ★ ★

(ULPIAN) If a slave-girl is pregnant when stolen, or becomes pregnant while stolen, the child, when born, is stolen property and regardless of whether at the time of birth the thief still has her, or she is with a possessor in good faith. However, in this latter case no action lies for the theft of the child.

★ ★ ★

(NERATIUS) If anyone takes possession as supposed heir of the property of someone thought to be dead but who is actually alive; he does not commit theft.

★ ★ ★

(PAUL) If a plaintiff sues for robbery he cannot sue for theft as well; but if in a robbery case he chooses to bring the theft action for double damages, he can also sue for robbery provided his total claim does not exceed four times the value of the property in question.

MEDIEVAL LANDMARKS

Katharine Scherman

FROM THE BIRTH OF FRANCE

On Clovis and the Lex Salica

During the . . . last three years of his life, [Clovis] issued the first written version of the *lex Salica*, the old German law by which the primitive tribes and, later, those affiliated with the empire as *foederati*, had ordered their lives. . . .

The work was executed by a team of Gallo-Roman lawyers and clerics, who clarified, rationalized and rendered into Latin (with some necessary Frankish words) the old Salic law. The code contains no pagan elements, but neither is it imbued with the precepts of Christianity. While Clovis ruled over a majority of Catholic Gallo-Romans, much of his Frankish minority, their titular masters, was not yet converted.

The code opens with a lofty prologue: "The illustrious Frankish people, founded by God, brave in war, firm in covenants of peace, high in purpose, superior in body, sound in integrity, distinguished in stature, bold, swift and fierce, converted to the Catholic faith and immune from heresy . . . This is the powerful people who, by fighting, shook from its neck the hard yoke of the Romans." The code moves from grandiloquence straight into practical matters. It is mainly a penal code: as such it expresses the problem and iniquities of a rather small rural population, the conquerors, settled among a larger class of subject people.

The Teutonic concept of the law differed from the Roman, which was community-oriented. In Germanic law the criminal's first liability was to the victim, and only secondarily, through him, to the public weal. This dual vision of crime entailed the primary compensation of the injured, along with secondary indemnity to the constituted authority. In tribal times punishment had been effected by violence: the blood feud was the only method the free Teutons had of correcting crime and suppressing disorder. The new code instituted, in place of personal vengeance, a graded series of punishments for which the payment of wergild could be substituted. Wergild, literally man-payment, was a levy of money or goods on the criminal or his family, half to be paid to the victim or his family, the other half to the state. The amount was proportionate to the grossness of the offense, and to the sex, age, position and general usefulness of the damaged citizen.

The highest wergild was commanded by the antrustions . . . not because they were of a higher class but because they were in the direct service of the king, having sworn a voluntary oath of perpetual fealty. Frankish Gaul had no hereditary aristocracy: after the king came the entire body of freemen, differentiated by their occupation, not by their

---

Developed from the warrior code of the Salian Franks, the lex Salica *was a cornerstone of law in western Europe in the early Middle Ages and a major contribution of Clovis (466–511), founder of the Frankish kingdom. Historian Scherman recounts some of the features of the Salic law in this brief excerpt from her recent study.*

birth. The antrustions were chosen by the king from all classes, and their position was not hereditary. They lived at court, superintended palace affairs and held themselves ready for any task their master might assign them, including war. The amount due for the murder of an antrustion was six hundred solidi (one solidus, a Roman gold coin whose descendant was the sou, was equal to one cow, and often the fine was paid in livestock). If he was killed while fighting the king's battle his body was valued at twenty-four hundred solidi. An ordinary Frankish freeman was worth two hundred solidi, but if he was under twelve—a potential warrior—this was tripled. Similarly escalated was the fine for killing a girl over twelve—that is, capable of bearing children. If she was pregnant her price was seven hundred. This was more than that of a priest, whose heirs could collect only six hundred, but not as much as a bishop, assessed at nine hundred. . . .

The lowest class in Gaul was the slave, whose master received only thirty solidi for his murder, somewhat more if he were skilled in an art or craft.

Below murder was a host of maledictions of greater or lesser atrocity, from rape and deliberate mutilation to thievery and insult. The minuteness of the inventory gives rise to the observation that this was indeed a barbarous age. But of course a penal code dealt exclusively with social violence. Its object, not its subject, was the majority of unventuresome citizenry existing guilelessly on farms and in peaceful middlesized towns. The Salic Law protected these honest citizens in their coming and going; it left no conceivable area of transgression unredressed.

Criminal mutilations included the cutting off of an ear or an unimportant finger: these were worth only one-third of the value of the nose, thumb or second finger (the one which drew the bow), and one-quarter that of an eye, which cost one hundred solidi. Castration and cutting out the tongue cost as much as the life of a Roman landowner.

The enumeration of thievery went from the flagrant to the picayune: in its lower categories were the stealing of a horse, a boat, a swineherd's bell, grapes or apples from a garden, an eel net, a hunting dog. It covered all kinds of poaching—misdeeds specially iniquitous to a people addicted to the hunt.

Among the punishable insults, to call a freemen a hare or a fox was only one-third as bad (three solidi) as to name a woman a harlot—unless she was one. Uninvited caresses were disfavored: to stroke a woman's hand or finger cost fifteen, to touch her bosom, thirty-five. Rape entailed a comparatively small wergild of sixty-two and a half. But adultery was severely penalized, bringing two hundred (from the man), and abortion was even more heavily indemnified. The discrepancy in the fines for these crimes is indicative of the Teutonic bias: though a woman's virtue was still honored as in tribal times, her chief value lay not in her person but in her potential as a mother.

If you could not pay, or refused to, a variety of punishments was prescribed, depending on the enormity of your crime and your position in society. If death were indicated this was performed by cleaving the skull with an axe, for the gentry; stoning, for the plebeian; hanging or drowning, for the coward, deserter or effeminate; for the slave, the slower, more degrading sentence of crucifying or breaking on the wheel. Punishments for lesser crimes included torture and mutilation: among the most heinous wrongdoing was property theft, for which the perpetrator could lose an eye for the first theft, a nose for the second, his life for the third. Flogging was a frequent chastisement. Worse than this were imprisonment and enslavement, dreaded above all by the free Franks. . . .

There was little in the code concerning civil law, most of that being administered under Roman law. The small section devoted to it dealt mainly with the inheritance of property. There were no wills: a man's personal property went equally to his children, male and female, while his real property descended only in the male line, each son receiving an equivalent portion. "Of Salic land no portion shall come to a woman; but the whole of the inheritance of the land shall come to the male sex." In the fourteenth century the *lex Salica* was erroneously invoked to justify the barring of women and any descendants through the female line from succession to the throne of France, and later, to that of some German kingdoms and duchies. But the actual Salic law and its successive emendations from the time of Clovis to that of Charlemagne had no political provisions. There is nothing in reference to the rights of succession, and almost no word of the powers and prerogatives of the king—except the crucial proviso that he is the final legal resource.

Clovis's *lex Salica* is an expressive picture of the society it protected: wealthy farmers living more or less pacifically side by side with legally inferior but more civilized conquered neighbors. Their farms were diversified, with cultivated fields, livestock, orchards, gardens and vineyards. Hawks, hounds, beehives and fishing boats added a spice of variation to placid rusticity. There is little reference to town life: the urban *modus vivendi* was not attractive to these country-oriented families whose fairly recent forebears still hunted and roved for their livelihood. Most of the malfeasance took the form of straightforward physical violence: assault, theft, and outrage to women. The simple Frankish felon was not yet educated in the subtleties of urban crime and the degeneracy which ulcerates the edges of more complex societies. . . .

But simplistic as it is legally, its codification by Clovis is a landmark. . . . It is a concrete expression of the unqualified prerogative of kingship, a concept new to the Franks. Traditionally their kings had been local chieftains elected by their warriors for the specific purpose of military enterprise; and their law had been developed for freemen and their leaders as equals, by these same warriors. Now the king, as supreme judge, was in practice outside the law.

William Sharp McKechnie

FROM MAGNA CARTA

Much ingenuity has been expended in the effort to discover which particular category of modern jurisprudence most accurately describes the Great Charter. Is it an enacted law, or a treaty; the royal answer to a petition; or a declaration of rights? Is it a simple pact, bargain, or agreement between contracting parties? Or is it a combination of two or more of these? Something has been said in favour of almost every possible view, perhaps more to the bewilderment than to the enlightenment of students of history uninterested in legal subtleties.

* * *

The essential nature of what took place at Runnymede, in June, 1215, is plain, when stripped of legal subtleties. A bargain was struck, between the King and his rebel magnates, that, in return for a renewal of fealty and homage, John would grant "to the freemen of England and their heirs for ever" the liberties enumerated in sixty-three chapters. No one thought of asking whether the transaction thus concluded was a "treaty" or a private "contract." The terms had to be drawn up in legal form, so as to bear record to the exact nature of the provisions, and also to the authenticity of John's consent. It was, therefore, reduced to writing, and the resulting document was naturally couched in the form invariably used for all irrevocable grants intended to descend from father to son, namely, a feudal charter, authenticated by the impression of the granter's seal—just as in the case of a grant of land, and with many of the clauses appropriate to such a grant.

John grants to the freemen of England and their heirs certain specified rights and liberties, as though these were so many hides of land. The legal effect of such a grant is hard to determine; and insuperable difficulties beset any attempt to expound its legal

---

In the year 1215, King John of England, long overzealous in taxing his barons to finance his wars, was forced to affix his seal to a charter establishing numerous basic rights, as demanded by the rebelling barons. William S. McKechnie, perhaps the foremost authority on Magna Carta, wrote extensively on the nature of the legendary document; this is a brief sample.

Magna Carta, signed by King John in 1215. British Library, London.

consequences in terms of modern law. In truth, the form and substance of Magna Carta are badly mated. Its substance consists of a number of legal enactments and political and civil rights; its form is borrowed from the feudal lawyer's book of styles for conferring a title to landed estate.

. . . It is misleading to describe phenomena of the thirteenth century in modern phraseology which would have been unintelligible to contemporaries. Yet, if it is necessary to make the attempt, Magna Carta may perhaps be regarded as an agreement partaking of the natures alike of a statute and a royal grant, of a public treaty and a private contract, yet identical with no one of these, but (in any view) enacting or proclaiming a number of rules and customs as binding in England, and reducing them to writing in the unsuitable form of a feudal charter granted by King John to the freemen of England and their heirs.

* * *

After every allowance has been made for the great and beneficent influence of Magna Carta, it may still be doubted whether the belief of enthusiasts in its excessive importance has been fully justified. Many other triumphs, almost equally important, have been won in the cause of liberty; and statutes have been passed embodying them. Why then should Magna Carta be extolled as the palladium of English liberties? Is not, when all is said, the extreme merit attributed to it mainly of a sentimental or imaginative nature? Such questions must be answered partly in the affirmative. Much of its value *does* depend on sentiment. Yet all government is, in a sense, founded upon sentiment—sometimes affection, sometimes fear: psychological considerations are all-powerful in the practical affairs of life. Intangible and even unreal phenomena have played an important part in the history of nations. . . .

It is no disparagement of Magna Carta, then, to confess that part of its power has been read into it by later generations, and lies in the halo, almost of romance, that has gathered round it in the course of centuries. It became a battle cry for future ages, a banner, a rallying point, a stimulus to the imagination. For a King, thereafter, openly to infringe the promises contained in the Great Charter, was to challenge public opinion—to put himself palpably in the wrong. For an aggrieved man, however humble, to base his rights upon its terms was to enlist the sympathy of all. Time and again, from the Barons' War against Henry III. to the days of John Hampden and Oliver Cromwell, the possibility of appealing to the words of Magna Carta has afforded a practical ground for opposition; an easily intelligible principle to fight for; a justified position to hold against the enemies of national freedom. To explain the exact way in which this particular document—dry as its details at first sight may seem—has fired the popular imagination, is a task that lies rather within the sphere of psychology than of history, as usually conceived. However difficult it may be to explain this phenomenon, there is no doubt of its existence. The importance of the Great Charter has increased, as traditions, associations, and aspirations have clustered more thickly round it.

Thus Magna Carta, in addition to its legal and political value, has a moral value of an equally emphatic kind. Apart from and beyond the salutary effect of the useful laws it contains, its moral influence has contributed to an advance in the national spirit, and therefore in the national liberties. Such considerations justify enthusiasts, who hold that the granting of Magna Carta was the turning-point in English history.

FROM THE TRIAL OF JOAN OF ARC

Testimony at Her Trial for Heresy and Witchcraft

A: I was thirteen when I had a Voice from God for my help and guidance. The first time that I heard this Voice, I was very much frightened; it was mid-day, in the summer, in my father's garden . . . I heard this Voice to my right, towards the Church; rarely do I hear it without its being accompanied also by a light. This light comes from the same side as the voice. Generally it is a great light . . .

Q: How long is it since you heard your Voices?

A: I heard them yesterday and today.

Q: What were you doing yesterday morning when the voice came to you?

A: I was asleep: the Voice awoke me.

Q: Was it by touching you on the arm?

A: It awoke me without touching me.

Q: Was it in your room?

Joan of Arc (1412–1431), leading a small French army, drove off superior English forces at the seige of Orléans. Captured in 1430 and condemned for witchcraft and heresy—as recorded in this excerpt from her trial—she was burned at the stake the following year.

A: Not so far as I know, but in the Castle.

Q: Did you thank it? and did you go on your knees?

A: I did thank it. I was sitting on the bed; I joined my hands; I implored its help. The Voice said to me: "Answer boldly; God will help thee." . . . *(Addressing herself to the Bishop of Beauvais:)* You say you are my judge. Take care what you are doing; for in truth I am sent by God, and you place yourself in great danger.

Q: Has this Voice sometimes varied its counsel?

A: I have never found it give two contrary opinions.

Q: This Voice that speaks to you, is it that of an Angel, or of a Saint, of from God direct?

A: It is the Voice of Saint Catherine and Saint Margaret. Their faces are adorned with beautiful crowns, very rich and precious.

Q: How do you know if these were the two Saints? How do you distinguish one from the other?

A: I know quite well it is they; and I can easily distinguish one from the other.

Q: How do you distinguish them?

A: By the greeting they give me. It is seven years now since they have undertaken to guide me. I know them well because they were named to me.

Q: What was the first Voice that came to you when you were about thirteen?

A: It was Saint Michael; I saw him before my eyes; he was not alone, but quite surrounded by the Angels of Heaven . . .

Q: Did you see Saint Michael and these Angels bodily and in reality?

A: I saw them with my bodily eyes as well as I see you; when they went from me, I wept. I should have liked to be taken away with them.

* * *

Q: What sign did you give to your King *(the Dauphin when she saw him for the first time)* that you came from God?

Boutet de Monvel. *The Trial of Joan of Arc.* 1911. Oil and gold leaf on canvas. 29¾ × 67½" (75.6 × 171.5 cm). The Corcoran Gallery of Art, Washington, D.C. William A. Clark Collection.

A: . . . The sign was that an Angel assured my King, in bringing him the crown, that he should have the whole realm of France, by the means of God's help and my labors; that he was to set me to work—that is to say, to give me soldiers; and that otherwise he would not be so soon crowned and consecrated.

Q: Of what material was the said crown?

A: It is well to know it was of fine gold; it was so rich that I do not know how to count its riches or to appreciate its beauty. The crown signified that my King should possess the Kingdom of France.

Q: Were there stones in it?

A: I have told you what I know about it.

Q: Did you touch or kiss it?

A: No.

Q: Did the Angel who brought it come from above, or along the ground?

A: He came from above,—I mean, he came at our Lord's bidding. He entered by the door of the chamber.

Q: Did he move along the ground from the door of the chamber?

A: When he came into the King's presence, he did him reverence, bowing before him and speaking the words I have told you about the sign. Then he reminded him of the beautiful patience he had shown in the face of the great tribulations which had come to him. And from the door of the chamber he stepped and moved along the ground as he came to the King. When the Angel came I accompanied him and went with him up the steps to the King's chamber, and the Angel went in first. And then I said to the King, "Sire, there is your sign—take it."

* * *

Q: Do you know if you are in the Grace of God?

A: If I am not, may God place me there; if I am, may God so keep me. I should be the saddest in all the world if I knew that I were not in the grace of God. But if I were in a state of sin, do you think the Voice would come to me? I would that every one could hear the Voice as I hear it. . . .

Q: Do you know if Saint Catherine and Saint Margaret hate the English?

A: They love what God loves; they hate what God hates.

Q: Does God hate the English?

A: Of the love or hate God may have for the English or of what he will do for their souls, I know nothing; but I know quite well that they will be put out of France, except those who shall die there, and that God will send victory to the French against the English.

Q: Was God for the English when they were prospering in France?

A: I do not know if God hated the French; but I believe that He wished them to be defeated for their sins, if they were in sin.

Q: Do the people of Domremy side with the Burgundians or with the opposite party?

A: I knew only one Burgundian at Domremy: I should have been quite willing for them to cut off his head—always had it pleased God.

Q: Had you in your youth any intention of fighting the Burgundians?

A: I had a great will and desire that my King should have his own Kingdom.

Q: Is it for any merit of yours that God sent you this Angel?

A: He came for a great purpose: I was in hopes that the King would believe the sign, and that they would cease to argue with me, and would aid the good people of Orleans. The Angel came for the merits of the King and of the good Duke d'Orleans.

Q: Why to you rather than to another?

A: It has pleased God so to do by a simple maiden, in order to drive back the enemies of the King.

* * *

Q: If the Church Militant tells you that your revelations are illusions, or diabolical things, will you defer to the Church?

A: I will defer to God, Whose Commandment I always do. . . . In case the Church should prescribe the contrary, I should not refer to any one in the world, but to God alone, Whose Commandment I always follow.

Q: Do you not then believe you are subject to the Church of God which is on earth, that is to say to our Lord the Pope, to the Cardinals, the Archbishops, Bishops, and other prelates of the Church?

A: Yes, I believe myself to be subject to them; but God must be served first.

Q: Have you then command from your Voices not to submit yourself to the Church Militant, which is on earth, not to its decision?

A: I answer nothing from my own head; what I answer is by command of my Voices; they do not order me to disobey the Church, but God must be served first.

Francis Cowper

"The Inns of Court"

The Inns of Court are unique. They are not merely schools of law. They are not merely lawyers' trade unions. They are not merely convivial social clubs. But they blend all three functions in the recognition that their members should be whole men, not just legal technicians, on the one hand, or hunters of fees and full employment, on the other.

No one knows their origin. Some guesses place it in Edward I's designs to stabilize the legal profession in the late 13th century. Certainly they were in existence by the mid 14th century. Their earliest extant records are those of Lincoln's Inn commencing in 1422, the year of the death of Henry V. One persuasive conjecture as to their original purpose was that bodies of lawyers, coming to London for the then relatively short law terms, took over a number of large houses as residential clubs which were used during the law vacations for the instruction of pupils. It may be so. Certainly by the 15th century a whole legal quarter had grown up along the suburban boundary between the commercial City of London and the royal City of Westminster where the judges sat in the King's palace. . . .

The system admirably exemplified the English genius for effective practical improvisation rather than long term planning dependent upon a whole complex of assumptions

---

London's ancient Inns of Court will probably always be mysterious in their origins. The two Temples take their names from the shadowy Order of the Knights Templar (12th–13th centuries). In Lincoln's Inn, Sir Thomas More applied himself to the demanding study of English law (as opposed to Roman law). Francis Cowper's 1979 article, excerpted here, takes an informative look, in contrasting profiles, at the nature of these curious legal institutions.

COLORPLATE 15

Fuero Juzgo. Manuscript. Seventh to eighth century. Biblioteca Nacional, Madrid. *This manuscript is an unofficial version, in Latin, of the Visigothic* Fuero Juzgo *(Book of Laws), which unified for the first time both Hispano-Roman and Roman laws. Its influence was felt in the greatest days of Spain, when that kingdom itself was a colonizing power.*

COLORPLATE 16 *(opposite)*

DIERIK (DIRK) BOUTS. *Justice of Emperor Otto III.* Right panel. 1470–1475. Oil on panel. 12′11″ × 6′7½″ (393.7 × 201.9 cm). Musées Royaux Des Beaux-Arts, Brussels. *Though he lived to be only twenty-two, Otto III (890–1002) had a grand vision of recreating the power of the Roman Empire as a Christian state and ranking the power of the secular government above that of the spiritual. As king, he secured the election of his twenty-three-year-old cousin as the first German pope (Pope Gregory V), and he was crowned Holy Roman emperor by this pope in 996. Otto having returned to Germany, a rebellious Roman nobleman, Crescentius II, drove Gregory V from Rome and replaced him with his own pope, John XVI. Consequently, in 997, Otto returned with his army to Italy, at last capturing Rome the following year. He ordered the torture and execution of Crescentius, deposed the antipope, and restored Gregory V to the papal throne. He also made Rome his residence and the empire's administrative heart. Upon Gregory's death in 999, Otto effected the installment of Sylvester II, a former tutor sympathetic to Otto's vision of himself as a theocratic emperor.*

The scene illustrated in this northern European Renaissance painting is from an account by the twelfth-century historian Godfrey of Viterbo. A count of Otto's court, accused of adultery with the empress, is executed in the left-hand panel (not shown here). In the panel shown, Otto, distrusting the empress, forces her to undergo trial by fire. She holds a piece of red-hot metal that has been heated in the burning embers at her feet. Since she is burned, the test "proves" her guilt, and she is burned at the stake (top of the panel).

COLORPLATE 17

Attributed to HENRY BRACTON. *On the Laws and Customs of England* Manuscript. Before 1268. Parchment. British Library, London. *The illustration in this manuscript, the earliest systematic treatise on English laws, pertains to Bracton's pronouncement, "Two things are necessary for a king who rules rightly, arms and laws."*

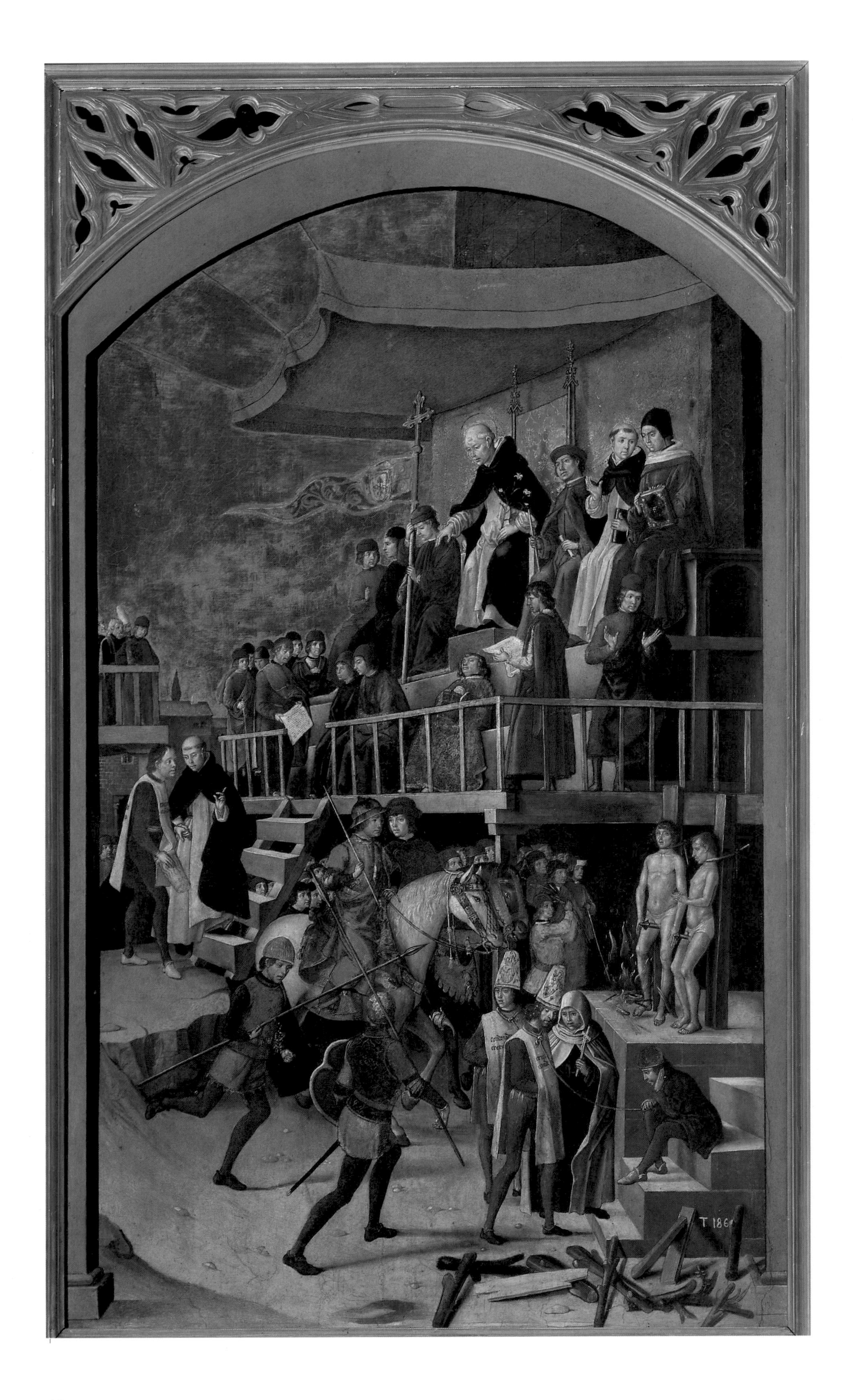
T 186

COLORPLATE 18 *(opposite)*

PADRO BERRUGUETE. *Saint Dominic Presiding over an Auto-da-fé.* c. 1475. Oil on wood. 60⅝ × 36¼" (154 × 92 cm). Prado Museum, Madrid. *Born in Castile in 1170, Dominic founded the order of Preaching Friars, also called the Dominican order, which was confirmed in 1216. He was instrumental in the Inquisition's heresy trials, which generally culminated in the ceremony and public execution known as auto-da-fé ("act of faith").*

Dominic is shown enthroned and holding lilies, symbols of the Virgin Mary. At the bottom right, two members of the Albigensian sect, a dualist heresy of the south of France, wear conical caps and tunics that identify them as the accused (a customary pretrial ignominy). They are led by a rope around the neck, held by a surprisingly indifferent jailer. Two others, who have already been condemned, are being burned at the stake.

COLORPLATE 19

RAPHAEL (RAFFAELLO SANZIO). *Gregory IX Receiving Decretals from Raymond da Peña Forte.* The Justice Wall in the Stanza della Segnatura. 1512. Fresco. The Vatican, Rome. *Pope from 1227 to 1241, Gregory IX promulgated the* Decretals, *a code of canon law that served as the basis of modern-day ecclesiastical law. Pope Julius II (pope 1503–1513) was the model for this painting.*

COLORPLATE 20

Artist unknown. *Judges in Their Robes*. From Lucas de Heere's *Corte Beschryŭinghe van Engheland, Schotland, Ende Irland, Vergader Uut de Beste Schryuers* (A Brief Description of England, Scotland, and Ireland, Collected from the Best Authors). Sixteenth century. Colored drawing on paper. 12 × 8″ (30.5 × 20.3 cm). British Library, London.

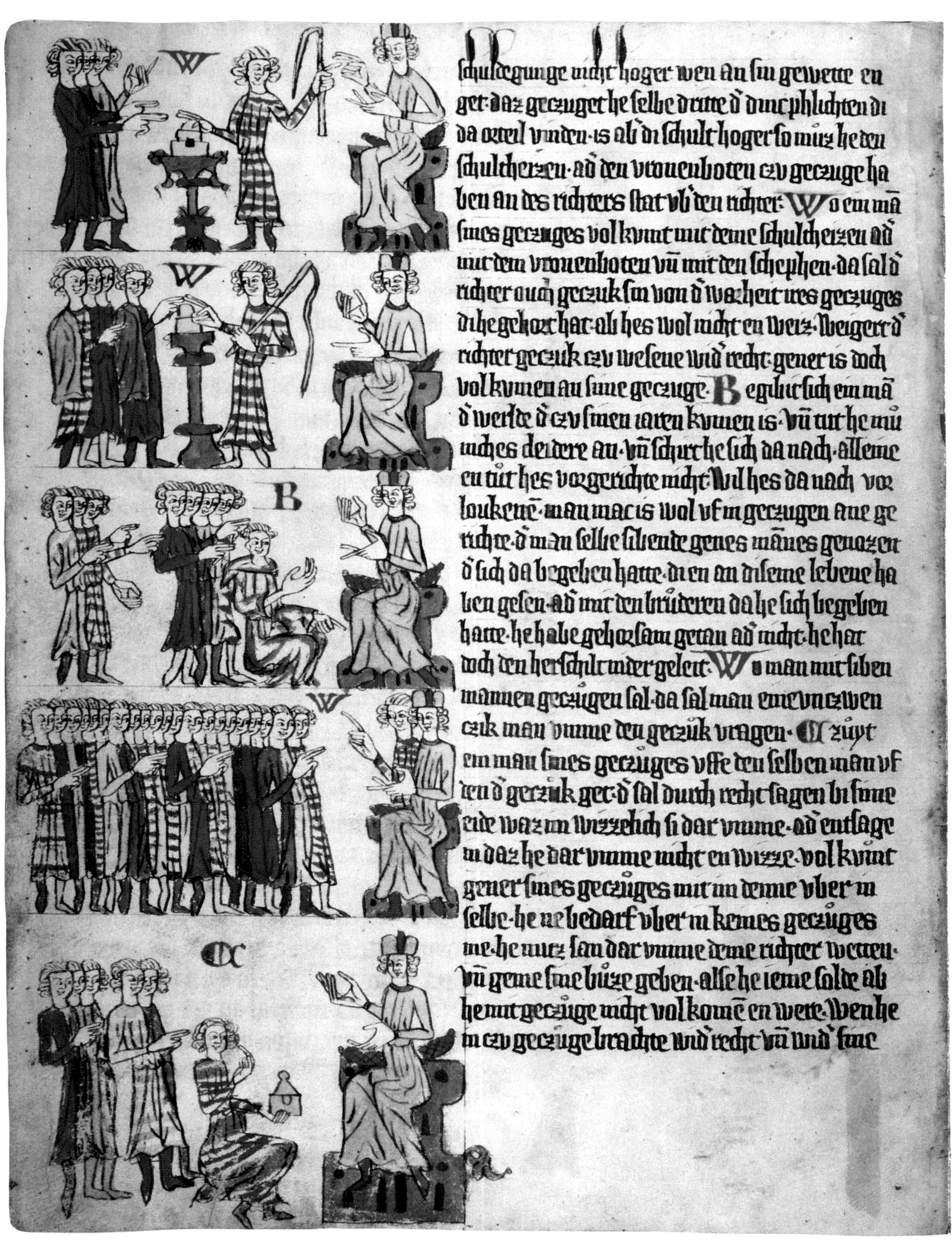

COLORPLATE 21

Mirror of Saxony. Illuminated manuscript. c. 1300–1315. Parchment. 11 13/16 × 9 1/4″ (30 × 23.5 cm). Universitätsbibliothek, Heidelberg. *This treatise on the law of the Saxons by the nobleman and jurist Eike von Repkow represents the beginning of German law writing and is our most important source on the Germanic perception of law in the Middle Ages.*

COLORPLATE 22

JEAN FOUQUET. *Trial of Duke of Alençon.* From Boccaccio's *Des Cas des Nobles Hommes et Femmes Malheureuses.* Illuminated manuscript. c. 1458. 13⅜ × 11″ (34 × 27.9 cm). Bayerische Staatsbibliothek, Munich. *Jean II, duke of Alençon, was tried and sentenced to death in Vendôme in 1458. Louis XVI repealed this sentence in 1461 and renewed the repeal in 1464 and 1467. However, in 1474 Jean was condemned again, this time for delivering the city of Alençon to the Bretons in the War of the Commonwealth. He died in 1476 in the home of a Parisian bourgeois who had served him in prison.*

and estimates of future contingencies and imponderables. Over the centuries the Inns of Court have adapted themselves to the changing conditions of society. Until the Civil War in the 17th century the instruction given in the Inns was almost wholly oral. The qualification to sit on the governing body of an Inn of Court was to hold one of the biannual Readings, courses of lectures onto which were grafted discussions, moots, or mock trials, and more informal bolts or siftings of doubtful points of law. Members of the Inn at all levels were expected to participate, the more senior assisting in the instruction of their juniors.

The Inns were residential colleges, communities living under scholastic discipline, and the great Hall of each was at once lecture room, dining room, club room, and, on the occasion of festivities like the keeping of Christmas, theatre and ballroom too. Not only prospective professional lawyers became members of the Inns Many rich young men were entered there to acquire enough law to manage their estates, act as Justices of the Peace or follow employment in the public service. They were expected to acquire not only law but also social accomplishments and the Christmas celebrations, which lasted till Candlemass on February 2nd, often centred round a mock prince and his court, serving the double purpose of inculcating courtly and diplomatic etiquette and providing an occasion for broad fun in topical satire and parody. When a Lord of Misrule took over, the excesses of the students' rags often gave grave concern to the governing Benchers.

The Civil War in the 17th century broke the continuity of the old order and attempts to reestablish it after the King's Restoration in 1660 gradually faded away. The framework of readings and moots disintegrated. The Inns of Court ceased to be residential colleges, and only dining in Hall as a qualification for call to the Bar carried on the tradition of the old community spirit. Printed books were now multiplied and a student, no longer depending on lecturers, read for the Bar. Legal education went underground and private pupillage became the accepted method of instruction. Throughout the 18th century the Inns of Chancery were steadily losing their grip on the professional lives of the attorneys and solicitors and becoming mere dining clubs, until in the 1830's the Law Society arose to take over their former functions, leaving them to wither away in total inutility. In particular the Law Society put professional qualification on the firm footing of those written examinations in which the pragmatic Victorians had so much faith.

Meanwhile the Inns of Court pursued their leisurely, gentlemanly way, producing an able and incorrupt Bar and, through it, an able and incorrupt, if somewhat Olympian, Bench. But the earnest, tidy, reformist spirit of the times and the quickening tempo of life in an increasingly industrialised nation could scarcely be expected to leave alone those enchanted islands of quiet in the heart of the modern whirlwind. Soon after the middle of the century examinations for call to the Bar were gradually introduced. In the 1870's the entire court system was remodelled and the serjeants-at-law, long professionally ailing and losing ground to the Queen's Counsel, were shorn of all their privileges. Leaving behind only the memory of their separate Inns, they returned, each man, to his original Inn of Court.

* * *

The Inns still train the Bar of England, now by providing a specialist finish to that knowledge of the law which the student has acquired at a university or elsewhere. By requiring him to dine in Hall and encouraging him to participate in after dinner moots, they induct him into the corporate spirit of the profession. They provide the libraries which he shares with the practising members of the Bar. They help the student to find men who will accept him as a pupil and impart to him the practical knowledge of court work without which even the most meticulous mastery of legal theory is mere bookworm stuff. . . .

LINCOLN'S INN

Each Inn has its own separate and distinct personality. Thus two historical accidents have especially influenced the development of Lincoln's Inn. First, in 1734, Lord Chancellor

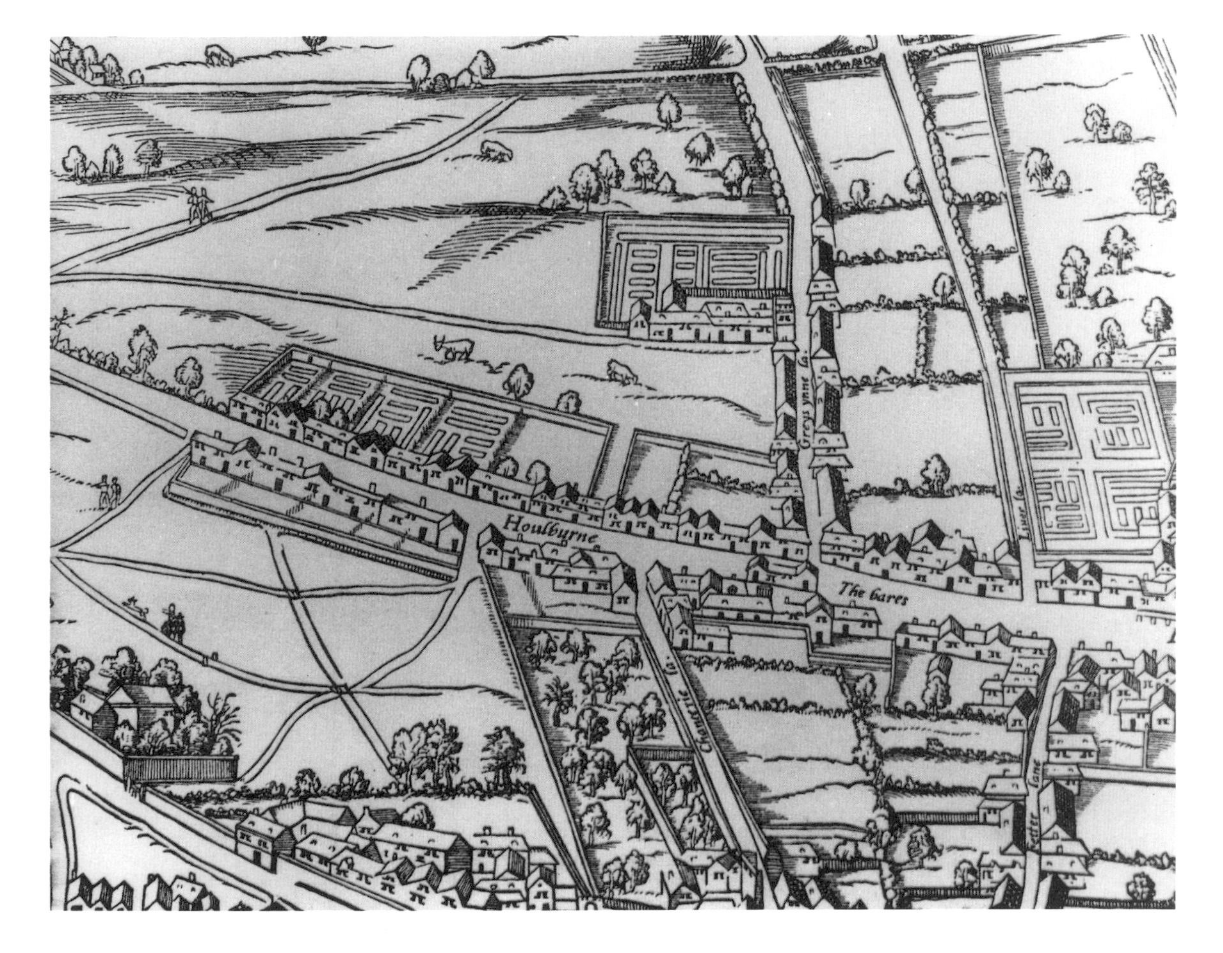

Ralph Agas. *Legal London*, detail. c. 1570. Engraving. Guild Hall Library, London. *At the top center is Gray's Inn, with its gardens. At the bottom center, just west of Chancery Lane, is Lincoln's Inn. Clementine Inn is to its left. Old Temple is in the center, at the east side of the intersection of Houlburne and Chancery Lane. Ely Place Gardens are at the far right.*

Talbot established his court at the upper end of its Hall, leaving only the lower part for dining and the other purposes of the Inn's communal life. Thereafter until the new Law Courts were opened in 1882 the Chancery judges sat within the Inn for, as the work of the Court increased and Vice-Chancellors were appointed to assist the Lord Chancellor, court rooms were erected close to the Hall to accommodate them. This meant that the Inn became a magnet for Chancery practitioners who moved in the rarified atmosphere of equity, that juster sort of justice, so much more esoteric than the rough and tumble practice of the common law. In the first chapter of *Bleak House*, with the Lord Chancellor sitting in the old Hall in the midst of a London fog, Dickens draws a remarkable picture of the mystique of equity practice moving in a learned labyrinth of trusts, settlements of great estates and the custody of infants, the Lord Chancellor's wards of court. The presence of so many learned men practising so refined and complex an art imparted to the Inn an atmosphere of a certain fastidious superiority, diluted though it was, since no Inn is all of a piece, by more robust matters attached to other branches of the law.

The cramped conditions in the old Hall used partly as a court eventually induced the Inn to build another, and in 1843 a very large and imposing neo-Tudor structure, with a fine library annexed to it, arose on the south-west part of the garden. Queen Victoria opened it in great state and the prestige of the Inn rose correspondingly.

* * *

GRAY'S INN

Perhaps Gray's Inn presents the greatest contrast to Lincoln's Inn. Sited beyond the northern extremity of Chancery Lane on the far side of Holborn, it was the remotest of all the Inns from the courts sitting at Westminster and, until late in the 17th century, it looked out over open country to the Hampstead and Highgate hills. Its day of glory came under the Tudors, when with new men like Thomas Cromwell, the Cecils and the Bacons, Nicholas and Francis, among its members, it was in the forefront of the changes which obliterated the mediaeval polity. In the Civil War its members were split almost evenly between King and Parliament and in the restless and conspiratorial England of the Restoration it was again divided, but a decline was setting in and it gradually ceased to be a breeding ground for the judiciary. Sir John Holt, Chief Justice under William and Mary, and Lord Raymond, Chief Justice under George I, were indeed trained at Gray's Inn, but as the 18th century progressed it became more and more of a backwater and by the middle of the 19th century its somnolence was almost complete. Calls to the Bar were numbered in ones and twos. When the new Law Courts in the Strand arose between Lincoln's Inn and the Temple the obvious convenience of immediate proximity to them drew the last of the practising Bar to those Inns, so that the chambers in Gray's Inn were abandoned to solicitors and architects.

But at this low ebb an energetic policy of revitalisation turned the tide. Scholarships were established. Moots, long abandoned in all the Inns, were recommenced at Gray's Inn and gradually the membership began to grow again.

* * *

Misfortune and revival had given Gray's Inn a character all its own, a curious combination of tenacity to its traditions, a robust and friendly informality among its members and a more intimate bond between the Benchers, the Bar and the students than was found in the other Inns. The seating at the long refectory tables was by seniority in messes of four and there were complex rules governing the obligations of members to toast one another individually and collectively by messes. Alleged breaches of custom were adjudicated upon by the senior barrister in Hall, "Mr. Senior," after the Benchers had retired to their private room, and the standard fine for a breach was a bottle of port. It was for Mr. Senior to give permission to smoke after an application by "Mr. Junior," the junior student, shouted across the Hall, often through a barrage of counter-shouting. Any evening in Hall might produce a spontaneous celebration with songs and recitations of all descriptions and assorted party tricks. There could be no greater contrast with the decorous proceedings at Lincoln's Inn. . . .

Till the outbreak of the second World War Gray's Inn was a peaceful harmony of predominantly late 17th and 18th century buildings. In the bombardments it was devastated. But it rose again and the first building to be completed was its well loved Elizabethan Hall, burnt from roof to cellar but now reproduced almost in replica, so that those who knew it of old were conscious of scarcely any difference. . . .

THE TEMPLE

At the lower end of Chancery Lane, beside the Thames, the twin Temples, the Inner Temple and the Middle Temple, were markedly different from Gray's Inn, perched at the top of Holborn Hill, and Lincoln's Inn, looking westward across Lincoln's Inn Fields, the great square which had once been fields indeed. There is a Georgian openness about Gray's Inn, and Lincoln's Inn too is full of light and air. The Temples, built on a site sloping down to the river, developed as a maze or warren of irregular courts and alleys with the strange Round Church of the Templars at its heart.

No one knows when the two Societies were founded or why precisely they co-existed as separate bodies or when the lawyers started adopting the conventional buildings to their own purposes. We do know that they were there in the time of Chaucer, for one of his Canterbury pilgrims was steward to one of the Temple Societies. . . .

INNER TEMPLE

The structure of life in the Inner Temple did not differ in essence from that of the other Inns. The senior members, the practitioners, concerned themselves with the instruction of the students by readings and moots. For their recreations there was the elaborate and extravagant ritual beauty of the masques and revels in the Hall. There was often trouble with turbulent students and sometimes political trouble, as when, during the revolt of the Earl of Essex in 1601, the Inner Temple bought a considerable quantity of arms and armour for the defence of the Queen and afterwards found itself financially embarrassed by the cost. A recurring preoccupation was the City of London's claim to jurisdiction over the Inn, consistently resisted by the members. Twice, when the Lord Mayor, invited to dine in the Hall, had insisted on coming in state, the City Sword, borne aloft as a symbol of his authority, was beaten down by the younger members. When in a frosty January in 1679 a tremendous fire broke out in the heart of the Temple, the Lord Mayor, imagining that now was the time to make good the City's claim, arrived with its Sword erect, the Inner Templars, turning from the blaze, beat it down again. The Mayor sulkily retired to a Fleet Street tavern and revenged himself by turning back the City fire engines.

* * *

The life of the Temple had not the cloistered calm of Lincoln's Inn. This was the realm of the common law, the bustling business of disputes over broken heads, broken contracts, street accidents, libel and slander and, of course, crime. It was in this atmosphere that the famous leaders of the Bar flourished, providing copy for the newspaper reporters by their speeches and their cross-examinations. Such a life produced robust characters like the keen yachtsman who built a dinghy in his one-man chambers in Crown Office Row, where he both lived and practised, and launched it at the Temple Stairs, or the King's Counsel whose pupil parties in King's Bench Walk were famous in the 1920's. After lashings of drink, everyone would stand on the tables, a sack of rats would be opened and emptied and terriers would be let loose to hunt them through the chambers. Such high jinks were exceptional but they were possible.

MIDDLE TEMPLE

The Middle Temple life was very like that in the Inner Temple, though it lacked the great expanses of tree-shadowed King's Bench Walk. Its buildings were more of a huddle, Elm Court, now vanished, between Pump Court and the back of Crown Office Row, Essex Court and Brick Court divided from each other by a pleasant red brick 18th century building. But the glory of the Middle Temple was and is its great Elizabethan Hall with its double hammer beams and its intricately carved gallery. The coloured effigy tomb of its builder, Edmund Plowden, stands in the Temple Church on the north side. He was the greatest lawyer of his time, but he sacrificed his career to his steadfastness in his faith as a Roman Catholic. When Elizabeth I came to the throne he was just about to receive the degree of serjeant-at-law, but his refusal to conform to the Queen's Established Church barred him from that and any other future promotion. Instead of migrating to Serjeants' Inn and becoming a judge he remained a member of the Middle Temple and it was he who was put in charge of the rebuilding of the Hall. It is his monument. That Hall, the fountain beside it, surrounded by trees, and the terrace overlooking the Inn's garden remain one of the most charming spots in any of the Inns.

* * *

THE INNS TODAY

The postwar period brought many changes to the life of the Inns of Court. The combination of the extension of popular education, the extraordinary increase in crime and of the spread of litigiousness following on the institution of legal aid, swelled the ranks of the students, clamorous for new "amenities" and privileges and impatient of discipline and restrictions, while the numbers of the practising Bar grew beyond precedent.

The problem of introducing so many aspirants to the practical skills of advocacy, as pupils to established practitioners, became acute, since practice is a very different thing from book learning and not every able, busy man is an effective teacher. So too the problem of finding physical accommodation in chambers for newcomers presented enormous difficulties. Where formerly it was normal to have a dozen men working in a set of chambers, it now became usual to have twenty or thirty. All this affected the atmosphere of work in the Inns which, with the social dominance of the motor car and the increased demand for parking space within their boundaries, much diminished their cloistered calm. Relaxations in the conventions of dress and demeanour, especially among the students, modified the tone and atmosphere of life in the Inns. So did the increasing female presence.

★ ★ ★

The present function of the Inns is to personalise the Bar, to superimpose on the technical legal skills the personal elements which must dominate them. In that spirit for six centuries the Inns have adapted themselves by their own innate instincts to the changing character of many successive states of society, from the beginning keeping alive the idea of the "free and lawful man." It is essential to our society that they should do so still.

Arthur R. Hogue

FROM ORIGINS OF THE COMMON LAW

"From Medieval Law to Modern Law"

Among the nations of western Europe the English alone have managed to bring essential elements of their medieval customary legal system into the modern world. This extraordinary achievement should not be taken for granted, because the common law has had powerful critics and opponents along the way. It has survived, moreover, through several periods of political crisis which seriously disturbed the balance between three elements fundamental in the English constitution—the prerogative of the Crown, the privileges of Parliament, and the individual liberties of personal security, personal liberty, and private property. At times practitioners of absolutism, both royal and popular, threatened to sweep aside the substance of common-law rules. At other times civil wars interrupted the operation of common-law courts. The history of English law and politics is much more than a slow broadening down from precedent to precedent. England has known periods of terrible violence and disorder. More than once the common-law system has been in peril of its life. Its continuity through almost eight centuries is unique in the history of European legal systems.

★ ★ ★

The common-law system survived enormous social and political changes along the road between the medieval and the modern world. Possibly the balance between Crown, parliament, and individual rights of the subject has been maintained over the centuries because so many Englishmen, common lawyers, country squires, and city merchants have been drawn into the operation of a legal system which has borne directly on the incidents of daily life. In their minds, title to property and enjoyment of personal liberty have been intimately associated with the perpetuation of the common law.

Of the several forces which have operated to preserve its essential character, two should be mentioned in any discussion of the vitality of common law. First, the early maturity of the common law made it a system of technical complexity before the end of the thirteenth century. Thereafter laymen could not hope to conduct their own litigation

---

In this excerpt from his well-known concise volume on the English body of general rules known as the common law, historian Arthur R. Hogue (1906–1985) affirms the vitality and continued adaptability of a legal system whose medieval development he traces particularly in the period from 1154 to 1307 (Henry II's through Edward II's reigns).

successfully without professional help from pleaders and attorneys. The appearance of a legal profession was soon followed by the appearance of Inns of Court. What they were precisely in their medieval beginnings is mere conjecture. They may have been hostels, clubs, and chambers as well as schools of legal education. Certain it is that before the end of the Middle Ages England had a legal profession in close touch with legal education in the Inns of Court, all located near the common-law courts at Westminster. Judges were chosen from the ranks of the legal profession. Judges, pleaders, attorneys, and students formed a professional community with an interest in perpetuating a legal system which they had mastered during training in the Inns of Court. There they had learned to think in patterns set forth in formulas of the common-law writs. Students at the Inns of Court heard lectures, disputed in moot courts, and argued cases put at the dinner table. This system of legal education, always in touch with actual legal controversies at Westminster, was beautifully suited to transmit common-law traditions from the medieval to the modern period. Medieval Inns of Court were private corporations and their histories were not all fortunate; many have disappeared. In the twentieth century four Inns of Court remain: Gray's Inn, Inner Temple, Lincoln's Inn, and Middle Temple.

A second notable factor working for the perpetuation of common law was, again, related to the early maturity of the system. Medieval common law was principally land law. Rules of land law, first enforced in the reign of Henry II, were later elaborated, especially in the time of Edward I, who provided for the alienation of freehold and for the creation of long-term family property arrangements by means of conditional gifts. Land was the principal source of wealth in the Middle Ages and so continued until the commercial and industrial revolutions created alternative sources of personal property, which in their turn fell under common-law rules. Thus for several centuries every family fortune in England has been protected and regulated by intricate rules of common law. At any period between the twelfth and the twentieth centuries, a complete overthrow of common-law rules and the courts administering them would have affected every property owner. Thanks to the rise of Parliament in the Middle Ages and to the medieval evolution of the House of Commons, English property owners thereafter had a channel for the expression of alarm and opposition to

Artist unknown. *Felon Taken to Prison*. 1523. Woodcut.

Artist unknown. *Drawing and Quartering*. c. 1514. Woodcut.

sudden, revolutionary changes in the law of Property. Economic interests with a voice in politics have also worked to perpetuate common law.

* * *

The legacy of medieval law [resides in] . . . the persistence and force in the modern world of some ideas which men of the Middle Ages incorporated in the common law of England.

Foremost among these is the idea of the supremacy of law, a concept also expressed in such phrases as "the rule of law" and "due process." This idea implies that there are limits to the power of ruling, that all government agencies and the law courts themselves must operate according to known rules and procedures. The rule of law was difficult to apply against medieval kings with absolutist policies and no regard for established customs. The rule of law is now difficult to apply in the face of modern ideas of sovereignty which admit no limitation on the power of ruling. But whatever the difficulties, the preservation of the rules of law, or due process, may be the only means of preserving the enjoyment of private rights and personal freedoms. What is required in the twentieth century is a much wider understanding of legal rights, how they have been gained, how they may be lost. For programs promising social justice and economic justice are certain to be unfulfilled unless the programs can be translated into legal rights protected by courts free to apply known rules. Many lawyers understand this; many laymen do not.

It is not easy to see how the rule of law will survive in the midst of revolutionary changes in population density, in technical complexity of communications systems, in commercial transportation, in banking, and, above all, in the production of atomic energy. The complexity of modern society has created problems beyond the capacity of legislators to regulate effectively by statute or of courts to solve by case law—so the argument runs for the creation of a self-directing bureaucracy. If problems are complex, turn them over to experts, specialists in the management of public transportation, communications, commerce, banking, and atomic energy. By means of a legislative act, commission experts with authority to control conditions within a certain field. This is the modern solution. But a government agency must accomplish its mission by ordering people to act or not to act. The commission must issue directives with the force of laws. The directives, however, are difficult to find and they are frequently changed. It is not always possible to discover precisely what the agency has ordered. Moreover, the agency may be the judge and interpreter of its own administrative orders. Problems of the government of complex industrial societies present serious threats to the continuance of the common-law system. The doctrine of the supremacy of law now confronts competition with a doctrine of government regulation by administrative orders. In the twentieth century many European nations have shown how easily "statism" can replace the rule of law. It is a peculiar quality of the Anglo-American legal system that it still retains respect for due process and for courts administering known rules.

A second idea inherited from the Middle Ages touches the work of courts in the legal system and the doctrine of judicial precedents. The dignity of medieval royal courts was impressive. As repositories of the legal tradition, royal judges in the Middle Ages exercised their right to control all matters of procedure—from judging the initial grounds of a legal action to the enforcement of a decision on it. When judges in medieval England failed to maintain the high standards of learning and disinterested action expected of them, English feudal barons, churchmen, and merchants insisted on reform. This appears in the Dictum of Kenilworth, Chapter 2, again in the Ordinances of 1311, Chapter 14, and in other places where public opinion demands justices learned in the law of the realm. In the Middle Ages common-law court decisions were recorded, and on special occasions the record was consulted, but for several centuries the common law lived more in the minds of its judges and practitioners than in plea rolls and reports. The law of the Middle Ages was largely judge-made, and whenever it was changed by deliberate action of the king's council or by Parliament, judges participated in the change. It is an essential feature of the common-law system that its principles are derived from decisions in actual cases in which, of course, judges play the principal part.

A third important legacy of the medieval law to the modern law is the writ system. This statement may seem absurd in light of the fact that nineteenth-century legislation abolished the writ system in England. But English lawyers could afford the luxury of throwing away the old forms of action only after the principles within those forms had become embedded in the law. After men have learned what constitutes a debt recoverable in the courts, the writ of Debt is unnecessary. And so with many other grounds of legal action, or causes of action, defined in the medieval writ system. Modern courts now recognize that a leaseholder is entitled to enjoy the full term of the lease and to recover both the lease and damages if he is ejected from the leased property. But the leaseholder's remedies were not taken for granted in the Middle Ages. They were acquired slowly in the form of actions associated with writs. The full catalog of writs known as the Register of Writs was the framework of the common law. When, in the present, a lawyer decides that his client has a good cause of action which the courts will recognize, he is drawing, more often than he may realize, on the medieval definition of that cause of action in one of the many formal writs.

The rule of law, the development of law by means of judicial precedents, the use of the jury to determine the material facts of a case, and the definition of numerous causes of action—these form the principal and valuable legacy of the medieval law to the modern law.

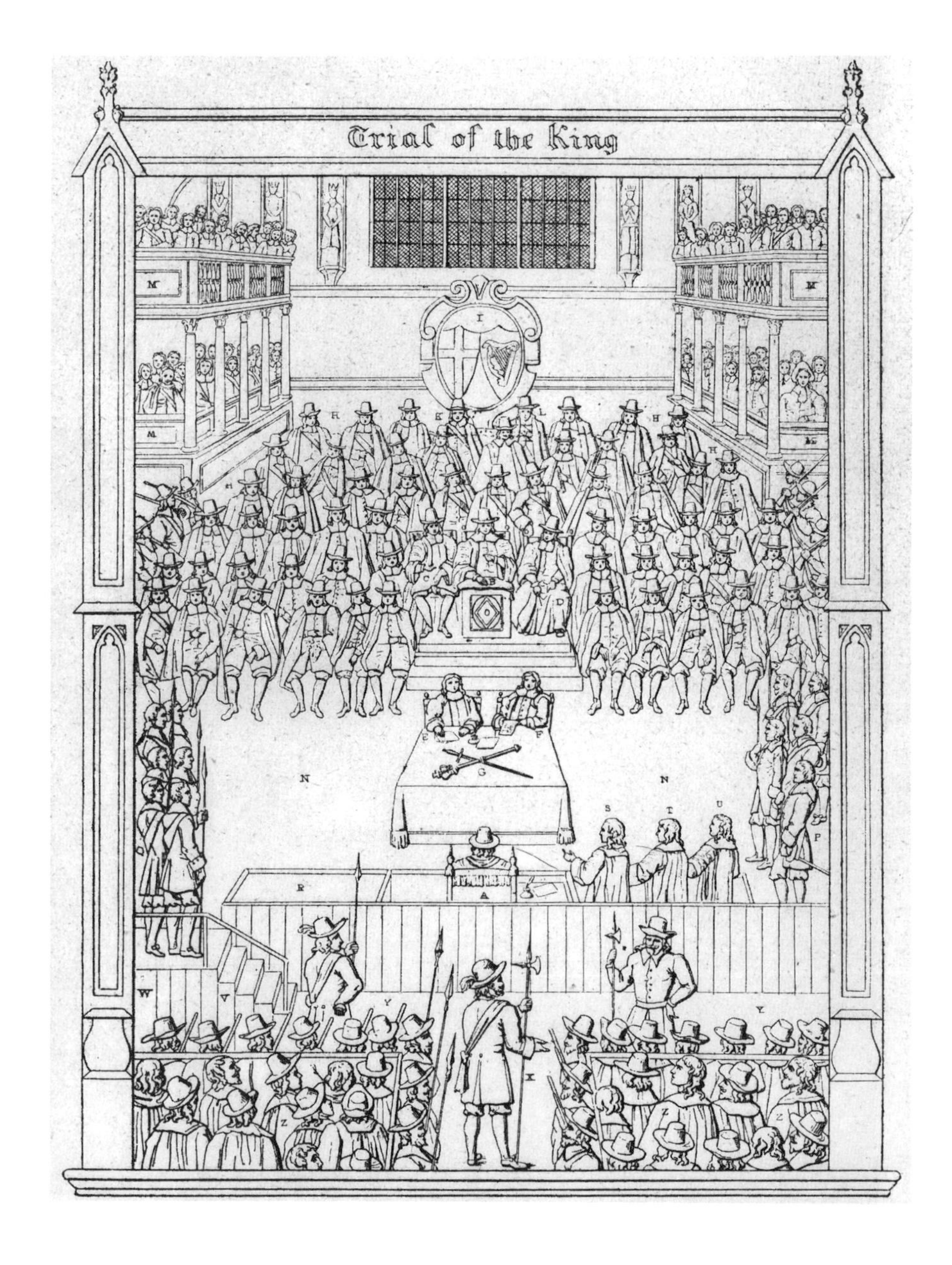

Artist unknown. *High Treason Trial Against Charles I.* c. 1649. Engraving. Westminster City Hall, London.
The king's trial occurred during the Puritan Revolution in London in January 1649.

ASIAN MILESTONES

Geoffrey MacCormack

"The T'ang Code: Early Chinese Law"

Although the T'ang code is the earliest of the Chinese codes to survive in its entirety, it was preceded by at least twelve hundred years of legal development and experiment. The first certainly known promulgation of written rules comes from the late sixth century B.C. In the centuries preceding the unification of the empire by the Ch'in and Han dynasties around 200 B.C. various states issued codes of law. Virtually nothing is known of their content. The Ch'in and Han regulated their empires by means of universally applicable codes. Something, but not a great deal, is known of these laws. With the collapse of the Han in 220 A.D., China again split up into separate states which issued their own codes. With the reunification of the empire by the Sui in 581 A.D. a new code was drawn up and applied to the whole empire, and it was this code which formed the basis of the code adopted by the early T'ang emperors in the succeeding century. . . .

Throughout the T'ang period the code underwent a number of modifications and revisions. The first T'ang emperor, Kao-tsu, established a commission to draft the provisions of a code; the result was promulgated in 624 A.D. It was revised several times after this, the final version appearing in 737 A.D. This is the one which is known today. It consists of 502 elliptically phrased articles with notes added to explain particular phrases. Even with the notes the articles were often too brief to be readily intelligible. Hence the third T'ang emperor, Kao-tsung, ordered a commission to compose an explanatory commentary. This commentary was issued in 653 A.D. and is as authoritative as the text of the code itself. It provides a fuller and clearer account of the rules stated in the articles and often adds many important qualifications.

* * *

The code provided for five classes of punishment: beheading, strangulation, exile for 3000 *li* or less, penal servitude for three years or less and beatings with a heavy or light stick, the latter ranging from ten to 50 blows and the former from 60 to 100. These punishments are more lenient or humane than those applied under earlier dynasties when various types of mutilation had been practised. For each offence, the type of death the number of years of exile or of penal servitude, or the number of blows with the heavy or light stick, is exactly prescribed. In cases where the punishment is exile, penal servitude or beating, the code frequently determines the quantity by means of the notion of degree. Each of these punishments is graded quantitatively into degrees. For example, every ten strokes of the stick counts as a degree. The code establishes the exact penalty for one situation and then

---

The T'ang dynasty (early 7th to early 10th centuries) represents the first great period of Chinese legal thought, yielding a code of law that was the basis of a strong central mechanism of government and finance. This is an excerpt from a highly informative overview by a prominent Scottish legal scholar, published in 1983.

deals with similar situations in which there is some important variable—and here variation in the status of the parties can be crucial—either by applying a different head of liability or by stating an increase or decrease by so many degrees in the punishment already established. Both methods may be employed. A common formula found in the code is: treat offence A as offence B and reduce or increase (as the case might be) one or more degrees.

Appreciation of the importance of status is fundamental to an understanding of the code. Chinese society at the time of the T'ang was divided into very clearly defined classes. The most important division was between officials or nobles, ordinary people who were free, and persons of servile status. Within the classes of officials and servile persons there were several sub-divisions. These classes were not equal under the law, a phenomenon related to the Confucian belief that there was a distinct form of behaviour proper to each of the classes of the people. The distribution of punishment varied according to the status either of the offender or of the victim or of both. One might expect slaves and other "inferior" persons to receive the heaviest punishments, at least where they offended in their behaviour towards a free person, and this is in fact the position in the code. One might also expect officials to be given some privileges, as is also the case. What is surprising is the extent of the privileges which they receive. The general principles section contains a mass of detailed rules on the special position of officials. These rules are of great complexity and the precise legal position of each official depends upon the particular grade or rank which he has. The main effect of the rules was to allow an official to bypass the punishment allocated for the ordinary case. For the most serious offences such as treason, showing disrespect to the emperor or killing one's parents (falling within the so-called "ten abominations") officials were not exempt from the operation of the ordinary law. But in other cases, including all the delicts which might be committed only by officials, they might be entitled to a reduction by one degree of the punishment prescribed for the offence, to a special consideration of their case by the emperor with the expectation that the normal penalty would be reduced, to ransoming themselves from punishment by the payment of copper or to exchanging their punishment for a surrender of their office. Of especial importance were the privileges to pay copper in lieu of punishment or to free oneself from punishment by giving up official position or rank. The range of the privileges open to an official depended upon his exact rank. Furthermore, an official's relatives received a degree of protection, exempting them from the full application of the penalties.

The position of officials under the code was not entirely one of privilege. They were subjected to what appears, from a modern point of view, to be a particularly strict liability. Where an official in the course of his duties made a mistake for which the code prescribed a punishment, his colleagues, both subordinate and superior, were also punished although they had neither participated in the mistake nor known about it. Again, the rules are detailed and worked out with great precision, but the basic principle is that the further removed in the hierarchy the official is from the one who committed the mistake, the less the degree of punishment. An official was made strictly liable in certain cases for breaches of good order in a district within his jurisdiction. In the case of the magistrate directly responsible for the district, it could, perhaps, be argued that the ground of his liability was his own carelessness in the discharge of his duties. But the magistrate of the province to which the district belonged was also made liable, albeit to a lesser degree. Here one cannot realistically speak of carelessness. In effect, the provincial officials were made liable for breaches of good order in a district over which they had no direct control. Furthermore, officials who acted as judges were made strictly liable for wrong judgments. Of course, the severity of the code in its wide distribution of liability was mitigated by the fact that the specific punishments imposed would normally be redeemable by surrender of office or payment of copper. The legal privilege of the official counter-balances and, to a certain extent, offsets the liability derived from his position.

The privileged position of officials under the code is a striking example of the influence of Confucian doctrines in the framing of the laws. A much quoted statement in the Li

Chi (Book of Rites) was "*Li* (used here in the sense of the proper behaviour expected of a gentleman) does not go down to the common people, punishment does not reach up to the Great Prefects (the officials)." Gentlemen or "superior men" (making up the officials class) were expected to behave in accordance with right principle without the threat of punishment for infringement. This view was not accepted by the adherents of a rival school of thought (legalism) for whom the laws (punishments) should apply in an equal fashion to all irrespective of rank. The code itself is an interesting mixture of the two opposed views. In form, the individual articles established the rule and the punishment for its infraction in a general fashion, and no special mention is made of officials unless the offence in question is one that can be committed only by an official. Hence, so far as the wording of the individual laws is concerned, the official is subject to the same penalty as anyone else. The Confucian influence is introduced through the medium of the section on general principles. This contains the rules defining the privileges available to officials and, in effect, exempting them from the ordinary punishment imposed for specific offences.

Equally prominent in the code is recognition of differences of status within the family. Its rules reflect the hierarchical structure of the patrilineal Chinese family in which agnatic relatives were expected to behave towards each other in well-defined ways. Members of the family ranked as senior or junior *vis-à-vis* each other, seniority being determined both by generation and age. A wife ranked as junior to her husband. The family head, in charge of the ancestral cult, was the eldest male of the senior generation. Juniors owed respect and obedience to seniors, particularly in the case of children and parents. Distance and seniority in relationship were marked by the period of time for which it was necessary to mourn a deceased relative. The period varied from three years for parents or paternal grandparents to three months for great-grandchildren.

Many provisions in the code regulate the behaviour of members of the family towards each other. What is striking to the modern eye is the extent to which the failure to exhibit proper behaviour is made an offence: for example, failure to observe the restrictions necessary for the period of mourning described for the death of a relative, failure to maintain the decorous conduct expected of a wife, failure to show proper respect to one's parents. In allocating penalties, the code paid most attention to the degree of relationship and the seniority of the individuals. For a junior member of the family to strike or curse a senior member who was a close relative was a very serious offence; on the other hand, it was no offence for a father to beat or curse his son. No greater offence could be committed than the killing of a father (even unintentionally) by his son; yet the intentional killing of a son by his father received a relatively light punishment and unintentional killing was not punished at all. With respect to property, it was a more serious offence to steal from a distant relative than a close one.

The code is concerned primarily with the detailing of administrative or military duties, the prescription of behaviour, and the allocation of penalties for the failure to carry out a duty or observe the prescribed behaviour. Hence, it has very little on what we would understand by the law of contract, succession or land ownership. Yet, precisely because of the wide variety of behaviour which the code deemed it necessary to enjoin by means of specific sanctions, one occasionally obtains glimpses of the rules regulating contracts, or the inheritance of property, or rights with respect to land. Much of what we call family law (marriage, divorce, adoption, relations between parent and child) is regulated in detail by the law because the Confucian ethic attached particular importance to the maintenance of proper behaviour of family members towards each other. The difference from the modern treatment is that the code, in effect, locates family law within the criminal law.

René David and John E. C. Brierley

FROM MAJOR LEGAL SYSTEMS IN THE WORLD TODAY

"Japanese Law"

The first landmarks in Japanese law appear in the Taika era which began in the year A.D. 646. Under Chinese influence, a form of state and moralistic planning was introduced by means, in particular, of a system of periodic distribution of the state rice plantations in proportion to the numbers to be fed and a strict division of society into "ranks." Each class was required to perform some specific task for the state, and legal compilations based on Chinese models known as *ritsu-ryō* spelled out the duties of each. They contain principally a series of prohibitions (*ritsu*) and rules of administration (*ryō*). These collections were commented upon in schools of law and administration for the enlightenment of the people. They contain no suggestion of the idea of *rights* but there is some notion of law in so far as they constitute a recording in writing of the duties of each person.

The land sharing system found in the *ritsu-ryō* of the seventh century, also based on Chinese ideas, functioned poorly in Japan. In the ninth and tenth centuries a seigneurial system developed to the detriment of the system of sharing of public land previously practised. The Japanese seigneurial unit (*shō*) appears to have been an inviolable domain enjoying certain fiscal privileges; the master of the *shō* changed his right to receive the products of the land, which he enjoyed as an hereditary public official, into a right of full ownership of extensive tracts of land; within the *shō* he had the powers of a sovereign.

Weaknesses in criminal justice, resulting insecurities and a series of civil wars led to the superimposition of a new feudal system at the end of the twelfth century. The emperor was deprived of any real power and his decline carried with it that of the courtier class (*kuge*) as well. Because of his sacred rights the emperor remained an important and revered figure but he no longer held any real power. He was above—but also quite outside—the military caste, unknown in China, which henceforth governed. The military caste (*buke, bushi, samurai*) lived according to its own personal, customary law (*buke-hō*). The ruling "code of chivalry" was founded on the idea of the duty of absolute faithfulness on the part of the vassal towards his overlord. There is once again no concept whatsoever of legal rights or duties. The vassal had no guarantee against the arbitrary action of the overlord; there was never any system of judgment by one's peers in Japan. Even the very idea that the vassal might have rights exercisable against his suzerain would have been shocking; their relationship was very much like that of father and son. There was, then, no concept of contract between them. . . .

For several centuries the warrior class ethic of the *buke* existed alongside the more detailed regulation of the *ritsu-ryō*; the latter continued to apply to those who did not belong to the warrior class. During the period of the Ashizaka Shoguns (1333–1573), following the Kamakura era (1185–1333), a period of anarchy and civil war ended with the triumph of the so-called "unitary" feudalism. The superiority of the warrior over the peasant was established; the local representatives of the military class (*jitō*) whose duty it was to ensure public order and collect taxes, secured for themselves the revenues of the *shō* which, until that time, they had shared. Japan, now divided between several powerful local and independent lords (*daymyō*) to whom the *jitō* were infeudated, was plagued by a series of private wars. The rules of the *ritsu-ryō* fell into a desuetude; only the ancient

---

The history of Japanese law—from its Chinese-influenced beginnings to its East-meets-West present—is briefly traced in this excerpt.

personal law of the *buke* remained in force and they soon replaced the territorial customs.

Until that time there were different social classes in Japan each ruled by its own particular *statut*. This inegalitarian structure was replaced in the fourteenth century by a strictly conceived hierarchy which in its own way excluded any idea of rights of an inferior as against his superior. Since there was no concept of contract or reciprocal legal obligations between the members of the warrior class, there were none, *a fortiori*, between the lords and those who tilled the land.

This hierarchical structure, in which any notion of rights was absent, was further re-enforced during the era of Tokugawa Shoguns (1603–1868) when the policy of isolation was inaugurated. As a reaction against European influences, Confucianism was made the official religion. A policy of close supervision and a system of denunciation began in 1597 with the organisation throughout the country of groups of persons, five in number called *goningumi*, charged with reporting all crimes, maintaining public order, informing the police of the movements of others or the presence of foreigners. The group, treated as an entity for fiscal and criminal purposes, had to agree before any form of judicial procedure could be instituted by one of its members. It intervened in the family affairs of each member by supplying either counsellors or witnesses, and it controlled the cultivation of land. This institution so deeply marked the Japanese mentality during the Tokugawa period that its traces are present even today.

This established order was considered at the time to be a natural and immutable social organisation. It was based on a strict separation of social classes (warriors, peasants, merchants) and their arrangement into a hierarchy. The whole way of life of a Japanese was determined on the basis of the class to which he belonged; the type of house inhabited, the type and colour of cloth worn and type of food consumed were all predetermined. The Shōgun of Ido, who was possessed of real power, did not consider that acting as a judge formed a normal part of his functions, and only in exceptional cases would he intervene in such capacity. His jurisdiction only developed in the eighteenth century; according to a decision of 1767, it covered 53 types of cases classified into two categories: major disputes and money disputes. But the policy of the central administration was always directed to maintaining rather than usurping the jurisdiction of the local courts. Justice continued, however, to be administered by the shōgun rather against his will and private persons were never recognised as having the right to institute an action. Judicial functions were never distinguished from other public duties. And in Japan, there were no law schools, no professional magistrates, judicial administration or legal professionals.

* * *

Whatever at this period might be considered law, or merely written rules, amounts really to no more than instructions given by superiors to inferiors. The inferior had only to obey; the mass of people, systematically kept in ignorance, was not protected in any way against any form of arbitrary action. There was no question of rights in the relations of persons from an inferior class with those of a superior class. And the idea of law, altogether absent with respect to persons belonging to different classes, was no more evident in relations between those of the same class. Just as in China, there was a sentiment amounting to abhorrence at the finality of solutions and the absence of shades of meaning which the very idea of law implies. A whole series of rules, in nature much closer to rules of propriety than morality, was developed in order to specify the conduct to be observed on all occasions when one individual came into contact with others. These rules of behaviour, analogous to the Chinese rites, were known as *giri*. . . .

The *giri* therefore replaced law and, according to some Japanese, even morality. It was spontaneously observed not so much because it corresponded to a series of moral values or strict duties but rather because social reprobation attached to its non-observance. It would be a source of shame, a loss of face, for a Japanese not to respect one of the *giri* in which he was involved. A code of honour, wholly customary, thus determined all forms of behavior. Until recent times, the system of the *giri* made any intervention of law in the western sense useless and even offensive.

★ ★ ★

Such was the picture of Japanese society at the beginning of the Meiji era in 1868. All these ancient structures then seemed to disappear as a result of a complete re-shaping of Japanese society. A democratic state of the western type replaced the former feudal state and an extraordinary development has placed Japan at the forefront of the world's trading nations. And now there is modern legislation linking Japanese law to the laws of the West, in particular the Romanist laws of the European continent. The legal works written in Japan confirm the impression that the legal system, legal thought and indeed the whole of society have been thoroughly westernised. The studies devoted to the philosophy of law written by Japanese expound western jurisprudential theories without making any mention of traditional and specifically Japanese ideas. A complete break between the ancient and the modern Japanese laws apparently exists. It is extremely rare for any reference ever to be made to the former law which has, moreover, never yet been completely described in a single work. Modern Japanese law is wholly attached to western law; Harada, a Japanese Romanist, has been able to establish that without exception *all* the articles of the Japanese Civil Code are derived from some western or Roman law.

★ ★ ★

The law of Japan . . . underwent very considerable change after 1945. There was no question at that time of returning to rules more in harmony with the genius of Japanese civilisation. The reforms introduced in a spirit of democratisation were American rather than Japanese in inspiration. A new constitution (1946), reforms in administrative organisation, the status of public officials, administrative jurisdictions and procedure resulted. There was also a radical re-organisation of the court structure and police, and some changes to the then existing codes were also made.

★ ★ ★

Since 1945, therefore, an Anglo-American influence has been at work on, and is sometimes in competition with, the Romanist influence. But the question is still very much open whether, behind this façade of westernisation, Japan really has undergone any kind of fundamental transformation and whether it has accepted the idea of justice and law such as understood in the West.

This question can be asked as readily in the field of private as in public law. In both cases the law is wholly state-made, copied from the West, and really only governs a very small part of Japan's social life. Western law does, after all, suppose a middle class, capitalist society made up of free individuals who establish their various relations on the basis of this liberty. Such a state of things is very far removed from the realities of Japan. It is true that Japanese *mores* are evolving, and they are approaching more and more, especially in urban society and among members of the younger generation, those presupposed by their law. But from all points of view Japanese society is still far from being a western society. The former habits and ways of thinking are still very much alive among the majority of Japanese, even those living in cities, the working classes and in commercial dealings. A state capitalism, or one developed by a small number of important businessmen, has grown up beside a very little changed peasant class closely linked to the industrial working class. A socially critical spirit has been slow to develop; the Confucian idea of an ordered hierarchy based on natural scheme of things is still very much alive. Individualism has never had very strong roots in Japan. Thus the social structures and the free atmosphere pre-supposed by western laws are present only to a very slight degree in Japan. Western laws were made for a rationalist milieu and their abstract conceptual structures are the product of a Cartesian outlook. In Japan the application of modern law runs counter to Japanese mystical sentimentalism, the outcome more of a poetic than a logical spirit, which has rendered the Japanese historically indifferent to the ideals of individual freedom and human dignity entertained in the West.

Mohandas K. Gandhi
On His Conviction for Sedition

I owe it perhaps to the Indian public and to the public in England to placate which this prosecution is mainly taken up that I should explain why from a stanch loyalist and cooperator I have become an uncompromising disaffectionist and non-cooperator. To the court too I should say why I plead guilty to the charge of promoting disaffection toward the government established by law in India.

My public life began in 1893 in South Africa in troubled weather. My first contact with British authority in that country was not of a happy character. I discovered that as a man and as an Indian I had no rights. More correctly, I discovered that I had no rights as a man because I was an Indian.

But I was not baffled. I thought that this treatment of Indians was an excrescence upon a system that was intrinsically and mainly good. I gave the government my voluntary and hearty cooperation, criticizing it freely where I felt it was faulty but never wishing its destruction.

* * *

I came reluctantly to the conclusion that the British connection had made India more helpless than she ever was before, politically and economically. A disarmed India has no power of resistance against any aggressor if she wanted to engage in an armed conflict with him. So much is this the case that some of our best men consider that India must take generations before she can achieve the Dominion status. She has become so poor that she has little power of resisting famines. Before the British advent, India spun and wove in her millions of cottages just the supplement she needed for adding to her meager agricultural resources. This cottage industry, so vital for India's existence, has been ruined by incredibly heartless and inhuman processes as described by English witnesses. Little do town dwellers know how the semistarved masses of India are slowly sinking to lifelessness. Little do they know that their miserable comfort represents the brokerage they get for the work they do for the foreign exploiter, that the profits and the brokerage are sucked from the masses. Little do they realize that the government established by law in British India is carried on for this exploitation of the masses. No sophistry, no jugglery in figures can explain away the evidence that the skeletons in many villages present to the naked eye. I have no doubt whatsoever that both England and the town dwellers of India will have to answer, if there is a God above, for this crime against humanity which is perhaps unequaled in history. The law itself in this country has been used to serve the foreign exploiter. My unbiased examination of the Punjab Martial Law cases has led me to believe that at least ninety-five per cent of convictions were wholly bad. My experience of political cases in India leads me to the conclusion that in nine out of every ten the condemned men were totally innocent. Their crime consisted in the love of their country. In ninety-nine cases out of a hundred justice has been denied to Indians as against Europeans in the courts of India. This is not an exaggerated picture. It is the experience of almost every Indian who has had anything to do with such cases. In my opinion, the administration of the law is thus prostituted consciously or unconsciously for the benefit of the exploiter.

The greatest misfortune is that Englishmen and their Indian associates in the administration of the country do not know that they are engaged in the crime I have attempted to describe. I am satisfied that many Englishmen and Indian officials honestly believe that they are administering one of the best systems devised in the world and that India is

---

Tried and convicted for seditious writings in support of the Indian nationalist movement in the early 1920s, Mohandas K. Gandhi (1869–1948) asked to receive that crime's severest penalty—as shown in this selection from Gandhi's closing statement to the judge on March 23, 1922.

Mahatma Gandhi. From *Life* magazine, July 15, 1946.
Photograph by Margaret Bourke-White.

making steady though slow progress. They do not know that a subtle but effective system of terrorism and an organized display of force on the one hand, and the deprivation of all powers of retaliation or self-defense on the other, have emasculated the people and induced in them the habit of simulation. This awful habit has added to the ignorance and the self-deception of the administrators. Section 124-A, under which I am happily charged, is perhaps the prince among the political sections of the Indian Penal Code designed to suppress the liberty of the citizen. Affection cannot be manufactured or regulated by law. If one has an affection for a person or system, one should be free to give the fullest expression to his disaffection, so long as he does not contemplate, promote, or incite to violence. But the section under which Mr. Banker [a colleague in nonviolence] and I are charged is one under which mere promotion of disaffection is a crime. I have studied some of the cases tried under it, and I know that some of the most loved of India's patriots have been convicted under it. I consider it a privilege, therefore, to be charged under that section. I have endeavored to give in their briefest outline the reasons for my disaffection. I have no personal ill will against any single administrator, much less can I have any disaffection toward the King's person. But I hold it to be a virtue to be disaffected toward a government which in its totality has done more harm to India than any previous system. India is less manly under the British rule than she ever was before. Holding such a belief, I consider it to be a sin to have affection for the system. And it has been a precious privilege for me to be able to write what I have in the various articles, tendered in evidence against me.

In fact, I believe that I have rendered a service to India and England by showing in non-cooperation the way out of the unnatural state in which both are living. In my humble opinion, non-cooperation with evil is as much a duty as is cooperation with good. But in the past, non-cooperation has been deliberately expressed in violence to the evildoer. I am endeavoring to show to my countrymen that violent non-cooperation only multiplies evil and that as evil can only be sustained by violence, withdrawal of support of evil requires complete abstention from violence. Nonviolence implies voluntary submission to the penalty for non-cooperation with evil. I am here, therefore, to invite and submit cheerfully to the highest penalty that can be inflicted upon me for what in law is a deliberate crime and what appears to me to be the highest duty of a citizen. The only course open to you, the judge, is either to resign your post, and thus dissociate yourself from evil if you feel that the law you are called upon to administer is an evil and that in reality I am innocent, or to inflict on me the severest penalty if you believe that the system and the law you are assisting to administer are good for the people of this country and that my activity is therefore injurious to the public weal.

COLORPLATE 23

Conjugal Law: Adulterous Wife Appearing in Court. Manuscript. Fifteenth century. Royal Library, El Escorial.

INGRES
1854.
et son bucher se change
dans les cieux

COLORPLATE 24 *(opposite)*

JEAN AUGUST DOMINIQUE INGRES. *Jeanne d'Arc au Sâcre de Charles VII* (Joan of Arc at the Coronation of Charles VII). 1851–1854. Oil on canvas. 94½ × 70¾" (240 × 178 cm). Louvre, Paris. *At the age of 13, the peasant girl Joan of Arc (1412–1431) believed herself selected by God to aid the dauphin of France (later King Charles VII) by lifting the nearly overwhelming English seige of Orléans. With a small army, the Maid of Orléans succeeded in driving off the English in 1429. After leading French forces in many battles, she was captured in 1430, sold to the English, and turned over to the Inquisition. Tried and condemned for heresy and witchcraft, she was burned at the stake in May 1431. Pope Benedict XV canonized Joan in 1920.*

COLORPLATE 25

Artist unknown. *Sir Thomas Lyttelton*. Before 1461. Oil on canvas. 83 × 48" (210.8 × 121.9 cm). The Honourable Society of the Inner Temple, London. *Sir Thomas Littleton (1407?–1481) earned reknown for his treatise on English land law,* Tenures *(1481 or 1482), the earliest printed work on English law. Sir Edward Coke's* Institutes of the Lawes of England *(1628) is a commentary on* Tenures.

COLORPLATE 26

Courtroom scene from *Le Coutume de Normandie*. Illuminated manuscript. 1450–1470. 6¾ × 4¾″ (16.8 × 12.2 cm). Rare Book Collection, Law Library, Library of Congress, Washington, D.C.
Meeting with officers of the Norman court, twelve men reach a decision on a legal dispute.

COLORPLATE 27

A Wager of Battel. From *Le Coutume de Normandie.* Illuminated manuscript. 1450–1470. 6¾ × 4¾″ (16.8 × 12.2 cm). Rare Book Collection, Law Library, Library of Congress, Washington, D.C. *In pre–trial-by-jury Europe, legal disputes were often settled by wagers of battel, in which the survivor of one-on-one conflict was considered the vindicated party. It was believed that the righteous hand of God guided the killing blow. The concept, which came to be introduced into England by the Normans, was used in both civil and criminal cases.*

COLORPLATE 28

Law Lecturer and His Class. Detail of a sarcophagus frieze. Fifteenth century. Marble. Museo Civico, Bologna.

COLORPLATE 29 *(opposite)*

CH'ANG HSIU. *Confucius.* From an album of portraits of well-known Chinese. c. 1770. Gouache on paper. 13³⁄₁₆ × 8″ (33.5 × 20.2 cm). Bibliothèque Nationale, Paris. *Confucius (K'ung Fu-tzu) (c. 552–479 B.C.), resigned as prime minister of the state of Lu (in present province of Shantung) c. 495 B.C., taking up the life of a peripatetic teacher. Confucianism is a practical philosophy involving ethics, family responsibilities, and good government, not a religion in the Western sense. His teachings are collected as maxims in the classic known as the* Analects.

至聖孔子
名丘字仲尼山東
兗州府曲阜縣人

COLORPLATE 30

Huejotzingo Codex. Manuscript. 1531. Harkness Collection, Library of Congress, Washington, D.C. *This codex was used as documentary evidence in a lawsuit brought against members of the First Audiencia of New Spain (1528–1531) by Hernando Cortes, conqueror of Mexico, in Tenochtitlán (now Mexico City). Aztec Indians are shown making heavy tribute payments to the First Audiencia. The illustration includes a standard with an image of the Virgin Mary.*

COLORPLATE 31 *(opposite)*

The Magistrates of Paris. From a compendium of the Ordinances of the City of Paris. c. 1500. Bibliothèque de l'Arsenal, Paris.

Le greffe
Le receueur
Le clerc

Sr. Thomas Moore Knt. Ld. CHANCELLOR. of ENGLAND
1530.

COLORPLATE 32 *(opposite)*

Artist unknown. *Sir Thomas More.* 1530. Oil on canvas. 22 9/16 × 17 5/8" (57.3 × 44.8 cm). Harvard Law Art Collection, Cambridge. *More (1478–1535), although a layman, was appointed lord chancellor of England in 1529. When Henry VIII, unhappily married to Catherine of Aragon, appointed himself head of the Church of England and granted himself an annulment of marriage, making possible his marriage to Anne Boleyn, More resigned in protest in 1532. For his refusal to support the Act of Succession, he was found guilty of high treason and beheaded. More was canonized in 1935.*

COLORPLATE 33

George Harlow. *The Court for the Trial of Queen Katharine.* From Shakespeare's *Henry VIII,* act 2, scene iv. c. 1817. Oil on canvas. 31½ × 41" (80 × 104 cm). Royal Shakespeare Theatre Picture Gallery, Stratford-upon-Avon. *King Henry VIII, anxious to marry Anne Boleyn, sought to have his marriage to Catherine of Aragon annulled on the grounds that she had previously been married to Arthur, his older brother—a case of incest in contemporary opinion. Pope Clement VII's refusal to grant the annulment provoked the desperate king to declare himself head of the Church of England, unbeholden to the Church of Rome. In this illustration, a dismayed Henry sits in the background while the papal legate glares out at the viewer.*

COLORPLATE 34

JAN VAN RAVENSTEYN. *The Hague Magistrates Receiving the Officers of the Civic Guard.* 1618.
Oil on canvas. 68 × 196$\frac{1}{16}$" (173 × 498 cm). Collection Haags Gemeentemuseum, The Hague.

34

COLORPLATE 35

PAUL VAN SOMER. *Sir Edward Coke.* 1616. Oil on canvas. 82½ × 48″ (209.6 × 121.9 cm). The Honourable Society of the Inner Temple, London. *Sir Edward Coke (1552–1634) is best known for his* Institutes, *a collection of treatises that constitutes the first textbook of modern common law. Coke was appointed chief justice of the Court of Common Pleas in 1606 and chief justice of King's Bench in 1613. Throughout his career Coke quarreled with his king, James I, and was eventually dismissed in 1616.*

COLORPLATE 36

GIOVANNI BATTISTA MORONI. *Bartolommeo Bonghi*. Inscribed and dated 1584. Oil on canvas. 40 × 32¼" (101.6 × 81.9 cm). The Metropolitan Museum of Art, New York. Museum purchase. *A distinguished jurist, Bonghi was doctor of both canon and civil law.*

COLORPLATE 37

ROBERT-FLEURY (JOSEPH NICOLAS ROBERT FLEURY). *Galileo Devant le Saint Office* (Galileo Before the Inquisition). 1847. Oil on canvas. 77⅜ × 121¼" (196.5 × 308 cm). Louvre, Paris. *Galileo Galilei (1564–1642) was denounced for heresy in advocating the Copernican system and admonished by Pope Paul V in 1616 to no longer defend that system. However, in 1632 he published his* Dialogo dei due Massimi Sistemi del Mondo, *again commending the heliocentric system; for this offense he was tried by the Inquisition and forced, for the sake of his life, to renounce the system he had championed.*

THE MODERN THRESHOLD

Francis Bacon

"Of Judicature"

Judges ought to remember that their office is *jus dicere,* and not *jus dare;* to interpret law, and not to make law, or give law. Else will it be like the authority claimed by the church of Rome, which under pretext of exposition of Scripture doth not stick to add and alter; and to pronounce that which they do not find; and by shew of antiquity to introduce novelty. Judges ought to be more learned than witty, more reverend than plausible, and more advised than confident. Above all things, integrity is their portion and proper virtue. *Cursed* (saith the law) *is he that removeth the landmark.* The mislayer of a mere-stone is to blame. But it is the unjust judge that is the capital remover of landmarks, when he defineth amiss of lands and property. One foul sentence doth more hurt than many foul examples. For these do but corrupt the stream, the other corrupteth the fountain. So saith Solomon, *Fons turbatus, et vena corrupta, est justus cadens in causâ suâ coram adversario* [A righteous man falling down before the wicked is as a troubled fountain or a corrupt spring]. The office of judges may have reference unto the parties that sue, unto the advocates that plead, unto the clerks and ministers of justice underneath them, and to the sovereign or state above them.

First, for the causes or parties that sue. *There be* (saith the Scripture) *that turn judgment into wormwood;* and surely there be also that turn it into vinegar; for injustice maketh it bitter, and delays make it sour. The principal duty of a judge is to suppress force and fraud; whereof force is the more pernicious when it is open, and fraud when it is close and disguised. Add thereto contentious suits, which ought to be spewed out, as the surfeit of courts. A judge ought to prepare his way to a just sentence, as God useth to prepare his way, by raising valleys and taking down hills: so when there appeareth on either side an high hand, violent prosecution, cunning advantages taken, combination, power, great counsel, then is the virtue of a judge seen, to make inequality equal; that he may plant his judgment as upon an even ground. *Qui fortiter emungit, elicit sanguinem* [Violent blowing makes the nose bleed]; and where the wine-press is hard wrought, it yields a harsh wine, that tastes of the grape-stone. Judges must beware of hard constructions and strained inferences; for there is no worse torture than the torture of laws. Specially in case of laws penal, they ought to have care that that which was meant for terror be not turned into rigour; and that they bring not upon the people that shower whereof the Scripture speaketh, *Pluet super eos laqueos* [He shall rain snares upon them]; for penal laws pressed are a *shower of snares* upon the people. Therefore let penal laws, if they have been sleepers of long, or if they be grown unfit for the present time, be by wise judges confined in the execution: *Judicis officium est, ut res, ita tempora rerum, &c.* [A judge must have regard to

---

The interests of Francis Bacon (1561–1626), English philosopher, lawyer, and courtier to Elizabeth I and James I, ranged widely, from literature and history to politics, law, and natural philosophy. Bacon's best-known writings are his aphoristic Essays *(1597–1625).*

the time as well as to the matter]. In causes of life and death, judges ought (as far as the law permitteth) in justice to remember mercy; and to cast a severe eye upon the example, but a merciful eye upon the person.

Secondly, for the advocates and counsel that plead. Patience and gravity of hearing is an essential part of justice; and an overspeaking judge is no well-tuned cymbal. It is no grace to a judge first to find that which he might have heard in due time from the bar; or to show quickness of conceit in cutting off evidence or counsel too short; or to prevent information by questions, though pertinent. The parts of a judge in hearing are four: to direct the evidence; to moderate length, repetition, or impertinency of speech; to recapitulate, select, and collate the material points of that which hath been said; and to give the rule or sentence. Whatsoever is above these is too much; and proceedeth either of glory and willingness to speak, or of impatience to hear, or of shortness of memory, or of want of a staid and equal attention. It is a strange thing to see that the boldness of advocates should prevail with judges; whereas they should imitate God, in whose seat they sit; who *represseth the presumptuous, and giveth grace to the modest*. But it is more strange, that judges should have noted favorites; which cannot but cause multiplication of fees, and suspicion of bye-ways. There is due from the judge to the advocate some commendation and gracing, where causes are well handled and fair pleaded; especially towards the side which obtaineth not; for that upholds in the client the reputation of his counsel, and beats down in him the conceit of his cause. There is likewise due to the public a civil reprehension of advocates, where there appeareth cunning counsel, gross neglect, slight information, indiscreet pressing, or an over-bold defense. And let not the counsel at the bar chop with the judge, nor wind himself into the handling of the cause anew after the judge hath declared his sentence; but on the other side, let not the judge meet the cause half way, nor give occasion for the party to say his counsel or proofs were not heard.

Artist unknown. *Francis Bacon*. Nineteenth century. Engraving.

Thirdly, for that that concerns clerks and ministers. The place of justice is an hallowed place; and therefore not only the bench, but the foot-pace and precincts and purprise thereof, ought to be preserved without scandal and corruption. For certainly *Grapes* (as the Scripture saith) *will not be gathered of thorns or thistles;* neither can justice yield her fruit with sweetness amongst the briars and brambles of catching and polling clerks and ministers. The attendance of courts is subject to four bad instruments. First, certain persons that are sowers of suits; which make the court swell, and the country pine. The second sort is of those that engage courts in quarrels of jurisdiction, and are not truly *amici curiae* [friends of the court], but *parasiti curiae* [parasites of the court] in putting a court up beyond her bounds, for their own scraps and advantage. The third sort is of those that may be accounted the left hands of courts; persons that are full of nimble and sinister tricks and shifts, whereby they pervert the plain and direct course of courts, and bring justice into oblique lines and labyrinths. And the fourth is the poller and exacter of fees; which justifies the common resemblance of the courts of justice to the bush whereunto while the sheep flies for defence in weather, he is sure to lose part of his fleece. On the other side, an ancient clerk, skilful in precedents, wary in proceeding, and understanding in the business of the court, is an excellent finger of a court; and doth many times point the way to the judge himself.

Fourthly, for that which may concern the sovereign and estate. Judges ought above all to remember the conclusion of the Roman Twelve Tables; *Salus populi suprema lex* [The supreme law of all is the weal of the people]; and to know that laws, except they be in order to that end, are but things captious, and oracles not well inspired. Therefore it is an happy thing in a state when kings and states do often consult with judges; and again when judges do often consult with the king and state: the one, when there is matter of law intervenient in business of state; the other, when there is some consideration of state intervenient in matter of law. . . . Let judges also remember, that Solomon's throne was supported by lions on both sides: let them be lions, but yet lions under the throne; being circumspect that they do not check or oppose any points of sovereignty. Let not judges also be so ignorant of their own right, as to think there is not left to them, as a principal part of their office, a wise use and application of laws. For they may remember what the apostle saith of a greater law than theirs; *Nos scimus quia lex bona est, modo quis eâ utatur legitime* [We know that the law is good, if a man use it lawfully].

Galileo Galilei

His Defense to the Inquisition

When asked if I had signified to the Reverend Father, the Master of the Holy Palace, the injunction privately laid upon me, about sixteen years ago, by the order of the Holy Office, not to hold, defend, or "in any way" teach the doctrine of the motion of the Earth and the stability of the Sun, I answered that I had not done so. And, not being questioned as to the reason why I had not intimated it, I had no opportunity to add anything further. It now appears to me necessary to state the reason, in order to demonstrate the purity of my intention, ever foreign to the practice of simulation or deceit in any operation I engage in.

I say, then, that, as at that time reports were spread abroad by evil-disposed persons

---

Galileo Galilei (1564–1642) was tried by the Inquisition for his writings in support of the discoveries of Copernicus, the father of modern astronomy. Galileo's written defense (here translated by scholar Giorgio de Santilana) of his teachings was submitted to his judges around May 12, 1632.

G. Bossi. *Galileo Galilei.* Nineteenth century. Engraving after a painting by Tintoretto.

to the effect that I had been summoned by the Lord Cardinal Bellarmine to abjure certain of my opinions and teachings and also to submit to penitence for them, I was thus constrained to apply to his Eminence and to solicit him to furnish me with an attestation, explaining the cause for which I had been summoned before him; which attestation I obtained in his own handwriting, and it is the same that I now produce with the present document. From this it clearly appears that it was merely announced to me that the doctrine attributed to Copernicus, of the motion of the Earth and the stability of the Sun, must not be held or defended; but that, beyond this general announcement affecting everyone, there should have been ordered anything to me in particular, no trace thereof appears in it.

Having, then, as a reminder, this authentic attestation in the hand-writing of the very person who informed me of the command, I made no further application of thought or memory with regard to the words employed in orally announcing to me the said order not to hold or defend the doctrine in question; so that the two articles of the order—in addition to the injunction not to "hold" or "defend" it—to wit, the words "not to teach it" and "in any way whatsoever"—which, I hear, are contained in the order enjoined on me, and registered—struck me as quite novel and as if I had not heard them before; and I do not think I ought to be disbelieved when I urge that in the course of fourteen or sixteen years I had lost all recollection of them, especially as I had no need to give any particular thought to them, having in my possession so authentic a reminder in writing. Now, if the said two articles be left out, and those two only be retained which are noted in the accompanying attestation, there is no doubt that the injunction contained in the latter is the same command as that contained in the decree of the Holy Congregation of the Index. Hence it appears to me that I have a reasonable excuse for not having notified to the Master of the Holy Palace about the command privately imposed upon me, it being the same as that of the Congregation of the Index.

Now, if so be my book was not subject to a stricter censorship than that made binding by the decree of the Index, it will, it appears to me, be sufficiently plain that I adopted the surest and most becoming method of having it guaranteed and purged of all shadow of taint, inasmuch as I handed it to the Supreme Inquisitor at the very time when many books dealing with the same matters were being prohibited solely by virtue of the said decree. After what I have now stated, I would confidently hope that the idea of my having knowingly and deliberately violated the command imposed upon me will henceforth be entirely banished from the minds of my most eminent and wise judges; hence those faults which are seen scattered throughout my book have not been artfully introduced with any concealed or other than sincere intention but have only inadvertently fallen from my pen, owing to a vainglorious ambition and complacency in desiring to appear more subtle than the generality of popular writers, as indeed in another deposition I have confessed; which fault I shall be ready to correct with all possible industry whenever I may be commanded or permitted by Their Most Eminent Lordships.

Lastly, it remains for me to beg you to take into consideration my pitiable state of bodily indisposition, to which, at the age of seventy years, I have been reduced by ten months of constant mental anxiety and the fatigue of a long and toilsome journey at the most inclement season—together with the loss of the greater part of the years to which, from my previous condition of health, I had the prospect. I am persuaded and encouraged to do so by the faith I have in the clemency and goodness of the most Eminent Lords, my judges; with the hope that they may be pleased, in answer to my prayer, to remit what may appear to their entire justice the rightful addition that is still lacking to such sufferings to make up an adequate punishment for my crimes, out of consideration for my declining age, which, too, humbly commends itself to them. And I would equally commend to their consideration my honor and reputation, against the calumnies of ill-wishers, whose persistence in detracting from my good name may be inferred from the necessity which constrained me to procure from the Lord Cardinal Bellarmine the attestation which accompanies this.

William Hogarth. *Hudibras and the Lawyer.* 1726. Pen and ink, brown and gray washes over pencil. 9¾ × 13¼″ (24.8 × 33.7 cm). Windsor Castle, Royal Library, London. © Her Majesty Queen Elizabeth II. *Samuel Butler's long satirical poem (1663–1678), illustrated here, attacks the Puritan hypocrisy.*

William Shakespeare

FROM HAMLET

On a Lawyer's Remains

Hamlet: There's another: why may not that be the skull of a lawyer? Where be his quiddities now, his quillities, his cases, his tenures, and his tricks? Why does he suffer this mad knave now to knock him about the sconce with a dirty shovel, and will not tell him of his action of battery? Hum! This fellow might in's time a great buyer of land, with his statutes, his recognizances, his fines, his double vouchers, his recoveries: is this the fine of his fines, and the recovery of his recoveries, to have his fine pate full of fine dirt? Will his vouchers vouch him no more of his purchases, and double ones too, than the length and breadth of a pair of indentures? The very conveyances of his lands will scarcely lie in this box; and must the inheritor himself have no more, ha?

Horatio: Not a jot more, my lord.

Hamlet: Is not parchment made of sheep-skins?

Horatio: Ay, my lord, and of calf-skins too.

Hamlet: They are sheep and calves which seek out assurance in that. . . .

Shakespeare (1564–1616) wrote Hamlet *around 1600–1601. In the famous graveyard scene, the prince of Denmark reflects with something less than reverence on a variety of earthly remains.*

William Shakespeare

FROM THE MERCHANT OF VENICE

Por. . . . Which is the merchant here, and which the Jew?

Duke. Antonio and old Shylock, both stand forth.

Por. Is your name Shylock?

Shy. Shylock is my name.

Por. Of a strange nature is the suit you follow;
Yet in such rule that the Venetian law
Cannot impugn you as you do proceed.
[To *Antonio.*] You stand within his danger, do you not?

Ant. Ay, so he says.

Por. Do you confess the bond?

Ant. I do.

In the trial scene of The Merchant of Venice *(1596), one of Shakespeare's sharpest heroines effects a "happy ending" by insisting on the letter of the law.*

Por. Then must the Jew be merciful.

Shy. On what compulsion must I? tell me that.

Por. The quality of mercy is not strain'd,
It droppeth as the gentle rain from heaven
Upon the place beneath: it is twice bless'd;
It blesseth him that gives and him that takes:
'Tis mightiest in the mightiest; it becomes
The throned monarch better than his crown;
His sceptre shows the force of temporal power,
The attribute to awe and majesty,
Wherein doth sit the dread and fear of kings;
But mercy is above this sceptred sway,
It is enthroned in the hearts of kings,
It is an attribute to God himself,
And earthly power doth then show likest God's
When mercy seasons justice. Therefore, Jew,
Though justice be thy plea, consider this,
That in the course of justice none of us
Should see salvation: we do pray for mercy,
And that same prayer doth teach us all to render
The deeds of mercy. I have spoke thus much
To mitigate the justice of thy plea,
Which if thou follow, this strict court of Venice
Must needs give sentence 'gainst the merchant there.

Shy. My deeds upon my head! I crave the law,
The penalty and forfeit of my bond.

Por. Is he not able to discharge the money?

Bass. Yes, here I tender it for him in the court;
Yea, twice the sum: if that will not suffice,
I will be bound to pay it ten times o'er,
On forfeit of my hands, my head, my heart.
If this will not suffice, it must appear
That malice bears down truth. And, I beseech you,
Wrest once the law to your authority:
To do a great right, do a little wrong,
And curb this cruel devil of his will.

Por. It must not be. There is no power in Venice
Can alter a decree established:
'Twill be recorded for a precedent,
And many an error by the same example
Will rush into the state. It cannot be.

Shy. A Daniel come to judgment! yea, a Daniel!
O wise young judge, how I do honour thee!

Por. I pray you, let me look upon the bond.

Shy. Here 'tis, most reverend doctor; here it is.

Por. Shylock, there's thrice thy money offer'd thee.

Shy. An oath, an oath, I have an oath in heaven:
Shall I lay perjury upon my soul?
No, not for Venice.

Por. Why, this bond is forfeit;
And lawfully by this the Jew may claim
A pound of flesh, to be by him cut off
Nearest the merchant's heart. Be merciful:
Take thrice thy money; bid me tear the bond.

Shy. When it is paid according to the tenour.
It doth appear you are a worthy judge;
You know the law, your exposition
Hath been most sound: I charge you by the law,
Whereof you are a well-deserving pillar,
Proceed to judgment: by my soul I swear
There is no power in the tongue of man
To alter me. I stay here on my bond.

Ant. Most heartily I do beseech the court
To give the judgment.

Por. Why then, thus it is:
You must prepare your bosom for his knife.

Shy. O noble judge! O excellent young man!

Por. For, the intent and purpose of the law
Hath full relation to the penalty,
Which here appeareth due upon the bond.

Shy. 'Tis very true! O wise and upright judge!
How much more elder art thou than thy looks!

Por. Therefore lay bare your bosom.

Shy. Ay, "his breast":
So says the bond:—doth it not, noble judge?—
"Nearest his heart": those are the very words.

Por. It is so. Are there balance here to weigh
The flesh?

Shy. I have them ready.

Por. Have by some surgeon, Shylock, on your charge,
To stop his wounds, lest he do bleed to death.

Shy. Is it so nominated in the bond?

Por. It is not so express'd; but what of that?
'Twere good you do so much for charity.

Shy. I cannot find it: 'tis not in the bond.

* * *

Por. . . . This bond doth give thee here no jot of blood;
The words expressly are "a pound of flesh:"
Then take thy bond, take thou thy pound of flesh;
But, in the cutting it, if thou dost shed
One drop of Christian blood, thy lands and goods
Are, by the laws of Venice, confiscate
Unto the state of Venice.

Gra. O upright judge! Mark, Jew: O learned judge!

Shy. Is that the law?

Por. Thyself shalt see the act;
For, as thou urgest justice, be assur'd
Thou shalt have justice, more than thou desir'st.

Gra. O learned judge! Mark, Jew: a learned judge!

Shy. I take this offer then: pay the bond thrice,
And let the Christian go.

Bass. Here is the money.

Por. Soft!
The Jew shall have all justice; soft! no haste:—
He shall have nothing but the penalty.

Gra. O Jew! an upright judge, a learned judge!

Por. Therefore prepare thee to cut off the flesh.
Shed thou no blood; nor cut thou less, nor more,
But just a pound of flesh: if thou tak'st more,
Or less, than a just pound, be it but so much
As makes it light or heavy in the substance,
Or the division of the twentieth part
Of one poor scruple, nay, if the scale do turn
But in the estimation of a hair,
Thou diest and all thy goods are confiscate.

Gra. A second Daniel, a Daniel, Jew!
Now, infidel, I have thee on the hip.

Por. Why doth the Jew pause? take thy forfeiture.

Shy. Give me my principal, and let me go.

Bass. I have it ready for thee; here it is.

Por. He hath refus'd it in the open court:
He shall have merely justice, and his bond.

Gra. A Daniel, still say I; a second Daniel!
I thank thee, Jew, for teaching me that word.

Shy. Shall I not have barely my principal?

Por. Thou shalt have nothing but the forfeiture,
To be so taken at thy peril, Jew.

Shy. Why, then the devil give him good of it!
I'll stay no longer question.

Por. Tarry, Jew:
The law hath yet another hold on you.
It is enacted in the laws of Venice,
If it be prov'd against an alien
That by direct or indirect attempts
He seek the life of any citizen,
The party 'gainst the which he doth contrive
Shall seize one half his goods; the other half
Comes to the privy coffer of the state;
And the offender's life lies in the mercy
Of the duke only, 'gainst all other voice.
In which predicament, I say, thou stand'st;
For it appears by manifest proceeding,

That indirectly and directly too
Thou hast contriv'd against the very life
Of the defendant; and thou hast incurr'd
The danger formerly by me rehears'd.
Down therefore and beg mercy of the duke.

Gra. Beg that thou mayst have leave to hang thyself:
And yet, thy wealth being forfeit to the state,
Thou hast not left the value of a cord;
Therefore thou must be hang'd at the state's charge.

Duke. That thou shalt see the difference of our spirits,
I pardon thee thy life before thou ask it.
For half thy wealth, it is Antonio's;
The other half comes to the general state,
Which humbleness may drive into a fine.

Por. Ay, for the state; not for Antonio.

Shy. Nay, take my life and all; pardon not that:
You take my house when you do take the prop
That doth sustain my house; you take my life
When you do take the means whereby I live.

Por. What mercy can you render him, Antonio?

Gra. A halter gratis; nothing else, for God's sake!

Ant. So please my lord the duke, and all the court,
To quit the fine for one half of his goods,
I am content; so he will let me have
The other half in use, to render it,
Upon his death, unto the gentleman
That lately stole his daughter:
Two things provided more, that, for this favour,
He presently become a Christian;
The other, that he do record a gift,
Here in the court, of all he dies possess'd,
Unto his son Lorenzo, and his daughter.

Duke. He shall do this, or else I do recant
The pardon that I late pronounced here.

Por. Art thou contented, Jew? what dost thou say?

Shy. I am content.

Por. Clerk, draw a deed of gift.

Shy. I pray you give me leave to go from hence;
I am not well. Send the deed after me,
And I will sign it.

Duke. Get thee gone, but do it.

Gra. In christening thou shalt have two godfathers;
Had I been judge, thou shouldst have had ten more,
To bring thee to the gallows, not the font.
[*Exit* SHYLOCK.]

Artist unknown. *Portia*. Nineteenth century. Engraving. 3¾ × 5¼″ (9.5 × 13.3 cm). Yale Law Art Collection, New Haven.

O. Hood Phillips

FROM SHAKESPEARE AND THE LAWYERS

"*The Trial in* The Merchant of Venice"

There is a fair measure of agreement among Shakespeare scholars that the trial scene in *The Merchant of Venice* (IV. I.) expresses the perennial conflict between law or strict justice on the one hand and mercy on the other, while the play itself (classed as a comedy) is primarily about a usurer rather than a Jew. Usury was condemned by Christian doctrine, though Christians practised it. Hebrew law forbad usury among Jews, but not between Jews and Gentiles. The main source of the story of Shylock's bond was probably Giovanni Fiorentino's *Il Pecorone* (1558), although we do not know of an English translation in Shakespeare's time. A recent influence on the play would be Marlowe's *Jew of Malta*. The Bond of Flesh and the Casket Choice both had long traditions, and they were linked together in some versions anticipating Shakespeare's union of the two themes.

There is a mass of lawyers' comment and criticism in various languages on the bond and the trial. . . . The judgments reached have varied from the high-flown philosophy of German jurists, through some not always very imaginative technical commentary, to a view not unlike that expressed by Professor Russell Brown concerning Portia: "Shakespeare at his most irresponsible."

* * *

The technical merits and demerits of one of the most riveting trials in literature have been much debated by legal experts. This is excerpted from an engaging survey of that ongoing discussion by scholar O. Hood Phillips.

Ezek Cowen, of New York, published in 1872 a fictitious report of an appeal in the Supreme Court of New York which anticipated some of the points brought forward later in the same year by the great German jurist, Rudolf von Ihering. Ihering, himself a Jew, commented on the trial in *Der Kampf ums Recht,* first published in 1872, without knowing that he had been anticipated by Cowen. Ihering concludes that justice was not done to Shylock. The bond was void as being contrary to good morals, and the judge should have refused to enforce it on this ground from the first. The weakness of Portia's judgment lies juridically in this, that as she did not decide against the validity of the bond on the ground of its being *contra bonos mores,* it was a wretched subterfuge, a miserable pettifogging trick, to forbid the shedding of blood that necessarily accompanied it. We might as well say that a person entitled to an easement may not leave footmarks on the land because this was not expressly mentioned in the grant. If the end ever justifies the means, why was the denial of right not revealed until after the sentence? In defeating Shylock's claim Portia abused the law of Venice. Ihering admits, however, that the poet is free to build up his own system of jurisprudence, and we need not regret that Shakespeare has done so here.

* * *

Pietscher, a German judge (Landsgericht-Präsident), wrote a pamphlet in 1881 strongly critical of Ihering's views on *The Merchant of Venice.* The play is not a tragedy about a Jew, says Pietscher, but a comedy about a merchant usurer. Shylock typifies the person who mercilessly insists on his legal rights. He cares nothing for the law, but is actuated by envy, hatred and greed. It is doubtful whether the contract would have been void as against good morals by the law of Venice at that time, but it is permissible to meet chicanery with chicanery. Thus the rogue is caught in his own snare. What Shylock really wanted was not the pound of flesh but Antonio's life, though he dared not say so. Anyway, a bargain of this nature must be strictly construed. In the end the outraged State of Venice demands atonement for abuse of private rights.

One of the best known German jurists of the late nineteenth century, Josef Kohler, always an opponent of Ihering's jurisprudence, accused Ihering of completely failing to understand the history of law. Nor did Kohler agree with Pietscher that cunning may be met with cunning. Portia's judgment may not be justifiable before the Forum of Jurisprudence, but it is an expression of the judge's feeling for right, a manifestation of the (late nineteenth-century) free-law movement. Mercy or equity prevails over the inhuman laws of older times. The moral and legal consciousness of a people must in time prevail over rigid formalism. The judgment was right; but the reasons were faulty, because a right granted to do something includes the right to do anything that is necessarily incidental thereto; also, a creditor is allowed to take less than that to which he is entitled. Although we would not dare openly to oppose an outdated legal rule, we may in a comedy evade it in a thousand ways. Thus the kingdom of Sarastro overcomes the powers of night. Shylock's catastrophe consists, first, in the injustice of being required to become a Christian; and secondly in the forfeiture of all his property. The forfeiture of some of his property would have been justifiable, but the sentence goes rather far. Shylock does not succumb, as Ihering said, under the weight of an unjust sentence. He crumbles because he knows in his conscience that his wrongful motives have been exposed. His demand was within the strict law of his own time, but it was an abuse of right.

An abuse of legal right is morally wrong, and to seek to take a person's life through abuse of right is against law as attempted murder. Shylock's criminality is somewhat lessened, however, by the fact that the court itself is not clear that it is an abuse of right. The only injustice done to Shylock is in treating him as if he had directly sought Antonio's life, whereas he merely made use of legal forms and judicial process. But, Kohler concludes in his Hegelian manner, a severe punishment is justified: even if we think the sentence unjust as being oppressive to the individual, yet it is all part of world history and the universal development of law, because the law on which Shylock relied was obsolete and the representatives of obsolete ideas must be crushed. Here Shakespeare, as a historian of law and right, surpassed even himself.

* * *

The American lawyer and legal author, Appleton Morgan, thought the trial scene in *The Merchant of Venice* showed a most consummate ignorance of all or any legal procedure. Another legal member of the Shakespeare Society of New York, William C. Devecmon, agreed that the trial was riddled with legal mistakes. Portia, as *amicus curiae* or referee, makes a number of rulings which are bad in law, in logic and in morals. In the result, her effort to vest Jessica with Shylock's property was as abortive and ridiculous as any or all of her judicial pronouncements. In this play Shakespeare not only manifests his lack of knowledge of the technique of the legal profession, Devecmon continues, but he shows a profound ignorance of law and of the fundamental principles of justice; unless we assume that the trial scene disregards all ideas of law, justice and morality for mere dramatic effect, although equal dramatic effect could have been attained without such sacrifice.

* * *

One of the most thoughtful and least accessible articles on the subject is that by Professor Paul Huvelin, of the Faculty of Law at the University of Lyon. The denouement of the play is Portia's judgment. But in what society does the process take place? We have to place ourselves at different points of view: the plot of the pound of flesh is derived from a primitive Germanic culture; the scene is laid in sixteenth-century Venice; the form of the bond and the legal procedure belong to late sixteenth-century England. By strict common law the object of the debt, after the three months have passed, is not the 3,000 ducats but the forfeit only. Equity, on the other hand, would not allow the creditor to take more than the principal, interest and fruits. The penalty of the pound of flesh would be illegal in modern law, but not in primitive law. Disagreeing with Ihering and Kohler, Huvelin inclines to think that Portia's judgment is right by strict law. The case is evidently tried by a court of common law. Shylock bungled in not stipulating in the bond that he might spill Antonio's blood, and that he might take from him a piece of flesh weighing a pound, *more or less*. Portia's decision is not only in accordance with law, it is also fundamentally equitable and humane. But the final condemnation of Shylock is arbitrary and without any juridical character. Portia, having rejected Shylock's arguments on grounds of strict law, could not apply equitable principles in sentencing him. The sentence is the work of vengeance rather than justice. But Shylock takes on a symbolic character, his humiliation clothing him with a sort of majesty. He falls, in beauty, like some legal Prometheus, thunderstruck. The feeling for dramatic beauty rather than the sense of legal right guided the dramatist in the latter part of the litigation. And Shakespeare was right because beauty, and not law, was required of him.

William Cole

FROM A ROD FOR THE LAWYERS

Courteous Reader,

Had not my affections to my countrymen more engaged me, than any particular enmity I have against the Lawyers' corrupt interest, by any damage I have sustained by them; I should have forborne publishing the ensuing lines. But if the very heathens could say,

---

In this sermonic selection from England during the Commonwealth, William Cole, a self-described "Lover of his Country," declares lawyers to be "the grand Robbers and Deceivers of the Nation; greedily devouring yearly many Millions of the People's Money." His discourse, oft-noted by legal historians, was published as a pamphlet in London in 1659.

Non solùm nobis nati sumus; we are not only born for ourselves, but that next to the duty we owe to God, we are bound, every individual man, to be a helpful member to his country; why should I, or any man keep silence, whilst this pestiferous generation of the Lawyers, runs from city to country, seeking whom they may devour? It is thy duty as well as mine, to cry aloud for justice against them.

★ ★ ★

That the Lawyers have only sought their own advantage, although to the total impoverishing the nation, consider this following.

I have often, both in city and country, made as near an enquiry as possibly I could, in a general way, what number of lawyers there might be in England and Wales, in all offices; as judges, masters of chancery, serjeants at law, counsellors, attorneys, solicitors, with the rest of the rabble; and I cannot find by calculation, but that there are, great and small, masters and servants, (by the best account I can estimate,) above thirty-thousand. Now consider at what high rates, the very meanest of these live: see but a very country hackney, and you will find he goeth clothed in a genteel garb, and all his family; he keeps company with the gentry, and yet usually quickly getteth an estate over and above his expences, which cannot possibly be less than one hundred and fifty pounds *per annum*. Now if such country-lawyers live at that rate, bring the judges, masters of rolls, counsellors, attorneys, registers, *cum multis aliis,* in the common law, chancery, and admiralty;

Artist unknown. *Lawyer's Coat of Arms*. 1692. Woodcut. 14¼ × 8⅜" (36.2 × 21.3 cm). Harvard Law Art Collection, Cambridge. *The sly fox atop this satiric coat of arms spouts legalese, two clients hold the scroll, and the motto* "Dum Vivo Thrivo" *(Where I live, I thrive) lies at their feet.*

and you will find, that this mercenary generation, one with another, do not receive less yearly from the people, in their law practice, (I say the number of thirty-thousand,) than two-hundred and fifty pounds *per annum* each man: what if some have but fifty, then know some have thousands; surely, I believe, that Prideaux and Maynard will not, nor can deny it. Now, at this rate, to say, two-hundred and fifty pounds, *per annum*, to each lawyer, these thirty-thousand receive seven-millions and half of money yearly, which is seventy-five hundred-thousand pounds: and what a charge are the people at, to attend their tedious and vexatious trials? Consider, what doth it cost to ride and go from all countries and towns to London, to attend the terms: it cannot be less than one million of money yearly, and to what purpose observe.

Whosoever contends in law against another, either for land, debt, or trespass, must, by the law, try his title, debt, or damage, by witness; after it hath been never so long delayed by sophistry, quirks, and quibbles of the lawyers. Now, therefore, it it must be of necessity proved at the last; why is it not better to have it tried in the neighbourhood, while it is fresh, green, and new, when the witnesses are alive; and in places, wherein their lives and conversations are known; than seven, ten, twenty, or thirty years after the suit is commenced, when knights of the post may be taken as witnesses, when the lawyers shall baffle and confound witness and jury by their impudent sophistry and prattle; when things at great courts-assizes are passed over in hugger-mugger, for want of time to examine them; there being more care taken to keep a precise hour for a dinner, than precisely and strictly to see the execution of justice and true judgment in behalf of the poor, the fatherless, the widow, and the orphan: and when either party sees he is like to have the worst, by common law, then they have liberty to remove unto the chancery, where a suit commonly depends as long as a buff coat will endure wearing; especially, if the parties have, as it is said, good stomachs and strong purses: but, when their purses grow empty, their stomachs fail; then, when no more corn is like to be brought to the lawyer's mill, it is usual to ordain some men to hear and end the business: but, alas! then it is too late, for then, probably, both parties, or at least one of them, are ruined utterly in prosecuting the suit, want of his stock, and following of his calling.

What a folly is it, that all bargains in trade and commerce, foreign and domestic, must unavoidably run into this channel, to be debated by lawyers, that understand it as little as they have uprightness; and be tried by jury-men, of which, probably, not one of the number hath the least knowledge in merchandise! What an injustice is it, that all wills must be proved in London, at such a vast charge and distance from the place, where the party deceased; where they usually cannot know the truth of things or little care whether they do or no, so their fees be paid; where they often either take no security at all, or if they do, it may be it is such that is as good as nothing; where every tapster or chamberlain, &c. that pretends himself a freeman, is legal security. How many fatherless, widows, and orphans are utterly ruined by this!

* * *

A WORD TO THE LAWYERS

"Ye have plowed wickedness, ye have reaped iniquity, ye have eaten the fruit of lyes"; Hosea x. 13. The spoil of the poor and fatherless is in our houses; ye are weighed in the balance of justice, ye are found as light as chaff; there is a wind risen up, that will blow your interest into the land of oblivion; all the mischiefs and evils, that ye have done in secret, are now discovered on the house-top: the cries of the wronged and oppressed, the lamentations of the widows, fatherless and orphans, God hath heard. Your wickedness is now, like the Amorites', at the height; the sword of justice is ready to cut it down; the decree is passed against your legal robberies: strive therefore now to learn peace and patience, and an honester calling; this will be your benefit and content. But, if ye will resist and gainsay, know this, that assuredly ye will perish in the attempt.

Sir William Blackstone

FROM COMMENTARIES ON THE LAWS OF ENGLAND

"Of Husband and Wife"

By marriage, the husband and wife are one person in law; that is, the very being or legal existence of the woman is suspended during the marriage, or at least is incorporated and consolidated into that of the husband; under whose wing, protection, and *cover*, she performs every thing; . . . Upon this principle, of an union of person in husband and wife, depend almost all the legal rights, duties, and disabilities that either of them acquire by the marriage. . . . A man cannot grant any thing to his wife, or enter into covenant with her, for the grant would be to suppose her separate existence; . . . A woman indeed may be attorney for her husband; for that implies no separation from, but is rather a representation of her lord. And a husband may also bequeath any thing to his wife by will; for that cannot take effect till the coverture is determined by his death. The husband is bound to provide his wife with necessaries by law, as much as himself: and if she contracts debts for them, he is obliged to pay them; but for any thing besides necessaries, he is not chargeable. . . . If the wife be indebted before marriage, the husband is bound afterward to pay the debt; for he has adopted her and her circumstances together. . . .

The husband also (by the old law) might give his wife moderate correction. For, as

---

The subjection of women as reflected in legal history, a topic debated pro and con by women as well as men, has commonly focused on this passage from the landmark text by the influential British jurist Sir William Blackstone (1723–1780). This glimpse of married women's legal "place" is drawn from the text of 1775.

AERT DE GELDER. *The Marriage Contract.* c. 1670. Oil on canvas. 37¼ × 56½" (94.6 × 143.5 cm). The Royal Pavillion Art Gallery and Museum, Brighton.

COLORPLATE 38

Artist unknown. *Francis Bacon*. After 1731. Oil on canvas. 79 × 50″ (200.7 × 127 cm). National Portrait Gallery, London.

COLORPLATE 39

JOHN HOSKINS. *John Selden.* Before 1664. Miniature on ivory. 1¾ × 1⁵⁄₁₆″ (4.4 × 3.3 cm). Harvard Law Art Collection, Cambridge. *John Selden (1584–1654) is best known for his writings on legal history.* Table Talk, *compiled posthumously by his secretary in 1689, is a collection of his most famous pronouncements on contemporary events.*

COLORPLATE 40

GEORGE DIXON. *Sir William Blackstone.* c. 1770. Miniature on ivory, framed in gold and set with pearls and turquoise. 1½ × 1″ (3.8 × 2.5 cm). Harvard Law Art Collection, Cambridge. *A legal professor at Oxford, Sir William Blackstone (1723–1780) was reknowned for his* Commentaries on the Laws of England *(1765–1769), among the finest historical accounts of English law and the first systematic analysis of the English legal system.*

COLORPLATE 41 *(opposite)*

EDWARD ALCOCK. *Portia and Shylock.* From Shakespeare's *The Merchant of Venice,* act 4, scene i. c. 1778. Oil on canvas. 26 × 20″ (66 × 51.2 cm). Yale Center for British Art, New Haven. Paul Mellon Fund.

COLORPLATE 42

PIETER DE BLOOT.
The Lawyer's Office.
1628. Oil on panel.
22⅜ × 32⅝″
(57 × 83 cm).
Rijksmuseum,
Amsterdam.

COLORPLATE 43

GOYA (FRANCISCO JOSÉ DE GOYA Y LUCIENTES). *Scene of the Inquisition*. 1812–1814. Oil on wood. 18 × 28¾″ (46 × 73 cm). Accademia di San Fernando, Madrid.

COLORPLATE 44

Painter unknown. *Louis XIV Presiding at the Council of the Parties.* Seventeenth century. Oil on canvas. 43⁵⁄₁₆ × 50⁷⁄₁₆″ (110 × 128 cm). Versaille, Paris.

COLORPLATE 45

ADRIAEN VAN OSTADE. *The Village Lawyer*. 1655. Oil on panel. 14⅝ × 11¾" (37 × 30 cm). Allentown Art Museum, Allentown, Pennsylvania. Samuel Kress Memorial Collection. 1961.

COLORPLATE 46

WILLIAM HOGARTH. *The Denunciation* (Woman Swearing a Child to a Grave Citizen). c. 1729. Oil on canvas. 19¾ × 26″ (50 × 66 cm). The National Gallery of Ireland, Dublin. *A paternity suit is the subject of this painting. An older woman points to the belly of a pregnant woman who swears her accusation on a Bible. The accused throws his hands upward in denial.*

COLORPLATE 47

WILLIAM HOGARTH. *Marriage à la Mode: The Marriage Contract.* 1743. Oil on canvas. 27 × 35″ (68.5 × 88.9 cm). The National Gallery, London. *In his series* Marriage à la Mode, *Hogarth provides a biting study of manners and mores, illustrated by an uproarious, all-too-human cast. Here, a marriage is being arranged between the son of the earl of Squanderfield and the daughter of the alderman. The earl has the lineage but not the funds; the alderman, having the wherewithal, seeks to improve his social status. The young woman's expression indicates that she is none too happy with her foppish fiancé (the black patch on the viscount's neck, moreover, is a conventional sign for venereal disease). Construction on the earl's new home (seen through the open window) has been interrupted due to lack of funds, but it will recommence once his son has married into the wealthy middle-class family. As another element in the melodrama, the young lawyer on the scene, Silvertongue, sharpening his quill pen, bends toward the bride-to-be with unmistakable intent.*

The scene is rich in symbolism. The coronets of the earl (considering his circumstances, flagrant ostentation) are ludicrously abundant, even branded on his hunting dogs. On the earl's family tree, the branch signifying a marriage between the Squanderfields and a nonnoble family has been lopped off by an ancestor, William, duke of Normandy.

COLORPLATE 48

NICOLAS LANCRET. *The Seat of Justice in the Parliament of Paris.* 1723. Oil on canvas. 22 × 32″ (56 × 81.3 cm). Louvre, Paris.

COLORPLATE 49

WILLIAM HOGARTH. *Bainbridge on Trial for Murder by a Committee of the House of Commons.* Engraving by J. Cook after a painting by Hogarth. Published June 1, 1803, by G. and J. Robinson, Pater Noster Row, London. 15¾ × 20½" (38.7 × 52 cm). Yale University Law School, New Haven. *Warden of the Fleet Prison, Bainbridge was notorious for his cruelty to prisoners. In 1728 and 1729, a parliamentary commission investigating prison conditions charged him with murder, but he was acquitted. The commission is shown examining some of the barbarous torture devices used in Bainbridge's prison; a shackled Bainbridge is presented to the judges.*

COLORPLATE 50

THOMAS ROWLANDSON and AUGUSTUS PUGIN. *Court of Common Pleas, Westminster Hall.* Plate 23 from R. Ackermann, *Repository of Arts* (London, June 1, 1808). Color aquatint by J.C. Stadler. 9⅛ × 10⅞" (23 × 27.6 cm). Harvard Law Art Collection, Cambridge.

COLORPLATE 51

ARMAND DE POLIGNAC. *The Trial Against Cadoudal.* c. 1794. Gouache on paper. 15⅜ × 19¼" (39 × 49 cm). Musée Carnavalet, Paris. *French royalist Georges Cadoudal (1771–1804), a leader of the band of smugglers known as the Chouans, part of the antirevolutionary uprisings of the Wars of the Vendée (1793–1794), was tried for participating in an English-backed assassination attempt on the life of Napoleon in 1803 and guillotined the following year.*

COLORPLATE 52

JACQUES LOUIS DAVID. *Tennis Court Oath.* 1789. Oil on canvas. 25⁹⁄₁₆ × 35⅛" (65 × 89 cm). Musée Carnavalet, Paris. *Barred on June 20, 1789, from their assigned meeting place in Versailles, having formed on June 17 a National Assembly to strengthen their voice in the Estates General, the deputies of the Third Estate (representing the nonprivileged classes, that is, neither the clergy nor the nobility) met at a nearby tennis court, where they swore not to disband until a written constitution had been established in France. This stands as one of the grandest acts of defiance culminating in the French Revolution. Louis XVI capitulated on June 27, ordering the First and Second Estates to meet with the Third Estate in the National Assembly.*

JAMES DOBIE.
A Breach of Promise (A Sure Case). 1895.
Etching after W. Denby Sadler.
13⅜ × 19″ (34 × 48.3 cm).
Library of Congress, Washington, D.C.

he is to answer for her misbehaviour, the law thought it reasonable to intrust him with this power of restraining her, by domestic chastisement. . . . But, with us, in the politer reign of Charles the second, this power of correction began to be doubted: and a wife may now have security of the peace against her husband; or, in return, a husband against his wife. . . .

These are the chief legal effects of marriage during the coverture upon which we may observe, that even the disabilities, which the wife lies under, are for the most part intended for her protection and benefit. So great a favourite is the female sex of the laws of England.

Georges Lefebvre

FROM THE COMING OF THE REVOLUTION

"The Rights of Man and Citizen"

It is a commonplace of counterrevolutionary polemics to find fault with the Declaration for being too philosophical and abstract. In reality it bears the strong imprint of the circumstances surrounding its birth; its "historical" character is evident both in what it includes and in what it omits, and in the unequal importance which it obviously places on different principles. If the patriots disregarded objections of whose cogency they were well aware, if they held to the idea of promulgating a Declaration, it is because in their

As historian Georges Lefebvre (1874–1959) has shown, the seventeen articles of the Declaration of the Rights of Man and Citizen (August 26, 1789) heralded the French Revolution in a positive enunciation of broad generalities—yet these had a negative "flip side" sharply pertaining to specific legal conditions under the absolutist rule of Louis XVI.

eyes it had an especially great *negative* value, in the sense that it condemned the practices of the Old Regime and prevented their revival. Its formulation of principles is in general terms, as is customary in legislative documents—nor were the American declarations any different in this respect—but for the members of the National Assembly and their contemporaries there was nothing abstract or even properly philosophical in such generalization, for under each article they mentally aligned concrete particularities from which they had suffered. Sovereignty belongs to the nation—i.e., France is no longer the property of the king. No obedience is owed except to the law—i.e., the arbitrary will of the king, and of his ministers and agents, is binding on no one. No man may be arrested or detained except by law—i.e., there shall be no more arrest by administrative orders merely. The accused is innocent until pronounced guilty—i.e., no restoration of torture. Citizens are equal before the law—i.e., there is no justification for the privileges. Resistance to oppression is allowable—i.e., the insurrection of July 14 was legitimate. And so on and on. As the historian [François Alphonse] Aulard put it, the Declaration is essentially the *death certificate of the Old Regime*.

This is why the preamble asserts that "ignorance, disregard or contempt of the rights of man are the sole causes of public misfortunes and governmental corruption," and that henceforth the citizens, by comparing the actions of government with "the aim of all political institutions," may "found their demands on simple and incontestable principles." It is also for the reasons suggested above that the Assembly did not favor the deductive order adopted by [Emmanuel Joseph] Sieyès, a true theoretical philosopher, or yet enumerate the various principles in the order we should prefer today, or with uniform emphasis. We have seen with what caution religious toleration was provided for, where to us it seems that freedom of conscience and worship deserve first place, or at least the most straightforward affirmation. If the Assembly judged otherwise, it was not only from a wish to spare the patriotic lower clergy, but also because many of the grievance-lists were indifferent to Protestants, hostile to Jews and outspokenly in favor of maintaining the preeminence of Catholicism; and also because the Assembly itself, being not at all "laic" in the present sense of the word, did not dream of depriving the Catholic Church (as was soon proved) of its monopoly of public worship, birth and marriage records, education and poor relief, but intended instead to bring the Church more closely than ever into the government of the State. Similarly, it would certainly be thought necessary today to insist upon the right of property and to define it and justify it, as Sieyès had done. The Assembly did not trouble to do so because it was a right which the Old Regime did not question. On the contrary, ministers and administrators of the eighteenth century always spoke of property with respect, in an altogether bourgeois manner. Property rights were appealed to by the aristocracy to defend their position as manorial lords. The only concrete complaint concerning property under the Old Regime was that the public authorities were often highhanded in making expropriations on the ground of public utility, negligent in compensating the owners, arbitrary in assessing values and slow in payment; and these are the faults aimed at in Article XVII, which at the same time was probably intended to legitimatize the requirement that the peasants should buy up the manorial dues. On the other hand, individual liberty is the subject of three articles, because administrative arrest and abuses of criminal procedure were a menace to all. The rule of law was insisted upon because under the Old Regime there was no legal requirement which might not be somehow evaded at the king's discretion. Equality of rights was treated at length because special privilege was the foundation of the social hierarchy. The thought in the Declaration looked to the past more than the future.

Nor are the silences in the Declaration less revealing. If there is any principle we should expect to find in it, it is the economic freedom which the bourgeoisie held to above all others. It will be sought in vain. One reason is that the Old Regime, since the suppression of gilds by Turgot and the removal of controls on the grain trade by Brienne, was no longer hostile to economic freedom. Another reason was division within the Third Estate itself on the matter of gilds and similar bodies.

The Declaration says nothing of the right of association, not because the Assembly meant to prohibit it purely and simply, for the clubs became one of the most solid pillars in revolutionary organization, but rather because it was inopportune to proclaim a right of association at a time when the clergy was to cease to be a "body," and when suppression of property in office was to put an end to the judicial "bodies" also.

The rights of assembly and petition, so much used by the revolutionaries themselves at the very moment, were likewise passed over in silence. Nor was anything said, though Sieyès had foreseen the question, of education and relief of the needy. These were matters of importance for the society of the future, not for the destruction of the Old Regime. They could wait, and were in fact comprised in Section Two of the Constitution as completed in 1791, because at that time the Assembly was oriented mentally toward the future, whereas in August 1789 its members were still hypnotized by the past.

Yet the past could not be separated from the future. Although the Declaration in the

Declaration of the Rights of Man and of the Citizen. c. 1789.
Musée Carnavalet, Paris.

Artist unknown. *Counsellor Cozen Consulting Cases.* 1773. Engraving. 14 × 10″ (35.6 × 25.4 cm). Rare Book Department, Free Library of Philadelphia. Hampton L. Carson Collection.

minds of its authors had for the moment an essentially negative meaning, it was none the less drawn up in a positive form, in which the preamble especially, while recalling what was to be condemned in the old order, indicated that the principles of the new order were also to be laid down. In this sense, too, in the eyes of the Assembly, the Declaration had a concrete meaning. They knew the kind of organization they wanted for France, and consequently how the principles proclaimed in the Declaration should be interpreted in practice. But whereas interpretation was not open to doubt when matters of the past were concerned, because everyone knew what was aimed at, it was subject to controversy when it turned to the future, since the future was still undetermined and was to be settled only by the Constitution itself. Principles expressed in general terms might be, in the judgment of many, logically contradictory to the arrangements made in the Constitution. Hence the strong current in favor of postponement: if one waited until the concrete task was accomplished, then the terms of the Declaration of Rights might be so adjusted as to be entirely consistent with it.

There is no foundation to the charge often made against the National Assembly, that it incited people to believe in an unlimited and arbitrary liberty and to demand a perfect equality. From Article IV it follows expressly that liberty is limited by law, and the first article stipulates that men are equal *in rights*, an equality carefully defined in other articles as an equality before the law. Nor would we be rash to suppose that the Assembly, in deciding not to mention "general felicity" as the purpose of political association, wished to prevent the transformation of juridical or civil equality into social equality, and to forestall those who might appeal to equality in demanding improvement of the lot of the poor. Even these precautions were not generally considered sufficient. Some deputies, notably churchmen such as Grégoire, suggested that the Declaration of Rights be supplemented with a Declaration of Duties; they were told that rights and duties were correlative, the right to liberty necessarily implying the duty to respect the liberty of others, as was set forth in Article IV. But in any case it is certain that the leaders of the Assembly felt no apprehension at the time. This is not because having read Rousseau they believed man by nature good—they were far more realistic than is often supposed. It is rather that they represented a triumphant class, full of energy and on the way to transforming the world. The bourgeoisie had no doubts of itself, nor did it doubt that the new order it had conceived, in accord with the laws of nature and the divine will, was destined forever to assure the welfare and progress of the human race. Warnings produced simply incredulity.

Yet the warnings were justified. From the standpoint of the bourgeoisie it would have been prudent to adopt the distinction drawn by Sieyès between equality of *rights* and equality of *means*. It would have been wise to include a definition of property. Without these safeguards the Declaration, if examined on a philosophical level and without regard to historical circumstances, can readily be interpreted in a socialistic sense, as was recognized by Aulard. And this is what has in fact happened.

Moreover, though liberty of the individual may imply a corresponding obligation toward other individuals, nothing in the Declaration affirms the obligations of all individuals to the national community. Such obligations may certainly be prescribed by law through restrictions on the rights of man in time of emergency; more than once, in fact, *habeas corpus* has been suspended in England and the state of siege declared in France. The Declaration might therefore well have stated that the right to liberty varies with circumstances, and that circumstances are to be judged by the community itself. This is what several deputies maintained in connection with the repression of counterrevolutionaries. Gouy d'Arsy had already argued that human rights could not be the same in wartime as in peace, and the same doctrine in 1793 and 1794 was to justify the emergency government of the Terror.

Yet nothing of this relativity of individual rights was retained in the Declaration. Silence on the matter was due to the circumstances. On the one hand, it was unnecessary to remind the Third Estate of its duties to itself or of its obligations under conditions of war, at a time when it had declared that it alone constituted the national community, when it was imposing an unqualified solidarity on its members and when it was in process of resisting all enemies both within and outside its ranks. On the other hand, since the rights of man had been invoked to destroy despotism and privilege, it was politically unwise to weaken their force by noting that in some eventualities they would have to be restricted.

But it is incumbent on us, who regard the Declaration as the foundation of constitutional law, so to understand and expound it as to forestall the objection that it contradicts certain practical necessities of social life. We must show its consistency with emergency needs. Our commentary must break the self-imposed silence of the Constituents, reestablish the ultimately relative character of the Declaration, admit the power inherent in the nation to restrict liberty when necessary for the public safety. Such a commentary would be entirely acceptable to the Constituents, who refrained from making it themselves only for practical reasons. The fact is, contrary to what is often maintained, that we cannot explain what the Constituents did and said simply as the result of abstract philosophical prepossessions, but only by taking account of the historical circumstances in which they acted.

It is likewise because they were affected by circumstances that they included the right of resistance to oppression in the Declaration. They intended by including it to legitimatize the insurrection of July 14, or a future insurrection if the Court should renew its appeal to force, and in fact did thus justify the October Days in advance. Had they been merely reasoning in the abstract they would probably have left out the right of resistance to oppression, since it was inconceivable to them, or at least highly unlikely, that any oppression could exist in the constitutional order which they were about to establish.

Of more immediate significance were the contradictions which soon revealed themselves between certain articles of the Declaration and the constitutional ideas developed by the Assembly. "All citizens," according to Article VI, "have the right to take part, *in person* or by their representatives," in the formation of the law. And Article XIV: "Citizens have the right, by themselves or through their representatives," to vote taxes. The phrase "in person" seemed to authorize the direct democracy attempted by the electoral districts of Paris. But the Assembly certainly meant to organize a purely *representative* government. The completed Constitution was not even submitted in 1791 to popular ratification. The legislature became the almost absolute master of the community. Amendment of the Constitution was surrounded with such formalities as to be impossible in less than ten years, and in addition the initiative had to come from the legislators, not from the people. As early as the law of December 12, 1789, there seemed to be a violation of Article VI. That article, referring to *all* citizens, seemed to call for universal suffrage, whereas the Assembly by the law of December 12 withheld the vote from those citizens whom it designated as "passive," those who did not pay taxes equal in value to three days' wages.

This inconsistency might have been avoided had the Declaration included an article prepared by Sieyès in July, which distinguished "active" from "passive" citizens, and which held voting to be a public function to which all were admissible, if only they could meet, as for any public function, the conditions prescribed by law as a guarantee of capacity. This was the doctrine half a century later of Guizot and Royer-Collard; the bourgeoisie reasoned in 1789 as later under Louis-Philippe. But in 1789 the democratic movement was not yet born, and the bourgeoisie expressed its thought in less measured and prudent language than it used later, since it did not foresee that its own political ascendancy would ever be questioned, and since even the Americans, who expressed themselves in the same way, were far from having arrived at universal suffrage.

Avoidance of such inconsistencies would indeed not have checked the course of history. The common people had fought to destroy the Old Regime and had forced the abolition of feudalism. It was chimerical to suppose that they would let themselves be excluded forever from the vote, in the name of a declaration which proclaimed men equal in rights. But thanks to the superb confidence of the bourgeoisie, its Declaration could become a charter of political and even social democracy, since it neither condemned the regulation of economic life nor subjected the right of property to any definition.

AMERICAN DAWNING

Cotton Mather

THE TRIAL OF MARTHA CARRIER

Martha Carrier was Indicted for the bewitching certain Persons, according to the Form usual in such Cases, pleading *Not Guilty*, to her Indictment; there were first brought in a considerable number of the bewitched Persons; who not only made the Court sensible of an horrid Witchcraft committed upon them, but also deposed, That it was *Martha Carrier*, or her Shape, that grievously tormented them, by Biting, Pricking, Pinching and Choaking of them. It was further deposed, That while this *Carrier* was on her Examination, before the Magistrates, the Poor People were so tortured that every one expected their Death upon the very spot, but that upon the binding of *Carrier* they were eased. Moreover the Look of *Carrier* then laid the Afflicted People for dead; and her Touch, if her Eye at the same time were off them, raised them again: Which Things were also now seen upon her Tryal. And it was testified, That upon the mention of some having their Necks twisted almost round, by the Shape of this *Carrier*, she replyed, *Its no matter though their Necks had been twisted quite off.*

Before the Trial of this Prisoner, several of her own Children had frankly and fully confessed, not only that they were Witches themselves, but that this their Mother had made them so. This Confession they made with great Shews of Repentance, and with much Demonstration of Truth. They related Place, Time, Occasion; they gave an account of Journeys, Meetings and Mischiefs by them performed, and were very credible in what they said. Nevertheless, this Evidence was not produced against the Prisoner at the Bar, inasmuch as there was other Evidence enough to proceed upon.

Benjamin Abbot gave his Testimony, That last March was a twelvemonth, this Carrier was very angry with him, upon laying out some Land, near her Husband's: Her Expressions in this Anger, were, *That she would stick as close to Abbot as the Bark stuck to the Tree; and that he should repent of it afore seven Years came to an End, so as Doctor Prescot should never cure him.* These Words were heard by others besides *Abbot* himself; who also heard her say, *She would hold his Nose as close to the Grindstone as ever it was held since his name was* Abbot. Presently after this, he was taken with a Swelling in his Foot, and then with a Pain in his Side, and exceedingly tormented. It bred into a Sore, which was launced by Doctor *Prescot*, and several Gallons of Corruption ran out of it. For six Weeks it continued very bad, and then another Sore bred in the Groin, which was also lanced by Doctor *Prescot*. Another Sore then bred in his Groin, which was likewise cut, and put him to very great Misery: He was brought unto Death's Door, and so remained until *Carrier* was

---

Cotton Mather (1663–1728), the Bostonian Puritan minister, counseled against the use of "spectre evidence" in the Salem witch trials that sent twenty people to their deaths during the hysteria from 1692 to 1694. At the request of Sir William Phips, the Massachusetts governor, he wrote trial accounts, such as this one for August 1692. The defendant, Martha Carrier, was convicted and died on the gallows on August 19, 1692.

A few LINES on

Magnus Mode, Richard Hodges & J. Newington Clark.

Who are Sentenc'd to ſtand one Hour in the

Pillory at Charleſtown;

To have one of their EARS cut off, and to be Whipped 20 Stripes at the public Whipping-Poſt, for making and paſſing Counterfeit DOLLARS, &c.

BEHOLD the villains rais'd on high !
(The *Poſt* they've got attracts the eye :)
Both Jews and Gentiles all appear
To ſee them ſtand exalted here ;
Both rich and poor, both young and old,
The dirty ſlut, the common ſcold :
What multitudes do them ſurround,
Many as bad as can be found.
And to encreaſe their ſad diſgrace,
Throw rotten eggs into their face,
And pelt them ſore with dirt and ſtones,
Nay, if they could would break their bones.
Their malice to ſuch height ariſe,
Who knows but they'll put out their eyes :
But pray conſider what you do
While thus expos'd to public view.
Juſtice has often done its part,
And made the guilty rebels ſmart ;
But they went on did ſtill rebel,
And ſeem'd to ſtorm the gates of hell.
To no good counſel would they hear ;
But now each one muſt looſe an EAR,

And they although againſt their will
Are forc'd to chew this bitter pill ;
And this day brings the villains hence
To ſuffer for their late offence ;
They on th' Pillory ſtand in view :
A warning firs to me and you !
The drunkards ſong, the harlots ſcorn,
Reproach of ſome as yet unborn.
But now the *Poſt* they're forc'd to hug,
But loath to take that nauſeous drug
Which brings the blood from out their veins,
And marks their back with purple ſtains.
From their diſgrace, now warning take,
And never do your ruin make
By ſtealing, or unlawful ways ;
(If you would live out all your days)
But keep ſecure from Theft and Pride ;
Strive to have virtue on your ſide.
Deſpiſe the harlot's flattering airs,
And hate her ways, avoid her ſnares ;
Keep clear from Sin of every kind,
And then you'll have true peace of Mind.

A Colonial broadside announcing the punishment of wrongdoers. Traditionally, the public gathered to witness such punishments. Eighteenth century. Historical Society of Pennsylvania, Philadelphia.

Woodcut of a woman being punished by ducking stool, a common means of law enforcement in the American Colonies. Seventeenth century. British Museum, London.

taken, and carried away by the Constable, from which very Day he began to mend, and so grew better every Day, and is well ever since.

Sarah Abbot also, his Wife, testified, That her Husband was not only all this while Afflicted in his Body, but also that strange extraordinary and unaccountable Calamities befel his Cattle; their Death being such as they could guess at no Natural Reason for.

Allin Toothaker testify'd, That *Richard,* the son of Martha *Carrier,* having some difference with him, pull'd him down by the Hair of the Head. When he Rose again, he was going to strike at *Richard Carrier;* but fell down flat on his Back to the ground, and had not power to stir hand or foot, until he told *Carrier* he yielded; and then he saw the shape of *Martha Carrier,* go off his breast.

This *Toothaker,* had Received a wound in the *Wars*; and he now testify'd, that *Martha Carrier* told him, *He should never be Cured.* Just afore the Apprehending of *Carrier,* he could thrust a knitting Needle into his wound, four inches deep; but presently after her being siezed, he was thoroughly healed.

He further testify'd, that when *Carrier* and he sometimes were at variance, she would clap her hands at him, and say, *He should get nothing by it;* whereupon he several times lost his Cattle, by strange Deaths, whereof no natural causes could be given.

John Rogger also testifyed, That upon the threatning words of this malicious *Carrier,* his Cattle would be strangely bewitched; as was more particularly then described.

Samuel Preston testify'd, that about two years ago, having some difference with *Martha Carrier,* he lost *a Cow* in a strange Preternatural unusual manner; and about a month after this, the said *Carrier,* having again some difference with him, she told him; *He had lately lost a Cow, and it should not be long before he lost another;* which accordingly came to pass; for he had a thriving and well-kept *Cow,* which without any known cause quickly fell down and dy'd.

Phebe Chandler testify'd, that about a Fortnight before the apprehension of *Martha Carrier,* on a Lordsday, while the Psalm was singing in the *Church,* this *Carrier* then took her by the shoulder and shaking her, asked her, *where she lived:* she made her no Answer, although as *Carrier,* who lived next door to her Fathers House, could not in reason but know who she was. Quickly after this, as she was at several times crossing the Fields, she heard a voice, that she took to be *Martha Carriers,* and it seem'd as if it was over her head. The voice told her, *she should within two or three days be poisoned.* Accordingly, within such a little time, one half of her right hand, became greatly swollen, and very painful; as also part of her Face; whereof she can give no account how it came. It continued very bad for some dayes; and several times since, she has had a great pain in her breast; and been so siezed on her leggs, that she has hardly been able to go. She added, that lately, going well to the House of God, *Richard,* the son of *Martha Carrier,* look'd very earnestly upon her, and immediately her hand, which had formerly been poisoned, as is abovesaid, began to pain her greatly, and she had a strange Burning at her stomach; but was then struck deaf, so that she could not hear any of the prayer, or singing, till the two or three last words of the Psalm.

One *Foster,* who confessed her own share in the Witchcraft for which the Prisoner stood indicted, affirm'd, that she had seen the prisoner at some of their *Witch-meetings,* and that it was this *Carrier,* who perswaded her to be a Witch. She confessed, that the Devil carry'd them on a pole, to a Witch-meeting; but the pole broke, and she hanging about *Carriers* neck, they both fell down, and she then received an hurt by the Fall, whereof she was not at this time recovered.

One *Lacy,* who likewise confessed her share in this Witchcraft, now testify'd, that she and the prisoner were once Bodily present at a *Witch-meeting in Salem Village*; and that she knew the prisoner to be a Witch, and to have been at a Diabolical sacrament, and that the prisoner was the undoing of her, and her Children, by enticing them into the snare of the Devil.

Another *Lacy,* who also confessed her share in this Witchcraft, now testify'd, that the prisoner was at the *Witch-meeting, in Salem Village,* where they had Bread and Wine administered unto them.

T. H. MATTESON.
Examination of a Witch.
1853. Oil on canvas.
39 × 53″
(99.1 × 134.6 cm).
Essex Institute, Salem,
Massachusetts.

In the time of this prisoners Trial, one *Susanna Sheldon*, in open Court had her hands Unaccountably ty'd together with a Wheel-band, so fast that without cutting, it could not be loosed: It was done by a *Spectre;* and the Sufferer affirm'd, it was the *Prisoners*.

Memorandum. This Rampant Hag, *Martha Carrier,* was the person, of whom the Confessions of the Witches, and of her own Children among the rest, agreed, That the Devil had promised her, she should be *Queen of Heb*.

The Earl of Birkenhead

FROM FAMOUS TRIALS OF HISTORY

"The Trial of Captain Kidd"

William Kidd, judged solely by his piratical career, did not display any marked ability, and cannot be ranked as a really great pirate. His claim to the notice of posterity rests upon two facts. First, that he, almost alone among their number, was sent out to catch, not to lead, pirates, but unmindful of his duty, turned from gamekeeper to poacher. The second remarkable circumstance of his career is that he nearly involved in his misdeeds no less a person than the Lord High Chancellor of Great Britain. . . .

In 1665, a Scots-born New York shipowner and sea captain named William Kidd (1645?–1701) was commissioned to root out the pirates preying on the ships of the East India Company and causing great losses to the merchants of the New England colonies. How the tables were turned is told in this excerpt.

At the end of the seventeenth century pirates infested these coasts and caused great losses to the merchants of New England. A trading vessel which continually passed along the Atlantic shores of North America must needs fall in with them. Kidd, in fact, knew many of them and their haunts, which excites suspicion that he was of assistance to them; else how did he escape their marauding propensities? But at the time no suspicion attached to him, and he was accustomed when in port to interest his merchant friends by outlining plans whereby the pirates could easily be suppressed. He was known as a skilful seaman, he was privy to the pirates' habits, he was experienced in the ways of sea warfare and had proved himself to be a courageous fighter. It was natural, when the authorities determined to tackle the problem of piracy seriously, that his claims for employment should receive early and favourable consideration. . . .

A small ship of 150 tons, named *The Adventure,* was purchased and fitted out at Plymouth. She sailed on 1st May, 1696, with a crew of 80, and carried 30 guns. Her destination was New York, where she arrived in July, with a French ship which she had captured as a prize on the voyage. At New York, Kidd gave out that he was bound for Madagascar, which was then a noted haunt of pirates, and called for volunteers. He made up his complement to 155, and set sail. For three years no authentic news of him reached England or America, but ugly rumours came that he had turned pirate, and friendly States began to protest that their ships were being seized. In December, 1698, the Government issued a Proclamation offering to pardon all pirates who surrendered to four named Commissioners and took service in the Navy, but Kidd was excepted by name. Orders were issued that he should be captured.

At last in 1699, he arrived at Boston in a small sloop. He was seized and protested that he had come to clear his name. All the ships he had taken were, he said, lawful prize. But he had been betrayed. Early in the year he had reached the West Indies in a ship called *The Quedagh Merchant.* His fame had preceded him, and he was refused supplies, but eventually, through an Englishman named Button, he managed to revictual at a small Spanish island. He there made his plans. He buried the bulk of his hoard on Gardner's Island, where probably it still remains, as the Government failed to find it. He then bought from Button a small sloop, in which he and some of his crew embarked, taking some of the treasure with them. *The Quedagh Merchant* he left in Button's charge, but no sooner had he sailed than that worthy sold the vessel to the Spaniards and set off for Boston to give information. He arrived before Kidd, who thereby lost the advantage that he had planned. Lord Bellamont realised that he had an important prisoner, and sent to England for instructions, and when they arrived Kidd was sent home for trial.

The news of his capture had caused great excitement. It was known that he had been sent out by Somers and his friends, who were now the object of fierce attacks in Parliament, and it was now certain that he had turned pirate. What an opportunity if only he would implicate them in his misdeeds! The Junto was on the eve of its fall, but the trial must take place in England, since Lord Bellamont might, if Kidd were tried in America, burke all the evidence reflecting on the syndicate. . . . On his arrival on 8th April, 1700, no time was lost in bringing him before the Bar of the House of Commons. It was a sad disappointment. He was half drunk and made a poor show. He would not admit that he was a pirate, and then and throughout never said a word that would implicate his employers. One of the most eager of the Members to have him examined angrily exclaimed: "I thought the fellow had only been a knave, but unfortunately he happens to be a fool likewise!" Perhaps Kidd was not such a fool. There would only have been his bare word. They were powerful Lords, even after their fall from power, and to seek to involve them necessarily deprived him of his only defence, as no doubt he clearly perceived.

* * *

The trials began at once. . .

Kidd refused to plead and asked for Counsel, who were then only allowed to argue points of law for the defence. When asked why, he explained that he wanted to put off the trial as long as possible in order to get his evidence. His papers had been seized,

William the Third by
the Grace of God of England Scotland France & Ireland

Captain Kidd's privateering commission, which carries a portrait of King William III. December 11, 1695. Public Record Office, London.

including the French passes, which showed that the captured vessels were lawful prize. A wrangle ensued, during which Kidd repeated that he "wasn't ready," and the Recorder very unjudicially retorted, "Nor never will, if you can help it." But he still refused and the Court proceeded to take the pleas of the others. More difficulty. Churchill, the first of them, wanted to raise the plea that he came in under the King's Proclamation, but he was told that he must first plead. So he pleaded Not Guilty, and so did all the others, of whom Owens and Mullins also claimed to have come in under the Proclamation. Then again Kidd was called on. He again refused, and repeated his protest about his papers, but eventually being informed that, if he refused to plead, the penalty was condemnation without trial, he gave way and pleaded not guilty.

* * *

The first indictment for piracy charged Kidd, and the nine men, Nicholas Churchill, James Howe, Robert Lamley, William Jenkins, Gabriel Loff, Hugh Parrot, Richard Barlicorn, Abel Owens, and Darby Mullins, with the piratical capture of *The Quedagh Merchant* on 30th January, 1697–8. In the course of this trial the story of Kidd's voyage was told in full.

After leaving New York in July, 1696, *The Adventure* reached Madagascar in July, 1697. The adventurer could have found ample employment at that nest of pirates, but instead he went off to the Red Sea and lay off a small island in the entrance called "Bab's Key," waiting for the Mocha fleet, consisting of Indian vessels trading between the Red Sea and India. He declared that he would ballast his ship with gold and silver. Three times he sent out boats to reconnoitre, and at last, on 14th August, 1697, the fleet came by. Kidd sailed into her midst and opened fire, but he was answered by a convoy, which he had not expected, and made a hurried flight.

Having thus miscarried in his first attempt, he cruised about off Arabia and India, capturing Arab and Indian vessels. The first ship taken hailed from Bombay. . . . In November they took a ship from Surat. Kidd hoisted French colours and went in chase of her, but she also hoisted French colours, and apparently had a French pass. She was taken to Madagascar. In December they took a ketch, and sent her adrift after plundering her. In January, 1697–8, they fell in with *The Quedagh Merchant.* The pirate hoisted French colours and overtook her. She was owned by some Armenians, who were on board. After that they boarded several vessels, and plundered them. Finally they decided to make for Madagascar, taking a native ship on the way. They arrived in May, 1698, and proceeded to a complete share out. The money and goods were divided separately, each into 160 shares. Kidd took 40 of each, and each seaman had one complete share of each, and each landsman one half share; but for equality of division some men had half a share in the money and a whole share in the goods.

At Madagascar they fell in with Captain Culliford on the pirate ship *Resolution*, which, before her capture, had been a merchantman named *The Mocha Frigate.* Culliford was a notorious freebooter, and Kidd's advent filled him and his band with alarm. They had heard of his commission, but not of his dereliction of duty. Their fears, however, were soon allayed, and the two bands fraternised. Their new friend swore that his soul would fry in hell before he harmed them, and he gave practical proof of his pacific intentions by supplying Culliford with two guns and ammunition and stores.

By this time *The Adventure* was foul and leaky, so she was destroyed. Kidd transferred to *The Quedagh Merchant*, but with the share out the cruise had come to an end. Several, including Bradinham, left him, and some of these joined Culliford. The rest sailed with him for the West Indies, where many rich prizes could be picked up. At this point the story ended, as the Crown had no evidence to show what had become of *The Quedagh Merchant* or how Kidd had managed to reach Boston in the sloop.

Palmer and Bradinham were the only witnesses for the prosecution. It is not easy to say why, since it came out that one of the Armenian owners of *The Quedagh Merchant* was actually in court.

. . .Kidd's defence suggested that in these piracies he was the unwilling follower of his own men, but he did not take that line on the actual charge of piracy. Possibly the

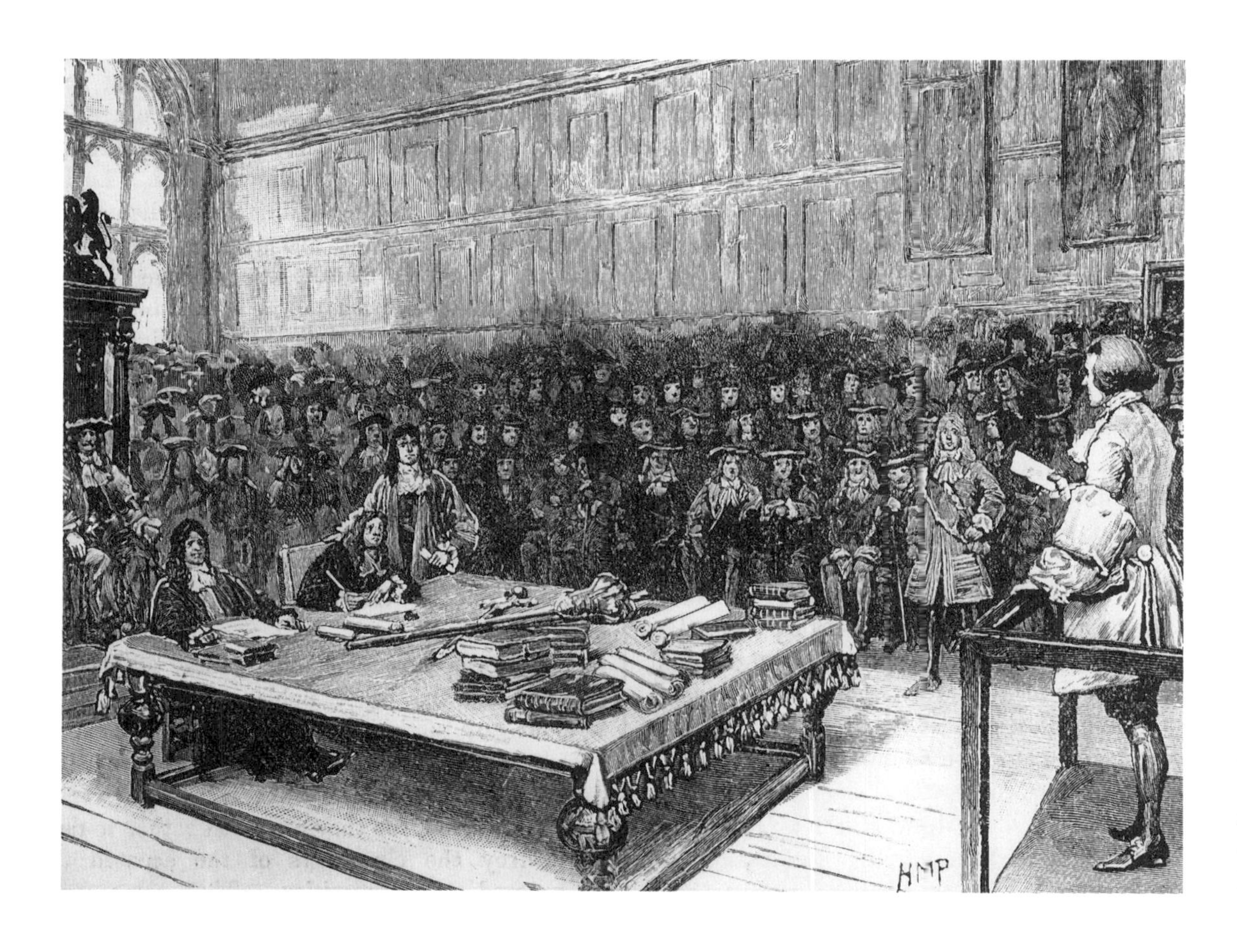

Engraving of Captain Kidd (right) testifying before the bar in the House of Commons on March 27, 1701. Nineteenth century.

presence of the owner warned him that there was evidence available as to what he had done at the capture. His defence now was that the ship had a French pass and was, therefore, lawful prize. Davis was called, and swore that, at Amboyna, Kidd had shown some papers in his presence to another captain, who said they were French passes, and offered to turn them into Latin. Davis did not explain what he or Kidd were doing at Amboyna, and certainly gave no evidence that the papers related to this vessel or that he had read them himself. Bradinham was interrogated, but all he knew was that Kidd had always said that the ships had French passes, but he had never seen them himself. . . .

Kidd called witnesses to impeach Bradinham's veracity and also as to his meritorious services in the former wars. He again called for the French passes, which he alleged Lord Bellamont had taken from him. They were never produced, nor did the prosecution ever attempt to prove that no such passes were found among Kidd's papers. It is indeed highly probable that some at least of the captured vessels had provided themselves with French passes. It was a time of war, for the news of the peace had not reached Indian waters, the seas swarmed with French privateers, and many mariners in such times took the precaution to procure passes from both sides. On the other hand, none of the nine men charged with Kidd ever said that the documents existed. Palmer said nothing about them, and Bradinham had only heard Kidd say that they existed. The nearest to proof was Davis' statement that Kidd had some papers which someone else examined and said were French passes. Perhaps the prosecution desired not to confuse the issue by a false point. Although Kidd, as a privateer, could lawfully seize such ships, yet it was his duty in such a case to bring them in for adjudication by a Court of Prize, and, with the captured ship, all her papers, not merely the pass. He had never attempted to do this, but by dividing the spoils at Madagascar had clearly shown that he had abandoned his letters of marque and was a mere filibuster. Kidd knew the procedure required. He had been a privateer before, and had actually brought in for adjudiction the lawful prize made by *The Adventure* on her voyage to New York. The Lord Chief Baron summed up. He ruled that the defence that the ships were lawful prize could only be sustained by evidence that the ships were French or were sailing under French passes. . . .

The prosecution then went on with a third indictment for the piratical seizure of an unknown native-owned ship in 16th September, 1697. The defences were the same. Mr. Justice Turton summed up, and the jury convicted the same seven.

Then came three more indictments, and the same verdicts followed.

After this Churchill and Mullins had still to meet two other charges. Captain Culliford and some of his crew were arraigned on a number of indictments charging them with piracy in seizing several ships, and they pleaded guilty. On two of these indictments Churchill and Mullins were also accused. They pleaded not guilty to raise the point of their surrender under the Proclamation, but eventually confessed guilt. The sentence for piracy is death by hanging, and this was pronounced upon all those who were convicted by Dr. Oxenden. Kidd had the last word. "It is a very hard sentence," he complained. "I am the innocentest person of them all. Only I have been sworn against by perjured persons."

On the 23rd May, 1701, he was taken to Execution Dock, and there hanged in the sight of all vessels using the Port of London.

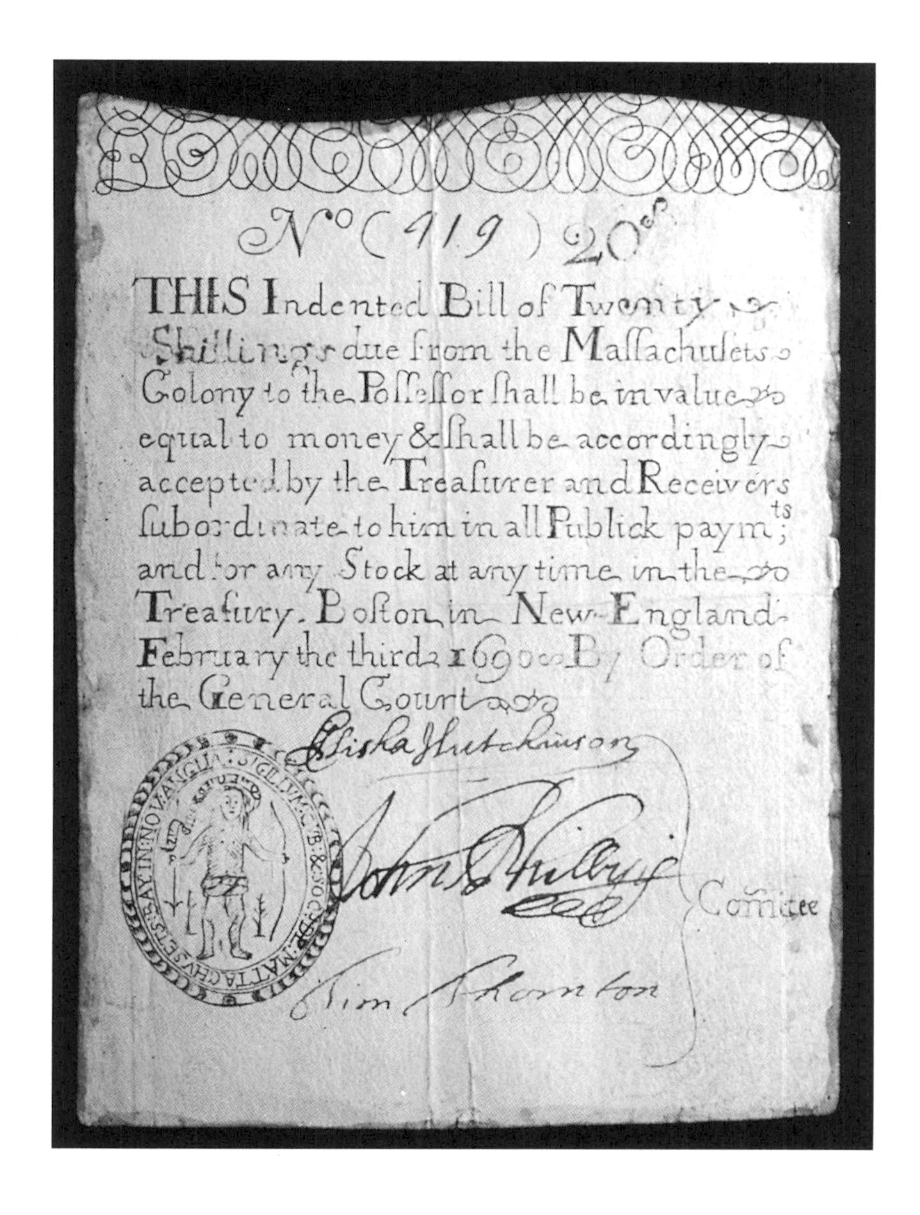
No (419) 20s

THIS Indented Bill of Twenty Shillings due from the Massachusets Colony to the Possessor shall be in value equal to money & shall be accordingly accepted by the Treasurer and Receivers subordinate to him in all Publick paym^ts and for any Stock at any time in the Treasury. Boston in New England February the third 1690 By Order of the General Court

Elisha Hutchinson
John Phillips
Tim Thornton
Comittee

Massachusetts Indenture Bill of
twenty shillings. 1690.
Library of Congress, Washington, D.C.

Benjamin Franklin

"Poor Richard's Opinion"

I know you lawyers can with ease
Twist words and meanings as you please;
That language, by your skill made pliant,
Will bend, to favor every client;
That 'tis the fee limits the sense
To make out either side's pretense,
When you peruse the clearest case,
You see it with a double face,
For skepticism's your profession,
You hold there's doubt in all expression.

Hence is the Bar with fees supplied,—
Hence eloquence takes either side;
Your hand would have but paltry gleaning
Could every man express his meaning.
Who dares presume to pen a deed
Unless you previously are feed?
'Tis drawn, and to augment the cost,
In dull prolixity engrossed;
And now we're well secured by law,
Till the next brother find a flaw.

Printer, author, inventor, scientist, diplomat, and public official Benjamin Franklin (1706–1790), using the name Richard Saunders, published Poor Richard's Almanack *from 1732 to 1757. This poem is taken from that popular mixture of standard almanac material and pithy, homespun sayings.*

John Peter Zenger

FROM A BRIEF NARRATIVE OF THE CASE AND TRYAL OF JOHN PETER ZENGER

Mr. Hamilton: May it please Your Honor; I am concerned in this cause on the part of Mr. Zenger, the defendant. The information against my client was sent me, a few days before I left home, with some instructions to let me know how far I might rely upon the truth of those parts of the papers set forth in the information and which are said to be libelous. And though I am perfectly of the opinion with the gentleman who has just now spoke, on the same side with me, as to the common course of proceedings, I mean in putting Mr. Attorney upon proving that my client printed and published those papers mentioned in the information; yet I cannot think it proper for me (without doing violence to my own principles) to deny the publication of a complaint, which I think is the right of every freeborn subject to make, when the matters so published can be supported with truth; and therefore I'll save Mr. Attorney the trouble of examining his witnesses to that point; and I do (for my client) confess that he both printed and published the two newspapers set forth in the information, and I hope in so doing he has committed no crime.

Mr. Attorney: Then if Your Honor pleases, since Mr. Hamilton has confessed the fact, I think our witnesses may be discharged; we have no further occasion for them.

Mr. Hamilton: If you brought them here, only to prove the printing and publishing of these newspapers, we have acknowledged that, and shall abide by it.

Mr. Chief Justice: Well, Mr. Attorney, will you proceed?

Mr. Attorney: Indeed, sir, as Mr. Hamilton has confessed the printing and publishing these libels, I think the jury must find a verdict for the King; for supposing they were true, the law says that they are not the less libelous for that; nay, indeed, the law says their being true is an aggravation of the crime.

Mr. Hamilton: Not so neither, Mr. Attorney, there are two words to that bargain. I hope it is not our bare printing and publishing a paper that will make it a libel. You will have something more to do before you make my client a libeler; for the words themselves must be libelous, that is, *false, scandalous, and seditious* or else we are not guilty.

Mr. Attorney: The case before the court is whether Mr. Zenger is guilty of libeling His Excellency the Governor of New York, and indeed the whole administration of the government. Mr. Hamilton has confessed the printing and publishing, and I think nothing is plainer than that the words in the information are *scandalous, and tend to sedition, and to disquiet the minds of the people of this province.* And if such papers are not libels, I think it may be said there can be no such thing as a libel.

Mr. Hamilton: May it please Your Honor; I cannot agree with Mr. Attorney: for though I freely acknowledge that there are such things as libels, yet I must insist at the same time that what my client is charged with is not a libel; and I observed just now that Mr. Attorney, in defining a libel, made use of the words *scandalous, seditious, and tend to disquiet the people*; but (whether with design or not I will not say) he omitted the word *false.*

German immigrant John Peter Zenger (1697–1746) exercised his "liberty to know, to utter, and to argue freely, according to conscience" by attacking the state administration in his newspaper, the New-York Weekly Journal. *His acquittal in the subsequent seditious libel trial (1735), in which he was defended by Andrew Hamilton of Philadelphia, helped establish freedom of the press in the United States.*

COLORPLATE 53

AMBROGIO LORENZETTI. *Allegory of Good Government*, detail. 1338–40. Fresco. Town Hall, Siena.
Seen in this beautiful fresco in the Sala della Pace (Room of Peace) of the Palazzo Pubblico of Siena, the figure of Wisdom floats gracefully above the majestic crowned figure of Justice, who metes out a sentence. The figure of Commutative Justice, to the right of Justice, gives money and alms to worthy recipients; to the left, Distributive Justice crowns one figure and decapitates another. Directly underneath, the twenty-four council members of the Sienese Republic are presided over by Concordia.

COLORPLATE 54

GIOTTO (GIOTTO DI BONDONE).
Justice. 1304. Fresco.
Cappella Scrovegni,
Padua.

COLORPLATE 55

GIOTTO (GIOTTO DI BONDONE).
Injustice. 1304. Fresco.
Cappella Scrovegni,
Padua.

S' IOB PROPhETA

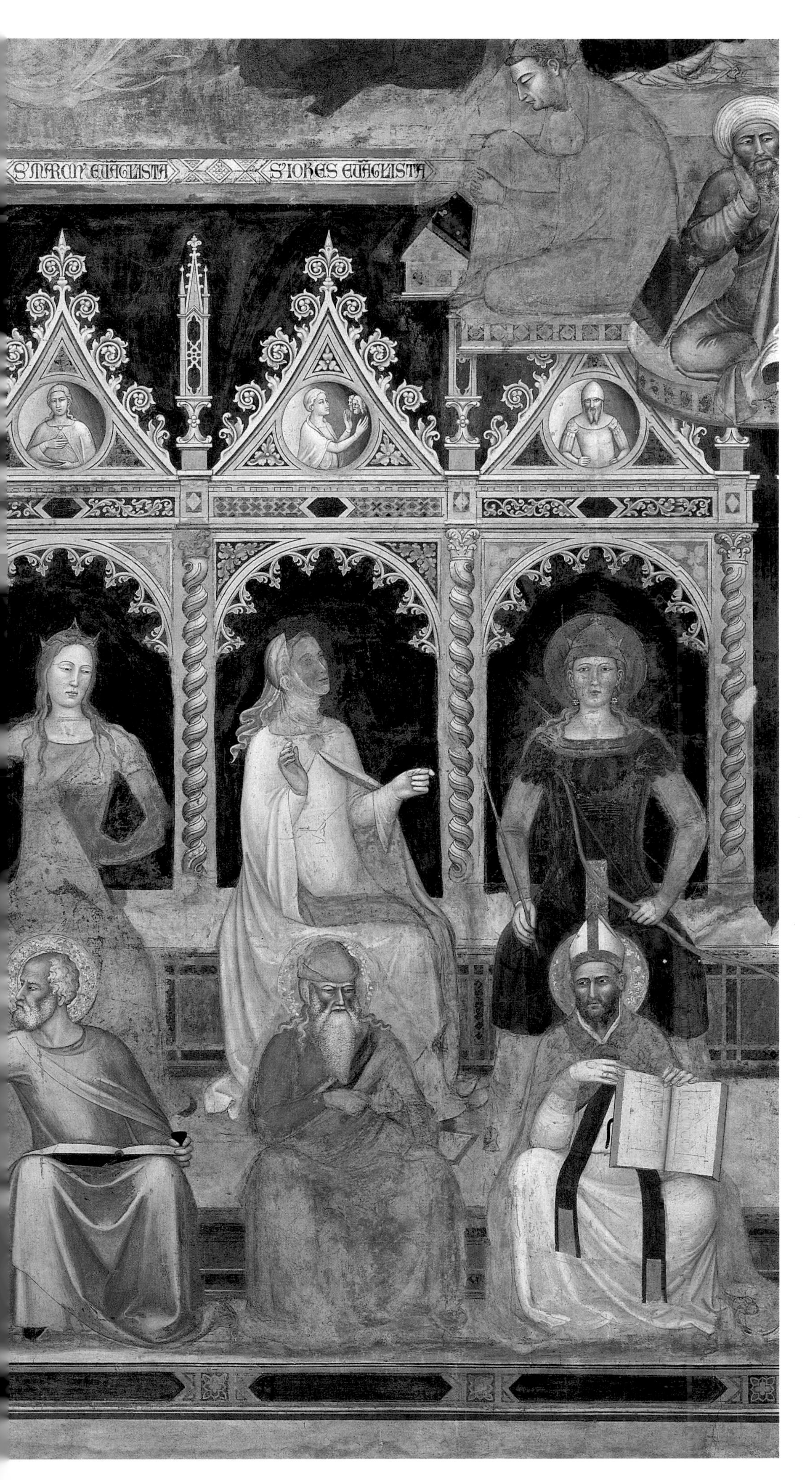

COLORPLATE 56

ANDREA DI BUONAIUTO (ANDREA DA FIRENZE). *Triumph of St. Thomas of Aquinas: Allegories of Civil and Canonic Law*. 1365. Fresco. Santa Maria Novella, Florence. *Reflecting the supreme power of the Church during the Italian Renaissance, particularly the Dominican role, this fresco focuses on ecclesiastical—as opposed to state or civil—government. Part of a large series in the Spanish Chapel of Santa Maria Novella, it graces what was originally the chapter house for the Dominican monks in Florence. Seen here are allegorical representations of civil and canonic law, along with those of several branches of theology.*

COLORPLATE 57

RAPHAEL (RAFFAELLO SANZIO). *Justice*. c. 1510. Mosaic. The Vatican, Rome.

COLORPLATE 58

ELIHU VEDDER. *Finished Study for Good Administration*. c. 1896. Oil on canvas on wood.
25 × 49" (63.6 × 124.5 cm). Williams College Museum of Art, Williamstown, Massachusetts.
Gift of Miss Anita Vedder.

COLORPLATE 59

ELIHU VEDDER. *Finished Study for Corrupt Legislation* c. 1896. Oil on canvas on wood.
25 × 49" (63.6 × 124.5 cm). Williams College Museum of Art, Williamstown, Massachusetts.
Gift of Miss Anita Vedder.

COLORPLATE 60

JOHN SINGER SARGENT. *Israel and the Law*. Study for the mural on the east wall of the Boston Public Library. c. 1903–1909. Oil on canvas. 37¾ × 59¼″ (95.9 × 150.5 cm). Courtesy William Vareika Fine Arts, Newport.

Mr. Attorney: I think I did not omit the word *false.* But it has been said already that it may be a libel notwithstanding it may be true.

Mr. Hamilton: In this I must still differ with Mr. Attorney; for I depend upon it, we are to be tried upon this information now before the court and jury, and to which we have pleaded *Not Guilty*, and by it we are charged with printing and publishing *a certain false, malicious, seditious, and scandalous libel.* The word *false* must have some meaning, or else how came it there?

Mr. Chief Justice: You cannot be admitted, Mr. Hamilton, to give the truth of a libel in evidence. A libel is not to be justified; for it is nevertheless a libel that it is *true.*

Mr. Hamilton: I am sorry the court has so soon resolved upon that piece of law; I expected first to have been heard to that point. I have not in all my reading met with an authority that says we cannot be admitted to give the truth in evidence upon an information for a libel.

Mr. Chief Justice: The law is clear that you cannot justify a libel.

* * *

Mr. Chief Justice: Mr. Hamilton, the court is of opinion you ought not to be permitted to prove the facts in the papers: these are the words of the book, *"It is far from being a justification of a libel that the contents thereof are true, or that the person upon whom it is made*

Artist unknown. *Andrew Hamilton Delivering Closing Speech to Jury in Trial of John Peter Zenger.* c. 1735. Illustration after a painting. New-York Historical Society.

had a bad reputation, since the greater appearance there is of truth in any malicious invective so much the more provoking it is."

Mr. Hamilton: These are Star Chamber cases, and I was in hopes that practice had been dead with the court.

Mr. Chief Justice: Mr. Hamilton, the court have delivered their opinion, and we expect you will use us with good manners; you are not to be permitted to argue against the opinion of the court.

Mr. Hamilton: With submission, I have seen the practice in very great courts, and never heard it deemed unmannerly to—

Mr. Chief Justice: After the court have declared their opinion, it is not good manners to insist upon a point in which you are overruled.

Mr. Hamilton: I will say no more at this time; the court, I see, is against us in this point; and that I hope I may be allowed to say.

Mr. Chief Justice: Use the court with good manners, and you shall be allowed all the liberty you can reasonably desire.

Mr. Hamilton: I thank Your Honor. Then, gentlemen of the jury, it is to you we must now appeal, for witnesses to the truth of the facts we have offered, and are denied the liberty to prove; and let it not seem strange that I apply myself to you in this manner. I am warranted so to do both by law and reason. The last supposes you to be summoned *out of the neighborhood where the fact is alleged to be committed;* and the reason of your being taken out of the neighborhood is *because you are supposed to have the best knowledge of the fact that is to be tried.* And were you to find a verdict against my client, you must take upon you to say the papers referred to in the information, and which we acknowledge we printed and published, are *false, scandalous, and seditious;* but of this I can have no apprehension. You are citizens of New York; you are really what the law supposes you to be, *honest and lawful men;* and, according to my brief, the facts which we offer to prove were not committed in a corner; *they are notoriously known to be true;* and therefore in your justice lies our safety. And as we are denied the liberty of giving evidence, to prove the truth of what we have published, I will beg leave to lay it down as a standing rule in such cases *that the suppressing of evidence ought always to be taken for the strongest evidence;* and I hope it will have that weight with you.

It is true in times past it was a crime to speak truth, and in that terrible Court of Star Chamber many worthy and brave men suffered for so doing; and yet even in that court, and in those bad times, a great and good man durst say, what I hope will not be taken amiss of me to say in this place, *to wit, the practice of informations for libels is a sword in the hands of a wicked king, and an arrant coward to cut down and destroy the innocent; the one cannot, because of his high station, and the other dares not, because of his want of courage, revenge himself in another manner.*

Mr. Attorney: Pray, Mr. Hamilton, have a care what you say, don't go too far neither, I don't like those liberties.

Mr. Hamilton: Sure, Mr. Attorney, you won't make any applications; all men agree that we are governed by the kings, and I cannot see the meaning of Mr. Attorney's caution, my well-known principles, and the sense I have of the blessings we enjoy under his present Majesty, makes it impossible for me to err, and, I hope, even to be suspected, in that point of duty to my king. May it please Your Honor, I was saying that notwithstanding all the duty and reverence claimed by Mr. Attorney to men in authority, they are not exempt from observing the rules of common justice, either in their private or public capacities; the laws of our mother country know no exemption.

I hope to be pardoned, sir, for my zeal upon this occasion: it is an old and wise caution *that when our neighbor's house is on fire, we ought to take care of our own.* For though, blessed be God, I live in a government where liberty is well understood and freely enjoyed, yet experience has shown us all (I'm sure it has to me) that a bad precedent in one government is soon set up for an authority in another; and therefore I cannot but think it mine and every honest man's duty that (while we pay all due obedience to men in authority) we ought at the same time to be upon our guard against power, wherever we apprehend that it may affect ourselves or our fellow subjects.

I am truly very unequal to such an undertaking on many accounts. And you see I labor under the weight of many years, and am borne down with great infirmities of body; yet old and weak as I am, I should think it my duty, if required, to go to the utmost part of the land where my service could be of any use in assisting to quench the flame of prosecutions upon informations, set on foot by the government, to deprive a people of the right of remonstrating (and complaining too) of the arbitrary attempts of men in power. Men who injure and oppress the people under their administration provoke them to cry out and complain; and then make that very complaint the foundation for new oppressions and prosecutions. I wish I could say there were no instances of this kind.

But to conclude: the question before the court and you, gentlemen of the jury, is not of small nor private concern, it is not the cause of a poor printer, nor of New York alone, which you are now trying. No! It may in its consequence affect every freeman that lives under a British government on the Main of America. It is the best cause. It is the cause of liberty; and I make no doubt but your upright conduct this day will not only entitle you to the love and esteem of your fellow citizens; but every man who prefers freedom to a life of slavery will bless and honor you as men who have baffled the attempt of tyranny, and, by an impartial and uncorrupt verdict, have laid a noble foundation for securing to ourselves, our posterity, and our neighbors that to which nature and the laws of our country have given us a right—the liberty both of exposing and opposing arbitrary power (in these parts of the world, at least) by speaking and writing the truth.

Mr. Chief Justice: Gentlemen of the jury. The great pains Mr. Hamilton has taken to show how little regard juries are to pay to the opinion of the judges, and his insisting so much upon the conduct of some judges in trials of this kind, is done, no doubt, with a design that you should take but very little notice of what I may say upon this occasion. I shall therefore only observe to you that, as the facts or words in the information are confessed: the only thing that can come in question before you is whether the words, as set forth in the information, make a libel. And that is a matter of law, no doubt, and which you may leave to the court. But I shall trouble you no further with anything more of my own, but read to you the words of a learned and upright judge in a case of the like nature.

> To say that corrupt officers are appointed to administer affairs is certainly a reflection on the government. If people should not be called to account for possessing the people with an ill opinion of the government, no government can subsist. For it is necessary for all governments that the people should have a good opinion of it. And nothing can be worse to any government than to endeavor to procure animosities; as to the management of it, this has been always looked upon as a crime, and no government can be safe without it be punished.

Mr. Hamilton: I humbly beg Your Honor's pardon; I am very much misapprehended if you suppose what I said was so designed.

Sir, you know I made an apology for the freedom I found myself under a necessity of using upon this occasion. I said there was nothing personal designed; it arose from the nature of our defense.

The jury withdrew, and in a small time returned, and being asked by the clerk whether they were agreed of their verdict, and whether John Peter Zenger was guilty of printing and publishing the libels in the information mentioned, they answered by Thomas Hunt, their foreman: *Not Guilty*. Upon which there were three huzzas in the hall, which was crowded with people, and the next day I was discharged from my imprisonment.

Jay F. Alexander

"Legal Careers in Eighteenth-Century America"

Those who settled upon the law as a career did not have to obtain the formalized education required today, and except for those able to attend the Inns of Court of London or study at European universities, legal training was acquired by an apprenticeship during which students read the law under the supervision of a practicing attorney. In fact, classroom instruction in the law was unavailable until George Wythe began offering courses at the College of William and Mary in 1779. . . .

Regardless of the route taken, it was recognized that preparation for a successful career necessitated "[a] tolerable share of learning." The selection of a lawyer under whom to study therefore represented a crucial decision, and the decision could be confusing. "I am determined," said Rufus King, "to study Law—where, how, and with whom—uncertain." Robert Troup, writing to his friend Aaron Burr in 1780, explained why he had declined to study under the same attorney chosen by Burr. "[He] is immersed in such an ocean of business," said Troup, "that I imagined it would be out of his power to bestow all the time and pains on our improvement we would wish."

Perhaps just as important, it was feared by Troup that he would be "more confined to the drudgery of copying in his office than I ought." The fear of "copying" duties expressed by prospective students reflects the conclusion of some contemporaries "[t]hat Attorneys were always lookt upon as so many Copyers and their knowledge only lay in knowing from whom to Copy Properly. Under the date of October 2, 1787, John Quincy Adams recorded his appraisal of this task. "I began to copy off, not a small volume, of forms for declarations. This is a piece of drudgery," he said, "which certainly does not carry its reward with it. . . .

Despite the fact that those serving clerkships assisted with office drudgery, they were charged for the opportunity to work with, and receive instructions from, a practicing attorney. "A Lawyer must have a Fee," lamented one student, "for taking me into his Office." For this student, it was arranged that a fee of one hundred dollars be paid when "convenient." Following the payment of the instructional fee, the costs of room and board had to be confronted. Rufus King, while serving as law clerk in 1777, complained that his total expenses were "exceeding high." . . .

Students who placed themselves under the direction of prominent attorneys sometimes found themselves forced into independent study. Charles Phelps, who served an apprenticeship with Theophilus Parsons between 1792 and 1795, estimated that his teacher was gone "three fourths of the time" attending courts in Massachusetts, New Hampshire, and Rhode Island. Joseph Story, who studied under the eminent Samuel Sewall, recalled being "left very much alone." Story understandably considered Sewall's "absence in Congress for about half the year . . . a serious disadvantage. . . . " Story lamented that because of those absences he was provided "no opportunity to ask for any explanation of difficulties, and no cheering encouragement to light up the dark and intricate paths of the law."

Students who confronted such periodic abandonment were forced to study independently, a perhaps frustrating but survivable situation. In fact, Thomas Jefferson, somewhat pessimistic concerning the student–lawyer relationship, was of the opinion that "[a]ll that is necessary for a student is access to a library, and directions in what order the books are to be read." Although Peter Van Schaack, like Jefferson, harshly condemned practicing lawyers as teachers, Van Schaack reached the conclusion that it was "in vain to put a law book into the hands of a lad without explaining difficulties to him as he goes along." Van

---

The eighteenth century was an era of avid diarists and correspondents. Their careful records lend great insight into the education and careers of colonial lawyers, as seen in this excerpt.

Schaack supported his opinion with a brief reminiscence. "For my part," he said, "how many hours have I hunted, how many books turned up for what three minutes of explanation from any tolerable lawyer would have made evident to me!"

⋆ ⋆ ⋆

After informing his father that he had decided to study law, John Jay received a reply warning him that it would be necessary to "attend to it with a firm resolution," and only "if possible" was he to take "a delight in it." If the experience of James Monroe was typical, that possibility was slight. When describing his studies under Thomas Jefferson, Monroe forsook the opportunity to cite pleasant memories and instead commented somewhat tersely that he "persevered in it" until he was able to enter the bar. Dirck Ten Broeck, studying under Alexander Hamilton, with "unremitted application," complained that his apprenticeship necessitated "the sacrifice of every pleasure." William Livingston, after being admonished by his father for the alleged "neglect" of his studies, responded by informing his father that in pursuit of his studies he had "read the greatest part of this winter till 12 and 2 o'clock at night, and . . . frequently rose at five in the morning, and read by candle-light." John Adams portrayed the seriousness with which he approached his legal studies by equating his room to "the cell of an Hermit." He was, however, not without friends. "Old Roman Lawyers, and dutch Commentators," he said, "are my constant Companions."

⋆ ⋆ ⋆

Many 18th century observers were of the opinion that Americans were quick to seek judicial settlement of their differences. For example, St. John de Crèvecoeur, a visitor from France, noted in his journal that one locality in particular was "famous for the litigious spirit of its inhabitants." From this de Crèvecoeur somewhat cynically predicted the "the lawyers will have all." Writing a description of the northern colonies in 1755,

PETER MAVERICK. *Judge Tapping Reeve.* Before 1831. Engraving after a painting by George Catlin. Courtesy of the Litchfield Historical Society, Connecticut. *Reeve was the founder of the Litchfield Law School.*

John Barrell expressed the opinion that there were "too many Law Suits!" By way of remedy, he suggested "[t]hat the Number of Lawyers may be limited." However, the fact that America was a young society, expanding at a phenomenal rate but often in an unorderly manner, offers another explanation for what de Crèvecoeur considered a litigious spirit. A doctor traveling through New Jersey in mid-century made a note in his journal which supports this contention. It was his belief that there were "so many doubtfull titles and rights that it creates an inexhaustible and profitable pool for the lawyers."

Whatever the source of litigation, the trials themselves were considered a source of entertainment. Gottlieb Mittelberger, following his arrival from Germany in 1750, observed that "[o]n court days young and old may enter the chamber and may listen to the cross-examinations and to the judgments, which often cause the listeners to burst into uproarious laughter." Thus the trials became a popular source of diversion for the community. Joseph Hadfield, an Englishman traveling in America in 1785, was a witness to this popularity. Upon reaching Worcester, Massachusetts, Hadfield saw that "in the town were assembled a great number of people, it being court day." In addition to explaining the custom of attending court day, Mittelberger related a case the spectators found particularly amusing. Mittelberger explained that an unmarried woman "who had gotten herself pregnant, wanted the man who was responsible for a husband." The woman accused the man of rape but was questioned why at the time of the alleged attack she failed to alarm other people in the house as to her plight. To this "she answered that if she had thought that this time she would become pregnant, then she would certainly have cried for help." Her reply found a responsive audience. "At this," Mittelberger reports, "young and old broke into great laughter; and the man was at once acquitted and set free."

If the account of Benjamin Chew is not exaggerated, the trials themselves could be marathon events, taxing an attorney's physical as well as mental stamina. Chew described a trial which "began on Thursday morning, and the proofs were not gone through till midnight." Although it was then agreed that "but two counsel should speak on each side," the move toward brevity was wasted when Chew's partner (John Dickinson) "butchered the cause most horribly" for three and one half hours. "It was after sunrise on Friday," said Chew, "before the plaintiff's counsel began, but before they had proceeded ¼ of an hour two of the jurymen were taken so ill that we were obliged to adjourn over to Saturday morning. . . ." Chew did not minimize the effect such trials had upon his constitution: "I am," he complained, "absolutely worn down by hard service. . . ."

Erwin C. Surrency

"The Lawyer and the Revolution"

In the events leading to the American Revolution, the role played by lawyers has been acknowledged by many. Observers of the revolutionary scene stated that the lawyers were the leaders of the Stamp Act mobs and similar accusations were made in Parliament. Thomas Gage, writing from Boston in December 1765, stated that "The Lawyers are the Source from whence the clamors have flowed in every Province." Yet, the role of a revolutionist is a strange one for the lawyer, since as a class, lawyers are among the most

---

Writing to London following the commotion caused by the enactment of the Stamp Act in 1765, Governor Colden of New York complained that "the Lawyers of this Place are the Authors, Promoters and Leaders" of resistance to the act. The influential part played by members of the colonial bar in events leading up to the American Revolution is discussed in this excerpt.

EDWARD SAVAGE.
Congress Voting Independence.
After 1788. Engraving
after a painting by
Robert Edge Pine and
Edward Savage. 19 × 25⅞″
(48.2 × 65.6 cm). Library of
Congress, Washington, D.C.

conservative elements in the community. Legal training emphasizes respect for past as well as present institutions. Then why should the majority of leaders in this revolutionary movement have been lawyers?

The events leading to the Revolution are well known and need not detain us here except to emphasize that a constitutional change was taking place in England at that time. At the end of the French and Indian War, the British government instituted a policy of closer supervision and control of her colonies in North America. As a part of this policy, it was felt that the colonies should bear more of the cost of the administration, including support of the soldiers sent to protect them. Ever since the founding of the colonies, each had been free to manage its own affairs with a minimum of supervision, and the acts of Parliament designed for their regulation had been successfully evaded. Suddenly, in 1764, the colonies became aware of a change of policy.

The first instance that foreshadowed the constitutional controversy with the mother country was the issuance of the Writs of Assistance in Massachusetts. With the death of George II and the ascent of George III to the throne, existing Writs of Assistance had terminated and colonial customs offices had to apply for new ones. . . .

The first step taken by Parliament to implement this new policy was through passage of the Sugar Act of 1764. This raised or lowered the tariffs on sugar, molasses, and other commodities. This was harmless enough; but a previous act provided that all violations of the revenue acts could be tried in the admiralty courts, and the British Navy was authorized to aid in the enforcement of the acts. Dealing with the local customs officials had been one thing; but dealing with the British Navy would be quite another. The merchants had developed such techniques for evading the Navigation Acts that even the mildest enforcement would have been inimical to their interests.

Nothing in this act would seem to us today as giving any reason to arouse the opposition of the lawyers. However, as a class, the lawyers occupied one of the highest positions in the society of that time, and were connected with the mercantile families through marriage or kinship. . . .

It was the passage of the Stamp Act itself which was the next step on the road leading to the American Revolution. The Ministry had attempted to find a tax that would raise revenue which the colonies would be willing to pay. In fact, the Stamp Act was announced a year before it was presented to Parliament with an invitation for the colonies to propose some form of taxation if this were not acceptable. Needless to say, no substitute was proposed, and the Stamp Act was passed without any controversy. The storm was to break after enactment.

The Stamp Act imposed stamp duties on newspapers, college diplomas, deeds, wills, all types of pleadings, and all types of documents essential to commerce. Certainly, no act could have been better conceived to affect adversely the interests of the members of the two most influential professions that molded public opinion, namely, lawyers and journalists. As is obvious from the items enumerated, the interests of both these groups were affected. All papers prepared by the lawyer were subject to the tax, leading the lawyer to believe his business would be ruined.

Theoretically, the lawyer would not pay these taxes but it would be his duty to see that the proper stamps were affixed to "any declaration, plea, replication, rejoinder, demurrer, or other pleading." Three pence on each of these would increase the cost of a law suit, for the losing party was generally taxed for the entire cost.

Fees that a lawyer could charge for his services were small and were regulated by statute. To complicate his economic plight further, the lawyer often failed to collect them. The members of the Virginia Bar published a notice in the *Virginia Gazette* that they would no longer take cases unless the fees were paid in advance. Probably the lawyer feared most the lessening of his business, for a person would put off making a will for a small estate where the tax was heavy. Too, the stamps attached to the document had to be paid in currency, whereas in some colonies, the lawyers' fees were expressed and paid in tobacco. Certainly, the stamp taxes would have an economic effect on his practice.

The Stamp Act was not popular in the colonies, for people, then as today, did not like paying taxes. What made this tax the more unpalatable to the colonists was the fact that it was imposed upon them by Parliament and not by their own legislative bodies. But taxes are always relative, and the fact that from hindsight they do not seem excessive or that the total tax load was very light should not blind us to the fact that in 1764, in the eyes of the colonists, the taxes appeared excessive.

When faced with an unpleasant situation, persons often react violently, and this was typical of the first reactions of the colonists when news of the passage of the Stamp Act was received in America. At this point, the leaders were generally the younger members of the leading families in the colonies. In Pennsylvania, the son of Chief Justice William Allen was the leader of the mob that forced the resignation of the newly appointed stamp agent. In Georgia, it was the sons of the Habershams and the Joneses who led the mobs. The "Liberty Boys," as those who opposed these acts were called, forced the resignation of the stamp agents in all the colonies and took upon themselves the responsibility of preventing the landing of the stamps. But none of this is a part of our story. . . .

The Liberty Boys were not satisfied to burn effigies and threaten the stamp agents with tar and feathers; they demanded that the Stamp Act be ignored and that legal business be conducted as usual. Of the judges, they demanded that the courts be opened without the stamps. The lawyer faced a delicate problem. Because of his training, the lawyer could not sanction ignoring the law, yet the sympathies of many in the legal profession were with the colonial cause. When the lawyers in all the colonies learned that the members of their profession had determined to suspend practice, conducting only that business that did not require stamps, they all followed this course of conduct.

In at least one colony, the legal profession did not assume the popular position with enough alacrity to please the Liberty Boys and thus aroused popular resentment. The lawyers of New York were accused of "snoring over the Liberties and Properties of their Fellow subjects in the most supine Indolence."

The resistance of the colonists caused the Superior Courts in all the colonies to close. In Massachusetts, while the courts were closed, the Sons of Liberty undertook to reopen the courts without the use of stamps. John Adams and James Otis, Jr. appeared before the Council on 18 December 1765 to urge the governor to reopen the courts. Adams argued that the Stamp Act was void and without binding force upon the colony because

Parliament did not have the authority to pass this statute. He quoted from the Magna Charta to the effect that justice would be denied no man and justice would be delayed to no man. Otis followed with tears in his eyes arguing that the wicked and unfeeling minister had caused the loyal subjects "the most insupportable oppression." He argued that the court should be open and that nothing warranted the stopping of the administration of justice but war, invasion, rebellion, or insurrection, quoting Coke's *Institute*. He continued by arguing that closing the courts was a dissolution of the government. He quoted Hugo Grotius to the effect that where there were no courts to which citizens could appear for justice, the only recourse must be to the law of nature. The governor stated that this argument as to the validity of the act should be addressed to the judges of the Superior Court and not to him; and he did not feel that the Executive could command the courts to act in any particular way.

* * *

During the period the Stamp Act was in force and the courts closed, the judges and the attorneys were divided over the question: Should the courts remain closed to all business or should they conduct business in those cases which did not require stamps? Apparently, the demands of the more radical elements that the courts proceed without the stamps was never seriously considered by the majority of the legal profession. The courts of general jurisdiction did not proceed with any business. This is understandable as these courts were held in the capitals of the colonies, and the judges were appointed by the Home Government.

The Sons of Liberty tried every device to force these courts to proceed without stamps. In South Carolina, the Sons of Liberty tried every economic pressure they knew to force the Chief Justice, Charles Skinner, to hold court without stamps. Obviously, this gentleman was stubborn, for neither economic pressures nor threats of physical violence made him accede to this request and his court remained closed during the entire period that the Stamp Act was in effect. We are told that he slept with loaded pistols by his side. Certainly, the procedure of the radical groups made the individual lawyers involved more inclined to follow the conservative approach. . . .

The suspension of the courts affected the incomes of the legal profession. The chief source of income for the lawyer of this era was appearances in court, and the fees he could receive for these services were regulated by statute. When the courts were closed, the lawyer was deprived of this income. The studies of some of the account books left by attorneys indicated that during the period of the Stamp Act, income fell by nearly one half. The number of fees collected by Patrick Henry fell from 557 in 1765 to 114 in 1766, and this number rose to 555 in 1767. The lawyers in New York, and doubtless all other colonies, were looking forward to the repeal of the act and a return of their income, and so expressed themselves, describing this period as one of famine. The legal profession suffered with all other colonists for their opposition to this tax. . . .

At this stage in American colonial history, violence could not win the support of the majority of the population regardless of their feelings in the struggle against the Stamp Act. What was needed was a postulation of political theories; and it was in doing this that the lawyers as a group made their greatest and most lasting contribution to the revolutionary controversy.

Along with the ministers of religion, the leading merchants in the Northern colonies, and certain plantation owners in the Southern colonies, the lawyers were the best educated of the colonists. Many of them had received their education in the Inns of Court in London, although the majority had studied law in the offices of American attorneys. Training then required reading books which would be considered today jurisprudential. Many of the lawyers had read such works as those by Pufendorf, Grotius, Hale's *History of the Common Law*, and Wood's *Institutes of Civil Law*. One authority has written that the training of the American lawyer "had been too casual and too scanty to contract their minds to statutes and precedents." A few were familiar with the works of the political theorists of Europe.

Legal training of this sort tends to make one respectful of past traditions and to create a profound reverence for the English Common Law. Certainly, at the time of the Revolution, the majority of American lawyers would have argued that the source of all their political liberties was the Common Law; but the importance of this argument has generally been overlooked by historians. Opposition to the Admiralty Courts established in America during this period centered around the virtues of the Common Law procedure rather than the admiralty proceedings without a jury. The colonists gave strong support to the trial by jury in the common law courts established in the colonies. Thus, it is not surprising that John Dickinson, in his *Letters from a Pennsylvania Farmer*, based his arguments partly on the legalistic approach, quoting from Coke's *Institutes*, a book that was required reading for any lawyer of that era. James Otis, author of *The Rights of the British Colonies*, argued from a similar point of view. Oxenbridge Thacher, a lawyer in Boston, in *Sentiments of a British American*, sought to analyze the Stamp Act, blending economic and legal reasoning.

* * *

Legal training stresses respect for law and government, and the lawyer espouses the settlement of disputes by legal procedures. In good conscience, many colonial lawyers could not support any illegal activity to overthrow a legal government. Joseph Galloway, of Pennsylvania, had participated in the Continental Congress and had proposed a plan of Union for the colonies, but as the radicals gained control, his legal conservatism caused him to become a Tory. Maryland lost her best known attorney, Daniel Dulany, as well as another attorney, George Chalmers, who later compiled a book of legal opinions of various officials in the British government whose offices handled colonial affairs. Massachusetts lost Jonathan Sewall, considered, in his day, one of the best attorneys. Pennsylvania lost its Chief Justice, William Allen, who died in exile in England before the end of the war. It has often been stated that this left the legal profession depleted of its ablest members. Although it was true that more than 130 lawyers left the colonies during the Revolution or by the end of the war, a sufficient body of able lawyers remained to re-establish the profession.

In formulating the constitutional arguments, the lawyers supplied the political leadership that made the Revolution possible. One need only to recall the names of prominent leaders of the colonial side, John Adams, Thomas Jefferson, John Jay, Robert Livingston, just to mention a few, to see the lawyer's significance as a group. It is not surprising that the lawyers were well represented as signers of the Declaration of Independence. Of the fifty-six signers, twenty-five were lawyers.

Another contribution made by the lawyers in the events leading up to the American Revolution lay in inducing the populace not to go to excessive lengths of zeal, as the people were to do in the French and other Revolutions. . . . When compared with other revolutions, the American Revolution is characterized by its lack of blood baths, mob violence and other extreme conduct so common to revolution. This is not to say that such conduct did not exist; but the instances were not frequent. This shortage of excessive conduct may be attributed in part to the conservative influence of the lawyers, who were the leaders, and their strong belief in an orderly legal process.

There is no evidence that any sizeable number of lawyers looked upon the Revolution as a means of legal reform, but two examples do suggest that there were some whose thoughts ran in this direction. Thomas Jefferson resigned from the Continental Congress to go into the Virginia General Assembly where he was the leader in revising the Virginia statutes, thus effecting lasting reforms. In Pennsylvania, the lawyers wrote into the first Constitution of that state the requirements that the Assembly would, as soon as practical, undertake a revision of the criminal laws, a step which was taken and completed by 1800 and followed in other states. The effects of the American Revolution on the law have never been adequately described.

In summary, the lawyers played a significant role in the events leading to the Revolution by providing the necessary leadership. The reason they were able to do this was in part due to their legal training and the active role which the lawyers had hitherto played in the government. At this time, the lawyer began a tradition of governmental service in which the American lawyer enjoys a nearly unique advantage.

Frank L. Dewey

FROM THOMAS JEFFERSON, LAWYER

On 20 May 1773 Jefferson joined his General Court brethren John Randolph, Edmund Pendleton, James Mercer, Patrick Henry, and Gustavus Scott in placing this exasperated notice in Purdie and Dixon's *Virginia Gazette:*

> The fees allowed by law, if regularly paid, would barely compensate our incesssant labors, reimburse our expenses, and the losses incurred by neglect of our private affairs; yet even these rewards, confessedly moderate, are withheld from us, in a great proportion, by the unworthy part of our clients. . . . After the 10th day of October next we will not give an opinion on any case stated to us but on payment of the whole fee, nor prosecute or defend any suit or motion unless the tax, and one half the fee, be previously advanced, except those cases only where we choose to act *gratis*.

To this notice Thomson Mason appended an equally testy message: "The subscriber by no means disapproves of the above resolution, but as he has long determined to quit his practice as an attorney, and practice only as a counsel in such causes as are ready for trial, he has declined signing the above, as he shall not engage in any cause for the future but such in which he shall previously receive an adequate satisfaction for his trouble, which they may be assured will not be less than the legal fees." . . .

The problem that Jefferson and his colleagues faced was that a case might take years to complete—how long depended on the type of case and how far advanced it was when the lawyer was retained. On the one hand, the fee was not wholly earned until the work had been completed. On the other hand, it was unfair to the lawyer to defer all compensation for an indefinite period. A compromise clearly made sense. Requiring a down payment of half the fee at the time of employment offered some protection against the irresponsible client while giving the lawyer an incentive to complete the work.

Although it had been Jefferson's practice to debit the client with the full fee when he was retained, he apparently had had no policy before the notice of 1773 about requiring a down payment. On rare occasions, he collected the full fee at the time he was retained. More often he was paid something on account, and most often he received nothing at that time. In fact, very often he advanced out of his own pocket the taxes and clerical fees that the client was supposed to pay to get the case started. According to the *Gazette* announcement, he would do so no more after 10 October 1773.

The *Gazette* notice spoke of "the unworthy part of our clients" who withheld payment. One of the prime offenders among Jefferson's nonpaying clients was his cousin George Jefferson, who retained him in two cases in 1769, one in 1770, two in 1771, two in 1772, and two in 1773 and never paid a shilling. Carter Henry Harrison, himself a lawyer, paid nothing for nine cases from 1768 to 1773. At the end of 1774 John Reid of Amherst still owed a balance of £17.10.0 on the twenty petitions for lapsed lands he brought to Jefferson in October 1770. Among those who had paid nothing against small

---

Thomas Jefferson (1743–1826) was a practicing lawyer from 1767 to 1774, before moving on to bigger, and some would say better, things. The financial (less than lucrative, generally honorable) aspects of his practice are discussed in this selection.

IN CONGRESS, JULY 4, 1776.

The unanimous Declaration of the thirteen united States of America,

When in the Course of human events, it becomes necessary for one people to dissolve the political bands which have connected them with another, and to assume among the powers of the earth, the separate and equal station to which the Laws of Nature and of Nature's God entitle them, a decent respect to the opinions of mankind requires that they should declare the causes which impel them to the separation. —— We hold these truths to be self-evident, that all men are created equal, that they are endowed by their Creator with certain unalienable Rights, that among these are Life, Liberty and the pursuit of Happiness. — That to secure these rights, Governments are instituted among Men, deriving their just powers from the consent of the governed, — That whenever any Form of Government becomes destructive of these ends, it is the Right of the People to alter or to abolish it, and to institute new Government, laying its foundation on such principles and organizing its powers in such form, as to them shall seem most likely to effect their Safety and Happiness. Prudence, indeed, will dictate that Governments long established should not be changed for light and transient causes; and accordingly all experience hath shewn, that mankind are more disposed to suffer, while evils are sufferable, than to right themselves by abolishing the forms to which they are accustomed. But when a long train of abuses and usurpations, pursuing invariably the same Object evinces a design to reduce them under absolute Despotism, it is their right, it is their duty, to throw off such Government, and to provide new Guards for their future security. — Such has been the patient sufferance of these Colonies; and such is now the necessity which constrains them to alter their former Systems of Government. The history of the present King of Great Britain is a history of repeated injuries and usurpations, all having in direct object the establishment of an absolute Tyranny over these States. To prove this, let Facts be submitted to a candid world. —— He has refused his Assent to Laws, the most wholesome and necessary for the public good. —— He has forbidden his Governors to pass Laws of immediate and pressing importance, unless suspended in their operation till his Assent should be obtained; and when so suspended, he has utterly neglected to attend to them. —— He has refused to pass other Laws for the accommodation of large districts of people, unless those people would relinquish the right of Representation in the Legislature, a right inestimable to them and formidable to tyrants only. —— He has called together legislative bodies at places unusual, uncomfortable, and distant from the depository of their public Records, for the sole purpose of fatiguing them into compliance with his measures. —— He has dissolved Representative Houses repeatedly, for opposing with manly firmness his invasions on the rights of the people. —— He has refused for a long time, after such dissolutions, to cause others to be elected; whereby the Legislative powers, incapable of Annihilation, have returned to the People at large for their exercise; the State remaining in the mean time exposed to all the dangers of invasion from without, and convulsions within. —— He has endeavoured to prevent the population of these States; for that purpose obstructing the Laws for Naturalization of Foreigners; refusing to pass others to encourage their migrations hither, and raising the conditions of new Appropriations of Lands. —— He has obstructed the Administration of Justice, by refusing his Assent to Laws for establishing Judiciary powers. —— He has made Judges dependent on his Will alone, for the tenure of their offices, and the amount and payment of their salaries. —— He has erected a multitude of New Offices, and sent hither swarms of Officers to harrass our people, and eat out their substance. —— He has kept among us, in times of peace, Standing Armies without the Consent of our legislatures. —— He has affected to render the Military independent of and superior to the Civil power. —— He has combined with others to subject us to a jurisdiction foreign to our constitution, and unacknowledged by our laws; giving his Assent to their Acts of pretended Legislation: —— For Quartering large bodies of armed troops among us: —— For protecting them, by a mock Trial, from punishment for any Murders which they should commit on the Inhabitants of these States: —— For cutting off our Trade with all parts of the world: —— For imposing Taxes on us without our Consent: —— For depriving us in many cases, of the benefits of Trial by Jury: —— For transporting us beyond Seas to be tried for pretended offences: —— For abolishing the free System of English Laws in a neighbouring Province, establishing therein an Arbitrary government, and enlarging its Boundaries so as to render it at once an example and fit instrument for introducing the same absolute rule into these Colonies: —— For taking away our Charters, abolishing our most valuable Laws, and altering fundamentally the Forms of our Governments: —— For suspending our own Legislatures, and declaring themselves invested with power to legislate for us in all cases whatsoever. —— He has abdicated Government here, by declaring us out of his Protection and waging War against us. —— He has plundered our seas, ravaged our Coasts, burnt our towns, and destroyed the lives of our people. —— He is at this time transporting large Armies of foreign Mercenaries to compleat the works of death, desolation and tyranny, already begun with circumstances of Cruelty & perfidy scarcely paralleled in the most barbarous ages, and totally unworthy the Head of a civilized nation. —— He has constrained our fellow Citizens taken Captive on the high Seas to bear Arms against their Country, to become the executioners of their friends and Brethren, or to fall themselves by their Hands. —— He has excited domestic insurrections amongst us, and has endeavoured to bring on the inhabitants of our frontiers, the merciless Indian Savages, whose known rule of warfare, is an undistinguished destruction of all ages, sexes and conditions. In every stage of these Oppressions We have Petitioned for Redress in the most humble terms: Our repeated Petitions have been answered only by repeated injury. A Prince, whose character is thus marked by every act which may define a Tyrant, is unfit to be the ruler of a free people. Nor have We been wanting in attentions to our Brittish brethren. We have warned them from time to time of attempts by their legislature to extend an unwarrantable jurisdiction over us. We have reminded them of the circumstances of our emigration and settlement here. We have appealed to their native justice and magnanimity, and we have conjured them by the ties of our common kindred to disavow these usurpations, which, would inevitably interrupt our connections and correspondence. They too have been deaf to the voice of justice and of consanguinity. We must, therefore, acquiesce in the necessity, which denounces our Separation, and hold them, as we hold the rest of mankind, Enemies in War, in Peace Friends. ——

We, therefore, the Representatives of the united States of America, in General Congress, Assembled, appealing to the Supreme Judge of the world for the rectitude of our intentions, do, in the Name, and by Authority of the good People of these Colonies, solemnly publish and declare, That these United Colonies are, and of Right ought to be Free and Independent States; that they are Absolved from all Allegiance to the British Crown, and that all political connection between them and the State of Great Britain, is and ought to be totally dissolved; and that as Free and Independent States, they have full Power to levy War, conclude Peace, contract Alliances, establish Commerce, and to do all other Acts and Things which Independent States may of right do. —— And for the support of this Declaration, with a firm reliance on the protection of divine Providence, we mutually pledge to each other our Lives, our Fortunes and our sacred Honor.

John Hancock

Button Gwinnett
Lyman Hall
Geo Walton.

Wm Hooper
Joseph Hewes,
John Penn

Edward Rutledge 1.

Thos Heyward Junr.
Thomas Lynch Junr.
Arthur Middleton

Samuel Chase
Wm. Paca
Thos. Stone
Charles Carroll of Carrollton

George Wythe
Richard Henry Lee
Th Jefferson
Benja Harrison
Thos Nelson jr.
Francis Lightfoot Lee
Carter Braxton

Robt Morris
Benjamin Rush
Benja. Franklin
John Morton
Geo Clymer
Jas. Smith
Geo. Taylor
James Wilson
Geo. Ross
Caesar Rodney
Geo Read
Tho M:Kean

Wm Floyd
Phil. Livingston
Frans. Lewis
Lewis Morris
Richd. Stockton
Jno Witherspoon
Fras. Hopkinson
John Hart
Abra Clark

Josiah Bartlett
Wm. Whipple
Saml Adams
John Adams
Robt Treat Paine
Elbridge Gerry
Step. Hopkins
William Ellery
Roger Sherman
Saml Huntington
Wm. Williams
Oliver Wolcott
Matthew Thornton

The Declaration of Independence. 1776.

amounts owed were Richard Bland, former governor Dinwiddie, and various merchant firms that were suing laggard debtors.

Jefferson should have anticipated that his experience in collecting from clients would be poor. He surely knew about John Mercer, who had advertised in Rind's *Virginia Gazette* of 19 February 1767: "The great number of debts due to me for the last seven years of my practice, and the backwardness of my clients (in attendance of whose business, I unhappily neglected my own) to make me satisfaction, would of itself, if I had had no other reason, have obliged me to quit my practice." Mercer said he was unable to pay his own debts and would be obliged to sue those who did not pay him by the end of the next General Court session. He went on to say that such legal work as he could do at home would be done only if paid for in advance. . . .

With this background, verified by his own experience, it is surprising that Jefferson indulged his clients so long. Even after 10 October when the more severe credit policy promulgated by the May *Gazette* notice went into effect, he did not consistently require the specified down payment.

The notice in the *Gazette* referred to the "confessedly moderate" fees allowed by law. The law in question was the "Act for regulating the Practice of Attornies," which provided in part: "Lawyers practising in the general court may demand or receive for an opinion or advice . . . one pound one shilling and sixpence, and in any suit at common law, other than the actions herein after mentioned, fifty shillings; in all chancery suits or real mixed or personal actions, where the title or bounds of land may come in question, five pounds." Charging more "for any of the above services, before he has performed the said services, or finished the said suits" made the offender subject to a penalty of £50 for every offense.

The fees permitted were indeed moderate. The basic fee of fifty shillings for a common law suit was the same as had been fixed by law in 1718. Marie Kimball rightly said: "No man could make a fortune on that basis. Indeed, in view of the prevailing habit of a leisurely settlement of debts, it was difficult even to make a fair living."

* * *

In two instances Jefferson took gratuities in clear violation of the law. In *Hite* v. *Fairfax* . . . , Jefferson was assisting Wythe in defending Lord Fairfax, the proprietor of Virginia's Northern Neck, in a very complicated chancery suit regarding land rights of settlers on proprietary land. Jefferson debited Fairfax £5 on 13 October 1768. In April 1769 he received £10 and, in April 1771, £20 more. The case had not been concluded when the payments were made. Since the payments came through Wythe, it may be assumed that he received comparable payments.

Another such case is *Muir* v. *Dade*. . . . Muir, Jefferson's client, sued the Reverend Townshend Dade, the rector of Fairfax Parish, for libel. The action was at common law; the ecclesiastical jurisdiction of the General Court was not involved. Therefore, the most Jefferson could legally receive before the case was finished was £2.10.0 plus advances. Yet he received three payments aggregating £10.10.0. . . .

Was it legal to agree with a client, before the services were completed, that a fee exceeding the legal amount would be paid at the conclusion of the case? The statute forbade not only receiving more than the legal fee before the services had been performed but also "exacting" or "demanding" more. The question is troublesome, but Jefferson made such agreements. . . .

He made contingent fee arrangements under which success would have paid off handsomely. The first such instance occurred in 1770 when Roger Thompson instructed Jefferson to institute a proceeding regarding certain land . . . Jefferson was to receive 30 pistoles (slightly more than £32) if he won, nothing if he lost. Unfortunately, Jefferson's records offer no further information about the matter. He took two other cases . . . in which he was to receive no fee if he lost and a large fee if he won—£30 and £20, respectively. He lost both. He took another batch of three cases . . . in which he was to receive no fee if he lost and only the normal fee if he won. He lost all three. . . .

When he strayed from the statutory scale, it was generally by charging less, not more, than the law allowed. In many cases, he made no charge at all. On four different occasions he defended his friend Francis Willis, Jr., in debt cases without charge. Others receiving like favors included George Wythe and Francis Eppes, his wife's brother-in-law. In several cases he acted gratis for persons alleging that they were being wrongfully held in slavery, and he charged nothing for representing other clients, who, he was told, were poor.

Jefferson charged nothing for general retainers, although they involved watching the docket repeatedly to see whether suits had been brought against the client. He would also watch the docket without charge for one who feared that a particular action might be brought against him and wanted Jefferson to represent him if it were. He charged nothing for cases taken over from George Wythe or John Blair, Jr., if Wythe or Blair had been paid. He often charged nothing in one case if he had been paid in a previous case with some relation to the second. In a caveat proceeding he charged no fee if he found that the land was patented. Several times he charged less than a full fee without recording why.

⋆ ⋆ ⋆

To sum up Jefferson's financial experience as a practicing lawyer, we can say that . . . his departures from the statutory scale were, with few exceptions, on the lenient side; and that if his debtors had been forthcoming, he would have earned a modest living. But his debtors disappointed him, and if any earnings remained after he had paid his expenses, they were a meager reward for his labor.

Thomas Paine

FROM COMMON SENSE

But where, says some, is the King of America? I'll tell you. Friend, he reigns above, and doth not make havoc of mankind like the Royal Brute of Britain. Yet that we may not appear to be defective even in earthly honors, let a day be solemnly set apart for proclaiming the charter; let it be brought forth placed on the divine law, the word of God; let a crown be placed thereon, by which the world may know, that so far we approve of monarchy, that in America THE LAW IS KING. For as in absolute governments the King is law, so in free countries the law *ought* to be King; and there ought to be no other. But lest any ill use should afterwards arise, let the crown at the conclusion of the ceremony, be demolished, and scattered among the people whose right it is.

To hasten an American declaration of independence, Thomas Paine (1737–1809) wrote the pamphlet Common Sense *(1776). Though outlawed in England, Paine, while defending the French Revolution in France, was jailed (1793–1794) for being an Englishman! He returned to America in 1802 and unfortunately lived out his life in poverty.*

Alexander Hamilton

THE FEDERALIST, no. 78

We proceed now to an examination of the judiciary department of the proposed government.

In unfolding the defects of the existing Confederation, the utility and necessity of a federal judicature have been clearly pointed out. It is the less necessary to recapitulate the

---

The Federalist *papers, eighty-five articles written from 1787 to 1788 by Alexander Hamilton (1755–1804), James Madison (1751–1836), and John Jay (1745–1829) to support the adoption of the Constitution, are considered classics of political writing.*

considerations there urged as the propriety of the institution in the abstract is not disputed; the only questions which have been raised being relative to the manner of constituting it, and to its extent. To these points, therefore, our observations shall be confined.

The manner of constituting it seems to embrace these several objects: 1st. The mode of appointing the judges. 2nd. The tenure by which they are to hold their places. 3rd. The partition of the judiciary authority between different courts and their relations to each other.

First. As to the mode of appointing the judges: this is the same with that of appointing the officers of the Union in general and has been so fully discussed in the two last numbers that nothing can be said here which would not be useless repetition.

Second. As to the tenure by which the judges are to hold their places: this chiefly concerns their duration in office, the provisions for their support, the precautions for their responsibility.

According to the plan of the convention, all judges who may be appointed by the United States are to hold their offices *during good behavior;* which is conformable to the most approved of the State constitutions, and among the rest, to that of this State. Its propriety having been drawn into question by the adversaries of that plan is no light symptom of the rage for objection which disorders their imaginations and judgments. The standard of good behavior for the continuance in office of the judicial magistracy is certainly one of the most valuable of the modern improvements in the practice of government. In a monarchy it is an excellent barrier to the despotism of the prince; in a republic it is a no less excellent barrier to the encroachments and oppressions of the representative body. And it is the best expedient which can be devised in any government to secure a steady, upright, and impartial administration of the laws.

Whoever attentively considers the different departments of power must perceive that, in a government in which they are separated from each other, the judiciary, from the nature of its functions, will always be the least dangerous to the political rights of the Constitution; because it will be least in a capacity to annoy or injure them. The executive not only dispenses the honors but holds the sword of the community. The legislature not only commands the purse but prescribes the rules by which the duties and rights of every citizen are to be regulated. The judiciary, on the contrary, has no influence over either the sword or the purse; no direction either of the strength or of the wealth of the society, and can take no active resolution whatever. It may truly be said to have neither FORCE nor WILL but merely judgment; and must ultimately depend upon the aid of the executive arm even for the efficacy of its judgments.

This simple view of the matter suggests several important consequences. It proves incontestably that the judiciary is beyond comparison the weakest of the three departments of power; that it can never attack with success either of the other two; and that all possible care is requisite to enable it to defend itself against their attacks. It equally proves that though individual oppression may now and then proceed from the courts of justice, the general liberty of the people can never be endangered from that quarter; I mean so long as the judiciary remains truly distinct from both the legislature and the executive. For I agree that "there is no liberty if the power of judging be not separated from the legislative and executive powers." And it proves, in the last place, that as liberty can have nothing to fear from the judiciary alone, but would have everything to fear from its union with either of the other departments; that as all the effects of such a union must ensue from a dependence of the former on the latter, notwithstanding a nominal and apparent separation; that as, from the natural feebleness of the judiciary, it is in continual jeopardy of being overpowered, awed, or influenced by its co-ordinate branches; and that as nothing can contribute so much to its firmness and independence as permanency in office, this quality may therefore be justly regarded as an indispensable ingredient in its constitution, and, in a great measure, as the citadel of the public justice and the public security.

The complete independence of the courts of justice is peculiarly essential in a limited Constitution. By a limited Constitution, I understand one which contains certain specified exceptions to the legislative authority; such, for instance, as that it shall pass no bills of attainder, no *ex post facto* laws, and the like. Limitations of this kind can be preserved in practice no other way than through the medium of courts of justice, whose duty it must be to declare all acts contrary to the manifest tenor of the Constitution void. Without this, all the reservations of particular rights or privileges would amount to nothing.

Some perplexity respecting the rights of the courts to pronounce legislative acts void, because contrary to the Constitution, has arisen from an imagination that the doctrine would imply a superiority of the judiciary to the legislative power. It is urged that the authority which can declare the acts of another void must necessarily be superior to the one whose acts may be declared void. As this doctrine is of great importance in all the American constitutions, a brief discussion of the grounds on which it rests cannot be unacceptable.

There is no position which depends on clearer principles than that every act of a delegated authority, contrary to the tenor of the commission under which it is exercised, is void. No legislative act, therefore, contrary to the Constitution, can be valid. To deny this would be to affirm that the deputy is greater than his principal; that the servant is above his master; that the representatives of the people are superior to the people themselves; that men acting by virtue of powers may do not only what their powers do not authorize, but what they forbid.

If it be said that the legislative body are themselves the constitutional judges of their own powers and that the construction they put upon them is conclusive upon the other departments it may be answered that this cannot be the natural presumption where it is not to be collected from any particular provisions in the Constitution. It is not otherwise to be supposed that the Constitution could intend to enable the representatives of the people to substitute their *will* to that of their constituents. It is far more rational to suppose that the courts were designed to be an intermediate body between the people and the legislature in order, among other things, to keep the latter within the limits assigned to their authority. The interpretation of the laws is the proper and peculiar province of the courts. A constitution is, in fact, and must be regarded by the judges as, a fundamental law. It therefore belongs to them to ascertain its meaning as well as the meaning of any particular act proceeding from the legislative body. If there should happen to be an irreconcilable variance between the two, that which has the superior obligation and validity ought, of course, to be preferred; or, in other words, the Constitution ought to be preferred to the statute, the intention of the people to the intention of their agents.

Nor does this conclusion by any means suppose a superiority of the judicial to the legislative power. It only supposes that the power of the people is superior to both, and that where the will of the legislature, declared in its statutes, stands in opposition to that of the people, declared in the Constitution, the judges ought to be governed by the latter rather than the former. They ought to regulate their decisions by the fundamental laws rather than by those which are not fundamental.

This exercise of judicial discretion in determining between two contradictory laws is exemplified in a familiar instance. It not uncommonly happens that there are two statutes existing at one time, clashing in whole or in part with each other and neither of them containing any repealing clause or expression. In such a case, it is the province of the courts to liquidate and fix their meaning and operation. So far as they can, by any fair construction, be reconciled to each other, reason and law conspire to dictate that this should be done; where this is impracticable, it becomes a matter of necessity to give effect to one in exclusion of the other. The rule which has obtained in the courts for determining their relative validity is that the last in order of time shall be preferred to the first. But this is a mere rule of construction, not derived from any positive law but from the nature and reason of the thing. It is a rule not enjoined upon the courts by legislative provision but adopted by themselves, as consonant to truth and propriety, for the direction of their conduct as interpreters of the law. They thought it reasonable that between the interfering acts of an *equal* authority that which was the last indication of its will should have the preference.

But in regard to the interfering acts of a superior and subordinate authority of an

COLORPLATE 61

J. H. MATTESON. *Trial of George Jacobs, August 5, 1692.* 1855. Oil on canvas. 39 × 53″ (99 × 134.6 cm). Essex Institute, Salem. *A patriarch of Salem, Massachusetts, during the witch craze, George Jacobs ridiculed the trials; consequently, he too was accused, tried, and executed.*

COLORPLATE 62

ROBERT FEKE. *Isaac Royall and His Family*. 1741. Oil on canvas. 56 3/16 × 77 3/4" (142.7 × 195.7 cm). Harvard Law Art Collection, Cambridge. *Royall (1719–1781, a loyalist refugee from Massachusetts, donated money and land that was sold and used to establish the first law professorship at Harvard.*

COLORPLATE 63

JOHN TRUMBULL. *The Declaration of Independence*. 1786. Oil on canvas. 21⅛ × 31⅛" (53.5 × 80.8 cm). Yale University Art Gallery, New Haven.

COLORPLATE 64

GEORGE COOKE. *Patrick Henry Arguing the "Parson's Cause."* c. 1830. Oil on canvas. 28 × 36" (71.1 × 91.4 cm). The Virginia Historical Society, Richmond. *Admitted to the bar in 1760, American patriot Patrick Henry (1736–1799) quickly achieved great reknown. In the case known as the Parson's Cause (1763), the authority of the colonial legislature to pay clerical salaries in money rather than in tobacco when the crop was poor was challenged by a minister and vetoed by the crown. Henry, arguing for the legislature, invoked the doctrine of natural rights and succeeded, inasmuch as the award to the plaintiff was held to a single penny.*

VIRGINIA

COLORPLATE 65

SAMUEL F. B. MORSE. *The Old House of Representatives.* 1822. Oil on canvas. 86½ × 130¾" (219.7 × 332 cm). The Corcoran Gallery of Art, Washington, D.C. Museum purchase.

COLORPLATE 66 *(opposite, above)*

GEORGE CATLIN. *Virginia Constitutional Convention of 1829–30.* 1829. Oil on canvas. 24½ × 33" (62.2 × 83.8 cm). The Virginia Historical Society, Richmond.

COLORPLATE 67 *(opposite, below)*

JUNIUS BRUTUS STEARNS. *Washington Addressing the Constitutional Convention.* 1856. Oil on canvas. 37½ × 54" (95.3 × 137.2 cm). Virginia Museum of Art, Richmond. Gift of Colonel and Mrs. Garbisch.

COLORPLATE 68

CHESTER HARDING. *John Marshall.* 1830. Oil on canvas. 95½ × 60¼" (242.8 × 153 cm). The Boston Athenaeum, Boston. Purchase. *John Marshall (1775–1835), a Federalist leader, was appointed chief justice of the United States Supreme Court in 1801. Among his most famous cases is* Marbury *v.* Madison *(1803), establishing the power of judicial review.*

original and derivative power, the nature and reason of the thing indicate the converse of that rule as proper to be followed. They teach us that the prior act of a superior ought to be preferred to the subsequent act of an inferior and subordinate authority; and that accordingly, whenever a particular statute contravenes the Constitution, it will be the duty of the judicial tribunals to adhere to the latter and disregard the former.

It can be of no weight to say that the courts, on the pretense of a repugnancy, may substitute their own pleasure to the constitutional intentions of the legislature. This might as well happen in the case of two contradictory statutes; or it might as well happen in every adjudication upon any single statute. The courts must declare the sense of the law; and if they should be disposed to exercise WILL instead of JUDGMENT, the consequence would equally be the substitution of their pleasure to that of the legislative body. The observation, if it proved anything, would prove that there ought to be no judges distinct from that body.

If, then, the courts of justice are to be considered as the bulwarks of a limited Constitution against legislative encroachments, this consideration will afford a strong argument for the permanent tenure of judicial offices, since nothing will contribute so much as this to that independent spirit in the judges which must be essential to the faithful performance of so arduous a duty.

This independence of the judges is equally requisite to guard the Constitution and the rights of individuals from the effects of those ill humors which the arts of designing men, or the influence of particular conjunctures, sometimes disseminate among the people themselves, and which, though they speedily give place to better information, and more deliberate reflection, have a tendency, in the meantime, to occasion dangerous innovations in the government, and serious oppressions of the minor party in the community. Though I trust the friends of the proposed Constitution will never concur with its enemies in questioning that fundamental principle of republican government which admits the right of the people to alter or abolish the established Constitution whenever they find it inconsistent with their happiness; yet it is not to be inferred from this principle that the representatives of the people, whenever a momentary inclination happens to lay hold of a majority of their constituents incompatible with the provisions in the existing Constitution would, on that account, be justifiable in a violation of those provisions; or that the courts would be under a greater obligation to connive at infractions in this shape than when they had proceeded wholly from the cabals of the representative body. Until the people have, by some solemn and authoritative act, annulled or changed the established form, it is binding upon themselves collectively, as well as individually; and no presumption, or even knowledge of their sentiments, can warrant their representatives in a departure from it prior to such an act. But it is easy to see that it would require an uncommon portion of fortitude in the judges to do their duty as faithful guardians of the Constitution, where legislative invasions of it had been instigated by the major voice of the community.

But it is not with a view to infractions of the Constitution only that the independence of the judges may be an essential safeguard against the effects of occasional ill humors in the society. These sometimes extend no farther than to the injury of the private rights of particular classes of citizens, by unjust and partial laws. Here also the firmness of the judicial magistracy is of vast importance in mitigating the severity and confining the operation of such laws. It not only serves to moderate the immediate mischiefs of those which may have been passed but it operates as a check upon the legislative body in passing them; who, perceiving that obstacles to the success of an iniquitous intention are to be expected from the scruples of the courts, are in a manner compelled, by the very motives of the injustice they meditate, to qualify their attempts. This is a circumstance calculated to have more influence upon the character of our governments than but few may be aware of. The benefits of the integrity and moderation of the judiciary have already been felt in more States than one; and though they may have displeased those whose sinister expectations they may have disappointed, they must have commanded the esteem and applause of all the virtuous and disinterested. Considerate men of every description ought to prize whatever will tend to beget or fortify that temper in the courts; as no man can be sure that he may not be tomorrow the victim of a spirit of injustice, by which he may be a gainer today. And every man must now feel that the inevitable tendency of such a spirit is to sap the foundations of public and private confidence and to introduce in its stead universal distrust and distress.

That inflexible and uniform adherence to the rights of the Constitution, and of individuals, which we perceive to be indispensable in the courts of justice, can certainly not be expected from judges who hold their offices by a temporary commission. Periodical appointments, however regulated, or by whomsoever made, would, in some way or other, be fatal to their necessary independence. If the power of making them was committed either to the executive or legislature there would be danger of an improper complaisance to the branch which possessed it; if to both, there would be an unwillingness to hazard the displeasure of either; if to the people, or to persons chosen by them for the special purpose, there would be too great a disposition to consult popularity to justify a reliance that nothing would be consulted but the Constitution and the laws.

There is yet a further and weighty reason for the permanency of the judicial offices which is deducible from the nature of the qualifications they require. It has been frequently remarked with great propriety that a voluminous code of laws is one of the inconveniences necessarily connected with the advantages of a free government. To avoid an arbitrary discretion in the courts, it is indispensable that they should be bound down by strict rules and precedents which serve to define and point out their duty in every particular case that comes before them; and it will readily be conceived from the variety of controversies which grow out of the folly and wickedness of mankind that the records of those precedents must unavoidably swell to a very considerable bulk and must demand long and laborious study to acquire a competent knowledge of them. Hence it is that there can be but few men in the society who will have sufficient skill in the laws to qualify them for the stations of judges. And making the proper deductions for the ordinary depravity of human nature, the number must be still smaller of those who unite the requisite integrity with the requisite knowledge. These considerations apprise us that the government can have no great option between fit characters; and that a temporary duration in office which would naturally discourage such characters from quitting a lucrative line of practice to accept a seat on the bench would have a tendency to throw the administration of justice into hands less able and less well qualified to conduct it with utility and dignity. In the present circumstances of this country and in those in which it is likely to be for a long time to come, the disadvantages on this score would be greater than they may at first sight appear; but it must be confessed that they are far inferior to those which present themselves under the other aspects of the subject.

Upon the whole, there can be no room to doubt that the convention acted wisely in copying from the models of those constitutions which have established *good behavior* as the tenure of their judicial offices, in point of duration; and that so far from being blamable on this account, their plan would have been inexcusably defective if it had wanted this important feature of good government. The experience of Great Britain affords an illustrious comment on the excellence of the institution.

EUROPEAN EPOCHS

Harold J. Berman

"Law and Belief in Three Revolutions"

As in the case of the German and English Revolutions, the most apparent and most comprehensive legal changes connected with the French Revolution were in the field of constitutional law. . . . A written constitution was adopted for the first time in French history. A republican form of government was instituted, with supreme power given to a legislative assembly elected by popular vote and responsive to public opinion. The church was subjected to state control insofar as that was necessary to protect religious toleration. The judiciary was confined to the application of statutory law. Most hereditary distinctions and social privileges of the aristocracy were abolished. Remnants of feudal law were abolished. In principle, equal civil rights were established for all.

In addition to constitutional law, other aspects of the French legal system underwent transformation. Of special importance was the unification of French law. Diversity of local customs, and especially the striking differences in legal traditions between the south and the north of France, were subordinated not only to a common written constitution and a unified system of legislation and adjudication but also to codification of criminal, civil, and commercial law on a national scale.

In civil law, the famous *Code civil* of 1804, in whose drafting Napoleon himself played a part, and which was intended to express the spirit of the Revolution, gave especially strong protection to rights of private property and contract. With the abolition of the remaining feudal dues and restrictions, ownership was defined broadly as the right to possess, use, and dispose of one's property as one wills, except as prohibited by law. A general contract law was formulated—rules applicable to all kinds of agreement; and the intention of the parties was made central to contractual obligation. Rescission of contract for gross unfairness ("lesion"), duress, or fraud, as well as for minority, was now permitted by law without the former requirement of royal consent. In tort law ("delict"), the principle was established that, as a general rule, liability should be based on fault: the doer of harm should not be civilly liable to the victim unless he intended to cause the harm or else caused it negligently. In family law, the state was accorded general jurisdiction over marriage and divorce. Marriage was viewed as any other civil contract, and divorce was obtainable by mutual consent, for cause, or for proven incompatibility. The father's disciplinary power over his wife and his children was restricted. Wives were accorded greater property rights and greater civil rights generally.

Striking law reforms were also introduced in the field of criminal law and procedure. Voltaire had not exaggerated when he wrote that French criminal law and procedure of

---

The law reforms that followed in the wake of the French Revolution in the late eighteenth and early nineteenth centuries—a reflection of the current philosophies' emphasis on equality of opportunity, natural rights, freedom of expression, and freedom of will—are discussed in this brief excerpt from the comprehensive article by Harvard Law Professor Harold J. Berman.

his time seemed to be "planned to ruin citizens." Although the Criminal Ordinance of 1670 had identified types of crimes and the punishments applicable to them, in fact public prosecutors and judges were free to indict and convict for acts not legally defined as crimes at all; moreover, there was no control over their actions, since proceedings were not public and no reports of the reasons for decisions were given. . . .

The arbitrariness and cruelty of the substantive criminal law was more than matched by that of the system of criminal procedure. . . . Suspects could be held indefinitely in prison, incommunicado, while under investigation—this under the notorious *lettres de cachet*. For capital offenses, of which there were a very large number (including not only treason and murder but also sacrilege, heresy, pandering, incest and others), torture could be applied to secure a confession. The judges, who had purchased their offices, were paid by the parties; additional fees were extorted by delays, and bribery was a common practice.

The penal policy of the Revolution was expressed forcefully in the Declaration of the Rights of Man and Citizen of August 1789. Among its provisions were the following:

—The law may inflict only such penalties as are strictly and clearly necessary.

—Retroactive laws are proscribed.

—Like offenses are to receive like punishments, regardless of the rank and station of the offender.

—The death penalty or infamous punishment cannot carry a vicarious infamy to the family of the condemned person.

—General confiscation of the property of a condemned person is abolished.

—A criminal action against a party dies when the party dies.

—There shall be no crime, no punishment, without a [previously enacted] law.

—There shall be a presumption of innocence.

In 1791 the fledgling Republic issued a comprehensive Penal Code. Characteristically, it was meticulous in its efforts to define crimes and to fix the severity of the punishments in proportion to the gravity of the crime. It aimed to curtail judicial discretion severely and to provide a predictable, graduated penalty structure. The 1791 Penal Code was revised in 1795. Ultimately it was replaced in 1810. The 1810 Code has served as the basic penal legislation in France—of course, with numerous amendments—until the present.

The 1810 Penal Code—like the 1804 Civil Code—bears the stamp of Napoleon's own ideas. Napoleon was in close touch with the five draftsmen of his Penal Code and with the Council of State which was responsible for accepting or rejecting it.

Napoleon's guiding principle, and that of his draftsmen, was general deterrence of crime, which he believed that the law could foster by intimidation, that is, by threat of penalty. Retribution was rejected, whether in the classical sense of exaction of a price for violation of the law (which I would call general retribution) or in the sense of vengeance (which I would call special retribution). The emphasis on deterrence was characteristic of the utilitarian philosophy which prevailed in the Enlightenment and was embodied in the Revolution. Criminal acts were to be punished because they were socially harmful—*not* because they violated the divine order or the cosmic order, *not* because they were morally wrong, *not* because they were against the traditions of the people. The punishment was to be primarily a deterrent to others. The goal of rehabilitation of the offender is, of course, consistent with utilitarianism and was reflected in the 1791 Code. In the 1810 Code, however, Napoleon opted for general deterrence, and against rehabilitation, as a guiding principle. "Prisons," said Napoleon, "are to punish prisoners, not to reform them." This was also consistent with utilitarianism, and with Beccaria's view that it is not a proper function of the law to enforce moral virtues.

In addition, Napoleon supported the reintroduction of branding for forgery, which the 1791 Code had eliminated. Confiscation of property was also reintroduced. Life imprisonment was ruled out, but not penal servitude for life. Only limited judicial discretion to move between minimum and maximum penalties was favored. There were other shifts in emphasis between 1791 and 1810, but the basic philosophy was the same: for Napoleon and his draftsmen, as for the draftsmen of 1791, as for Beccaria and the *philosophes* in the generation after 1750, the criminal law was to be, above all, a rational instrument of the state, intended by its nature to deter potential criminals by threat of penalties. Of Luther's first two uses of the law—the political and the theological—only the first was kept; the third use, the educational (to guide the faithful to virtue), stressed by Calvinism, was also discarded ("Prisons are to punish prisoners, not to reform them").

Artist unknown. *The Lawyers Are Met, a Terrible Shew*. c. 1760. Hand-colored mezzotint after a watercolor by Robert Dighton. Printed by and for Bowles and Carver. 9¾ × 12⅝″ (22.9 × 32.1 cm). British Museum, London.

WILLIAM HOGARTH. *The Industrious 'Prentice: Alderman of London, the Idle One, Brought Before Him and Impeach'd by His Accomplice.* 1747. Engraving. 10 × 13¼" (25.4 × 33.7 cm). British Museum, London.

Charles Dickens

FROM BLEAK HOUSE

"In Chancery"

Who happen to be in the Lord Chancellor's court this murky afternoon besides the Lord Chancellor, the counsel in the cause, two or three counsel who are never in any cause, and the well of solicitors before mentioned? There is the registrar below the Judge, in wig and gown; and there are two or three maces, or petty-bags, or privy purses, or whatever they may be, in legal court suits. These are all yawning; for no crumb of amusement ever falls from JARNDYCE and JARNDYCE (the cause in hand), which was squeezed dry years upon years ago. The shorthand writers, the reporters of the court, and the reporters of the newspapers, invariably decamp with the rest of the regulars when Jarndyce and Jarndyce comes on. Their places are a blank. Standing on a seat at the side of the hall, the better to peer into the curtained sanctuary, is a little mad old woman in a squeeze bonnet, who is always in court, from its sitting to its rising, and always expecting some incomprehensible judgment to be given in her favor. Some say she really is, or was, a party to a suit; but no one knows for certain, because no one cares. She carries some small litter in a reticule which she calls her documents; principally consisting of paper matches and dry lavender. A sallow prisoner has come up, in custody, for the half-

---

After leaving school at fifteen, Charles Dickens (1812–1870) worked as a clerk in a solicitor's office and a short-hand reporter in law courts. These experiences left him with a lasting contempt for the law, as can be seen in this excerpt from his 1852–53 novel.

dozenth time, to make a personal application "to purge himself of his contempt"; which, being a solitary surviving executor who has fallen into a state of conglomeration about accounts of which it is not pretended that he had ever any knowledge, he is not at all likely ever to do. In the meantime his prospects in life are ended. Another ruined suitor, who periodically appears from Shropshire, and breaks out into efforts to address the Chancellor at the close of the day's business, and who can by no means be made to understand that the Chancellor is legally ignorant of his existence after making it desolate for a quarter of a century, plants himself in a good place and keeps an eye on the Judge, ready to call out "My Lord!" in a voice of sonorous complaint, on the instant of his rising. A few lawyers' clerks and others who know this suitor by sight, linger, on the chance of his furnishing some fun, and enlivening the dismal weather a little.

Jarndyce and Jarndyce drones on. This scarecrow of a suit has, in course of time, become so complicated, that no man alive knows what it means. The parties to it understand it least; but it has been observed that no two Chancery lawyers can talk about it for five minutes, without coming to a total disagreement as to all the premises. Innumerable children have been born into the cause; innumerable young people have married into it; innumerable old people have died out of it. Scores of persons have deliriously found themselves made parties in Jarndyce and Jarndyce, without knowing how or why; whole families have inherited legendary hatreds with the suit. The little plaintiff or defendant, who was promised a new rocking-horse when Jarndyce and Jarndyce should be settled, has grown up, possessed himself of a real horse, and trotted away into the other world. Fair wards of court have faded into mothers and grandmothers; a long procession of Chancellors has come in and gone out; the legion of bills in the suit have been transformed into mere bills of mortality; there are not three Jarndyces left upon the earth perhaps, since old Tom Jarndyce in despair blew his brains out at a coffee-house in Chancery Lane; but Jarndyce and Jarndyce still drags its dreary length before the Court, perennially hopeless.

Jarndyce and Jarndyce has passed into a joke. That is the only good that has ever come of it. It has been death to many, but it is a joke in the profession. Every master in Chancery has had a reference out of it. Every Chancellor was "in it," for somebody or other, when he was counsel at the bar. Good things have been said about it by blue-nosed, bulbous-shoed old benchers, in select port-wine committee after dinner in hall. Articled clerks have been in the habit of fleshing their legal wit upon it. The last Lord Chancellor handled it neatly, when correcting Mr. Blowers the eminent silk gown who said that such a thing might happen when the sky rained potatoes, he observed, "or when we get through Jarndyce and Jarndyce, Mr. Blowers"—a pleasantry that particularly ticked the maces, bags, and purses.

How many people out of the suit, Jarndyce and Jarndyce has stretched forth its unwholesome hand to spoil and corrupt, would be a very wide question. From the master, upon whose impaling files reams of dusty warrants in Jarndyce and Jarndyce have grimly writhed into many shapes; down to the copying-clerk in the Six Clerks' Office, who has copied his tens of thousands of Chancery-folio-pages under that eternal heading; no man's nature has been made better by it. In trickery, evasion, procrastination, spoilation, botheration, under false pretenses of all sorts, there are influences that can never come to good. The very solicitors' boys who have kept the wretched suitors at bay, by protesting time out of mind that Mr. Chizzle, Mizzle, or otherwise, was particularly engaged and had appointments until dinner, may have got an extra moral twist and shuffle into themselves out of Jarndyce and Jarndyce. The receiver in the cause has acquired a goodly sum of money by it, but has acquired too a distrust of his own mother, and a contempt for his own kind. Chizzle, Mizzle, and otherwise, have lapsed into a habit of vaguely promising themselves that they will look into that outstanding little matter, and see what can be done for Drizzle—who was not well used—when Jarndyce and Jarndyce shall be got out of the office. Shirking and sharking, in all their many varieties, have been sown broadcast by the ill-fated cause; and even those who have contemplated its history from the outermost circle of such evil, have been insensibly tempted into a loose way of letting bad

Phiz (Hablot Knight Browne). *Lawyer's Office.* From Charles Dickens's *Pickwick Papers.* 1837. Engraving. Rare Books and Manuscript Division, The New York Public Library. Astor, Lenox, and Tilden Foundations.

things alone to take their own bad course, and a loose belief that if the world go wrong, it was, in some offhand manner, never meant to go right.

Thus, in the midst of the mud and at the heart of the fog, sits the Lord High Chancellor in his High Court of Chancery.

"Mr. Tangle," says the Lord High Chancellor, latterly something restless under the eloquence of that learned gentleman.

"Mlud," said Mr. Tangle. Mr. Tangle knows more of Jarndyce and Jarndyce than anybody. He is famous for it—supposed never to have read anything else since he left school.

"Have you nearly concluded your argument?"

"Mlud, no—variety of points—feel it my duty tsubmit—ludship," is the reply that slides out of Mr. Tangle.

"Several members of the bar are still to be heard, I believe?" says the Chancellor, with a slight smile.

Eighteen of Mr. Tangle's learned friends, each armed with a little summary of eighteen hundred sheets, bob up like eighteen hammers in a pianoforte, make eighteen bows, and drop into their eighteen places of obscurity.

"We will proceed with the hearing on Wednesday fortnight," says the Chancellor. For, the question at issue is only a question of costs, a mere bud on the forest tree of the parent suit, and really will come to a settlement one of these days.

The Chancellor rises; the bar rises; the prisoner is brought forward in a hurry; the man from Shropshire cries, "My lord!" Maces, bags, and purses, indignantly proclaim silence, and frown at the man from Shropshire.

"In reference," proceeds the Chancellor, still on Jarndyce and Jarndyce, "to the young girl—"

"Begludship's pardon—boy," says Mr. Tangle, prematurely.

"In reference," proceeds the Chancellor, with extra distinctness, "to the young girl and boy, the two young people . . . "

(Mr. Tangle crushed.)

"Whom I directed to be in attendance today, and who are now in my private room, I will see them and satisfy myself as the expediency of making the order for their residing with their uncle."

Mr. Tangle on his legs again.

"Begludship's pardon—dead."

"With their," Chancellor looking through his double eye-glass at the papers on his desk, "grandfather."

"Begludship's pardon—victim of rash action—brains."

Suddenly a very little counsel, with a terrific bass voice, arises, fully inflated, in the back settlements of the fog, and says, "Will your lordship allow me? I appear for him. He is a cousin, several times removed. I am not at the moment prepared to inform the Court in what exact remove he is a cousin; but he *is* a cousin."

Leaving this address (delivered like a sepulchral message) ringing in the rafters of the roof, the very little counsel drops, and the fog knows him no more. Everybody looks for him. Nobody can see him.

"I will speak with both the young people," says the Chancellor anew, "and satisfy myself on the subject of their residing with their cousin. I will mention the matter to-morrow morning when I take my seat."

The Chancellor is about to bow to the bar, when the prisoner is presented. Nothing can possibly come of the prisoner's conglomeration, but his being sent back to prison; which is soon done. The man from Shropshire ventures another remonstrative "My lord!" but the Chancellor, being aware of him, has dexterously vanished. Everybody else quickly vanishes too. A battery of blue bags is loaded with heavy charges of papers and carried off by clerks; the little mad old woman marches off with her documents; the empty court is locked up. If all the injustice it has committed, and all the misery it has caused, could only be locked up with it, and the whole burnt away in a great funeral pyre—why so much the better for other parties than the parties in Jarndyce and Jarndyce!

HONORÉ DAUMIER. *Counsel for the Defense*. Before 1879. Crayon, ink, and wash on paper. 9 × 13¾″ (22.9 × 34.9 cm). The Phillips Collection, Washington, D.C.

Lewis Carroll

FROM ALICE'S ADVENTURES IN WONDERLAND

"Alice's Evidence"

"Here!" cried Alice, quite forgetting in the flurry of the moment how large she had grown in the last few minutes, and she jumped up in such a hurry that she tipped over the jury box with the edge of her skirt, upsetting all the jurymen onto the heads of the crowd below, and there they lay spreading about, reminding her very much of a globe of goldfish she had accidentally upset the week before.

"Oh, I *beg* your pardon!" she exclaimed in a tone of great dismay, and began picking them up again as quickly as she could, for the accident of the goldfish kept running in her head, and she had a vague sort of idea that they must be collected at once and put back into the jury box, or they would die.

"The trial cannot proceed," said the King in a very grave voice, "until all the jurymen are back in their proper places—*all,*" he repeated with great emphasis, looking hard at Alice as he said so.

Alice looked at the jury box, and saw that in her haste she had put the Lizard in head downward, and the poor little thing was waving its tail about in a melancholy way, being quite unable to move. She soon got it out again, and put it right. "Not that it signifies much," she said to herself; "I should think it would be *quite* as much use in the trial one way up as the other."

As soon as the jury had a little recovered from the shock of being upset, and their slates and pencils had been found and handed back to them, they set to work very diligently to write out a history of the accident, all except the Lizard, who seemed too much overcome to do anything but sit with its mouth open, gazing up into the roof of the court.

"What do you know about this business?" the King said to Alice.

"Nothing," said Alice.

"Nothing *whatever?"* persisted the King.

"Nothing whatever," said Alice.

"That's important," the King said, turning to the jury.

They were just beginning to write this down on their slates, when the White Rabbit interrupted. *"Un*important, your Majesty means, of course," he said in a very respectful tone, but frowning and making faces at him as he spoke.

*"Un*important, of course, I meant," the King hastily said, and went on to himself in an undertone, "important—unimportant—unimportant—important—" as if he were trying which word sounded best.

Some of the jury wrote it down "important," and some "unimportant." Alice could see this, as she was near enough to look over their slates; "but it doesn't matter a bit," she thought to herself.

At this moment the King, who had been for some time busily writing in his notebook, called out, "Silence!" and read out from his book, "Rule Forty-two. *All persons more than a mile high to leave the court."*

Everybody looked at Alice.

Charles Lutwidge Dodgson (1832–1898), better known by his pseudonym, Lewis Carroll, wrote his classic dreamworld novels ostensibly for a real child, Alice Liddle, but with intellectual concerns suitable for an adult.

"I'm not a mile high," said Alice.

"Nearly two miles high," added the Queen.

"You are," said the King.

"Well, I shan't go, at any rate," said Alice. "Besides, that's not a regular rule; you invented it just now."

"It's the oldest rule in the book," said the King.

"Then it ought to be Number One," said Alice.

The King turned pale, and shut his notebook hastily. "Consider your verdict," he said to the jury in a low, trembling voice.

"There's more evidence to come yet, please, your Majesty," said the White Rabbit, jumping up in a great hurry; "this paper has just been picked up."

"What's in it?" said the Queen.

"I haven't opened it yet," said the White Rabbit, "but it seems to be a letter, written by the prisoner to—to somebody."

"It must have been that," said the King, "unless it was written to nobody, which isn't usual, you know."

"Whom is it directed to?" said one of the jurymen.

"It isn't directed at all," said the White Rabbit; "in fact, there's nothing written on the *outside."* He unfolded the paper as he spoke, and added, "It isn't a letter after all; it's a set of verses."

"Are they in the prisoner's handwriting?" asked another of the jurymen.

"No, they're not," said the White Rabbit, "and that's the queerest thing about it." (The jury all looked puzzled.)

"He must have imitated somebody else's hand," said the King. (The jury all brightened up again.)

"Please your Majesty," said the Knave, "I didn't write it, and they can't prove I did; there's no name signed at the end."

"If you didn't sign it," said the King, "that only makes the matter worse. You *must* have meant some mischief, or else you'd have signed your name like an honest man."

There was a general clapping of hands at this; it was the first really clever thing the King had said that day.

"That *proves* his guilt," said the Queen.

"It proves nothing of the sort!" said Alice. "Why, you don't even know what they're about!"

"Read them," said the King."

The White Rabbit put on his spectacles. "Where shall I begin, please, your Majesty?" he asked.

"Begin at the beginning," the King said gravely, "and go on till you come to the end; then stop."

These were the verses the White Rabbit read:

"They told me you had been to her,
And mentioned me to him:
She gave me a good character,
But said I could not swim.

He sent them word I had not gone
(We know it to be true):
If she should push the matter on,
What would become of you?

I gave her one, they gave him two,
You gave us three or more;
They all returned from him to you,
Though they were mine before.

If I or she should chance to be
Involved in this affair,
He trusts to you to set them free,
Exactly as we were.

My notion was that you had been
(Before she had this fit)
An obstacle that came between
Him, and ourselves, and it.

Don't let him know she liked him best,
For this must ever be
A secret, kept from all the rest,
Between yourself and me."

SIR JOHN TENNIEL. Trial scene from Lewis Carroll's *Alice's Adventures in Wonderland.* 1865. Engraving.

"That's the most important piece of evidence we've heard yet," said the King, rubbing his hands; "so now let the jury—"

"If any one of them can explain it," said Alice (she had grown so large in the last few minutes that she wasn't a bit afraid of interrupting him), "I'll give him sixpence. *I* don't believe there's an atom of meaning in it."

The jury all wrote down on their slates, *"She* doesn't believe there's an atom of meaning in it," but none of them attempted to explain the paper.

"If there's no meaning in it," said the King, "that saves a world of trouble, you know, as we needn't try to find any. And yet I don't know," he went on, spreading out the verses on his knees, and looking at them with one eye; "I seem to see some meaning in them, after all. '—*said I could not swim*'—you can't swim, can you? ' he added, turning to the Knave.

The Knave shook his head sadly. "Do I look like it?" he said. (Which he certainly did *not*, being made entirely of cardboard.)

"All right, so far," said the King, and he went on muttering over the verses to himself: "*We know it to be true*'—that's the jury, of course—'*I gave her one, they gave him two*'—why, that must be what he did with the tarts, you know—"

"But it goes on, '*They all returned from him to you,*' " said Alice.

"Why, there they are!" said the King triumphantly, pointing to the tarts on the table. "Nothing can be clearer than *that*. Then again—'*before she had this fit*'—you never had fits, my dear, I think?" he said to the Queen.

"Never!" said the Queen furiously, throwing an inkstand at the Lizard as she spoke. (The unfortunate little Bill had left off writing on his slate with one finger, as he found it made no mark; but he now hastily began again, using the ink that was trickling down his face, as long as it lasted.)

"Then the words don't *fit* you," said the King, looking around the court with a smile. There was a dead silence.

"It's a pun!" the King added in an angry tone, and everybody laughed. "Let the jury consider their verdict," the King said, for about the twentieth time that day.

"No, no!" said the Queen. "Sentence first—verdict afterward."

"Stuff and nonsense!" said Alice loudly. "The idea of having the sentence first!"

"Hold your tongue!" said the Queen, turning purple.

"I won't!" said Alice.

"Off with her head!" the Queen shouted at the top of her voice Nobody moved.

"Who cares for you?" said Alice (she had grown to her full size by this time). "You're nothing but a pack of cards!"

Gilbert Abbott à Beckett

FROM THE COMIC BLACKSTONE

"Of the Rise, Progress, and Gradual Improvement of the Laws of England"

We now propose to take a survey of the whole judicial history of England; and boldly grasping the constitutional theodolite, we proceed to take the levels, mark out the gradients, and observe the cuttings along the whole line of British Law. The periods and intermediate stations through which we intend to pass are six: 1. From the earliest times to the Norman Conquest, a short and not a very easy stage. 2. From the Norman Conquest to the reign of King Edward I, which will be very uphill work. 3. From thence to the Reformation, in which we shall observe that the gradients were somewhat rapid. 4. From the Reformation, to the Restoration of Charles II, where the cuttings were very

---

Gilbert Abbott à Beckett (1811–1856) was an original staff member for Punch, *the British humor magazine. As an author of lampoons such as* The Comic History of England, *he also took on Sir William Blackstone's famous text* Commentaries on the Laws of England. *This excerpt is but one of many flippant chapters from that spoof.*

severe. 5. From thence to the Revolution in 1688, where the tunnelling must be heavy considering what was gone through. And 6. From the Revolution to the present time, where we arrive at the terminus of our work.

1. And first let us look at the Ancient Britons, who, we are told, "never committed their laws to writing, possibly for want of letters"—a reason that reminds us of the excuse of the angler who did not go out fishing, because, in the first place, there were no fish. Though in our day we hear of French without a Master, the Druids were not such clever fellows as to be able to achieve writing without letters, or penmanship without an alphabet. Antiquarians tell us no trace of a letter is to be found among the British relics, and if they have been looking for some correspondence with the Druidical postmark, we are not surprised at the search for letters having proved vain.

When we consider the number of different nations that broke in upon Britain, we must not wonder at the hodge-podge they made of our early laws; for what with the Romans thrashing the Britons, the Picts pitching into the Saxons, and the Normans drubbing the Danes, it is impossible to say who gave its early judicial system to England, though it is clear that they gave it to one another in magnificent style.

The first attempt to model the constitution was by Alfred, who, having whacked his enemies, might be called a modeller in whacks, and who divided the whole country into hundreds, as we have since learned to divide our walnuts and our coals. He made himself the head reservoir of justice, and laid it on—sometimes rather too thick—to every part of the nation. He was the first literary monarch who ever sat upon the Saxon mile-stone, which was the substitute in those days for the British throne, and we hail him as a brother author; for he wrote the first law book that England ever saw. Among the Saxon laws we find the constitution of Parliaments, the election of magistrates, the descent of the crown, and other institutions preserved to the present day; and not only preserved but potted and garnered up in the bosom of the British Constitution, where we hope they will long remain.

2. The Norman Conquest made considerable alteration, and introduced the forest laws, which threw the game into the king's hands, vesting every beast of the field and fowl of the air in the sovereign, as in one vast hamper, which hampered the people to the very last degree. William also introduced the trial by combat, for he wished the people to learn to lick each other, having taught them to lick the dust. During this period of our legal history, feudal tenures came into full growth, and they at last had the effect of irritating the barons, in the reign of John, to demand that splendid piece of parchment, which every one puffs but nobody reads—as is sometimes the case with a well-advertised book—that enormous palladium of our liberties, called Magna Charta. We shall not describe the contents of this glorious specimen of penmanship, for every Briton of course has it at his fingers' ends, and having learnt it at school, hangs it in his study at home, that he may remember that it regulates the time and place of holding a court leet, among other privileges even still more precious than the one to which we allude.

3. The third period commences with Edward the First, our English Justinian—a title that savours of quackery, like the Irish Paganini, the American Braham, and other foreign editions of distinguished men. Among other achievements, he first established a repository for the public records, which, perhaps, stood on the very ground now occupied by the horse repository in St. Martin's Lane.

The laws went on improving until the time of Henry the Seventh, when that monarch and his ministers, being hard up, resorted to every method of making money, and only considered what was "likely to pay."

4. Our fourth period brings us to Henry the Eighth, who introduced the bankrupt laws, and several other legal measures; having imbibed a taste for law studies while lodging at Honey and Skelton's, the hair-dressers at the top of Inner Temple Lane—and it is said that the rival family came to be called the house of Tu-dor, because there are two doors to the house alluded to—a piece of antiquarian affection and learned foppishness in which we do not believe.

The children of Henry the Eighth did little for the law; but Elizabeth extended the royal prerogative, which she seemed to consider as elastic as a piece of Indian rubber, and she used it to rub out many of the dearest privileges of the people.

On the accession of James the First, he found the sceptre too heavy for his hand, a discovery that was subsequently made by James the Second, who very prudently dropped it, when he could no longer manage it, instead of holding on like Charles the First, who was little better than half a sovereign, and ultimately paid the forfeit of a crown.

5. The fifth period brings us to the Restoration, and this reminds us that the British constitution is a good deal like Smith and Baber's floor-cloth manufactory at Knightsbridge, which has been destroyed, restored, rebuilt, repaired, burnt down, and raised up at least half-a-dozen different times. The British constitution seems, like a cat, to have nine lives, for it has received within our recollection several death blows; but, no matter from what height it is thrown, it always comes upon its feet again. It was in the period after the Restoration, that the *Habeas Corpus* Act was passed, which is said to be a second *Magna Charta*, and must therefore be a good deal like butter upon bacon, for if *Magna Charta* was a bulwark and a palladium, we did not require another bulwark and another palladium before the first had been regularly worn out.

6. From the Revolution to the present time is the sixth and last division of our subject, and we are happy to say that this period has been fertile of really useful reforms. These amendments have been noticed in other portions of this work, and it is needless to recapitulate them here.

FRANCISCO GOYA. *¡Qual la Descañonan!* (Oh, How They Pluck Out Her Quills!). From *Los Caprichos*, plate 21. 1797–1798. Etching and aquatint. 8½ × 5⅞″ (21.7 × 14.8 cm). The Metropolitan Museum of Art, New York. Gift of M. Knoedler and Co., 1918. *In one of Goya's greatest allegorical etchings, a prostitute owl, or bird of night, has fallen into the corrupt hands of the law, depicted as predatory animals. A constable on the right and a notary on the left pluck off her earrings as the district judge conceals the robbery.*

THOMAS ROWLANDSON. *Botheration*. 1793. Aquatint. 9½ × 13¾" (24.1 × 34.9 cm). British Museum, London.

Laurie Adams

FROM ART ON TRIAL

"The Brush or the Pen?"

In challenging Ruskin in the courts, Whistler's litigious personality led him into one of the most celebrated trials involving works of art. Although Ruskin had indeed made the libelous comments and had undeniably called the artist a "Cockney coxcomb," it was Whistler who actually brought the libel to the attention of the general public. Ruskin's monthly pamphlet had a small audience, and had Whistler not felt impelled to bring the lawsuit, the remarks would most probably have gone unnoticed. Whistler's tendency toward violence erupted into physical fights on several occasions throughout his lifetime, but the trial that Whistler instigated became a battle between opposed intellectual principles. On one level, the puritanical views of Ruskin would be pitted against the more modern views of Whistler, and there is irony in the fact that Whistler had had to struggle against the very puritanism within himself that he would now be fighting in court. On another level, the new Impressionist style would be on trial against London's artistic establishment as canonized by the Royal Academy. Even more universal in the world of creativity was the opposition of artist and critic. As Whistler himself said, it was a trial "between the Brush and the Pen."

That simple phrase evokes a number of associations that go far deeper than its surface

---

Charged with "flinging a pot of paint in the public's eye" with his semi-abstract canvas Nocturne in Black and Gold, *the painter James A. M. Whistler (1834–1904) sued the esteemed critic who penned the insult, John Ruskin (1819–1900). In this selection from her 1976 study, art historian Laurie Adams examines the highly publicized trial and the issues it raised.*

COLORPLATE 69

J. B. MAUZAISSE. *Le Code Napoléon Coronne par le Temps* (The Napoleonic Code Crowned by Time). 1833. Oil on canvas. 51½ × 63″ (131 × 160 cm). Le Musée National de Château de Malmaison, Rueil, France.

MARSHÆSEA PRISON
SOUTHWARK

COLORPLATE 70 *(opposite, above)*

THOMAS ROWLANDSON. *Marshalsea Prison.* 1820. Watercolor on paper. 5¾ × 9¼" (14.6 × 23.5 cm). Boston Public Library, Boston. *Established in 1376, the Marshalsea Prison was located in Southwark, London. Among the debtors who languished behind its walls was the father of Charles Dickens. The future novelist, forced to support his family in his father's absence, got an unwelcome close look at the hardness of life for the lower classes in Victorian London, an experience that would serve him throughout his career. Along with the other prisons in Southwark, it was demolished in the nineteenth century.*

COLORPLATE 71 *(opposite, below)*

THOMAS ROWLANDSON. *Reading the Will.* Early nineteenth century. Watercolor on paper. 6 × 9¼" (15.2 × 23.5 cm). Boston Public Library, Boston.

COLORPLATE 72

OTTO ERDMANN. *Reading the Will.* 1886. Oil on canvas. 38½ × 49½" (97.8 × 125.7 cm). Christie's, London.

COLORPLATE 73

JEAN LOUIS FORAIN. *The Counsel's Speech.* 1910. Oil on canvas. 23⅝ × 28¾″ (60 × 73 cm). Private collection.

COLORPLATE 74

HONORÉ DAUMIER. *Three Lawyers*. Before 1879. Oil on canvas. 16 × 13″ (40.6 × 33 cm).
The Phillips Collection, Washington, D.C.

COLORPLATE 75

SPY (SIR LESLIE WARD). *Bench and Bar (with the Earl of Malsbury). Vanity Fair* supplement, December 5, 1891. Colortype. 13¾ × 19½″ (35 × 49.5 cm). Harvard Law Art Collection, Cambridge.

COLORPLATE 76

ABRAHAM SOLOMON. *Waiting on the Verdict.* 1859. Oil on board.
14 × 16″ (35.6 × 40.6 cm). Tunbridge Wells Museum and Art Gallery, Kent.

COLORPLATE 77

VINCENT VAN GOGH. *Prisoners' Round*. After Doré. 1890. Oil on canvas. 31½ × 25¼" (80 × 64 cm). Pushkin Museum of Fine Arts, Moscow.

reference to artist and critic. Impressionism was very much a style of the Brush, while the Pen suggested the linear qualities of neoclassical and Pre-Raphaelite painting. And again, while on the surface the trial would pit Brush against Pen, it would mirror the old conflict within Whistler's own development as an artist, his progressive rejection of the linear and his assumption of impressionistic use of color. Finally, on an even deeper psychological level, the erotic symbolism of Brush and Pen can hardly escape notice. If one is to believe Whistler's own statement in his 1867 letter to Fantin-Latour, he certainly associated the Brush, and its reference to color, with sensuous female qualities, while the Pen had the obvious masculine significance of control and mastery.

After a delay of over a year, caused in part by Ruskin's mental illness, the trial began. It lasted for two days—from November 25 to November 26, 1878. Sir John Walter Huddleston and a special jury heard the case in the Court of Exchequer in Westminster. Whistler's case was prepared by Anderson Rose, who had handled the artist's constant financial problems, and it was argued by counsel Mr. Serjeant Parry and Mr. William Petheram. Burne-Jones, the Pre-Raphaelite painter, handled Ruskin's case since the critic had suffered a breakdown several weeks before the trial opened.

Ruskin's spell of madness was but one stage in a steady march toward mental decline. As early as 1874, he referred to periods of confusion and despondency, and the following year, he broke down before his students during an Oxford lecture. Starting in the 1860s, Ruskin had recorded terrifying erotic dreams in his diaries. There is considerable poetic justice and psychological truth in the fiercely moralizing Ruskin's hallucinations, shortly before the trial, in which Satan assumed the form of a black cat and commanded him to perform various obscene acts. The Satanic cat leaped at Ruskin from behind a *mirror*, thus confirming that the critic himself was ordering this distinctly unpuritanical form of behavior. As might be expected under the circumstances, Ruskin's doctor forbade him to appear in the courtroom.

Attorney General Sir John Holker, and his junior counsel, Charles Bowen, argued Ruskin's case. Both sides had difficulty in persuading artists to testify. Eventually, each produced three witnesses. In addition, Whistler testifed in his own behalf.

At 11:00 A.M. Monday, November 25, the trial began. For the theatrically inclined Whistler, the court setting must have indeed been a stage. The courtroom was crowded with an audience of celebrities. On the surface the case was a libel suit dealing with the matter of Whistler's wounded vanity. In fact, however, it dealt with a far more complex set of issues.

Serjeant Parry opened the case for Whistler on a rather tentative note:

> I speak for Mr. Whistler, who has followed the profession of an artist for many years, while Mr. Ruskin is a gentlemen well known to all of us, and holding perhaps the highest position in Europe or America as an art critic. Some of his words are destined to immortality, and it is the more surprising, therefore, that a gentleman holding such a position could traduce another in a way that would lead that other to come into a court of law to ask for damages. The jury, after hearing the case, will come to the conclusion that a great injustice has been done. Mr. Whistler. . . . is not merely a painter, but has likewise distinguished himself in the capacity of etcher, achieving considerable honors in that department of art. He has been an unwearied worker in his profession, always desiring to succeed, and if he had formed an erroneous opinion, he should not have been treated with contempt and ridicule. . . .
>
> Mr. Ruskin pleaded that the alleged libel was privileged as being a fair and *bona fide* criticism upon a painting which the plaintiff had exposed to public view. But the terms in which Mr. Ruskin has spoken of the plaintiff are unfair and ungentlemanly, and are calculated to do, and have done him, considerable injury, and it will be for the jury to say what damages the plaintiff is entitled to.

On the other hand, the Attorney General's opening statement for Ruskin was a forceful apology for the critic's philosophy of life and defense of his art criticism. What would become of the arts without criticism as an inspiration and a spur to excellence? This was the thrust of his opening remarks. Unfortunately, continued the Attorney General, Ruskin would be unable to appear in his own defense owing to illness:

> That gentleman, it is well known, has devoted himself for years to the study of art. From 1869 he has been Slade Professor at Oxford: he has written much on art, and judging from his works it is obvious that he is a man of the keenest susceptibility. He has a great love and reverence for art and a special admiration for highly finished pictures. His love for art almost amounts to idolatry, and to the examination of the beautiful in art he has devoted his life.

⋆ ⋆ ⋆

Art is characteristically elevated to a sphere above the ordinary so that, in some circles, it seems to be the last of the great religions. This is never more evident than in the social distinction between the rich man who collects nothing and the rich man who collects "art." Culture, with a capital *C*, is considered something of a moral virtue and has been for centuries.

Ironically enough, these attitudes are more apt to occur among the patrons of art than among the artists themselves. Certainly the vast majority of artists, writers, and all varieties of performers, work for money and fame. Whistler himself, especially in his later years, resented the success of his contemporaries. "Poverty," said Whistler, "may induce industry, but it does not produce the fine flower of painting. The test is not poverty, it's money. . . . If I had had, say, three thousand pounds a year, what beautiful things I could have done."

For Ruskin, on the other hand, an artist was not entitled to a single farthing for which he had not struggled furiously. His attorney hammered away on this issue: "You offer that picture to the public as one of particular beauty, as a work of art, and which is fairly worth two hundred guineas?"

"I offer it as a work which I have conscientiously executed and which I think is worth the money," Whistler replied flatly. "I would hold my reputation upon this, as I would upon any of my other works."

Rossetti testified that in his view 200 guineas "is the full value of the picture," while Burne-Jones disagreed, "seeing how much careful work men do for much less." Again the amount, rather than the quality of the work, was emphasized.

Thus the celebrated libel trial between Whistler and Ruskin became a vehicle for the expression of opposing philosophies of art and art criticism. In the summation for Whistler, Serjeant Parry concluded:

> His [Ruskin's] decree has gone forth that Mr. Whistler's pictures are worthless. He has not supported that by evidence. He has not condescended to give reasons for the view he has taken, he has treated us with contempt, as he treated Mr. Whistler. He has said: "I, Mr. Ruskin, seated on my throne of art, say what I please and expect all the world to agree with me." Mr. Ruskin is great as a writer, but not as a man; as a man he has degraded himself. His tone in writing the article is personal and malicious.
>
> Mr. Ruskin's criticism of Mr. Whistler's pictures is almost exclusively in the nature of a personal attack, a pretended criticism of art which is really a criticism upon the man himself, and calculated to injure him. It was written recklessly, and for the purpose of holding him up to ridicule and contempt. Mr. Ruskin has gone out of his way to attack Mr. Whistler personally and must answer for the consequences of having written a damnatory attack upon the painter. That is what is called pungent criticism—but it is defamatory, and I hope that you, gentlemen of the jury, will mark your disapproval by your verdict.

Ruskin's counsel closed by saying that the critic had given his opinion of Whistler's painting and that he held that opinion still.

The judge's final words to the jury left no doubt that Whistler had been libeled. The jury's task would be to assess the amount of damages, although here, too, the judge made his own feelings eminently clear:

> There are certain words by Mr. Ruskin, about which I should think no one would entertain a doubt: those words amount to libel. It is of the last importance that a critic should have full latitude to express the judgments he has honestly formed, and for that purpose there is no reason why he should not use ridicule as a weapon; but a critic should confine himself to criticism, and not make it the veil for personal censure, nor allow himself to run into reckless and unfair attacks merely for the love of exercising his power of denunciation. The question for the jury is, did Mr. Whistler's idea of art justify the language used by Mr. Ruskin? And the further question is whether the insult offered—if insult there has been—is of such a gross character as to call for substantial damages. Whether it is a case for merely contemptuous damages to the extent of a farthing, or something of that sort, indicating that it is one which ought never to have been brought into court, and in which no pecuniary damage has been sustained; or whether the case is one which calls for damages in some small sum as indicating the opinion of the jury that the offender has gone beyond the strict letter of the law.

The jury found for Whistler. Damages to be awarded: one farthing. The judge, in turn, refused to assess costs. This decision presented little financial problem for Ruskin, but for Whistler it proved to be a considerable hardship; he would soon find himself bankrupt. Ruskin reacted to his moral defeat by resigning his Slade Professorship at Oxford, as Whistler had said he should. "Let him resign his present professorship," declared the artist, "to fill the chair of Ethics at the University. As master of English literature, he has a right to his laurels, while, as the populariser of pictures he remains the Peter Parley of painting."

George Bernard Shaw, in his usual down-to-earth way, offered a sobering comment on the case. Whistler, he said, should have based his case on commercial damage rather than artistic conscience. "In talking about his artistic conscience," Shaw declared, "he could only raise a farthing—that being all conscience is worth in the eyes of the law!"

W. S. Gilbert

FROM TRIAL BY JURY

"The Judge's Song"

When I, good friends, was called to the Bar,
I'd an appetite fresh and hearty,
But I was, as many young barristers are,
An impecunious party.
I'd a swallow-tail coat of a beautiful blue—
A brief which was brought by a booby—
A couple of shirts and a collar or two,
And a ring that looked like a ruby!

In Westminster Hall I danced a dance,
Like a semi-despondent fury;
For I thought I should never hit on a chance
Of addressing a British Jury—
But I soon got tired of third-class journeys,
And dinners of bread and water;
So I fell in love with a rich attorney's
Elderly, ugly daughter.

Sir William Schwenck (W. S.) Gilbert (1836–1911) was called to the bar in 1863, but his real calling lay in comic verse and light operas. This selection is the earliest Gilbert and Sullivan patter-song for which Sir Arthur Sullivan's music survives.

The rich attorney, he wiped his eyes,
And replied to my fond professions:
"You shall reap the reward of your enterprise,
At the Bailey and Middlesex Sessions.
You'll get used to her looks," said he,
"And a very nice girl you'll find her—
She may very well pass for forty-three
In the dusk, with a light behind her!"

The rich attorney was as good as his word:
The briefs came trooping gaily,
And every day my voice was heard
At the Sessions or Ancient Bailey.
All thieves who could my fees afford
Relied on my orations,
And many a burglar I've restored
To his friends and his relations.

At length I became as rich as the GURNEYS—
And incubus then I thought her,
So I threw over that rich attorney's
Elderly, ugly daughter.
The rich attorney my character high
Tried vainly to disparage—
And now, if you please, I'm ready to try
This Breach of Promise of Marriage!

WILLIAM HOGARTH. *The Bench*. 1758. Engraving. 8½ × 8¼" (21.6 × 21 cm). British Museum, London.

HONORÉ DAUMIER. From *Lawyers and Litigants*. c. 1845. Lithograph. 14¼ × 10″ (36.2 × 25.4 cm). Harvard Law Art Collection, Cambridge. *"Be sure to respond to me, and I will reply back . . . This will lead to two more defense speeches that we can charge our clients for!"*

HONORÉ DAUMIER. "The Lawyer's Victory." From *The Beautiful Days of Life*. c. 1845. Lithograph. 14¼ × 9¾" (36.2 × 24.8 cm). Harvard Law Art Collection, Cambridge. *"Come close to my heart; you are acquitted! Between you and me, you deserved to be sent to the gallows because you are a downright scoundrel . . . But, anyhow, it is always pleasant to save your fellow man's head!" (The thief, quite touched, pinches his defender's purse, just to take a souvenir of esteem and friendship.)*

HONORÉ DAUMIER. "Neighbors in Front of the Judge." From *The Beautiful Days of Life*. c. 1845. Lithograph. 7½ × 9⅞" (19 × 25.1 cm). Harvard Law Art Collection, Cambridge. *"Well, I still won my trial and you will not be so proud anymore, Mrs. Stuck-up . . . since the judge sentenced you to go back home, back-to-back with me!"*

HONORÉ DAUMIER. From *People of Justice*. c. 1845. Lithograph. 7½ × 9⅞" (19 × 25.1 cm). Harvard Law Art Collection, Cambridge. *"My dear fellow, what can I say . . . We have had a misfortune . . . I could not prove your innocence this time . . . but for your next theft I hope to be more fortunate."*

Guy de Maupassant

"Hippolyte's Claim"

The fat Justice of the Peace, with one eye closed and the other half-open, is listening with evident displeasure to the plaintiffs. Once in a while he gives a sort of grunt that foretells his opinion, and in a thin voice resembling that of a child, he interrupts them to ask questions. He has just rendered judgment in the case of Monsieur Joly against Monsieur Petitpas, the contestants having come to court on account of the boundary of a field which has been accidentally over-stepped by Monsieur Petitpas's farmhand, while the latter was plowing.

Now he calls the case of Hippolyte Lacour, vestryman and ironmonger, against Madame Céleste Césarine Luneau, widow of Anthime Isidore Luneau.

Hippolyte Lacour is forty-five years old; he is tall and gaunt, with a clean-shaven face and long hair, and he speaks in a slow, singsong voice.

Madame Luneau appears to be about forty years of age. She is built like a prize-fighter, and her plain dress is stretched tightly over her portly form. Her enormous hips hold up her overflowing bosom in front, while in the back they support the great rolls of flesh that cover her shoulders. Her face, with strongly cut features, rests on a short, fat neck, and her strong voice is pitched at a key that makes the windows and the eardrums of her auditors vibrate. She is about to become a mother and her huge form protrudes like a mountain.

The witnesses for the defense are waiting to be called.

His Honor Begins: Hippolyte Lacour, state your complaint.

The Plaintiff Speaks: Your Honor, it will be nine months on Saint-Michael's day that the defendant came to me one evening, after I had rung the Angelus, and began an explanation relating to her barrenness.

The Justice of the Peace: Kindly be more explicit.

Hippolyte: Very well, your Honor. Well, she wanted to have a child and desired my participation. I didn't raise any objection, and she promised to give me one hundred francs. The thing was all cut and dried, and now she refuses to acknowledge my claim, which I renew before your Honor.

The Justice: I don't understand in the least. You say that she wanted a child! What kind of child! Did she wish to adopt one?

Hippolyte: No, your Honor, she wanted a new one.

The Justice: What do you mean by a new one?

Hippolyte: I mean a newborn child, one that we were to beget as if we were man and wife.

The Justice: You astonish me. To what end did she make this abnormal proposition?

Hippolyte: Your Honor, at first I could not make out her reasons, and was taken a little aback. But as I don't do anything without thoroughly investigating beforehand, I called on her to explain matters to me, which she did. You see, her husband, Anthime Isidore, whom you knew as well as you know me, had died the week before, and his money reverted to his family. This greatly displeased her on account of the loss it meant, so she went to a lawyer who told her all about what might happen if a child should be born to

---

Henri René Albert Guy de Maupassant (1850–1893) was the preeminent writer of short fiction in nineteenth-century France. This selection shows the master in a facetious vein.

her after ten months. I mean by this that if she gave birth to a child inside of ten months following the death of Anthime Isidore, her offspring would be considered legitimate and would entitle her to the inheritance. She made up her mind at once to run the risk, and came to me after church, as I have already had the honor of telling you, seeing that I am the father of eight living children, the eldest of whom is a grocer in Caen, department of Calvados, and legitimately married to Victoire-Elisabeth Rabou—

The Justice: These details are superfluous. Go back to the subject.

Hippolyte: I am getting there, your Honor. So she said to me: "If you succeed, I'll give you one hundred francs as soon as I get the doctor's report." Well, your Honor, I made ready to give entire satisfaction, and after eight weeks or so I learned with pleasure that I had succeeded. But when I asked her for the hundred francs she refused to pay me. I renewed my demands several times, never getting so much as a pin. She even called me a liar and a weakling, a libel which can be destroyed by glancing at her.

The Justice: Defendant, what have you to say?

Madame Luneau: Your Honor, I say that this man is a liar.

The Justice: How can you prove this assertion?

Madame Luneau (red in the face, choking and stammering): How can I prove it? What proofs have I? I haven't a single real proof that the child isn't his. But, your Honor, it isn't his, I swear it on the head of my dead husband.

The Justice: Well, whose is it, then?

Madame Luneau (stammering with rage): How do I know? How do—do I know? Everybody's, I suppose. Here are my witnesses, your Honor, they're all here, the six of them. Now make them testify, make them testify. They'll tell—

The Justice: Collect yourself, Madame Luneau, collect yourself and reply calmly to my questions. What reasons have you to doubt that this man is the father of the child you are carrying?

Madame Luneau: What reasons? I have a hundred to one, a hundred? No, two hundred, five hundred, ten thousand, a million and more reasons to believe he isn't. After the proposal I made to him, with the promise of one hundred francs, didn't I learn that he wasn't the father of his own children, your Honor, not the father of one of 'em?

Hippolyte (calmly): That's a lie.

Madame Luneau (exasperated): A lie! A lie, is it? I guess his wife has been seen by everybody around here. Call my witnesses, your Honor, and make them testify.

Hippolyte (calmly): It's a lie.

Madame Luneau: It's a lie, is it? How about the red-haired ones, then? I suppose they're yours, too?

The Justice: Kindly refrain from personal attacks, or I shall be obliged to call you to order.

Madame Luneau: Well, your Honor, I had my doubts about him, and said I to myself, two precautions are better than one, so I explained my position to Césaire Lepic, the witness who is present. Says he to me, "At your disposal, Madame Luneau," and he lent me his assistance in case Hippolyte should turn out to be unreliable. But as soon as the other witnesses heard that I wanted to make sure against any disappointment, I could have had more than a hundred, your Honor, if I had wanted them. That tall one over there, Lucas Chandelier, swore at the time that I oughtn't to give Hippolyte Lacour a cent, for he hadn't done more than the rest of them who had obliged me for nothing.

Hippolyte: What did you promise for? I expected the money, your Honor. No mistake with me—a promise given, a promise kept.

Madame Luneau (beside herself): One hundred francs! One hundred francs! One hundred francs for that, you liar! The others there didn't ask a red cent! Look at 'em, all six of 'em! Make them testify, your Honor, they'll tell sure. (To Hippolyte.) Look at 'em, you liar! they're as good as you. They're only six, but I could have had one, two, three, five hundred of 'em for nothing, too, you robber!

Hippolyte: Well, even if you'd had a hundred thousand—

Madame Luneau: I could, if I'd wanted 'em.

Hippolyte: I did my duty, so it doesn't change matters.

Madame Luneau (slapping her protuberant form with both hands) Then prove that it's you that did it, prove it, you robber! I defy you to prove it!

Hippolyte (calmly): Maybe I didn't do any more than anybody else. But you promised me a hundred francs for it. What did you ask the others for, afterward? You had no right to. I guess I could have done it alone.

Madame Luneau: It is not true, robber! Call my witnesses, your Honor; they'll answer, sure.

The Justice called the witnesses in behalf of the defense. Six red, awkward individuals appeared.

The Justice: Lucas Chandelier, have you any reason to suppose that you are the father of the child Madame Luneau is carrying?

Lucas Chandelier: Yes, sir.

The Justice: Célestin-Pierre Sidoine, have you any reason to suppose that you are the father of the child Madame Luneau is carrying?

Célestin-Pierre Sidoine: Yes, sir.

The four other witnesses testified to the same effect.

The Justice, after a pause, pronounced judgment: Whereas the plaintiff has reasons to

Artist unknown. *Old Bailey Justice After Dinner.* Late eighteenth century. Etching. 7¾ × 8¼" (19.7 × 21 cm). Harvard Law Art Collection, Cambridge.

believe himself the father of the child which Madame Luneau desired, Lucas Chandelier, Célestin-Pierre Sidoine, and others, have similar, if not conclusive reasons to lay claim to the child.

But whereas Mme. Luneau had previously asked the assistance of Hippolyte Lacour for a duly stated consideration:

And whereas one may not question the absolute good faith of Hippolyte Lacour, though it is questionable whether he had a perfect right to enter such an agreement, seeing that the plaintiff is married, and compelled by law to remain faithful to his lawful spouse:

Therefore the Court condemns Madame Luneau to pay an indemnity of twenty-five francs to Hippolyte Lacour for loss of time and unjustifiable abduction.

Oscar Wilde

FROM THE BALLAD OF READING GAOL

I know not whether Laws be right,
Or whether Laws be wrong;
All that we know who lie in gaol
Is that the wall is strong;
And that each day is like a year,
A year whose days are long.

Oscar Fingal O'Flahertie Wills Wilde (1854–1900), Irish playwright, novelist, poet, and coiner of barbed bon mots, *was convicted of sodomy, amid great scandal, and imprisoned from 1895 to 1897. The ballad based on his ordeal was written anonymously in 1898.*

Oscar Wilde relaxing during his lecture trip in America. 1882.

Cinq Centimes

ERNEST VAUGHAN

L'AURORE

Littéraire, Artistique, Sociale

J'Accuse...!

LETTRE AU PRÉSIDENT DE LA RÉPUBLIQUE

Par ÉMILE ZOLA

LETTRE

A M. FÉLIX FAURE

Président de la République

Front page of *L'Aurore*, regarding the handling of the Dreyfus affair. January 1898.

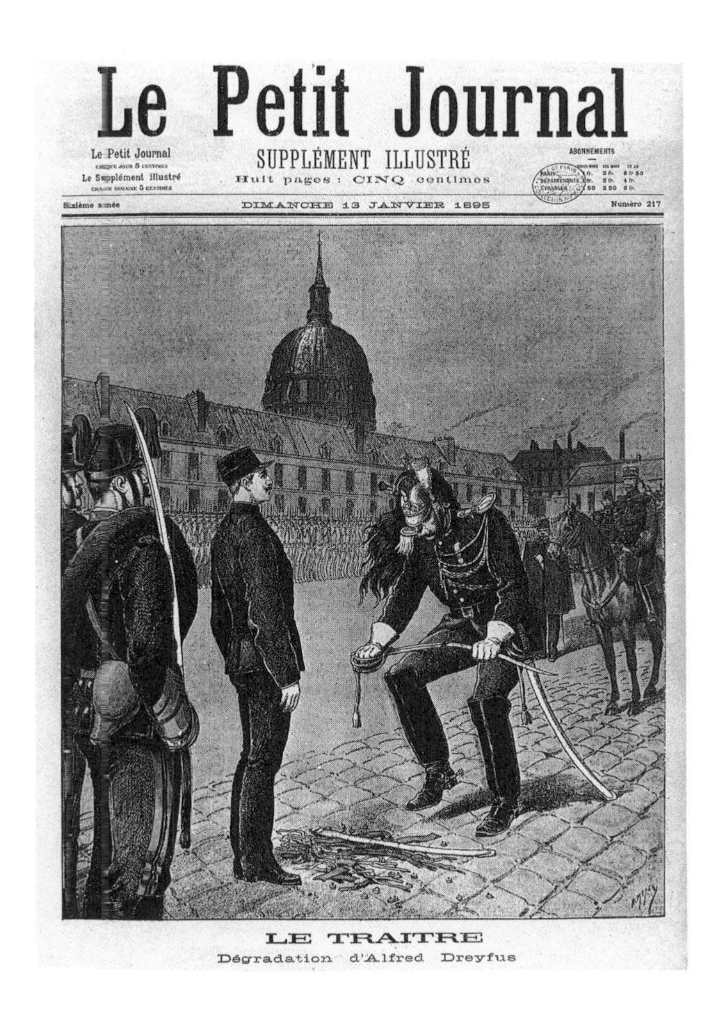
Le Petit Journal

Le Petit Journal

Le Supplément illustré

SUPPLÉMENT ILLUSTRÉ

Huit pages : CINQ centimes

ABONNEMENTS

Sixième année

DIMANCHE 13 JANVIER 1895

Numéro 217

LE TRAITRE

Dégradation d'Alfred Dreyfus

Artist unknown. *The Degradation of Dreyfus*. Cover illustration for the supplement for *Le Petit Journal*. January 1895. Collection, Library of the History of the City of Paris.

Emile Zola

FROM J'ACCUSE! . . .

January 13, 1898

Mr. President,

. . . Here is Dreyfus before the court-martial. The most rigorous secrecy is preserved. A traitor might have opened the frontier to the enemy and led the German emperor clear to the Nôtre Dame cathedral and no more extreme measures of silence and mystery would have been taken. The nation is horror-stricken, the most terrible details are whispered of monstrous treasons that make all history cry out; obviously, the whole nation bows to the court. No punishment is severe enough for the criminal; the country will applaud the public degradation, she will want the guilty man to stay eternally on his rock of infamy,

---

The most celebrated episode in the life of novelist Emile Zola (1840–1902) is his intervention in the case of Alfred Dreyfus (1859–1935), a Jewish French army officer falsely convicted of treason. Zola was found guilty of libel for attacking the army in his open letter to President Félix Faure, yet in 1904 Dreyfus was acquitted.

devoured by the remorse. Is there any truth in those whispered unmentionable things, capable of setting all Europe aflame, that they must needs be buried in the deep secrecy of star-chamber proceedings? No. Behind those doors there were only romantic and insane notions, and the imaginings of a Major du Paty de Clam. All these efforts were merely to hide the most ridiculous and bizarre of serial romances. To be assured of that one has only to study carefully the bill of indictment read before the court-martial.

Ah! the inanity of that accusation! That a man could have been condemned on such a charge is a prodigy of iniquity. I challenge honest people to read it and not be overcome with indignation, and not cry out their revulsion at the superhuman expiation of the man on Devil's Island.

Dreyfus, it is shown, knows several languages: crime; he works hard: crime; no compromising papers are found in his home; crime; he goes occasionally to the country of his origin: crime; he endeavors to learn everything: crime; he is not easily worried: crime; he is worried: crime. And the simplicity of all these concoctions, pompous assertions in a vacuum! We were told of fourteen charges in the accusation; in the end we find only one, that of the *"bordereau";* and we learn even, that the experts were not unanimous on this, that one of them, M. Gobert, was roughly handled for not having come to the desired conclusion. . . . It is a family trial, one is completely among friends, and it must be remembered, finally, that the General Staff made the trial, judged it, and has just merely reaffirmed its judgment.

⋆ ⋆ ⋆

Here then, Mr. President, are the facts that explain how a judicial error could have been committed; and the moral proofs, the prosperous situation of Dreyfus, the absence of motives, his continual cry of innocence, combine to show him a victim of the extraordinary imaginings of Major du Paty de Clam, and of the clerical milieu in which he found himself, of the whole persecution, in short, of "the dirty Jews" that dishonors our time.

And now we arrive at the Esterhazy affair.

I shall not make an exposition of the doubts, then the certainty of M. Scheurer-Kestner. But while he was making researches for his part, grave incidents were taking place within the General Staff itself. Colonel Sandherr had died, and Lieutenant-Colonel Picquart had succeeded him as chief of the Secret Service. It was in this function that the latter found one day a little dispatch addressed to Major Esterhazy by the agents of a foreign power. His duty was to open an investigation. It is clear that he never acted against the wishes of his superiors. He reported his findings to General Gonse, then General Billot, then Minister of War. These researches lasted from May to September, 1896, and what must be cried out loud to all is that General Gonse was convicted of the guilt of Esterhazy, that General Billot and General Boisdeffre never doubted that the *"bordereau"* was the work of Esterhazy; the inquest of Picquart's had made that conclusion inevitable. But the emotion was extraordinary, for the condemnation of Esterhazy involved fatedly the revision of the Dreyfus verdict and it was this of all things that the General Staff wished to avoid at all cost.

There must have been, then, a psychological moment steeped in anguish for them. Observe that General Billot, new Minister of War, was as yet in no way compromised in the previous affair. His hands were clean; he could have established the truth. He dared not; in terror no doubt of public opinion, certainly also in fear of abandoning the whole General Staff, Boisdeffre, Gonse and the others, not to mention numerous subordinates involved. And so there was nothing but a moment of struggle between his conscience and what he felt to be the army's interests. When that moment had passed, it was already too late. He had involved himself, he was compromised. And since then his responsibility has only grown; he has taken upon his own account the crimes of others; he is more guilty than they for he was in a position to render justice, and he has done nothing. Do you understand that! Here it is a year since Generals Billot, Boisdeffre and Gonse know that Dreyfus is innocent and they keep the fearful thing to themselves! And those men sleep, and they have wives and children they love!

* * *

This then, Mr. President, is the Esterhazy affair: a guilty man who had to be exculpated for "reasons of state." For two months past we have been forced to look at this fine spectacle, hour by hour. . . . And we have seen General Pellieux, then Major Ravary conduct a dishonorable investigation from which scoundrels emerge purified and honest men besmirched. And then, at length, they convoked the court-martial.

* * *

Such then, Mr. President, is the simple truth. It is the fearful truth. It will persist as a great stain upon your administration. I suspect that you have no power in this matter, that you are the prisoner of the Constitution and of your situation. You have, none the less, your duty as a man, on which you will doubtless reflect and which you will fulfill. In any event, I do not despair in the least of ultimate triumph. I repeat with more intense conviction: the truth is on the march and nothing will stop her! It is only today that this affair has begun, since it is only now that sides have definitely been taken: on the one hand, the culprits who want no light at all on the business; on the other, lovers of justice who would lay down their lives for it. I have said elsewhere and I say again, when the truth is buried underground, it grows, it chokes, it gathers such an explosive force that on the day when it bursts out, it blows everything up with it. We shall soon see whether we have not laid the mines for a most far-reaching disaster of the near future.

But this letter is long, Mr. President, and it is time to conclude.

I ACCUSE COLONEL DU PATY DE CLAM of having been the diabolical agent of the judicial error, unconsciously, I prefer to believe, and of having continued to defend his deadly work during the past three years through the most absurd and revolting machinations.

I ACCUSE GENERAL MERCIER of having made himself an accomplice in one of the greatest crimes of history, probably through weak-mindedness.

I ACCUSE GENERAL BILLOT of having had in his hands the decisive proofs of the innocence of Dreyfus and of having concealed them, and of having rendered himself guilty of the crime of lèse humanity and lèse justice, out of political motives and to save the face of the General Staff.

I ACCUSE GENERAL BOISDEFFRE AND GENERAL GONSE of being accomplices in the same crime, the former no doubt through religious prejudice, the latter out of esprit de corps.

I ACCUSE GENERAL DE PELLIEUX AND MAJOR RAVARY of having made a scoundrelly inquest, I mean an inquest of the most monstrous partiality, the complete report of which composes for us an imperishable monument of naïve effrontery.

I ACCUSE THE THREE HANDWRITING EXPERTS, MM. Belhomme, Varinard and Couard, of having made lying and fraudulent reports, unless a medical examination will certify them to be deficient of sight and judgment.

I ACCUSE THE WAR-OFFICE of having led a vile campaign in the press, particularly in *l'Eclair* and in *l'Echo de Paris* in order to misdirect public opinion and cover up its sins.

I ACCUSE, LASTLY, THE FIRST COURT-MARTIAL of having violated all human right in condemning a prisoner on testimony kept secret from him, and I ACCUSE THE SECOND COURT-MARTIAL of having covered up this illegality by order, committing in turn the judicial crime of acquitting a guilty man with full knowledge of his guilt.

In making these accusations I am aware that I render myself liable to articles 30 and 31 of Libel Laws of July 29, 1881, which punish acts of defamation. I expose myself voluntarily.

As to the men I accuse, I do not know them, I have never seen them, I feel neither resentment nor hatred against them. For me they are only entities, emblems of social malfeasance. The action I take here is simply a revolutionary step designed to hasten the explosion of truth and justice.

I have one passion only, for light, in the name of humanity which has borne so much and has a right to happiness. My burning protest is only the cry of my soul. Let them dare then to carry me to the court of appeals, and let there be an inquest in the full light of the day!

I am waiting.

Mr. President, I beg you to accept the assurances of my deepest respect.

Kenneth C. H. Willig

"The Bar in the Third Reich"

The experience of the legal profession in the Third Reich proved to be one of extreme frustration and abject humiliation. It saw its international and domestic reputation evaporate upon the altar of bizarre Nazi legal/racial institutions; its ethics denigrated to fearful compliance with whimsical standards of justice, and its entire *raison d'être* challenged by the emergence of an anti-legal, anti-rational, new philosophy of state power. Yet, for all its admitted prostitution to National Socialism, it was never accorded a genuine position in the reorganization of German society. The Nazis remained distrustful of German lawyers and consistently viewed the "mystique" of the law ideologically oriented sociopolitical goals.

In the case of the civil service which was virtually monopolized by jurists on the higher levels, compromises were effected by both the legal bureaucracy and the regime to insure the continuity of government and the implied legitimacy which trailed in its wake. Judges, prosecutors, law professors and other juridical officials were still essentially bureaucrats who could be "organized" and controlled through the traditional channels of state service: loyalty to the omnipotent position of the state as postulated by German legal positivism, job security and official discipline. While these methods were partially successful in ridding German officialdom of its legal scruples, they ignored the basic issue of dealing with the majority of German lawyers who were to be found outside the bureaucracy in private practice.

The solution which the Hitler state embarked upon was the gradual elimination of the lawyer's role in modern society as an independent servant of justice. Instead, the entire profession was to be transformed into a facile instrument for state, i.e., National Socialist, rule. This confrontation from 1933 to 1945 between the German Bar and National Socialism witnessed a major reversal in the historical development of the legal profession.

* * *

On the same day the civil service was purged, the regime enacted a law which Aryanized and "cleansed" the legal profession. Jews could no longer be admitted to the Bar and those already in practice were automatically disbarred with the exception of World War I veterans and legal practitioners pre-dating the establishment of the Weimar republic. Even in this restricted group of "privileged" Jews, the right to be a public defender, charity lawyer, tax-law advisor, liquidator, or sequestor was denied. . . .

Jews were not the only victims of the new Bar. Communists and other politically

---

The humiliations and perils facing members of the German bar under a Führer outspoken in his condemnation of lawyers are detailed in this excerpt from an article by historian Kenneth C. H. Willig.

unreliable elements were deemed ineligible to be attorneys. Since their numbers were not inordinately large, this brought little disruption to the profession The elimination of women jurists was an entirely different matter. The Weimar era had seen a large influx of women into the labor and professional markets. To some extent this could be blamed on the inverse female/male ratio in Germany due to the First World War, but also was a by-product of women receiving an increasingly higher level of education in democratic Germany.

Given the subordinate, albeit glorified, place of women in Nazi ideology and the unstable employment situation, it seemed natural that women would be de-emancipated in the Third Reich. With regard to the legal profession this certainly proved to be the case. Women were basically excluded from entering the Bar and subjected to a rigid quota system for attending law school. In 1934 they were also summarily dismissed from government service and those few who were permitted to remain had no hope of advancement. For women jurists this blocked the major avenue of employment, a situation only slightly altered because of personnel shortages during the war.

Simply reducing the number of practicing attorneys might have satisfied the profession's desire for reform, but it was only the first step for the Nazi regime. The entire German Bar was reorganized and centralized twice during the Third Reich in 1934 and 1935. . . . Finally in 1936 the old statute of 1878 was abrogated and in its place the Nazis promulgated a new National Lawyer's Code *(RRAO)*.

The new code was aimed at completely controlling the professional activities of the Bar and insuring its adherence to National Socialist legal doctrines. Professional/educational qualifications were no longer deemed adequate for practicing law. Instead stress was placed upon political awareness and the proper conduct for a "Legal Guardian of the People." Under the new provisions a candidate for the Bar after receiving his law degree had to spend a one year probationary period in the courts, though not in the capacity of a practicing attorney. At the end of that year and with the concurrence of the regional director of the *BNSDJ* [Association for National Socialist German Jurists] he was first licensed as an attorney-assessor in which service he spent the next three years. Thus four years after leaving the university and only after having proved himself worthy of the honor, i.e., a firm National Socialist, was he duly admitted into the German Bar. As part of his initiation into the legal profession he swore an oath of personal loyalty to Adolf Hitler which bound him in obedience to the *Fuehrer* till death.

The new constitution of the German Bar declared in its preamble "The lawyer is a free servant of the law . . . an indispensible organ of the administration of Justice, and as such a pillar of the German people. . . . ." The term "free," just as the word "independent" in regard to the judiciary, was a highly qualified semantic of Nazi legal rhetoric which had to be interpreted in a "spiritual" rather than literal sense. The new member of the Bar was free to practice his profession as long as he exercised his legal skills in complete harmony with the demands of Nazi legal theory, i.e., "The source of all German legal thought is the *NSDAP*. . . . As a lawyer he was subjected to the same onerous obligations to the party, whether a member or not, as the bureaucrat. He also had the added pressure of being professionally housed in a Nazi creation which strictly regulated his occupational, and thereby economic and social, survival.

* * *

The threat of disbarment was a serious one which carried the added possibility of future criminal proceedings. Under the Hitler regime the grounds for disbarment were extended from three to seven. The majority of the cases brought before the legal Honor Court revealed the new attitude towards what was to be the norm of ethical and professional conduct. Some cases dealt with infractions of the lawyer's new responsibilities totally outside his former juridical functions. Thus lawyers were fined or suspended for failing to give the Hitler Salute, while common grounds for disbarment were not voting in elections or plebescites. Another series of offenses which warranted disbarment may be termed racial. One lawyer was disbarred because during an argument with his father which was overheard, the latter claimed he was the son of a Jewish mother, while in another case the son of a converted Jew lost his license because he erroneously appeared on the Jewish Community list. One of the rare female lawyers was driven from the profession because she was seen playing chess and drinking coffee with a fellow tenant who was known to be Jewish. Finally, there was a category of offenses directly related to the basic role of the attorney, his position as a legal counselor. . . .

Once a lawyer undertook to defend a client he was immediately plagued by difficulties. In penal cases he had to contend with an initial series of disabilities due to Nazi legal innovations. If the court was the Supreme Court or the People's Court he had to receive permission to plead, which in the first case required the approval of the Justice Ministry, the Leader of the *BNSDJ*, the president of the Court, and the president of the *RRAK* [National Lawyer's Chamber], and in the second, the president of the People's Court who could withdraw such consent at any time, even during the actual trial process, for such infractions as too strenuous a defense effort. The lawyer's communications with his client were subject to the prosecutor's pleasure as was the availability of evidence and witnesses. . . .

If he somehow managed to surmount these difficulties, which included preparing a defence within the new twenty-four hour rule between issuing a warrant and the actual trial, he was faced by a second battery of disadvantages which required that he tread a very delicate line of defense that neither antagonized the court nor injured this client. In failure, not only was his client the loser but he himself might be disbarred, ruined or even liable to criminal prosecution. A lawyer who failed to prevent his client from committing perjury or making slanderous statements in court, i.e., anti-Nazi remarks, was considered an accomplice in the crime.

* * *

Fears of the concentration camp, as well as disbarment, made attorneys who were not already inclined to allow their devotion to National Socialism to override a sense of professional ethics extremely reticent to take up the defense for politically sensitive clients or issues. Ironically, the *Gestapo* was forced to resort to the threat of the concentration camp to compel attorneys to defend "enemies of the state" when the regime believed it to be necessary for public opinion.

For all the pressures and control exerted upon the Bar, lawyers never seemed able to mollify the inherent hostility of the *NSDAP* to their profession. As late as 1942, after the reorganization of the Justice Ministry, Martin Bormann was complaining about the continued objectivity of lawyers and even submitted a list of offending attorneys who were to be punished for statements made during defense arguments. Hitler himself certainly left no doubt as to his personal feelings both before and after his 1942 public tirade against the legal profession and revelled in calling lawyers "traitors," "idiots" and "absolute cretins":

> The lawyer's profession is essentially unclean, for the lawyer is entitled to lie to the court. . . . The lawyer looks after the underworld with as much love as owners of shoots taking care of their game during the closed season. There will always be some lawyer who will jiggle with the facts until the moment comes when he will find extenuating circumstances. . . .

Perhaps most galling to the *Fuehrer* was the failure of the German Bar to completely disassociate itself from the traditions of the normative *Rechtsstaat*:

> The lawyer doesn't consider the practical repercussions of the application of the law. He persists in seeing each case in itself . . . They cannot understand that in exceptional times new laws are valid. . . .

To bring the Bar to this necessary realization a further control factor was added in October 1944 when the Justice Minister, Theirack, began to publish "Lawyers' Letters" which were monthly public reprimands for "errors" made by named attorneys. In the first issue Theirack described the responsibilities of the lawyer as twofold: the defense of the individual racial-comrade and the legal protection of the entire racial community, but he failed to offer any concrete suggestion as to how this dichotomy could be harmoniously resolved. Instead he simply reiterated Nazi legal policy that an attorney's duty was not restricted to formal legal concepts of cases vis-à-vis the legal Codes, but also to the larger legal/political questions of the times. Thus for example, German women who "fraternized" with POWs were not to be defended in view of the restrictions in the application of paragraph 4 of the "Law for the Protection of German Military Potential," but according to the "healthy legal instincts of the German people," the unwritten law of protecting the German racial strain, especially in time of war. The Bar did not seem to appreciate Theirack's public review of their activities and shortcomings. There was a general feeling of "nit-picking" which was not dispelled by his attacking such serious cases of legal/professional misconduct as using the formal letter salutation of "Honored Sir," when writing to a client who was convicted of a felony.

Between all the attacks the *NSDAP* levied at the Bar, the public dismay in trial verdicts, and the constant compromising of traditional legal principles, the Bar on the whole suffered a tremendous loss of prestige. The two principal Nazi legal organs, the *BNSDJ* and the Academy for German Law, should, under normal circumstances, have been powerful and influential organizations. Instead, it was all too obvious how impotent both were and this was further exacerbated by the fall from Grace of their patron saint, Hans Frank, after his abortive crusade for a return to normative legal values in 1942.

* * *

The Nazis had an aversion to lawyers because they appeared to represent an alien ideology, formal normative law, and were as ubiquitous as the bureaucratics they also despised. The whole strategy of Nazi policy towards the Bar was armed at its extinction; not in the literal sense, but in terms of the continuity of a "free" profession. The Nazis wanted a unified legal administration which could carry out orders efficiently and obediently. The Bar was the loose link in the chain. Consequently, the regime accelerated its process of treating lawyers as civil servants, whether the members of the free profession were willing to admit it or not. The purges, obligations, and restrictions were almost identical with those found in the new Nazi Civil Service Code. The clearest indication of Nazi intent came in 1943 when even the harmless dignity of their own Honor Court was denied the legal profession and all German lawyers were placed under the jurisdiction of the *Dienststrafgericht*, the disciplinary court for the civil bureaucracy. The same law decreed a mandatory retirement age for all attorneys at 65, just as was already the case for civil servants.

None of this was haphazard or accidental. Hitler had hinted at this scheme to bureaucratize the legal profession at the beginning of the war,

> Let the profession be purified, let it be employed in public service. Just as there is a Public Prosecutor, let there be only Public Defenders. . .

Consequently, by the end of the Third Reich the Nazis had solved their problem of how to handle the German lawyer. There were no longer any "servants of justice," just servants of the state, i.e., the NS-state.

Nazi defendants in Nuremberg war crimes trial. Hermann Goering, in light-colored uniform, listens to testimony. November 12, 1945.

Robert H. Jackson

Summation of the Prosecution at Nuremberg

We charge unlawful aggression but we are not trying the motives, hopes, or frustrations which may have led Germany to resort to aggressive war as an instrument of policy. The law, unlike politics, does not concern itself with the good or evil in the *status quo,* nor with the merits of grievances against it. It merely requires that the *status quo* be not attacked by violent means and that policies be not advanced by war. We may admit that overlapping ethnological and cultural groups, economic barriers, and conflicting national ambitions created in the 1930s, as they will continue to create, grave problems for Germany

---

Supreme Court Justice Robert Houghwout Jackson (1892–1954) was chief U.S. prosecutor in the International Military Tribunal at Nuremberg. His writings on the trial include The Case Against the Nazi War Criminals *(1946) and* The Nürnberg Case *(1947).*

as well as for the other peoples of Europe. We may admit too that the world had failed to provide political or legal remedies which would be honorable and acceptable alternatives to war. We do not underwrite either the ethics or the wisdom of any country, including my own, in the face of these problems. But we do say that it is now, as it was for sometime prior to 1939, illegal and criminal for Germany or any other nation to redress grievances or seek expansion by resort to aggressive war.

Let me emphasize one cardinal point. The United States has no interest which would be advanced by the conviction of any defendant if we have not proved him guilty on at least one of the counts charged against him in the Indictment. Any result that the calm and critical judgment of posterity would pronounce unjust would not be a victory for any of the countries associated in this prosecution. But in summation we now have before us the tested evidences of criminality and have heard the flimsy excuses and paltry evasions of the defendants. The suspended judgment with which we opened this case is no longer appropriate. The time has come for final judgment and if the case I present seems hard and uncompromising, it is because the evidence makes it so.

★ ★ ★

Of one thing we may be sure. The future will never have to ask, with misgiving: "What could the Nazis have said in their favor?" History will know that whatever could be said, they were allowed to say. They have been given the kind of a trial which they, in the days of their pomp and power, never gave to any man.

But fairness is not weakness. The extraordinary fairness of these hearings is an attribute of our strength. The prosecution's case, at its close, seemed inherently unassailable because it rested so heavily on German documents of unquestioned authenticity. But it was the weeks upon weeks of pecking at this case by one after another of the defendants that has demonstrated its true strength. The fact is that the testimony of the defendants has removed any doubts of guilt which, because of the extraordinary nature and magnitude of these crimes, may have existed before they spoke. They have helped write their own judgment and condemnation.

But justice in this case has nothing to do with some of the arguments put forth by the defendants or their counsel. We have not previously and we need not now discuss the merits of all their obscure and tortuous philosophy. We are not trying them for possession of obnoxious ideas. It is their right, if they choose, to renounce the Hebraic heritage in the civilization of which Germany was once a part. Nor is it our affair that they repudiated the Hellenic influence as well. The intellectual bankruptcy and moral perversion of the Nazi regime might have been no concern of International Law had it not been utilized to goose-step the *Herrenvolk* across international frontiers. It is not their thoughts, it is their overt acts which we charge to be crimes. Their creed and teachings are important only as evidence of motive, purpose, knowledge, and intent.

★ ★ ★

It is against such a background that these defendants now ask this Tribunal to say that they are not guilty of planning, executing, or conspiring to commit this long list of crimes and wrongs. They stand before the record of this trial as bloodstained Gloucester stood by the body of his slain King. He begged of the widow, as they beg of you: "Say I slew them not." And the Queen replied, "Then say they were not slain. But dead they are. . . . " If you were to say of these men that they are not guilty, it would be as true to say there has been no war, there are no slain, there has been no crime.

Reginald L. Hine

FROM CONFESSIONS OF AN UN-COMMON ATTORNEY

. . . The office in Portmill Lane (sometimes, in pleasant banter, styled Chancery Lane) was housed in a comely Jacobean building. It had two front doors, and several bolt holes or back doors. A stranger, ringing the bell, would be puzzled by the lack of any apparent welcome. Somewhat mysteriously, the door would open, but only half an inch, the catch being released by a wired device, worked by a clerk far too busy and superior to descend from his high engrossing stool. If the stranger entered at his peril, and, in his ignorance, asked to see "Mr. Hawkins," he was once again abashed. "Sorry you can't, he died in 1877." But there was a deferred welcome within, and strangers became clients, and clients developed into friends.

It would not be correct to describe the interior as comely. Like most lawyers' offices (but why, why, why!) the rooms—littered with files, the dust of ages upon them—looked dishevelled and untidy. The wall-papers were of the mock varnished and grained pine in favour a century before, though if you explored with a penknife you might light upon five or six other specimens, each more attractive than the one above. The windows were made to open; but a ponderous legalistic atmosphere hung about the chambers: a curious conglomerate of parchment, sealing wax, corroding ink, calf bindings, stale tobacco, escaping gas, and myriad decaying matters. But very soon one became "part and parcel" of all this; one accepted, one even liked one's surroundings; they were all of a piece with the antiquity of the firm; one was proud to be able to smell one's way back to Elizabethan times.

Then there were other attractions. One's fancy was caught by the double doors of some of the principal rooms, an inner door of baize, warranted to muffle the guiltiest of intimate confessions. The room I occupied possessed a secret chamber, opened by a hidden spring in the wall, large enough to conceal a confidential clerk if earshot evidence of a ticklish interview were needful. Everywhere one came upon cupboards, some of them undisturbed for centuries, filled with family skeletons and other surprising things. One of the first I opened contained the reports and the account books of the celebrated McAdam (1756–1836), whom the firm, as clerks to the local Turnpike Trusts, had called in to macadamize and improve the Hitchin-to-Welwyn and Hitchin-to-Bedford roads. In another cupboard I came upon a marked catalogue of the sale of Byron's furniture and books, and I remembered that on 13th July 1824 his funeral cortège passed through Hitchin, with a black slave and a Greek attendant, and that some of Hawkins & Co.'s clients had been privileged, for one memorable moment, to take up the precious casket enshrining the poet's heart, and hold it in their hands, and that one of the women Friends was "scandalously reported to have kissed it." Tied up with a bundle of title-deeds in another cupboard I found two letters from the Cromwellian and Restoration poet, Andrew Marvell, written when member for Hull in 1670, and complaining that no one could expect promotions, spiritual or temporal, unless he made his court to the king's mistress, the Duchess of Cleveland.

On a shelf in that same cupboard, deep in dust, reposed the draft of a Bill introduced into the House of Commons in 1770, forbidding any woman "to impose upon, seduce, or betray into Matrimony any of His Majesty's subjects by means of scent, paints, cosmetic washes, artificial teeth, Spanish wool, iron stays, hoops, high-heeled shoes, or bolstered hips." Any marriage so contrived was to be null and void.

In this excerpt, Reginald L. Hine (1883–1949), attached for thirty-five years to Hawkins & Co. of Hitchin, one of England's oldest law firms, describes several impressions from those years.

THE EXPANDING UNION

G. Edward White

"The Working Life of the Marshall Court, 1815–1835"

When the 1815 term began, the Supreme Court had no courtroom in which to conduct its business. L'Enfant's original plan for Washington had included a site, approximately equidistant between the proposed White House and the proposed Capitol, on which a building for the Court would be erected. That plan had been approved in 1791, and by 1815 the skeletons of an executive mansion and a legislative building were evident on the Washington landscape. At the Supreme Court site, however, there was nothing except the swamps of Goose Creek, the estuary that flowed between Capitol Hill and the White House, creating "wet, marshy ground covered with weeds and wampopins where sportsmen shot ortolan, where cattle formed paths in zigzag courses, . . . and where fishermen often took their spoil, especially at full tide."

The Supreme Court was therefore forced to hold court in a room in the Capitol, originally on the first floor, and, after 1810, in the basement. In 1814, the Court lost even these quarters when British troops burned the Capitol, seriously damaging the basement courtroom. An 1816 report to Congress by Benjamin Latrobe, the architect of the Capitol, noted that "[g]reat efforts were made to destroy the Court-room, which was built with uncommon solidity, by collecting into it and setting fire to the furniture of the adjacent rooms." The result was that "the columns [of the courtroom] were cracked exceedingly" and its "condition [rendered] dangerous."

The uninhabitable condition of the courtroom forced the justices to hold court in a nearby private home for the next two years. In 1817 they returned to the Capitol in "a room temporarily filled up for their occupation," and by the 1819 term they were back in their basement courtroom. Even the refurbished courtroom was apparently unimpressive. A newspaper correspondent noted in 1824 that visiting the courtroom was "like going down a cellar." To find the room, "[a] stranger might traverse the dark avenues of the Capitol for a week [seeking] a room which is hardly capacious enough for a ward justice." Another observer suggested that the courtroom had "a certain cellarlike aspect," giving "the impression of justice being done in a corner."

Inside the courtroom a rail separated the justices from lawyers arguing cases; another rail separated the lawyers from the public. The justices' seats, which consisted of chairs behind individual mahogany desks, were slightly elevated. From that elevation the court-

---

In this excerpt the author describes in detail the life of a Supreme Court forced to meet in a basement room of an unfinished Capitol and whose justices lived and worked together in a boardinghouse and sometimes decided a case within days. John Marshall (1755–1835) served as chief justice from 1801 to 1835.

Artist unknown. *First Merchant Exchange.* Nineteenth century. Watercolor on paper. 4½ × 5⅞″ (11.5 × 15 cm). Emmet Collection, Miriam and Ira D. Wallach Division of Art, Prints, and Photographs, The New York Public Library. Astor, Lenox, and Tilden Foundations. *The First Merchant Exchange served as the site of the first sessions of the U.S. Supreme Court.*

room sloped down about two or three feet to the chairs and tables for lawyers, then rose again, higher than the justices' area, to enable spectators in chairs, settees, and sofas to observe the proceedings. There were no antechambers or robing rooms for the justices; they put on their robes in full view of the spectators and wore no wigs. Visitors to the Court passed in and out with no apparent restrictions. A florid speech by a famous lawyer such as William Pinkney or Daniel Webster might pack the galleries, but at the close of the oration the courtroom would be nearly empty. An argument before the Court was regarded as something of a social occasion; numerous eyewitnesses testified to the desirability of the courtroom as a place to meet members of the opposite sex.

Between 1815 and 1835 the Supreme Court sat from the first Monday in February or the second Monday in January through the second or third week in March. The justices heard arguments from 11 a.m. to 4 p.m. with no break for lunch. No time limits were imposed on lawyers arguing before the Court, and arguments sometimes lasted as long as six days. The work load of the Marshall Court was fairly substantial. During their brief sessions in Washington, the justices rendered an average of forty majority opinions per year. Although this is less than a third of the 139 opinions the Court averaged between 1970 and 1980, the Marshall Court had less than a fourth of the time the current Court has to consider a case.

When the justices were not hearing oral arguments, they spent little time working at the Capitol. Although there is evidence that they irregularly met in a conference room there, the justices had no offices or chambers in the building. The justices also did not have a support staff to manage nor did they have a library in which to do research. Other than to hear oral arguments, the justices had little reason to remain at the Capitol.

On the conclusion of formal argument, the justices tended to retire to their boardinghouse. From 1815 to 1830 all the justices lived together, without their families, in one of these houses. The particular boardinghouse varied from year to year, and during the summer months the justices would correspond with one another about arrangements.

Boardinghouses were a principal focus of political and social relationships in early nineteenth-century Washington. The unfinished character of the city—roads ranged from dusty or muddy to nonexistent, a swamp separated Capitol Hill from the White House, and Georgetown, the most established population center, was five virtually impassable miles from the Capitol—combined with the temporary residency of members of Congress to produce a clustering of boardinghouses around the Capitol. Although the executive branch of government had more permanence among its staff and tended to draw all but its highest-level employees from the pool of local residents, Congress was staffed by a transient population who saw the boardinghouses in which they resided as symbols of their regional and political identities. In choosing to live in a Capitol Hill boardinghouse and to remain in Washington for only a temporary period, the justices, although ostensibly permanent members of the Washington community by virtue of their life tenure, adopted the congressional rather than the executive pattern of residence. The boardinghouse became the nerve center of their existence in Washington.

Not all of the justices' time, however, was spent either in the courtroom or in the boardinghouse. Although one study of Washington life concluded that the Marshall Court justices "lived . . . a reclusive existence," the justices' correspondence suggests a more active social life. John Marshall's letters to his wife, who remained in Richmond, testify to regular attendance at dinners, balls, and other social functions. Marshall would complain of the demands on his time, but he did not seem to turn down many invitations. In 1818 a New York newspaper noted that Washington's "season of greatest festivity" began "after the Supreme Court commences its session" and that "there are now tea and dining parties daily." Five years later Charles Ingersoll remarked that the justices "begin a day's session . . . after robing & taking their places, by receiving from the Marshal their cards of invitation and taking up their pens to answer them before the list of cases is called for hearing." Ingersoll criticized the justices "for dining out so continually," although he asked "how can they help it under this raging star." In the face of this evidence, Joseph Story's remark that "I scarcely go to any places of pleasure or fashion" needs to be taken in context.

One should remember, however, that the justices only spent between six weeks and two months in Washington. A much larger portion of their time was spent serving as judges on the United States Circuit Courts. There were six of these courts before 1807 and seven thereafter to the end of Marshall's tenure. The circuit courts embraced various regions and varied widely in size and accessibility, with the Third Circuit, consisting of Pennsylvania and New Jersey, being the most compact and manageable, and the Seventh Circuit, consisting of Kentucky, Ohio, and Tennessee, being by far the most expansive and time consuming. The circuits were conceived primarily as courts of original jurisdiction for certain kinds of cases, such as serious crimes, copyrights and patents, piracy, slave and Indian cases, designated civil suits involving amounts over five hundred dollars, and diversity of citizenship cases. Their jurisdiction, in all but the first three sets of cases, was concurrent with the state courts, and cases in which diversity of citizenship existed and the amount in dispute exceeded five hundred dollars could be removed from state to federal courts. In addition, the circuit courts had appellate jurisdiction from the limited class of cases that originated in the federal district courts. The district courts were located within the boundaries of states, with approximately one court per state.

The staffing of the circuit courts was peculiar in that no circuit court judges were appointed. Instead the circuit courts were composed of the Supreme Court justice assigned to that circuit and a district judge from the locality in which the circuit court had been established. In theory, the Supreme Court justices would serve as itinerant "experts," bringing "the sense of the Supreme Court" to the localities, and the district judges would be conversant in local law.

Joseph Story's travels on the First Circuit, embracing the states of New Hampshire, Massachusetts, and Rhode Island, provide a microcosm of circuit riding. Story's circuit duties commenced with the opening of court in Boston on or about May 1. From Boston he went to Portland or Wiscasset, Maine; then to Portsmouth or Exeter, New Hampshire; then to Providence or Newport, Rhode Island, ending his spring circuit about June 27. Another circuit term began on or about October 1 and lasted until about November 27.

The geography of Story's circuit, which consisted of almost two thousand miles of traveling, made it possible for him to return sporadically to Salem, Massachusetts, where he lived until September 1829, when he moved to Cambridge to assume the Dane Professorship at Harvard Law School. Story's letters reveal that his time in court was not particularly extensive, nor did he spend considerable time in transit. The very fact that Story accepted the Dane Professorship suggests that he anticipated being able to be in Cambridge for a good portion of the academic year, notwithstanding his circuit duties. Other justices, however, with less compact circuits, needed to allocate much more time for travel. Before being appointed to the Court and assigned to the new Ninth Circuit, Justice John McKinley allegedly called his prospective position "certainly the most onerous and laborious of any in the United States."

Artist unknown. *Dane Hall.* 1832. Lithograph. 5¾ × 6⅞" (14.6 × 17.5 cm). Harvard Law Art Collection, Cambridge. *Dane Hall, named for Nathan Dane, one of the founders of Harvard Law School, was dedicated in 1832 and housed the law school until 1833.*

Charles Warren

FROM HISTORY OF THE HARVARD LAW SCHOOL

"The First Decade"

So far as is known the Law School started with one student—Charles Moody Dustin; and the number entering during the first year was six.

The principal instruction was of course given by Professor Stearns, although the fifteen lectures of Judge Parker as Royall Professor were considered a branch of the Law Department and were attended by the law students, during May and June in the Third Term, when they were given three or four times a week, at ten o'clock in the morning.

The method of instruction employed during the first decade of the law school, founded in 1817, is described in this excerpt by American author and lawyer Charles Warren (1868–1954). Warren, assistant attorney general of the United States from 1914 to 1918, was awarded the Pulitzer Prize for The Supreme Court in United States History *(1922).*

No record is extant showing the exact course of study in the early years of the School; but it probably followed along the same general lines as that described in the report made by Professor Stearns to the Board of Overseers, in 1825:

> A course of study has been drawn up with much care, under the advice of the judges of the Supreme Court and other distinguished jurists, and with reference to a term of 3 years within which period it can be established. . . .
>
> In the first place a reading of *Blackstone,* more or less particular, of the whole work. This practise has been found by experience to be highly useful. It aids the student in fixing his attention, enables him more readily to acquaintance with the technical terms and language of the law, and the same time to obtain a more distinct view of that admirable outline of the science. . . . For those gentlemen who do not pursue the study of the law as a Profession, the plan of instruction is varied by substituting for what relates to the practice, a more extended course of reading on the Civil Law, the Law of Nations, Constitutional Law and Political Economy.

The first description of the method of instruction is contained in Professor Stearns' report to the Overseers, Jan. 9, 1826:

> The experience of eight years since the Law School was established has led to several considerable improvements upon its original plan; and the utility of the present system of instruction seems to be fully evinced by the industry, limitation, and rapid improvement of the student.
>
> The regular exercises of the School are the following, viz.:
>
> 1. *Recitations and Examinations* in several of the most important text books, such as *Blackstone's Commentaries, Cruise on Real Property, Saunders on Uses, Fearne on Remainders,* etc.
>
> In these exercises the points of difference between the law of England and of our own country are carefully distinguished and the grounds and occasions of the difference are fully explained to the students.
>
> 2. *Written lectures* embracing a general course of legal instruction, in which those parts of our system of jurisprudence in which we do not adopt the law of England are particularly noticed, and the grounds of our departure from it are explained and illustrated by the decisions and practice of our own courts.
>
> 3. *A Moot Court* in which questions are regularly argued (often at considerable length) before the Professor, who pronounces an opinion. In these fictitious actions the pleadings, bills of exceptions, demurrers to evidence, special verdicts and motions in arrest of judgment or for a new trial are drawn up in form by the students.—During the argument those students who are not of counsel are employed in taking minutes, with a view to the acquisition of facility and accuracy preparatory to practice. The cases to be argued are of course, adapted to the progress of the respective students in their professional studies. But they are strongly urged to engage in them very soon after their commencement; it having been found by experience that no other exercise is so powerful an excitement to industry and emulation or so strongly interests the students in their professional pursuits.
>
> 4. *Debating Clubs* including all the members of the Law School in which some question (generally in moral philosophy, political economy, or civil polity) which admits an extended and free discussion, is debated once a week with a view to improvement in extempore elocution.
>
> 5. *Written dissertations* by the student upon some title or branch of the law or the history of some department of legal or political science.

Most of the students at this time, as appears from the *First Record Book of the Law School (1817–1840),* had had nearly two years study in a law office prior to entering the School, and were thus supposed to be grounded on the technical details of practice.

Stephen Vincent Benét
FROM THE DEVIL AND DANIEL WEBSTER

The stranger came in—very dark and tall he looked in the firelight. He was carrying a box under his arm—a black, japanned box with little air holes in the lid. At the sight of the box, Jabez Stone gave a low cry and shrank into a corner of the room.

"Mr. Webster, I presume," said the stranger, very polite, but with his eyes glowing like a fox's deep in the woods.

"Attorney of record for Jabez Stone," said Dan'l Webster, but his eyes were glowing too. "Might I ask your name?"

"I've gone by a good many," said the stranger carelessly. "Perhaps Scratch will do for the evening. I'm often called that in these regions."

Then he sat down at the table and poured himself a drink from the jug. The liquor was cold in the jug, but it came steaming into the glass.

"And now," said the stranger, smiling and showing his teeth, "I shall call upon you, as a law-abiding citizen, to assist me in taking possession of my property."

Well, with that the argument began—and it went hot and heavy. At first, Jabez Stone had a flicker of hope, but when he saw Dan'l Webster being forced back at point after point, he just scrunched in his corner, with his eyes on that japanned box. For there wasn't any doubt as to the deed or the signature—that was the worst of it. Dan'l Webster twisted and turned and thumped his fist on the table, but he couldn't get away from that. He offered to compromise the case; the stranger wouldn't hear of it. He pointed out the property had increased in value, and state senators ought to be worth more; the stranger stuck to the letter of the law. He was a great lawyer, Dan'l Webster, but we know who's the King of Lawyers, as the Good Book tells us, and it seemed as if, for the first time, Dan'l Webster had met his match.

Finally, the stranger yawned a little. "Your spirited efforts on behalf of your client do you credit, Mr. Webster," he said, "but if you have no more arguments to adduce, I'm rather pressed for time"—and Jabez Stone shuddered.

Dan'l Webster's brow looked dark as a thundercloud.

"Pressed or not, you shall not have this man!" he thundered. "Mr. Stone is an American citizen, and no American citizen may be forced into the service of a foreign prince. We fought England for that in '12 and we'll fight all hell for it again!"

"Foreign?" said the stranger. "And who calls me a foreigner?"

"Well, I never yet heard of the dev—of your claiming American citizenship," said Dan'l Webster with surprise.

"And who with a better right?" said the stranger, with one of his terrible smiles. "When the first wrong was done to the first Indian, I was there. When the first slaver put out for the Congo, I stood on her deck. Am I not in your books and stories and beliefs, from the first settlements on? Am I not spoken of, still, in every church in New England? 'Tis true the North claims me for a Southerner and the South for a Northerner, but I am neither, I am merely an honest American like yourself—and of the best descent—for, to tell the truth, Mr. Webster, though I don't like to boast of it, my name is older in this country than yours."

"Aha!" said Dan'l Webster, with the veins standing out in his forehead. "Then I stand on the Constitution! I demand a trial for my client!"

"The case is hardly one for an ordinary court," said the stranger, his eyes flickering. "And, indeed, the lateness of the hour—"

In this excerpt from one of the best-known stories of Stephen Vincent Benét, published in Thirteen O'Clock *(1937), Old Scratch locks horns with the great American lawyer and orator Daniel Webster (1782–1852) in a trial over a man's soul.*

"Let it be any court you choose, so it is an American judge and an American jury!" said Dan'l Webster in his pride. "Let it be the quick or the dead. I'll abide the issue!"

"You have said it," said the stranger, and pointed his finger at the door. And with that, and all of a sudden, there was a rushing of wind outside and a noise of footsteps. They came, clear and distinct, through the night. And yet, they were not like the footsteps of living men.

"In God's name, who comes so late?" cried Jabez Stone, in an ague of fear.

"The jury Mr. Webster demands," said the stranger, sipping at his boiling glass. "You must pardon the rough appearance of one or two; they will have come a long way."

And with that the fire burned blue and the door blew open and twelve men entered, one by one.

If Jabez Stone had been sick with terror before, he was blind with terror now. For there was Walter Butler, the loyalist, who spread fire and horror through the Mohawk Valley in the times of the Revolution; and there was Simon Girty, the renegade, who saw white men burned at the stake and whooped with the Indians to see them burn. His eyes were green, like a catamount's, and the stains on his hunting shirt did not come from the blood of the deer. King Philip was there, wild and proud as he had been in life, with the great gash in his head that gave him his death wound, and cruel Governor Dale, who broke men on the wheel. There was Morton of Merry Mount, who so vexed the Plymouth Colony, with his flushed, loose, handsome face and his hate of the godly. There was Teach, the bloody pirate, with his black beard curling on his breast. The Reverend John Smeet, with his strangler's hands and his Geneva gown, walked as daintily as he had to the gallows. The red print of the rope was still around his neck, but he carried a perfumed handkerchief in one hand. One and all, they came into the room with the fires of hell still upon them, and the stranger named their names and their deeds as they came, till the tale of twelve was told. Yet the stranger had told the truth—they had all played a part in America.

"Are you satisfied with the jury, Mr. Webster?" said the stranger mockingly, when they had taken their places.

The sweat stood upon Dan'l Webster's brow, but his voice was clear.

"Quite satisfied," he said. "Though I miss General Arnold from the company."

"Benedict Arnold is engaged upon other business," said the stranger, with a glower. "Ah, you asked for a justice, I believe."

He pointed his finger once more, and a tall man, soberly clad in Puritan garb, with the burning gaze of the fanatic, stalked into the room and took his judge's place.

"Justice Hathorne is a jurist of experience," said the stranger. "He presided at certain witch trials once held in Salem. There were others who repented of the business later, but not he."

"Repent of such notable wonders and undertakings?" said the stern old justice. "Nay, hang them—hang them all!" And he muttered to himself in a way that struck ice into the soul of Jabez Stone.

Then the trial began, and, as you might expect, it didn't look anyways good for the defense. And Jabez Stone didn't make much of a witness in his own behalf. He took one look at Simon Girty and screeched, and they had to put him back in his corner in a kind of swoon.

It didn't halt the trial, though; the trial went on, as trials do. Dan'l Webster had faced some hard juries and hanging judges in his time, but this was the hardest he'd ever faced, and he knew it. They sat there with a kind of glitter in their eyes, and the stranger's smooth voice went on and on. Every time he'd raise an objection, it'd be "Objection sustained," but whenever Dan'l objected, it'd be "Objection denied." Well, you couldn't expect fair play from a fellow like this Mr. Scratch.

It got to Dan'l in the end, and he began to heat, like iron in the forge. When he got up to speak he was going to flay that stranger with every trick known to the law, and the judge and jury too. He didn't care if it was contempt of court or what would happen to him for it. He didn't care any more what happened to Jabez Stone. He just got madder

FRITZ EICHENBERG. *Jurors.* From Stephen Vincent Benét's *The Devil and Daniel Webster.* 1955. Engraving. Rare Books and Manuscripts Division, New York Public Library.

and madder, thinking of what he'd say. And yet, curiously enough, the more he thought about it, the less he was able to arrange his speech in his mind.

Till, finally, it was time for him to get up on his feet, and he did so, all ready to bust out with lightnings and denunciations. But before he started he looked over the judge and jury for a moment, such being his custom. And he noticed the glitter in their eyes was twice as strong as before, and they all leaned forward. Like hounds just before they get the fox, they looked, and the blue mist of evil in the room thickened as he watched them. Then he saw what he'd been about to do, and he wiped his forehead, as a man might who's just escaped falling into a pit in the dark.

For it was him they'd come for, not only Jabez Stone. He read it in the glitter of their eyes and in the way the stranger hid his mouth with one hand. And if he fought them with their own weapons, he'd fall into their power; he knew that, though he couldn't have told you how. It was his own anger and horror that burned in their eyes; and he'd have to wipe that out or the case was lost. He stood there for a moment, his black eyes burning like anthracite. And then he began to speak.

He started off in a low voice, though you could hear every word. They say he could call on the harps of the blessed when he chose. And this was just as simple and easy as a man could talk. But he didn't start out by condemning or reviling. He was talking about the things that make a country a country, and a man a man.

And he began with the simple things that everybody's known and felt—the freshness of a fine morning when you're young, and the taste of food when you're hungry, and the new day that's every day when you're a child. He took them up and he turned them in his hands. They were good things for any man. But without freedom, they sickened. And when he talked of those enslaved, and the sorrows of slavery, his voice got like a big bell. He talked of the early days of America and the men who had made those days.

It wasn't a spread-eagle speech, but he made you see it. He admitted all the wrong that had ever been done. But he showed how, out of the wrong and the right, the suffering and the starvations, something new had come. And everybody had played a part in it, even the traitors.

Then he turned to Jabez Stone and showed him as he was—an ordinary man who'd had hard luck and wanted to change it. And, because he'd wanted to change it, now he was going to be punished for all eternity. And yet there was good in Jabez Stone, and he showed that good. He was hard and mean, in some ways, but he was a man. There was sadness in being a man, but it was a proud thing too. And he showed what the pride of it was till you couldn't help feeling it. Yes, even in hell, if a man was a man, you'd know it. And he wasn't pleading for any one person any more, though his voice rang like an organ. He was telling the story and the failures and the endless journey of mankind. They got tricked and trapped and bamboozled, but it was a great journey. And no demon that was ever foaled could know the inwardness of it—it took a man to do that.

The fire began to die on the hearth and the wind before morning to blow. The light was getting gray in the room when Dan'l Webster finished. And his words came back at the end to New Hampshire ground, and the one spot of land that each man loves and clings to. He painted a picture of that, and to each one of that jury he spoke of things long forgotten. For his voice could search the heart, and that was his gift and his strength. And to one, his voice was like the forest and its secrecy, and to another like the sea and the storms of the sea; and one heard the cry of his lost nation in it, and another saw a little harmless scene he hadn't remembered for years. But each saw something. And when Dan'l Webster finished he didn't know whether or not he'd saved Jabez Stone. But he knew he'd done a miracle. For the glitter was gone from the eyes of judge and jury, and, for the moment, they were men again, and knew they were men.

"The defense rests," said Dan'l Webster, and stood there like a mountain. His ears were still ringing with his speech, and he didn't hear anything else till he heard Judge Hathorne say, "The jury will retire to consider its verdict."

Walter Butler rose in his place and his face had a dark, gay pride on it.

"The jury has considered its verdict," he said, and looked the stranger full in the eye. "We find for the defendant, Jabez Stone."

With that, the smile left the stranger's face, but Walter Butler did not flinch.

"Perhaps 'tis not strictly in accordance with the evidence," he said, "but even the damned may salute the eloquence of Mr. Webster."

With that, the long crow of a rooster split the gray morning sky, and judge and jury were gone from the room like a puff of smoke as if they had never been there. . . .

Orma Linford

"The Mormons, the Law, and the Territory of Utah"

In 1851, an Illinois physician who was contemplating a move west wrote to Brigham Young for information about Utah. Among his questions was: "Have you adopted the common law of England as the law of the territory, or have you a special code by which you are governed?" Young replied, "We have not adopted the common law of England, nor any other general law of old countries, any further than the extending over us the

---

The many trials and tribulations suffered by the early followers of the Church of Jesus Christ of Latter-Day Saints at the hands of state and local governments caused them to set up their own legal system in far-off Utah, as recounted in this excerpt.

constitutional laws of the United States, by Congress, has produced that effect." He then explained the kind of "common law" that was in effect:

> We have a few Territorial laws, principally directory in their provisions and operation. And we have a *common law* which is written upon the tablets of the heart, and "printed on the inmost parts, whose executors and righteousness, and whose exactors are peace"; one of its golden precepts is "Do unto others as you would they should do unto you." This common law we seek to establish throughout the valleys of the mountains; and shall continue our exertions for its adoption as long as we shall continue to exist upon the earth, until all nations shall bow in humble acquientscence thereto.

★ ★ ★

R.N. Baskin, a non-Mormon attorney who arrived in 1865, found a special reason for bemoaning the absence of the common law. He claimed that applicable English criminal law had become the common law of the colonies when they gained independence. Since bigamy was punishable in England, if the common law had been adopted in Utah, polygamy would have been a crime from the beginning, and much of the battle in Congress and later in the federal courts over the Mormon practice of plural marriage could have been avoided.

Brigham Young had no use for technicalities and fine points of legal procedure, either. He urged that the courts should not be crippled with ancient and unwieldly practices, "as though there had been made no advancement in the sciences of the law." Accordingly, the first judiciary act of the Territory provided that "all technical forms of actions and pleadings are hereby abolished."

★ ★ ★

At the beginning of the life of the Church, the Saints did not appear to have prejudices against the legal profession, but by 1838 the Saints had been worn down by the law, lawyers, judges, and legal proceedings.

In a "political motto" issued on March 29, 1838, the Church warned, "Woe to . . . all who invent or seek out unrighteous and vexatious lawsuits, under the pretext and color of law, or office."

In April of 1838, the Church high council found one of the early Church leaders guilty on six charges of practicing law "for the sake of filthy lucre," wanting his temporal affairs free from Church domination, urging lawsuits among Saints, and making false accusations. . . .

This antagonism was absorbed by Brigham Young as he grew in importance in the ranks of the Church membership. In March, 1845, he said:

> I swear by the God of Heaven that we will not spend money in feeing Lawyers. All the lawsuits that have been got up against the Saints have been hatched up to fee lawyers, tavernkeepers, etc. I had rather have a six shooter than all the Lawyers in Illinois.

In his reply to the Illinois doctor, quoted above, Young also had some strident rhetoric for the legal profession:

> [A]nd the earth shall be redeemed from the thraldom that wicked and corrupt men have entangled her through their "entangling alliances," specious and unmeaning pretences, servile and absurd acquiescence in the whims, caprices, dictation of profound ignoramuses, who being entitled through a little brief authority, to wear a cap or a feather, a surplice or a robe, a garter or a star, would be thought to be men of "legal learning" and would if they could fasten their peculiar dogmas upon all succeeding generations.

This animosity toward those who plied the law as a profession likewise found its way into the Utah statute books. While legislative opposition to lawyers was by no means

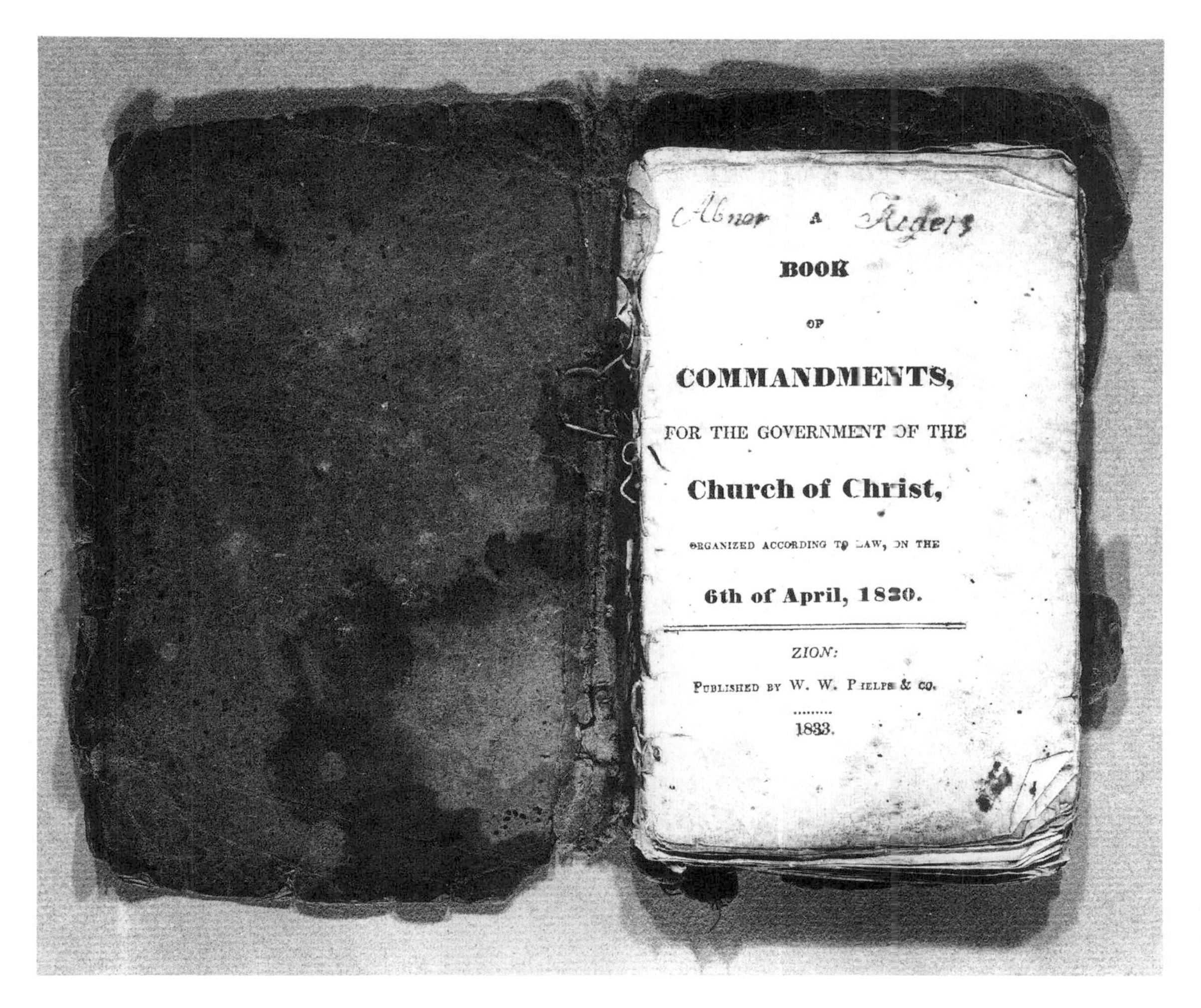

Artist unknown. Title page and cover for Joseph Smith's *A Book of Commandments for the Government of the Church of Christ.* 1833. The Huntington Library, San Marino, California. *Most copies of this volume of Mormon Law, published during the Mormons' settlement of Missouri, were destroyed in a fire just after they were printed.*

new to the American scene, such statutory antagonism had largely ceased elsewhere, and the Mormon revival had a distinctly original flavor. Upon his arrival in the Territory, Baskin's attention was drawn immediately to laws regulating attorneys. While Section 1 of an act of February 18, 1852, guaranteed the right to counsel, the second section provided that:

> No person or persons, employing counsel in any of the courts of this Territory, shall be compelled by any process of law to pay the counsel so employed, for any services rendered as counsel, before or after, or during the process of trial in the case.

★ ★ ★

In 1880, Franklin D. Richards, one of the Twelve Apostles of the [Latter-day Saints] Church said, "Theoretically, church and state are one. If there were no Gentiles and no other government, there would be no Civil Law." This is an apt summary of the fundamentalist Mormon attitude. However, the coming of civil government modified the Mormons' ideas to a certain degree. They grew to approve of judges and courts to enforce penal sanctions at least in serious cases. And they grudgingly came to accept civil power to declare status and dispose of uncontested or ex parte matters, such as granting divorces and processing estates. But they deplored litigation and could think of few forms of life lower than lawyers.

STATE OF GEORGIA v. NEGRO MAN SLAVE PETER

Georgia
Elbert County

Ira Christian, Clerk of the Inferior Court of said county, In the name and behalf of the citizens of Georgia charge and accuse Peter, a negro man slave of said county belonging to one Bedford Harper, with the offence of murder.

For that the said Peter not having the fear of God before his eyes, but being moved and seduced by the instigation of the devil, on the twenty eighth day of May in the year eighteen hundred and thirty seven, with force and arms, at the House of one William Alexander in said county, in and upon a certain negro man slave by the name of Ben, belonging to the said Alexander, in the peace of God & said state then and there being, then and there wilfully, feloniously, of his malice aforethought, did make an assault upon the said Peter with a certain knife, of the value of six cents, which he the said Peter in his right hand then and there had and held, the said negro Ben in and upon the left side of him the said Ben, and in and upon the Belly of him the said Ben, then and there feloniously, willfully, and of his malice aforethought, did strike and thrust, giving to the said negro Ben then and there with the knife aforesaid in and upon the said left side and upon the belly of him the said negro Ben, two mortal wounds of breadth of three Inches each, and of the depth of six inches each, & then & there struck said Ben with a chair on the head of him the said Ben, of which said mortal wounds the said negro man Ben on the day aforesaid in the county aforesaid at the House aforesaid died. And so the said Ira Christian, Clerk as aforesaid, says that the said negro Slave Peter, the said negro Slave Ben in manner and form aforesaid, feloniously, wilfully, and of his malice aforethought did kill and murder contrary to the laws of said state, the good order peace and dignity thereof.

Court for the trial of
negro slave Peter
30th June 1837.

Ira Christian
Clerk of Inferior
Court of Elbert County.
William Alexander
Prosecutor.

* * *

State of Georgia
vs
A negro man named
Peter

Evidence in the above stated case.
Jordan the property of Joseph Terry. Sworn. Saith was at the house of Wm. Alexander in last month on Sunday. The commencement of the difficulty was (Peter Told) Ben told Peter he wanted him explain those tales that had been told. Ben told Peter he wanted him to say if did tell those tales. Peter said he would be damned if he would not die on the cause before he would be scandelized so. Peter struck Benn on the side. Ben then collared Peter and Pushed him towards the wall. Peter went out at the door & struck Ben again. Saw two wounds one on the left side & one on the Belly.

So little importance was attached to the records of trials of slaves in the American South that many have vanished. This record, preserved in an Alberton, Georgia, courthouse, documents a murder trial held in 1837.

COLORPLATE 78

GILBERT CHARLES STUART. *John Jay*. 1794. Oil on canvas. 51½ × 40⅛" (130.9 × 101.9 cm). National Gallery of Art, Washington, D.C. Lent by Peter Jay. *A coauthor (along with Alexander Hamilton and James Madison) of the* Federalist *papers, John Jay (1745–1829) served as president of the Continental Congress in 1778–1779 and was the secretary for foreign affairs from 1784 to 1789, chief justice of the Supreme Court from 1789 to 1795, and governor of New York from 1795 to 1801.*

COLORPLATE 79

ASHER BROWN DURAND. *James Kent.* c. 1836. Oil on canvas. 30³⁄₁₆ × 25³⁄₁₆″ (76.7 × 64 cm). Harvard Law Art Collection, Cambridge. *James Kent (1763–1847) was the first professor of law at Columbia College, chief justice of New York's State Supreme Court, and chancellor of its Chancery Court. His* Commentaries on the American Law, *published between 1826 and 1830, based on Sir William Blackstone's* Commentaries, *is an American legal classic.*

COLORPLATE 80

FRANCIS ALEXANDER. *Portrait of Daniel Webster, "Black Dan."* 1835. Oil on canvas. 30 × 25" (76.2 × 63.5 cm). Hood Museum of Art, Dartmouth College, Hanover. Gift of Dr. George C. Shattuck, Class of 1803. *His allegiance to the Union above all considerations led Congressman Daniel Webster (1782–1852) to support the Compromise of 1850, which turned former supporters among the antislavery forces against him. They turned a nickname from Webster's Dartmouth days, "Black Dan" (referring to his complexion), into an epithet of abuse.*

COLORPLATE 81

HORACE BUNDY. *A Vermont Lawyer*. 1841. Oil on canvas. 44 × 35½″ (111 × 90.2 cm).
National Gallery of Art, Washington, D.C. Gift of Edgar William and Bernice Chrysler Garbisch.

COLORPLATE 82

LOUIS SCHULTZE. *Dred Scott*. 1881. Oil on canvas. 27 × 30" (68.5 × 76.2 cm). Missouri Historical Society, St. Louis. *Transported in 1834 from Missouri, a slave state, to Illinois, a free state, and then to the Minnesota Territory, the slave Dred Scott sued in 1846 for his freedom since he was residing in a free territory. The Supreme Court ruled on March 6, 1857, against Scott, holding that blacks could not sue in federal courts, and the Missouri Compromise of 1820, forbidding slavery in parts of the territory of the Louisiana Purchase, was unconstitutional.*

COLORPLATE 83

FREDERICK PORTER VINTON. *Christopher Columbus Langdell.* 1892. Oil on canvas. 50⅛ × 40¼″ (127.3 × 102 cm). Harvard Law Art Collection, Cambridge. *Christopher Columbus Langdell (1826–1906) was dean of Harvard Law School and developed the case method for studying law.*

COLORPLATE 84

NELLIE MATHES HORNE. *Belva Ann Bennett Lockwood.* 1913. Oil on canvas. 69¾ × 40″ (177.1 × 101.6 cm). National Portrait Gallery, Smithsonian Institution, Washington, D.C. Transfer from the National Museum of American Art. Gift of the Committee on Tribute to Mrs. Belva Ann Lockwood through Mrs. Anna Kelton Wiley, 1917. *Denied access to formal law studies at the National University Law School in Washington, D.C., because of sexist discrimination, Belva Ann Bennett Lockwood (1830–1917) studied with a private tutor and was admitted to the bar in 1873. She eventually became the first woman lawyer to argue before the U.S. Supreme Court.*

COLORPLATE 85

CHARLES SYDNEY HOPKINSON. *Oliver Wendell Holmes.* 1930. Oil on canvas. 95 × 59½″ (241.3 × 151 cm). Harvard Law Art Collection, Cambridge. *In 1902, President Theodore Roosevelt named Holmes to the U.S. Supreme Court, expecting that he would be a liberal ally. However, Holmes's dedication to the Constitution did not necessarily serve to promote Roosevelt's partisan positions.*

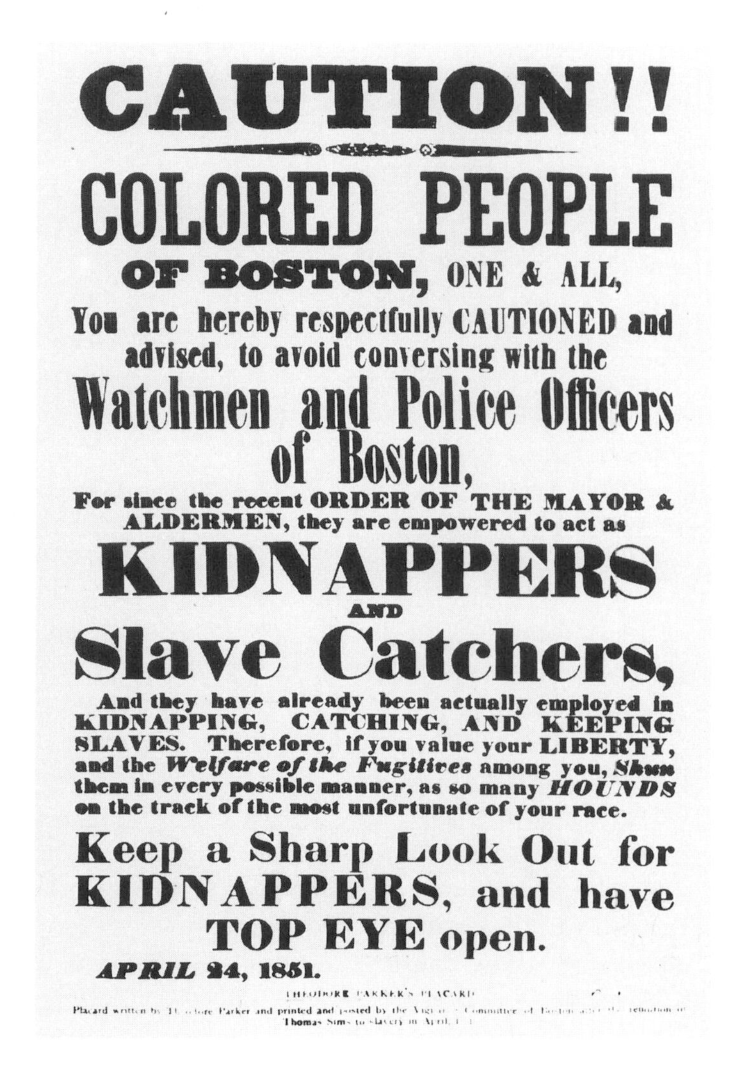

CAUTION!!

COLORED PEOPLE

OF BOSTON, ONE & ALL,

You are hereby respectfully CAUTIONED and advised, to avoid conversing with the

Watchmen and Police Officers of Boston,

For since the recent ORDER OF THE MAYOR & ALDERMEN, they are empowered to act as

KIDNAPPERS

AND

Slave Catchers,

And they have already been actually employed in KIDNAPPING, CATCHING, AND KEEPING SLAVES. Therefore, if you value your LIBERTY, and the *Welfare of the Fugitives* among you, *Shun* them in every possible manner, as so many *HOUNDS* on the track of the most unfortunate of your race.

Keep a Sharp Look Out for KIDNAPPERS, and have TOP EYE open.

APRIL 24, 1851.

Broadside issued by the Vigilance Committee of Boston that shows the concern of some Bostonians regarding the Fugitive Slave Law of 1850. April 24, 1851.
Rare Books Division, Library of Congress, Washington, D.C.

CROSS EXAMINATION

Ben asked Peter to come to his (Ben's) house. The chest on which Peter Lay was on the right side of the house. Ben was towards the door. Eddy said Peter did tell those tales. When Peter struck Ben first, Ben was standing with his hand on Peter. Did not appear to be pressing his hands on Peter. Ben was on the side of the door when Peter struck him the second Blow, which was on the Belly. After Peter struck Ben the second Blow, Peter fell, & Ben fell on him. When they were take up & apart Peter got a chair & struck Ben when Ben collared Peter. Peter shouted or made a noise trying to shout. Peter fell by going Backwards. Ben stumbled out & fell on Peter. While Peter & Ben were talking saw Peter have a knife scraping his nails. Neither appeared angry at first. Ben asked Peter twice to confess the lie that was told. Ben told Peter he did not want to have any difficulty with him.

* * *

William Alexander being sworn saith the transaction took place on the 28th May at his house in this county. When he heard the noise he ran down from his own house. When he saw them Ben was standing up & Peter took up a chair & struck Ben. He, Mr. Alexander, took up a piece of wood & struck Peter. Peter then ran off. The chair was at Peter's door. Told Peter not to strike Ben but he did so. A shirt exhibited now in court is the one which Ben had on when he died. Ben died of the wound inflicted on him then & there. Supposed he died of the wound inflicted on his side. Probed the wound under the breat thinks it was 3 inches deep. Saw no blood about his head.

CROSS [EXAMINATION]

When Peter struck Ben with the chair he appeared to strike with all his strength. The wound was about one Inch below his left Breast & about 2½ inches deep. [The witness] struck Peter about the head. The noise that Brot him from his house was the noise described by first witness Jordan.

Doct. Thos. F. Gibbs sworn. Saith the wound below the Breast. Thinks a puncture of the heart would [cause] instant death. Thinks three inches would have entered the heart. The wound or blow on the head might have caused the death of the negroe.

Bedford J. Hamilton Sworn. Saw Peter on the Tuesday after the affray. One of his eyes Blood shotten & a Bruise on the back of his head.

Fred. Banks Sworn. Saw Peter on Monday corrobarated Mr. Hamilton's Testimony.

C. W. Christian, J.I.C.
Thomas J. Heard, J.I.C.
William Jones, J.I.C.
Jerimiah S. Warren, J.I.C.
Thomas Johnston, J.I.C.

VIRDICT OF THE JURY & SENTENCE
of the Court

The State
vs
Peter a Negro Slave

Murder,
We the Jury find the prisoner
Guilty of Murder June 30th 1837
John G. Deadwyler
Foreman

You, Peter, will be taken by the proper Officer from the Bar of the court to the common Jail of this county, and there be kept in close and safe custody untill the twenty Eighth day of July next, and on that day, between the hours of ten o'clock in the forenoon and three o'clock in the afternoon, you will be taken from thence by the proper officer to the public gallows, to be erected in or near to the village of Elberton, and their be hung by the Neck untill you are dead. And may the Lord have Mercy upon Your Soul. This 30th June 1837.

* * *

Executed the within Sentence of the court by hanging Peter a slave by the Neck untill dead this 28th day of July 1837.

Wm. W. Downer, Sheff.

Irving Younger

"Abraham Lincoln, Esq."

"I do not care to speak ill of any man," said Dr. Johnson, "but I have heard that he is an attorney." Unkinder still to mark a man's birthday by remembering him at the bar. It is the plain truth, however, that Lincoln was a lawyer, one of the best and most successful of his time.

He was a litigator, specializing in courtroom work of all sorts. Unusually skillful at presenting complicated appellate issues simply and persuasively, he argued 243 cases in

---

In the years between log cabin and White House, the self-taught Abraham Lincoln (1809–1865) practiced law in Springfield, Illinois, where he was noted not only for his shrewdness and common sense, but also for his fairness and honesty.

Abraham Lincoln
in Springfield, Illinois.
February 1861.

the Illinois Supreme Court. He represented the Illinois Central Railroad in 40 lawsuits which took him to courthouses throughout the Midwest. When Isham Reavis applied to read law in Lincoln's office, he received this reply:

> I am from home too much of my time, for a young man to read law with me advantageously. If you are resolutely determined to make a lawyer of yourself, the thing is more than half done already. It is but a small matter whether you read with anybody or not. I did not read with anyone. Get the books and read and study them till you understand them and their principal features; and that is the main thing. It is of no consequence to be in a large town while you are reading. I read at new Salem, which never had three hundred people living in it. The books and your capacity for understanding them are just the same in all places. Always bear in mind that your resolution to succeed is more important than any other one thing.
>
> Very truly,
> Your friend,
> A. Lincoln

Lincoln's powers were at their most impressive before juries. The widow of a veteran of the Revolution had retained a claim agent to help her collect a pension of $500. Forgetting to specify a fee in advance, the widow was dismayed to learn that the agent was keeping half the pension for himself. She sued. Her lawyer was Lincoln, who outlined his summation to the jury as follows:

> No contract. Not professional services. Unreasonable charge. Money retained by defendant—not given by plaintiff. Revolutionary War. Describe Valley Forge

The board that tried Lincoln's assassins. 1867.

privation. Ice. Soldiers' bleeding feet. Plaintiff's husband. Soldier leaving home for army. SKIN DEFENDANT. Close.

In 1858, William "Duff" Armstrong was tried in the Circuit Court of Illinois for the murder of James Metzker on the night of August 29, 1857. The State's star witness was Charles Allen, who testified on direct examination that he had seen Armstrong strike Metzker in the eye with a slingshot.

According to one young lawyer present in the courtroom, Lincoln "sat with his head thrown back, his steady gaze apparently fixed upon one spot of the blank ceiling, entirely oblivious to what was happening around him, and without a single variation of feature or noticeable movement of any muscle of his face."

Finally, Lincoln arose and cross-examined:

Q: Did you actually see the fight?

A: Yes.

Q: And you stood very near to them?

A: No, it was 150 feet or more.

Q: In the open field?

A: No, in the timber.

Q: What kind of timber?

A: Beech timber.

Q: Leaves on it are rather thick in August?

A: It looks like it.

Q: What time did all this occur?

A: Eleven o'clock at night.

Q: Did you have a candle there?

A: No, what would I want a candle for?

Q: How could you see from a distance of 150 feet or more, without a candle, at 11:00 at night?

A: The moon was shining real bright.

Q: Full moon?

A: Yes, a full moon.

At this point, Lincoln drew out of his back pocket a blue-covered almanac, opened it slowly to the astronomical table for the night in question, and placed it before the witness. He continued his cross-examination:

Q: Does not the almanac say that on August 29 the moon was barely past the first quarter instead of being full?

A: (No answer.)

Q: Does not the almanac also say that the moon had disappeared by 11:00?

A: (No answer.)

Q: Is it not a fact that it was too dark to see anything from 50 feet, let alone 150 feet?

A: (No answer.)

Armstrong was acquitted.

Nor was Lincoln's virtuosity limited to matters of fact. In 1841, the Illinois Supreme Court decided that a promissory note was unenforceable where the note had been given in payment for a black girl. "The sale of a free person is illegal," said the court, "and that being the consideration of the note, that is illegal also, and consequently no recovery can be had upon the note."

But was the girl free to begin with? Yes, answered the court, because no person, whatever the person's color, can be enslaved in Illinois, and the reason for that was the reason suggested by the winning lawyer. The Northwest Ordinance of 1787, enacted before the formation of the United States of America and the adoption of the Constitution, forbade slavery in the states yet to be created in the Northwest Territory. The winning lawyer was Abraham Lincoln.

Lincoln's interest in law and lawyers continued through his days in the White House, where it sometimes manifested itself in unlikely circumstances. Take, for example, Nathan Goff.

Until a year before his death in 1920, Goff had been one of West Virginia's senators and before that, working backward, a judge of the United States Court of Appeals for the Fourth Circuit, a congressman, President Hayes's Secretary of the Navy, United States Attorney for the District of West Virginia, and a member of the West Virginia state legislature. While serving on the circuit court, Goff had presided over a hearing on the reorganization of the Long Island Traction Company. The arguments ended at noon, whereupon the judge invited all counsel to lunch at his home and, over coffee, told the following experience of his youth.

In 1861, as an eighteen-year-old native of the fiercely antislavery region of western Virginia (two years later to become West Virginia), Goff joined the Union army. He distinguished himself at Second Bull Run and by 1864 held the rank of major in the Fourth West Virginia Cavalry. In a skirmish near Moorfield, his horse shot out from under him, Goff was captured and sent to the notorious Libby Prison in Richmond. The Confederacy saw him as a citizen of Virginia traitorously fighting for the North, and so confined him to the cellar of the prison, a kind of death row reserved for capital offenders. There Goff devoted his nights to fighting off Libby Prison's sleek and fearless rats and his days to reading and rereading the only book he could find in that noisome place, a volume of Blackstone's Commentaries.

One Major Thomas D. Armesy, a Confederate officer, had been tried by the Union army as a spy and sentenced to death. The Confederate government announced that if Armesy died, so would Goff. Informed of this, Goff wrote President Lincoln:

> If Major Armesy is guilty, he should be executed, regardless of its consequences to me. The life of a single soldier, no matter who he may be, should not stand in the way of adherence to a great principle.

A few weeks later Armesy and Goff were exchanged. Proceeding to the War Department in Washington, Goff was directed by the duty officer to report immediately to President Lincoln. He walked the few blocks to the White House, where a reception was in progress. Faint from hunger and weighing no more than a hundred pounds, Goff stood in the line of guests being greeted by the President. When he came to Goff, Lincoln said, "Well, Major, what can I do for you?"

"I was ordered to report to you, sir," Goff replied.

"My God," explained Lincoln, "then you are Major Goff."

Lincoln sent Goff to an adjoining room. An hour passed, during which a butler brought Goff a plate of chicken sandwiches and a glass of milk. Then Lincoln entered. He listened quietly to Goff's description of conditions at Libby Prison and, when Goff was done, asked, "Are you strong enough to tell this again to Secretary Stanton?"

"Yes, sir," Goff answered.

Lincoln sent for Stanton, to whom Goff repeated everything. "Stanton, I've told you that these stories of Libby Prison are true," said Lincoln. "Those boys must be brought home."

After Stanton left, Lincoln said to Goff, "Well, inasmuch as you've been reading Blackstone under such unique conditions, perhaps you have determined to become a lawyer." Goff replied that he had been thinking about it. "Can I do anything further for you?" asked Lincoln. Goff mentioned two of his fellow inmates at Libby and said that he hoped Lincoln might secure their release by an exchange of prisoners.

"Major," Lincoln replied, "all that I can say to you is that the plight of your friends shall be attended to as you wish, and you can now have the satisfaction of knowing that, even before admission to the Bar, you have won your first case."

Don E. Fehrenbacher

FROM THE DRED SCOTT CASE

On Friday morning, March 6, 1857—a crisp, clear day for residents of Washington, D.C.—public attention centered on a dusky, ground-level courtroom deep within the Capitol. The Senate chamber directly above was quiet; Congress had adjourned on March 3. The inauguration ceremonies of March 4 were over, and James Buchanan had begun settling into his role as the fifteenth President. Now it was the judiciary's turn to be heard, as though the three branches of government were passing in review before the American people. Ordinarily, the Supreme Court carried on its business before a small audience

---

In 1857, the U.S. Supreme Court set the stage for the upcoming Civil War when it ruled 7 to 2 against Dred Scott, a slave who claimed freedom due to his temporary residency in Illinois, a "free" state.

FRANK LESLIE'S ILLUSTRATED NEWSPAPER

No. 82.—VOL. IV.] NEW YORK, SATURDAY, JUNE 27, 1857. [PRICE 6 CENTS.

TO TOURISTS AND TRAVELLERS.

We shall be happy to receive personal narratives, of land or sea, including adventures and incidents, from every person who pleases to correspond with our paper.

We take this opportunity of returning our thanks to our numerous artistic correspondents throughout the country, for the many sketches we are constantly receiving from them of the news of the day. We trust they will spare no pains to furnish us with drawings of events as they may occur. We would also remind them that it is necessary to send all sketches, if possible, by the earliest conveyance.

VISIT TO DRED SCOTT—HIS FAMILY—INCIDENTS OF HIS LIFE—DECISION OF THE SUPREME COURT.

While standing in the Fair grounds at St. Louis, and engaged in conversation with a prominent citizen of that enterprising city, he suddenly asked us if we would not like to be introduced to Dred Scott. Upon expressing a desire to be thus honored, the gentleman called to an old negro who was standing near by, and our wish was gratified. Dred made a rude obeisance to our recognition, and seemed to enjoy the notice we expended upon him. We found him on examination to be a pure-blooded African, perhaps fifty years of age, with a shrewd, intelligent, good-natured face, of rather light frame, being not more than five feet six inches high. After some general remarks we expressed a wish to get his portrait (we had made efforts before, through correspondents, and failed), and asked him if he would not go to Fitzgibbon's gallery and have it taken. The gentleman present explained to Dred that it was proper he should have his likeness in the "great illustrated paper of the country," overruled his many objections, which seemed to grow out of a superstitious feeling, and he promised to be at the gallery the next day. This appointment Dred did not keep. Determined not to be foiled, we sought an interview with Mr. Crane, Dred's lawyer, who promptly gave us a letter of introduction, explaining to Dred that it was to his advantage to have his picture taken to be engraved for our paper, and also directions where we could find his domicile. We found the place with difficulty, the streets in Dred's neighborhood being more clearly defined in the plan of the city than on the mother earth; we finally reached a wooden house, however, protected by a balcony that answered the description. Approaching the door, we saw a smart, tidy-looking negress, perhaps thirty years of age, who, with two female assistants, was busy ironing. To our question, "Is this where Dred Scott lives?" we received, rather hesitatingly, the answer, "Yes." Upon our asking if he was home, she said,

"What white man arter dat nigger for!—why don't white man 'tend to his own business, and let dat nigger 'lone? Some of dese days dey'll steal dat nigger—dat are a fact."

ELIZA AND LIZZIE, CHILDREN OF DRED SCOTT.

Engraving of Dred Scott, his wife, and his children.
From *Frank Leslie's Illustrated Newspaper*. June 27, 1857.

and with only perfunctory notice from the press, but today the journalists were out in force and the courtroom was packed with spectators. A murmur of expectancy ran through the crowd and greeted the nine black-robed jurists as they filed into view at eleven o'clock, led by the aged Chief Justice. Acrimonious debate in the recent Congress had once again failed to settle the paramount constitutional and political issue of the decade. The Court, however, was ready to terminate the long struggle over slavery in the territories and, incidentally, decide the fate of a man named Dred Scott.

Neither of the two litigants was present in the courtroom. Scott remained at home in St. Louis, still a hired-out slave eleven years after he had taken the first legal step in his long battle for freedom. As for his alleged owner, John F.A. Sandford languished in an insane asylum and within two months would be dead. But then, both men had been dwarfed by the implications of their case and were now mere pawns in a much larger contest.

Roger B. Taney, who in eleven days would be eighty years old, began reading from a manuscript held in tremulous hands. For more than two hours the audience strained to hear his steadily weakening voice as he delivered the opinion of the court in *Dred Scott v. Sandford.* Other opinions followed from some of the concurring justices and from the two dissenters. When they were finished at the end of the next day, only one thing was absolutely clear. Nine distinguished white men, by a vote of 7 to 2, had decided in the court of last resort that an insignificant, elderly black man and his family were still slaves and not free citizens, as they claimed.

What else had been decided was fiercely debated then and ever afterward. Critics argued that on some points Taney did not speak for a majority of the justices. Yet none of his eight colleagues directly challenged Taney's explicit assertion that his was the official opinion of the Court, and in popular usage on all sides the "Dred Scott decision" came to mean the opinion read by the Chief Justice. Critics also insisted that Taney's most important pronouncement was extrajudicial, but only the Court itself, in later decisions, could legally settle such a question by accepting or rejecting the pronouncement as established precedent. Rightly or not, permanently or not, the Supreme Court had written two new and provocative rules into the fundamental law of the nation: first, that no Negro could be a United States citizen or even a state citizen "within the meaning of the Constitution"; and second, that Congress had no power to exclude slavery from the federal territories, and that accordingly the Missouri Compromise, together with all other legislation embodying such exclusion, was unconstitutional.

Stephen Vincent Benét
FROM JOHN BROWN'S BODY

★ ★ ★

So, in the cupolaed Courthouse there in Charlestown,
When the jail-guards had carried in the cot
Where Brown lay like a hawk with a broken back,
I hear the rustle of the moving crowd,
The buzz outside, taste the dull, heavy air,
Smell the stale smell and see the country carts
Hitched in the streets.
For a long, dragging week
Of market-Saturdays the trial went on.
The droning voices rise and fall and rise.
Stevens lies quiet on his mattress, breathing
The harsh and difficult breath of a dying man,
Although not dying then.
Beyond the Square
The trees are dry, but all the dry leaves not fallen—
Yellow leaves falling through a grey-blue dusk,
The first winds of November whirl and scatter them. . . .
Read as you will in any of the books,
The details of the thing, the questions and answers,
How sometimes Brown would walk, sometimes was carried,
At first would hardly plead, half-refused counsel,
Accepted later, made up witness-lists,
Grew fitfully absorbed in his defense,
Only to flare in temper at his first lawyers
And drive them from the case.

★ ★ ★

No once can say
That the trial was not fair. The trial was fair,
Painfully fair by every rule of law,
And that it was made not the slightest difference.
The law's our yardstick, and it measures well
Or well enough when there are yards to measure.

In 1859, the abolitionist John Brown (1800–1859) organized a bloody slave insurrection at Harpers Ferry, Virginia. He was convicted of murder and treason and later hanged. The events are described in this excerpt from the epic poem, written in 1928 by the American poet and author Stephen Vincent Benét (1893–1943), who was awarded the Pulitzer Prize.

Measure a wave with it, measure a fire,
Cut sorrow up in inches, weigh content.
You can weigh John Brown's body well enough,
But how and in what balance weigh John Brown?

* * *

And yardstick law
Gave him six weeks to burn that hoarded knowledge
In one swift fire whose sparks fell like live coals
On every State in the Union.
Listen now,
Listen, the bearded lips are speaking now,
There are no more guerilla-raids to plan,
There are no more hard questions to be solved
Of right and wrong, no need to beg for peace,
Here is the peace unbegged, here is the end,
Here is the insolence of the sun cast off,
Here is the voice already fixed with night.

* * *

JOHN BROWN'S SPEECH

I have, may it please the Court, a few words to say.

In the first place I deny everything but what I have all along admitted: of a design on my part to free slaves. . . .

Had I interfered in the matter which I admit, and which I admit has been fairly proved . . . had I so interfered in behalf of the rich, the powerful, the intelligent, or the so-called great . . . and suffered and sacrificed, what I have in this interference, it would have been all right. Every man in this Court would have deemed it an act worthy of reward rather than punishment.

I see a book kissed which I suppose to be the Bible, or at least the New Testament, which teaches me that all things whatsoever I would that men should do unto me, I should do even so to them. It teaches me further to remember them that are in bonds as bound with them. I endeavored to act up to that instruction. I say I am yet too young to understand that God is any respecter of persons. I believe that to have interfered as I have done, as I have always freely admitted I have done in behalf of His despised poor, I did no wrong, but right. Now, if it is deemed necessary that I should forfeit my life for the furtherance of the ends of justice and mingle my blood further with the blood of my children and with the blood of millions in this slave country whose rights are disregarded by wicked, cruel and unjust enactments, I say, let it be done.

Let me say one word further. I feel entirely satisfied with the treatment I have received on my trial. Considering all the circumstances, it has been more generous than I expected. But I feel no consciousness of guilt. I have stated from the first what was my intention and what was not. I never had any design against the liberty of any person, nor any disposition to commit treason or incite slaves to rebel or make any general insurrection. I never encouraged any man to do so but always discouraged any idea of that kind.

Let me say also, in regard to the statements made by some of those connected with me, I hear it has been stated by some of them that I have induced them to join with me. But the contrary is true. I do not say this to injure them, but as regretting their weakness. Not one but joined me of his own accord, and the greater part at their own expense. A number of them I never saw, and never had a word of conversation with, till the day they came to me, and that was for the purpose I have stated.

Now I have done.

The voice ceased. There was a deep, brief pause.
The judge pronounced the formal words of death.
One man, a stranger, tried to clap his hands.
The foolish sound was stopped.
There was nothing but silence then.
No cries in the court,
No roar, no slightest murmur from the thronged street,
As Brown went back to jail between his guards.
The heavy door shut behind them.
There was a noise of chairs scraped back in the court-room,
And that huge sigh of a crowd turning back into men. . . .

Stephen J. Riegel

"The Persistent Career of Jim Crow"

Right after the Civil War, blacks often went to court to protect their newly won freedom and to win access to formerly exclusive public accommodations. *The New York Times* observed caustically, "There is no class of people here that are fonder of the pleasures of court proceedings, and of becoming parties to controversies in them, than the newly infranchised [sic] citizens." Whenever blacks "believe their rights assailed or threatened, a rush is made to some court or other for redress." In his decision shortly after the passage of the Civil Rights Act of 1875, Judge Halmer Emmons of the Circuit Court of Tennessee noted "the exceptional conditions which attend these [civil rights] complaints" and "the excited condition of those classes whom the law was intended to affect."

★ ★ ★

Some of the public accommodation cases were brought by black people who had been totally excluded from public establishments, such as inns, restaurants, or theatres. These suits arose most frequently under the 1875 Civil Rights Act during its lifetime (1875–1883) and were often successful. In 1876, the federal government prosecuted a Philadelphia hotel manager for refusing to accommodate a black minister when rooms were available and some white guests even offered to share their room with him. District Court Judge John Cadwalader instructed the jury that the case against the defendant "appears to be proved" and the jury imposed a $500 fine. Few of these exclusion cases are found in the legal reporters (perhaps because their outcomes were so obvious) but contemporary news stories reported other courts awarding damages to plaintiffs who were excluded from theatres, music halls, restaurants, inns, and bars. A Washington, D.C. court imposed a prison sentence on a restaurant owner in 1883 for refusing to serve a black. Occasionally, judges denied relief by employing a very narrow reading of what constituted "other places of amusement" under the 1875 act. A New York federal commissioner, for example, ruled that ice cream parlors did not fall under the act and thus could refuse to serve certain customers.

Some proprietors, it appears, allowed blacks into their establishments, but charged them outrageous prices or provided them with inferior accommodations. A few cases arose in which black patrons who had purchased first-class tickets to theatres sought to enforce their right to truly first-class accommodations. Successful verdicts were reported

---

By 1841 the term "Jim Crow"—derived from a song by "Jim Crow" Rice, the father of American minstrelsy—was being applied to those sections within racially segregated facilities that were intended for black people. This excerpt from a legal scholar's recent study examines the evolution of the "separate but equal" doctrine in lower federal courts.

in Texas, Illinois, and Virginia. Another decision held that an inn must give all patrons "equal privileges . . . at a uniform rate of charge," but accepted the innkeeper's right to "designate certain places or seats for customers," thus allowing him to set up separate first-class sections for blacks and whites.

Generally, however, blacks did not assert their civil rights in hotels, restaurants, and theatres very frequently (especially in the South) and they were largely excluded from such places during this period, except for those which catered to blacks. Their inaction here probably resulted from their self-respect and desire not to intrude where they were not wanted. In response to the passage of the Civil Rights Act of 1875, an influential Southern Black minister, J. C. Weaver, instructed his people "to patronize and encourage their own race, as far as comfortable accommodations are practicable" and care little about theatres and other places of amusement. As late as 1895, *The New York Times* stated that local blacks did not resort to hotels, theatres, restaurants, and clubs, "where they are now unwelcome."

Blacks' access to public conveyances—railroads, steamships, and streetcars—was much greater and more important for obvious reasons. If a black traveler needed to patronize a hotel or restaurant, there were generally separate establishments which catered to blacks. If he wanted to travel, however, there were no independent black transportation services (except on a very local level). Thus, it is not surprising that most of the public accommodations cases concerned blacks' rights to accommodations on public conveyances.

None of the reported cases involved blacks who had been totally excluded from conveyances. Rather, in all, blacks had been admitted to segregated accommodations which were generally inferior to comparable white accommodations of the same price, and they sued for the right to "equal" treatment under the 1875 act or the fourteenth amendment.

The factual circumstances of these cases were often very similar. For example, in *Murphy v. Western & A.R.R.* in 1885, a black man had purchased a first-class ticket on a two-car train from Georgia to Tennessee. He took a seat in the car "for ladies and those who escorted them" and remained there without complaint for the early part of the trip. When two white women got on the train, their male companions told him to leave the car. Mr. Murphy refused to move and the men proceeded to assault him and throw him into the second car, the "smoking car" (often referred to as the "Jim Crow" car in the cases of this period) which was occupied by blacks and whites. Witnesses testified that passengers in the ladies' car had "no objection to plaintiff's retaining his seat" and told the assailants to leave him alone.

Federal Judge David Key of Tennessee, an ex-Confederate officer, instructed the jury that railroad cars may be segregated by race "so as to avoid complaint and friction" if equal accommodations were provided for black and white passengers. But, he continued, "[t]here is no equality of right, when the money of the white man purchases luxurious accommodations amid elegant company, and the same amount of money purchases for the black man inferior quarters in a smoking car." Since Murphy had purchased a first-class ticket and there was no black first-class car, he had a right to sit in the white "ladies' " car. The jury awarded damages to the plaintiff to be paid by his assailants and also the railroad company because its employees "made no effort to prevent the mischief."

It is difficult to determine from this case and others whether black plaintiffs just wanted "equal" accommodations—whether racially segregated or not—or whether they really desired integrated accommodations. Many blacks apparently were more concerned about enjoying first-class facilities on a train (and avoiding the unpleasantness of second-class accommodations and passengers) than about sitting with white people. Weaver, the black preacher mentioned above, advised "decent" blacks in 1875 to accept segregated first-class accommodations on public conveyances since "I would prefer a seat . . . with those by whom I could be cordially entertained." But if no such accommodation is available and "you are crowded upon by base and reckless beings," he added, then blacks should enter the whites' car.

This economic class factor was very evident in *Logwood v. Memphis & C.R.*, a case in which a "proper" black woman had purchased a first-class ticket on a two-car train. She was denied entrance to the "ladies' car" but refused to enter the other car, where there was "swearing and smoking and whiskey drinking," and she got off the train.

The federal judge, balancing the conflicting considerations of racial caste and economic class, also adopted the "separate but equal" doctrine. Railroad carriers might reasonably separate races in some circumstances, he remarked, but to do so, they "must treat all passengers paying the same price alike." If the carrier furnished for white ladies "a car with special privileges of seclusion and other comforts, the same must be substantially furnished for colored ladies."

★ ★ ★

In 1883, four black women brought suit in district court in Maryland against a steamboat owner for putting them in "first-class" rooms in the black section of the boat which they claimed were inferior to the white first-class rooms. The testimony revealed that the black cabins were "offensively dirty; that the mattresses in the berths were defaced; that sheets were wanting or soiled" and "that there were no blankets and no conveniences for washing." The white first-class rooms, by contrast, were "clean, pleasant, and inviting." Judge John Erskine rejected the owner's claim that the small number of first-class black passengers made it too expensive to keep up their cabins. He awarded damages to the women, stating that "[t]he right of the first-class colored passenger was to have first-class accommodation according to the standard" of the white cabin.

Careful scrutiny was also evident in *Heard v. Georgia R.R.*, a case involving accommodations on passenger trains before the newly-formed Interstate Commerce Commission in 1888. A black minister "of education and decorous behavior" had filed a complaint for being assigned to a so-called first-class car for blacks in Georgia. It consisted of "half of a dingy old car" filled with "fumes of tobacco smoke and whiskey." In its answer to the complaint, the railroad company maintained that the only difference between the black and white first-class cars "related to matters aesthetical only . . . rather than in those which affect the substantial conditions of safety, comfort and convenience." The Commission ruled against the railroad and ordered it to "cease and desist from subjecting colored passengers to such undue and unreasonable prejudice and disadvantage." The Commission strongly rejected, however, petitioner's position that the Interstate Commerce Act required the racial integration of passenger cars: "Identity . . . in the sense that all must be admitted to the same car and that under no circumstances segregation can be made, is not indispensable to give effect to the statute."

Mark Twain

FROM ROUGHING IT

The mountains are very high and steep about Carson, Eagle and Washoe Valleys—very high and very steep, and so when the snow gets to melting off fast in the Spring and the warm surface-earth begins to moisten and soften, the disastrous land-slides commence. The reader cannot know what a land-slide is, unless he has lived in that country and seen the whole side of a mountain taken off some fine morning and deposited down in the valley, leaving a vast, treeless, unsightly scar upon the mountain's front to keep the

---

Samuel Langhorne Clemens (1835–1910), or Mark Twain, was a journalist in Nevada before becoming America's foremost humorist. In this selection, Twain relates a tall tale of justice in the frontier America of 1872.

circumstance fresh in his memory all the years that he may go on living within seventy miles of that place.

General Buncombe was shipped out to Nevada in the invoice of Territorial officers, to be United States Attorney. He considered himself a lawyer of parts, and he very much wanted an opportunity to manifest it—partly for the pure gratification of it and partly because his salary was Territorially meagre (which is a strong expression). Now the older citizens of a new territory look down upon the rest of the world with a calm, benevolent compassion, as long as it keeps out of the way—when it gets in the way they snub it. Sometimes this latter takes the shape of a practical joke.

One morning Dick Hyde rode furiously up to General Buncombe's door in Carson city and rushed into his presence without stopping to tie his horse. He seemed much excited. He told the General that he wanted him to conduct a suit for him and would pay him five hundred dollars if he achieved a victory. And then, with violent gestures and a world of profanity, he poured out his griefs. He said it was pretty well known that for some years he had been farming (or ranching as the more customary term is) in Washoe District, and making a successful thing of it, and furthermore it was known that his ranch was situated just in the edge of the valley, and that Tom Morgan owned a ranch immediately above it on the mountain side. And now the trouble was, that one of those hated and dreaded land-slides had come and slid Morgan's ranch, fences, cabins, cattle, barns and everything down on top of *his* ranch and exactly covered up every single vestige of his property, to a depth of about thirty-eight feet. Morgan was in possession and refused to vacate the premises—said he was occupying his own cabin and not interfering with anybody else's—and said the cabin was standing on the same dirt and same ranch it had always stood on, and he would like to see anybody make him vacate.

"And when I reminded him," said Hyde, weeping, "that it was on top of my ranch and that he was trespassing, he had the infernal meanness to ask me why didn't I *stay* on my ranch and hold possession when I see him a-coming! Why didn't I *stay* on it, the blathering lunatic—by George, when I heard that racket and looked up that hill it was just like the whole world was a-ripping and a-tearing down that mountain side—splinters, and cord-wood, thunder and lightning, hail and snow, odds and ends of hay stacks, and awful clouds of dust!—trees going end over end in the air, rocks as big as a house jumping 'bout a thousand feet high and busting into ten million pieces, cattle turned inside out and a-coming head on with their tails hanging out between their teeth!—and in the midst of all that wrack and destruction sot that cussed Morgan on his gate-post, a-wondering why I didn't *stay and hold possession!* Laws bless me, I just took one glimpse, General, and lit out'n the county in three jumps exactly.

"But what grinds me is that that Morgan hangs on there and won't move off'n that ranch—says it's his'n and he's going to keep it—likes it better'n he did when it was higher up the hill. Mad! Well, I've been so mad for two days I couldn't find my way to town—been wandering around in the brush in a starving condition—got anything here to drink, General? But I'm here *now*, and I'm a-going to law. You hear *me!*"

Never in all the world, perhaps, were a man's feelings so outraged as were the General's. He said he had never heard of such high-handed conduct in all his life as this Morgan's. And he said there was no use in going to law—Morgan had no shadow of right to remain where he was—nobody in the wide world would uphold him in it, and no lawyer would take his case and no judge listen to it. Hyde said that right there was where he was mistaken—everybody in town sustained Morgan; Hal Brayton, a very smart lawyer, had taken his case; the courts being in vacation, it was to be tried before a referee, and ex-Governor Roop had already been appointed to that office and would open his court in a large public hall near the hotel at two that afternoon.

The General was amazed. He said he had suspected before that the people of that Territory were fools, and now he knew it. But he said rest easy, rest easy and collect the witnesses, for the victory was just as certain as if the conflict were already over. Hyde wiped away his tears and left.

At two in the afternoon referee Roop's Court opened, and Roop appeared throned

Frontier law office established just after the Oklahoma Land Rush. 1889. Collection University of Oklahoma Library, Norman.

among his sheriffs, the witnesses, and spectators, and wearing upon his face a solemnity so awe-inspiring that some of his fellow-conspirators had misgivings that maybe he had not comprehended, after all, that this was merely a joke. An unearthly stillness prevailed, for at the slightest noise the judge uttered sternly the command:

"Order in the Court!"

And the sheriffs promptly echoed it. Presently the General elbowed his way through the crowd of spectators, with his arms full of law-books, and on his ears fell an order from the judge which was the first respectful recognition of his high official dignity that had ever saluted them, and it trickled pleasantly through his whole system:

"Way for the United States Attorney!"

The witnesses were called—legislators, high government officers, ranchmen, miners, Indians, Chinamen, negroes. Three fourths of them were called by the defendant Morgan, but no matter, their testimony invariably went in favor of the plaintiff Hyde. Each new witness only added new testimony to the absurdity of a man's claiming to own another man's property because his farm had slid down on top of it. Then the Morgan lawyers made their speeches, and seemed to make singularly weak ones—they did really nothing to help the Morgan cause. And now the General, with exultation in his face, got up and made an impassioned effort; he pounded the table, he banged the law-books, he shouted, and roared, and howled, he quoted from everything and everybody, poitry, sarcasm, statistics, history, pathos, bathos, blasphemy, and wound up with a grand war-whoop for free speech, freedom of the press, free schools, the Glorious Bird of America and the principles of eternal justice! [Applause.]

When the General sat down, he did it with the conviction that if there was anything in good strong testimony, a great speech and believing and admiring countenances all around, Mr. Morgan's case was killed. Ex-Governor Roop leant his head upon his hand for some minutes, thinking, and the still audience waited for his decision. Then he got up and stood erect, with bended head, and thought again. Then he walked the floor with long, deliberate strides, his chin in his hand, and still the audience waited. At last he returned to his throne, seated himself, and began, impressively:

"Gentlemen, I feel the great responsibility that rests upon me this day. This is no ordinary case. On the contrary it is plain that it is the most solemn and awful that ever man was called upon to decide. Gentlemen, I have listened attentively to the evidence, and have perceived that the weight of it, the overwhelming weight of it, is in favor of the plaintiff Hyde. I have listened also to the remarks of counsel, with high interest—and especially will I commend the masterly and irrefutable logic of the distinguished gentleman who represents the plaintiff. But gentlemen, let us beware how we allow mere human testimony, human ingenuity in argument and human ideas of equity, to influence us at a moment so solemn as this. Gentlemen, it ill becomes us, worms as we are, to meddle with the decrees of Heaven. It is plain to me that Heaven, in its inscrutable wisdom, has seen fit to move this defendant's ranch for a purpose. We are but creatures, and we must submit. If Heaven has chosen to favor the defendant Morgan in this marked and wonderful manner; and if Heaven, dissatisfied with the position of the Morgan ranch upon the mountain side, has chosen to remove it to a position more eligible and more advantageous for its owner, it ill becomes us, insects as we are, to question the legality of the act or inquire into the reasons that prompted it. No—Heaven created the ranches and it is Heaven's prerogative to rearrange them, to experiment with them, to shift them around at its pleasure. It is for us to submit, without repining. I warn you that this thing which has happened is a thing with which the sacrilegious hands and brains and tongues of men must not meddle. Gentlemen, it is the verdict of this court that the plaintiff, Richard Hyde, has been deprived of his ranch by the visitation of God! And from this decision there is no appeal."

Buncombe seized his cargo of law-books and plunged out of the court-room frantic with indignation. He pronounced Roop to be a miraculous fool, an inspired idiot. In all good faith he returned at night and remonstrated with Roop upon his extravagant decision, and implored him to walk the floor and think for half an hour, and see if he could not figure out some sort of modification of the verdict. Roop yielded at last and got up to walk. He walked two hours and a half, and at last his face lit up happily and he told Buncombe it had occurred to him that the ranch underneath the new Morgan ranch still belonged to Hyde, that his title to the ground was just as good as it had ever been, and therefore he was of opinion that Hyde had a right to dig it out from under there and—

The General never waited to hear the end of it. He was always an impatient and irascible man, that way. At the end of two months the fact that he had been played upon with a joke had managed to bore itself, like another Hoosac Tunnel, through the solid adamant of his understanding.

Karen Berger Morello

FROM THE INVISIBLE BAR

"The First Women Lawyers"

After graduating in 1873 from the National University Law School in Washington, D.C., with much difficulty because of prejudice against women students, Lockwood built up a practice in the Capitol area. She handled cases in police and probate courts, filed divorce and support proceedings and tried to specialize in claims against the United States government. Her interest in this area of the law began with a visit from a client who wanted

---

In this selection from her history of women in law, Karen Berger Morello tells the story of Belva Ann Lockwood (1830–1917), who fought against sexual discrimination in the bar and eventually became the first woman lawyer to argue before the U.S. Supreme Court.

representation in a suit against the government for infringement of her husband's patent on the design of a torpedo boat. Lockwood was not admitted to the United States Court of Claims, but she filed her power of attorney and a certificate with the court and asked attorney A. A. Hosmer to move her admission. When the five-man court convened, Belva Lockwood's admission was the first matter on the calendar. After Hosmer completed his oral argument, Chief Judge Charles Drake looked Lockwood over, then said, "Mistress Lockwood, you are a woman." Silence. Then, "This cause will be continued for a week. The court will recess for ten minutes." Lockwood, who never forgot the incident, remarked, "For the first time in my life I began to realize that it was a crime to be a woman, but it was too late to put in a denial, so I pled guilty." The following week Lockwood returned to the Court of Claims, and on the advice of counsel she was accompanied by her husband, Ezekiel Lockwood. This time Judge Drake sternly noted, "Mistress Lockwood, you are a married woman." Sensing the implication that she was barred from practicing law because of the doctrine of *feme covert*, Lockwood answered, "Yes but may it please the court, I am here with the consent of my husband." Drake replied, "Madam, women do not speak in this courtroom. You will sit down." The case was continued for another week. After several more adjournments, attorney Charles W. Horner filed an application for admission on Lockwood's behalf. But Horner had no better results than Hosmer or Lockwood herself had had—Judge Charles Nott, in delivering the decision of the court, said, "The position which this court assumes is that under the laws and Constitution of the United States a court is without power to grant such an application and that a woman is without legal capacity to take the office of attorney. The request is denied." Lockwood was not prepared to give up entirely. Unable to represent her client in court she schemed to win the case another way. Lockwood prepared the legal briefs in the case, then trained her client, Mrs. von Cort, to read them in open court, since no judge could prevent a citizen from pleading her own case. But Lockwood knew this method of practicing law could not continue. Ahead of her were countless cases needing to be argued in court—among them *Webster Raines* v. *United States*.

Mr. and Mrs. Raines had disagreed about whether Belva Lockwood should represent them. Mrs. Raines was determined to hire Lockwood as their attorney, but her husband thought their case might be seriously jeopardized by the restrictions placed on Lockwood

David Dudley Field addressing the first women's law class at New York University, then called the University of the City of New York. April 10, 1891. New-York Historical Society.

COLORPLATE 86

A. A. WIGHE. *Trial by Jury*. 1849. Oil on canvas. 34¾ × 47¾" (88 × 121 cm).
Museum of Art, Rhode Island School of Design, Providence. Gift of Edith Jackson Green and Ellis Jackson.

COLORPLATE 87

DAVID GILMORE BLYTHE. *Trial Scene*. 1860–1863. Oil on canvas. 22 × 27″ (56 × 68.6 cm). Memorial Art Gallery, University of Rochester. Marion Stratton Gould Fund.

COLORPLATE 88

JOHN MULVANEY. *Preliminary Trial of a Horse Thief: Scene in a Western Justice's Court.* 1877. Chromolithograph. 21⅛ × 28½″ (53.7 × 72.4 cm). The Bancroft Library, University of California, Berkeley.

COLORPLATE 89

George Caleb Bingham.
The County Election.
1851–1852. Oil on canvas.
35 7/16 × 48 3/4″ (90 × 123.8 cm).
St. Louis Art Museum.
Museum purchase.

COLORPLATE 90

HORACE PIPPIN. *John Brown Going to His Hanging.* 1942. Oil on canvas. 24⅛ × 30¼" (61.2 × 76.8 cm). The Pennsylvania Academy of the Fine Arts, Philadelphia. John Lambert Fund. *An active abolitionist from 1849, John Brown (1800–1859) was prominent among antislavery forces in the Kansas Territory, achieving notice nationwide for his part in the Pottawatomie Massacre (1856) in reprisal for the murder of Free-Soil fighters by supporters of slavery. Seeking headquarters in Maryland and Virginia, he attacked the federal arsenal at Harpers Ferry, Virginia, on October 16, 1859. He was captured, convicted, and hanged for murder, but his deeds were to serve as a symbol of truth and courage for Union forces during the Civil War.*

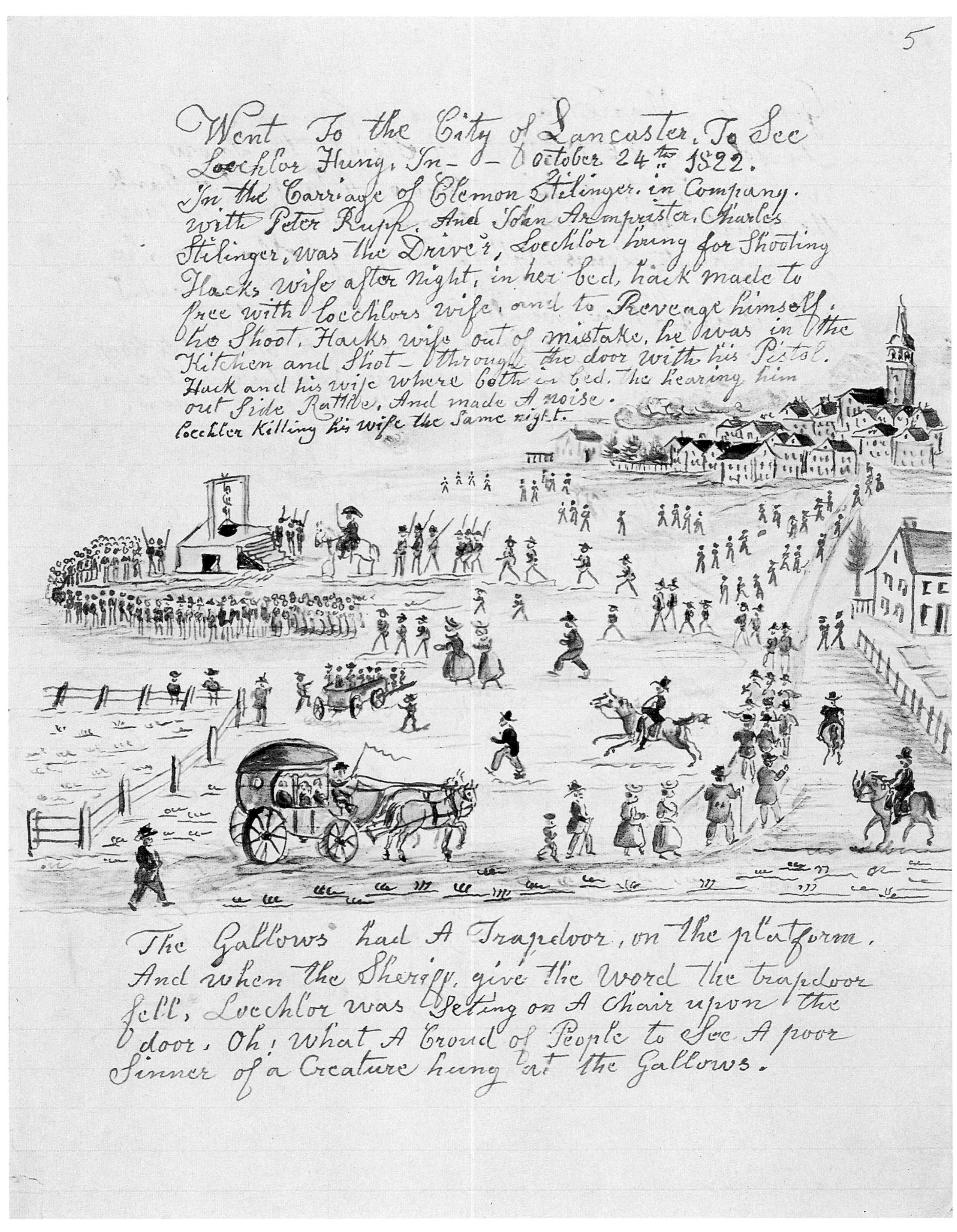

COLORPLATE 91

LEWIS MILLER. *"Went to the City of Lancaster, To See Loechlor Hung, In October 14th, 1822 . . . "*
c. 1840. Ink and watercolor on paper. Approximately 13⅛ × 10½" (33.2 × 26.7 cm).
The Historical Society of York County, York, Pennsylvania.

COLORPLATE 92

MARY FRANKLIN. *A Class at the University of Pennsylvania Law School.* 1879.
Oil on canvas. Framed, 42 × 30″ (106.7 × 76.2 cm). Collection of the Honorable Morris S. Arnold.

in the Court of Claims. Lockwood managed to convince them that it would be only a little while longer before she would be eligible for admission to the federal courts. The wording of the federal statute for admission to the United States Supreme Court was the basis for her assumption. It held that "any attorney in good standing before the highest court of any State or Territory for the space of three years shall be admitted to this court when presented by a member of this bar." With no restrictions in the statute regarding gender Lockwood was certain she would be able to take her clients' case all the way up to the Supreme Court. In the meantime she would try her luck again with the Court of Claims—this time with client Webster Raines close at her side.

When the *Raines* case was called, Judge Nott was amazed to see Lockwood daring to make another appearance before him. "Madam," he asked, "what are you doing in my courtroom?" But he apparently did not want to hear the answer because when Lockwood attempted to explain her reason for being there Nott cut her off: "Mrs. Lockwood, if you dare speak, I shall hold you in contempt." Webster Raines tried to intervene, even demanding that the judge let him proceed with the attorney of his choice, but Judge Nott ordered Raines to go out and get himself a "capable" lawyer.

Making no secret of her annoyance, Belva Lockwood conferred with her clients and realized they would have no other choice but to hire substitute counsel for the oral argument. After her replacement finished presenting his case before the court, Lockwood complained that "he said very badly in three days what I could have said well in one hour." Worse yet, they lost. The only optimistic note was that on appeal Belva Lockwood might possibly argue the case before the United States Supreme Court, since its admissions statute was not gender restrictive.

The opportunity arose in October 1876. Lockwood retained attorney Albert G. Riddle to move her admission to the Supreme Court and expected to have little difficulty in getting through the process. But as soon as Riddle stated his purpose, Chief Justice Morrison R. Waite announced that the matter of Mrs. Lockwood's admission would have to be taken under advisement. One week later the Chief Justice delivered the opinion of the Court:

> By the uniform practice of the court, from its organization to the present time, and by the fair construction of its rule, none but men are admitted to practice before it as attorneys and counselors. This is in accordance with immemorial usage in England, and the law and practice in all the states until within a recent period; and the court does not feel called upon to make a change, until such change is required by statute, or a more extended practice in the highest courts of the States. . . . As this court knows no English precedent for the admission of women to the bar, it declines to admit, unless there shall be a more extended public opinion or special legislation.

News of the Supreme Court's decision outraged Lockwood and supportive members of the bar. Myra Bradwell was the first to ridicule Chief Justice Waite in the pages of the *Chicago Legal News:*

> The opinion delivered by Waite, C.J., refusing Mrs. Lockwood a license to practice in the Supreme Court of the United States . . . was unsound, and contrary to the practice of the court in every case since its organization. The same reasoning which the Chief Justice used to exclude Mrs. Lockwood, would compel every attorney who appears in the Supreme Court of the United States to wear a gown and wig. Women have never been admitted to practice in Westminster Hall, and therefore Mrs. Lockwood is denied the right to practice in the United States Supreme Court. Counsellors have never been allowed to practice in Westminster Hall, and other superior courts in England, unless they wore gowns and wigs, and therefore it follows that they should not be allowed to practice in the Supreme Court of the United States without these necessary articles.

Belva Lockwood realized she would have to take the matter to Congress. She drafted a bill specifically providing for the admission of women to the federal courts and persuaded Representative Benjamin F. Butler to submit it to the House Judiciary Committee. The bill, and a second one she drafted, never got to the floor of the House. But finally, in April 1878, the House did pass Bill No. 1077—"An Act to Relive Certain Legal Disabilities of Women," which gave women attorneys access to the federal courts. Lockwood knew the battle would be even more difficult in the Senate and she publicly urged women to "get up a fight all along the line." She buttonholed senators in the corridors of the Capitol and cultivated the interest of the courthouse reporters who had always found Belva to be a lively source for articles. The favorable publicity she received in turn brought in more mail and more supporters.

Senators Aaron Sargent of California and Joseph McDonald of Indiana proved to be the greatest supporters of the bill in the Senate. In an impassioned argument, Sargent said:

> Mr. President, the best evidence that members of the legal profession have no jealousy against the admission to the Bar of women who have the proper learning, is shown by that document which I hold in my hand, signed by one hundred and fifty-five lawyers of the District of Columbia, embracing the most eminent men in the ranks of that profession [exhibiting a petition in support of the bill].
>
> Where is the propriety in opening our colleges, our higher institutions of learning, or any institutions of learning to women and then, when they have acquired in the race with men the cultivation for higher employments, to shut them out? There certainly is none.
>
> Some excellent lady lawyers in the United States are now practicing at the Bar, behaving themselves with propriety, acceptably received before courts and juries; and when they have conducted their cases to a successful issue, or to an unsuccessful one in any court below, why should the United States Courts, to which an appeal may be taken, and where their adversary of the male sex may follow the case up, why should they be debarred from appearing before those tribunals.

On February 7, 1879, the "Lockwood" bill passed the Senate; shortly thereafter President Rutherford B. Hayes signed it into law. The Washington *Star* said: "The credit for this victory belongs to Mrs. Belva Lockwood of this city, having been refused admission to the bar of the United States Supreme Court, appealed to Congress and by dint of hard work has finally succeeded in having her bill passed by both houses."

C. L. Sonnichsen

FROM ROY BEAN

Long before the coaches jarred to a halt in the shadow of the Langtry water tank, the greenhorns in the smoking car would have full information, some of it true, about the Law West of the Pecos, as Roy Bean called himself. With their curiosity already on edge they would take in the handful of adobe buildings which was Langtry, the little station and the big water tank, and finally the small frame shack twenty steps north of the tracks

---

Approaching the west Texas settlement that Roy Bean (1825?–1903) named after his glamorous mistress Lillie Langtry, railroad passengers bask in the legend of the notorious, self-appointed justice of the peace. This selection by Charles L. Sonnichsen (1901–) is taken from his standard biography of the wild west "judge" published in 1943.

Judge Roy Bean holding court in Langtry, Texas. 1900.

with a covered porch in front and signs plastered over it: THE JERSEY LILLY: JUDGE ROY BEAN NOTARY PUBLIC. LAW WEST OF THE PECOS.

Someone would say, "There he is!" And there he would be—a sturdy, gray-bearded figure with a Mexican sombrero on his head and a portly stomach mushrooming out over his belt, waiting on his porch for the swirl of business and excitement which always came at train time. You could see at a glance that he was as rough as a sand burr and tough as a boiled owl, but you realized also that he was a genuine character with plenty of salt in him.

If you came back more than once and really got to know the old man, you found that he was a curious mixture of qualities. First you noticed that he was almost innocent of book learning, that he was egotistical and opinionated, that he regarded cheating you as good clean fun, and that he drank too much and washed too little. Once you got used to these drawbacks, however, you found that you had to like and even admire him. He was really a tough old rooster and had been a godsend to the ranger force when in 1882 they got him his commission as justice of the peace to help clean up the railroad construction camps. At the same time he concealed under his horny hide a heart which was not without soft spots. Children and animals liked him, and that is supposed to prove something. Then too, he was often generous in his own high-handed, tyrannical way. The poor Mexicans in the neighborhood would not have known what to do without his benevolent bullying. Finally, he had a color and flavor, authentic and attractive, which made people take an interest in him and forget about his profanity, unscrupulousness, and dirt. . . .

They told about the time he held an inquest over a dead body on which he had found forty dollars and a pistol. He fined the corpse forty dollars for carrying concealed weapons. . . .

They told about his habit of divorcing couples he had married, though he had no legal right to do so, explaining that he only "aimed to rectify his errors"

★ ★ ★

For a while he lived the epic he imagined. He really was the Law in those parts for a few years. It was two hundred miles to the nearest justice court and naturally he had things his own way. Before long civilization and lawyers moved in on him, but by that time his saga was started and his position was assured. He became in the minds of other men a sort of Ulysses of West Texas—a man of craft and action combined—a figure of colorful peculiarities and great resourcefulness. His fame was no surprise to him, though it was to a great many other people, for he had been convinced all along that he was no ordinary citizen. He probably thought his recognition was, if anything, considerably overdue.

And so when the train pulled into Langtry, there he was on his porch. He always exposed himself at train time so people could see him. He was sure they would want to.

Oliver Wendell Holmes, Jr.

"The Path of the Law"

I wish, if I can, to lay down some first principles for the study of this body of dogma or systematized prediction which we call the law, for men who want to use it as the instrument of their business to enable them to prophesy in their turn, and, as bearing upon the study, I wish to point out an ideal which as yet our law has not attained.

The first thing for a business-like understanding of the matter is to understand its limits, and therefore I think it desirable at once to point out and dispel a confusion between morality and law, which sometimes rises to the height of conscious theory, and more often and indeed constantly is making trouble in detail without reaching the point of consciousness. You can see very plainly that a bad man has as much reason as a good one for wishing to avoid an encounter with the public force, and therefore you can see the practical importance of the distinction between morality and law. A man who cares nothing for an ethical rule which is believed and practised by his neighbors is likely nevertheless to care a good deal to avoid being made to pay money, and will want to keep out of jail if he can.

I take it for granted that no hearer of mine will misrepresent what I have to say as the language of cynicism. The law is the witness and external deposit of our moral life. Its history is the history of the moral development of the race. The practice of it, in spite of popular jests, tends to make good citizens and good men. When I emphasize the difference between law and morals I do so with reference to a single end, that of learning and understanding the law. For that purpose you must definitely master its specific marks, and it is for that that I ask you for the moment to imagine yourselves indifferent to other and greater things.

I do not say that there is not a wider point of view from which the distinction between law and morals becomes of secondary or no importance, as all mathematical distinctions vanish in presence of the infinite. But I do say that that distinction is of the first importance for the object which we are here to consider, a right study and mastery of the law as a business with well understood limits, a body of dogma enclosed within definite lines. I have just shown the practical reason for saying so. If you want to know the law and nothing else, you must look at it as a bad man, who cares only for the material consequences which such knowledge enables him to predict, not as a good one, who finds his reasons for conduct, whether inside the law or outside of it, in the vaguer sanctions of conscience. The theoretical importance of the distinction is no less, if you would reason on your subject aright. The law is full of phraseology drawn from morals, and by the mere force of language continually invites us to pass from one domain to the other without perceiving it, as we are sure to do unless we have the boundary constantly before our minds. The law talks about rights, and duties, and malice, and intent, and negligence, and so forth, and nothing is easier, or, I may say, more common in legal reasoning, than to take these words in their moral sense, at some stage of the argument, and so to drop into fallacy. For instance, when we speak of the rights of man in a moral sense, we mean to mark the limits of interference with individual freedom which we think are prescribed by conscience, or by our ideal, however reached. Yet it is certain that many laws have been enforced in the past, and it is likely that some are enforced now, which are condemned by the most enlightened opinion of the time, or which at all events pass the limit of interference as many consciences would draw it. Manifestly, therefore, nothing but confusion of thought can result from assuming that the rights of man in a moral sense

---

Oliver Wendell Holmes, Jr. (1841–1935), was appointed to the Supreme Court in 1902 by President Theodore Roosevelt, a position Holmes occupied until he was ninety-one. This excerpt comes from a talk given to students at Boston University Law School in 1897.

Oliver Wendell Holmes, Jr.
Justice of the U.S. Supreme Court. 1902–1932.

are equally rights in the sense of the Constitution and the law. No doubt simple and extreme cases can be put of imaginable laws which the statute-making power would not dare to enact, even in the absence of written constitutional prohibitions, because the community would rise in rebellion and fight, and this gives some plausibility to the proposition that the law, if not a part of morality, is limited by it. But this limit of power is not coextensive with any system of morals. For the most part it falls far within the lines of any such system, and in some cases may extend beyond them, for reasons drawn from the habits of a particular people at a particular time. I once heard the late Professor Agassiz say that a German population would rise if you added two cents to the price of a glass of beer. A statute in such a case would be empty words, not because it was wrong, but because it could not be enforced. No one will deny that wrong statutes can be and are enforced, and we should not all agree as to which were the wrong ones.

The confusion with which I am dealing besets confessedly legal conceptions. Take the fundamental question, What constitutes the law? You will find some text writers telling you that it is something different from what is decided by the courts of Massachusetts, or England, that it is a system of reason, that it is a deduction from principles of ethics or admitted axioms or what not, which may or may not coincide with the decisions. But if we take the view of our friend the bad man we shall find that he does not care two straws for the axioms or deductions, but that he does want to know what the Massachusetts or English courts are likely to do in fact. I am much of this kind. The prophecies of what the courts will do in fact, and nothing more pretentious, are what I mean by the law.

AMERICAN MODERNITY

FROM THE CONSTITUTION OF THE UNITED STATES

The 18th & 21st Amendments

AMENDMENT XVIII

SECTION 1. After one year from the ratification of this article the manufacture, sale, or transportation of intoxicating liquors within, the importation thereof into, or the exportation thereof from the United States and all territory subject to the jurisdiction thereof for beverage purposes is hereby prohibited.

SECTION 2. The Congress and the several States shall have concurrent power to enforce this article by appropriate legislation.

SECTION 3. This article shall be inoperative unless it shall have been ratified as an amendment to the Constitution by the legislatures of the several States as provided in the Constitution, within seven years from the date of the submission hereof to the States by the Congress.

★ ★ ★

AMENDMENT XXI

SECTION 1. The eighteenth article of amendment to the Constitution of the United States is hereby repealed.

SECTION 2. The transportation or importation into any State, Territory, or possession of the United States for delivery or use therein of intoxicating liquors, in violation of the laws thereof, is hereby prohibited.

SECTION 3. This article shall be inoperative unless it shall have been ratified as an amendment to the Constitution by conventions in the several States, as provided in the Constitution, within seven years from the date of the submission hereof to the States by the Congress.

The Prohibition Era, a product of the Temperance movement, began in 1919 with the ratification of the Eighteenth Amendment. By the mid-twenties the "Noble Experiment" was in trouble, due to public outrage at the rise of gangsterism and bootlegging. Repeal came in 1933 with the ratification of the Twenty-first Amendment.

Federal agents destroying barrels of beer during Prohibition. 1920s.

Clarence Darrow

FROM THE STORY OF MY LIFE

The Scopes Trial

I was in New York not long after the arrest of Mr. Scopes, and saw that Mr. Bryan had volunteered to go to Dayton to assist in the prosecution. At once I wanted to go. My object, and my only object, was to focus the attention of the country on the progamme of Mr. Bryan and the other fundamentalists in America. I knew that education was in danger from the source that has always hampered it—religious fanaticism. To me it was perfectly clear that the proceedings bore little semblance to a court case, but I realized that there was no limit to the mischief that might be accomplished unless the country was roused to the evil at hand. So I volunteered to go. With me went my friends, Dudley Field Malone and Arthur Garfield Hays. With Mr. Bryan volunteering on the one side, the matter soon attracted the interest of the entire country and the rest of the world.

Most of the newspapers treated the whole case as a farce instead of a tragedy, but they did give it no end of publicity. Not only was every paper of importance in America represented, but those of many foreign lands. Most of the local lawyers of Dayton were

---

In this excerpt from his autobiography, the great defense attorney Clarence Darrow (1857–1938) gives his version of the 1925 "Monkey Trial" of John T. Scopes, a high school teacher accused of teaching Darwinism. Darrow, who in more than fifty capital cases lost not one client to execution, took the Fundamentalist prosecuting attorney William Jennings Bryan (1860–1925) apart "like a dollar watch."

lined up on the side of the prosecution. We did have one local lawyer, but at the last minute he ran away from the case in fear and trepidation. The sentiment of the town and the State was more than he could face.

Mr. Bryan was the logical man to prosecute the case. He had not been inside a courtroom for forty years, but that made no difference, for he did not represent a real case; he represented religion, and in this he was the idol of all Morondom. His scientific attitude was epigrammatically stated in various speeches and interviews regarding what he did not know about science. He said that he was "not so much interested in the age of rocks as in the Rock of Ages." This left nothing more to be said by him to his credulous disciples who filled every hall and tent and crowded every grove when he appeared and defended The True Faith. A lecture advertisement by him on "The Prince of Peace" found men and boys clinging to the rafters when there were rafters, and to the limbs of trees when there were groves. Such a meeting in the countryside was an event. They were all there regardless of admission fees. As to science, his mind was an utter blank. He was willing to believe with Genesis that the earth was less than six thousand years old.

Mr. Bryan did not know that the monuments of Egypt, giving the genealogy of their kings and the dates of their reigns ran back more than seven thousand years. He closed his eyes to the ages between this day and the time of the primitive man. The endless centuries that rolled away while the lower animals fought and evolved and lived and perished ages before man arrived was a story of which he had never learned; neither did he know of the millions of ages when the earth sped in its path around the sun before it was fitted for any life, animal or vegetable. About all of this his mind was void. The solid rocks that were laid down millions of years ago meant not a thing to Mr. Bryan; their conflict with Genesis was settled with the sanctimonious sophomoric: "I am more interested in the Rock of Ages than in the age of rocks."

Mr. Bryan was like the traditional boy passing the graveyard at night—he was whistling to keep up his courage. His very attitude showed that he was frightened out of his wits lest, after all, the illusions of his life might be only dreams.

On the other hand, I had been reared by my father on books of science. Huxley's books had been household guests with us for years, and we had all of Darwin's as fast as they were published. Such books as Tyler's "Primitive Culture," Lysle's "Geology," Draper, Lecky, Winwood Reade, Buckle, Tyndall, and Spencer also were on my father's shelves, and later were on mine, and most of them I had read. They had long been my companions. For a lawyer, I was a fairly grounded scientist. Mr. Arthur G. Hays had also been educated in science and had an open and acute mind. I do not remember hearing Mr. Dudley F. Malone express an opinion as to whether he was convinced of the soundness of evolution. I presume he was never specially interested in the subject. He put his allegiance on a higher ground, as did we all. More than most men that one meets, Mr. Malone believes in freedom, in the right of every one to investigate for himself, and he resented the interference of the State in its effort to forbid or control the convictions and mental attitudes of men. Mr. John Neal had for years been a fighter for liberal causes, and must have been lonely indeed in these contests.

Associated with Mr. Bryan were his son, William, from Los Angeles (where he was assistant district attorney), the district attorney of that section of Tennessee, and four Dayton lawyers. When Mr. Bryan arrived in Dayton he was met by a throng of people. From the newspaper accounts one would judge the whole country was out to receive the defender of the faith. His reception proved that he was the ruler of "the Bible belt." The newspaper representatives flocked around him for crumbs of information, asking what he thought would be the outcome of the combat; and among other statements by him he said that this case was to be "a fight to the death."

The next morning I read Mr. Bryan's reply with some surprise. I had not realized that it was to be such a conflict. I arrived a day or two later. There was no torchlight parade to greet me as I stepped off the train. I did not miss it much, with the thermometer blazing away toward the hundred mark, where it remained nearly all the time that we were there. The sun did its best and worst to give us a hot time, if nothing else was had.

Still, there were some people at the depot to meet me; I was received most kindly and courteously, at that. As a matter of fact, all through the event down there people treated us with extreme consideration in many ways, in spite of the fact that they must have been shocked by my position in the case. The banker of the town went off to the foothills for a family treat in order that we should have a cottage to ourselves in the village, which was so crowded that it became practically impossible to get accommodations of any sort, although every imaginable preparation was made for taking care of the multitude expected from near and far to bask before the master, Mr. Bryan.

All the farm products and dairy supplies and other provisions had been contracted for by the hotel and the little restaurants and boarding houses and the lunch counter in Robinson's drug store, so that any one wanting a bottle of milk or pound of butter had to skirmish about for some one willing to spare that much, or, more likely, tell of some farmer out in the real country who might have some to sell if one had a way of going out there to see. Worst of all, ice was well-nigh unattainable, so that one sweltering Sunday night, when we returned from a week-end absence of so-called rest, it was enough to make one almost believe in miracle-making when we opened our icebox and found it stocked with a slab of ice, milk and cream and butter, and even a choice cantaloupe for Monday breakfast.

Our next-door neighbor, Mr. Wilbur, and all the others on our short street, were always doing such things for us. And one day, when a message came from the family up in the hills inquiring if we were comfortable or if they could do anything to make us more so, we felt that we had tasted and would ever after recognize that far-famed "true Southern hospitality."

Most of the lawyers employed by the State were courteous and kindly and we all got along exceedingly well. But especially General Ben MacKenzie and his son, whom we took to be stolid Scotchmen, became most agreeable and even lovable, so that a strong affection developed between us which I am sure will continue so long as we live. After all, men in all lands and at all times have been found human and loving outside their religious attitudes.

When the reporters came to me to forecast what we should undertake, or what result we expected, I said very little. I can always tell more about such matters when they are over with. It is more or less embarrassing to have to take back what one has stated, and one really cannot tell a reporter that he may lose his case.

As I loitered along, getting into my clothes that first morning, trying to imagine how the venture would begin and end in that warped company that I was about to meet, my eyes caught sight of things glistening on the walls in the sunshine streaming in, and lo and behold, if they weren't strangely tinselled framed mottoes with assurances that "The Lord will provide," and "Jesus loves you," and "Put your trust in Him." How could I doubt myself after that?

The large red-brick courthouse stood in the middle of a square, such as one sees in much larger towns; the walks radiated from the building to the four corners of the square and were shaded by trees that one did not need to be religious to call a godsend. At the top of the grand staircase we entered the largest courtroom that I have ever seen, all freshly painted in glazed finish the same color as the glaring sun pouring in from all sides. With a population said to be about one thousand and five hundred, Dayton surprised us with a courtroom designed to accommodate at least one thousand of its townpeople, besides all the dwellers of all the hills roundabout, who were allowed to stand solidly jammed into the aisles and against the walls. Any case that had to be tried in a courtroom was an event to them, it seemed, and provision had been made for vast audiences at such times. And this was one of those times. In a crescent outside the huge rail were ranged over one hundred magazine and newspaper representatives from the four winds and beyond, one felt; one man was from England, one was from Canada each sat with poised pencil and eagle eye the entire sweep of the curve as we filed in, ready to record the feature story of his life.

The judge was a quiet and affable man. He had been elected on a fluke, due to some

Clarence Darrow (left) and William Jennings Bryan at the Scopes Trial in Dayton, Tennessee. 1925.

political mixup. The judge called a special grand jury to indict John T. Scopes. This indicates how seriously that part of Tennessee viewed the heinous offense of teaching evolution, which they all pronounced as though the word began with double EE. The special grand jury was not legal, as the regular grand jury was to convene in a few weeks and the statute provided that a special grand jury could not be called excepting as a certain length of time intervened before the regular jury would assemble and be available.

But even though the statute forbade the calling of the special jury, the crime was so terrible that the case could not be delayed. Then, too, there were other towns in the State that wanted the case, and the judge meant that Dayton should have the honor of prosecuting the boy for teaching science, and he himself would have the glory of defending The Faith. I might also mention that the judge's term would soon expire, and he wanted to run again. Of course, I do not know that this had anything to do with his illegally calling the special grand jury to stop the spread of infidelity in the shortest possible time. And if John T. Scopes was found guilty, the highest penalty that could be inflicted upon him would be a one-hundred-dollar fine. Still, the treason against religion was reason enough for ignoring the law and resorting to a special session to bar the teaching of "EEvolution" in Tennessee.

Tennessee seemed to understand the significance of the battle. Especially did Dayton. Fences, bridges, buildings, streets were placarded with giant signs, and mammoth banners swung from tree to tree in the courtyard that could be easily read a block away summoning the community to *"Come to Jesus," "Prepare to meet thy Maker"*—and the slogan of all the section, greeting one at every turn, was *"Read your Bible daily."*

Certainly Tennessee can never be blamed if our souls were not saved that hot summer, in that torrid land that might have inspired one to beware of ever going to a hotter clime.

★ ★ ★

It was morning in Tennessee. And it was midsummer. Tennessee must be very close to the equator; or maybe the crust is very thin under this little sin-fearing section, or, where could such hellish heat come from?

The bailiff was calling the court to order, "Tennessee versus Scopes." The judge was sinking into his seat beneath a monster sign, saying, *"Read your Bible daily."* He had a palmleaf fan in one hand, and in the other the Bible and the statutes. As he laid these down on his desk I wondered why he thought he would need the statutes. To the end of the trial I did not know. Judge Raulston wriggled down into his high-backed chair and two tall policemen hopped forward close to his shoulder with Southern courtesy and big palm fans which they fluttered above and around his serious, shining brow. The policemen seemed to appreciate the arduous mental labor going on beneath the skull of the man under their wings.

Down below, at a long table, near the judge's bench, sat William Jennings Bryan, wearing as few clothes as possible. So few, indeed, that had he seen some girl so arrayed he would have considered her a bad sort, and straightway turned his head the other way. His shirt sleeves were rolled up as high as they would go, and his soft collar and shirt front were turned away from his neck and breast about as far as any one less modest would venture; not for the fray, but because of the weather. In his hand was the largest palmleaf fan that could be found, apparently, with which he fought off the heat waves—and flies.

Around Mr. Bryan sat several young men who were to be his field marshals in this great Waterloo of science. We were facing another big banner dangling from the ceiling over the chairs inside the bar of justice, awaiting the jury, to remind them also to *"Read your Bible daily."* And in other places in the courtroom were other specimens of this. It looked as though there might have been a discount for ordering a wholesale lot.

This important battle between Revealed Religion and Infidelity had been likened to the Crusaders under Richard the Lion-Hearted, instead of Waterloo. Anyhow, there sat Bryan, fanning himself, looking limp and martyr-like between assaults upon the flies that found a choice roosting-place on his bald, expansive dome and bare, hairy arms. He slapped away at them with the big fan, constantly and industriously. Somehow, he did not look like a hero. Or even a Commoner. He looked like a commonplace fly-catcher. It is this picture of Bryan that abides with me. Of course, hair, or the lack of it, has nothing to do with intellect, and much less learning; but then, the day was hot, and sticky, and one cannot look like a hero unless he dresses and poses for the part. And, even then, he should be engaged in something more heroic than swishing flies.

I did not use a fan myself. I had something else to do and think about. Feeling as I did, I would have had to work the fan so fast that it would have made me still hotter. All over the ceiling and walls, from chandeliers and side-brackets, and extra sockets, swung electric wires that were attached to electric fans. It looked as though they might have bought fans wholesale, too. But only the backs of these were turned toward us! All those fans were set to cool the fevered feelings of the judge, the jury, the prosecution and the different distinguished natives invited from day to day to sit alongside "His Honor." And all their friends, the flower of Dayton, and Mr. Bryan and his friends sat in social state as cool and comfortable as possible over in the shady section, opposite our sun-scorched side. As Southern gentlemen, they must have been sorry that there were not enough fans to go around, nor one wee socket left for "the defense."

The lawyers, ranged around Mr. Bryan like a human halo, looked very glum, as though contemplating the safety of their souls, while at our table, in spite of the temperature, were signs of light-heartedness and even frivolity. We must have looked as though we were doomed, so far as being eligible for heaven was concerned, and so were getting the most we could out of Tennessee.

I try never to take things too seriously; if I did, I would have been wiped out long ago. As to the Dayton case, from the beginning it seemed to be a joke. And I was satisfied that it would be only that if we could get the world to see it in its right light, which we did.

The courtroom was packed, and still the people crowded together in the hallways, on the staircases; and the yard, too, was filling up. Spectators had come from near and far. "Hot dog" booths and fruit peddlers and ice-cream venders and sandwich sellers had sprung into existence like mushrooms on every corner and everywhere between, mingling with the rest, ready to feed the throng. Evangelist tents were propped up at vantage points around the town square, where every night one not knowing what was going on would have thought hordes of howling dervishes were holding forth. In reality, they were crying out against the wickedness of Darwin and the rest of us, and advocating as substitutes cool meadows and melodious harps in KINGDOM COME. There was no reason why they should not be prohibitionists, for they were so elated and intoxicated by their religious jags that they needed no other stimulants. Then, too, they had become so immunized to common liquor through their brand of "White Mule" that it required something else to give them any "kick," and religion was doing the trick for some of the most hard-soaked, or sun-baked sinners.

When the courtroom was packed just short of bursting apart, it seemed, the judge ordered the doors closed over the sweltering audience, and with great solemnity and all the dignity possible announced that Brother Twitchell would invoke the Divine blessing. This was new to me. I had practiced law for more than forty years, and had never before heard God called in to referee a court trial. I had likewise been to prize fights and horse races, and these were not opened with prayer. After adjournment we went to the judge and told him that in a case of this nature, especially, we did not consider it fair or suitable to play up their side by opening court proceedings with prayer; it was not a form of church service; it was a trial in a court; and at best it was an unfair weapon to introduce, particularly as the case had a religious aspect.

The lawyers for the prosecution seemed shocked that such an objection and request should be presented. Prayer surely could do no harm. But, of course, it is easy for a lawyer to seem shocked.

Before the opening of the next session I arose and stated what had happened in the matter, pointed out the character of the case, and made my objection to the court opening the proceedings with prayer. The judge overruled the motion, of course. The people assembled looked as though a thunderbolt had stunned them, and the wrath of the Almighty might be hurled down upon the heads of the defense. None of them had ever heard of any one objecting to any occasion being opened or closed or interspersed with prayer. That there should be no dearth of preachers, the court had appointed a committee of church members to keep us supplied, so that there would be a new one at every session of the trial.

I made a complete and aggressive opening of the case. I did this for the reason that we never at any stage intended to make any arguments in the case. We knew that Mr. Bryan was there to make a closing speech about "The Prince of Peace" and the importance of "The Rock of Ages" above the "age of rocks" and that the closing address he meant should thrill the world was doubtless prepared for the press in manifold copies before he left Florida, and that it would be for the consumption and instruction of those who knew nothing about either "The Rock of Ages" or "the age of rocks." We knew that such of the assembled multitudes as had the capacity to understand would refuse to learn. By not making a closing argument on our side we could cut him out.

We realized that a jury drawn from Dayton, Tenn., would not permit a man to commit such a heinous crime as Scopes had been guilty of and allow him to go scot-free. However, there were questions to be argued concerning the meaning of the statute, and what power the legislature had to make the teaching of science a criminal offense.

Then, too, we expected to introduce evidence by experts as to the meaning of the word "evolution" and whether it was inconsistent with "religion" under correct definition of both words. We had assembled many of the best scientists of America to cover these subjects, and Mr. Bryan had given out that he would offer proof that science was in conflict with religion. We knew the names of some of his witnesses, but at the last moment Mr. Bryan's witnesses did not appear, as we feared they would not.

The State brought in a number of bright little boys who were pupils of the school taught by Mr. John T. Scopes. They told how Mr. Scopes had tried to poison their young minds and imperil their souls by telling them that life began in the sea from a single cell that gradually developed into the different structures that are now scattered over the earth. The boys said, on cross-examination, that they did not see how this had done them any harm, but Mr. Bryan and the judge knew better. When court adjourned for luncheon I overheard one of the small boys saying to another, "Don't you think Mr. Bryan is a little narrowminded?" Plainly, both of these boys had already been corrupted by Scopes. I am afraid their souls will be lost.

* * *

The judge had admitted one of our witnesses to give testimony as to the meaning of the word "evolution" and to describe the process of it as taught. This was Doctor Metcalf, of Oberlin College, a man whose attainments were everywhere recognized. Then I called Mr. W. J. Bryan as an expert on the meaning of the word "religion." At once every lawyer for the prosecution was on his feet objecting to the proceeding. The judge asked me if I considered it important. I reminded him that the statute was based on a conflict between evolution and religion, and that we were entitled to prove the meaning of the words so that the jury could determine whether there was any conflict. Mr. Bryan relieved the situation by saying that he was perfectly willing to take the stand, that he was ready to defend religion anywhere against any infidel. He said that he wanted to go on the stand on condition that I would go. I said that they could put me on at any time they wished and I would try to answer their questions. And of course this left the judge with nothing to decide.

* * *

When Mr. Bryan took the stand, I began by asking him concerning his qualifications to define religion, and especially fundamentalism, which was the State religion of Tennessee. In response to my questions he said that he had been a student of religion all his life, that he was familiar with a great deal of literature concerning Christianity and the Bible; that he had lectured on religious subjects at religious meetings and Chautauqua gatherings for years; that for a long time he had been conducting a Bible class at Miami on Sundays during the winter season, and that for a number of years he had written weekly syndicate letters for various publications extending over the country; that he had spoken on evolution in many college towns in the North and had been active in getting the Tennessee statute through the legislature and in urging similar statutes in various other States.

Then I proceeded with questions that brought out points illustrating the fundamentalists' ideas of the Bible and religion. These questions were practically the same that I had prepared and had published in a Chicago paper two years earlier. These questions were prepared because Mr. Bryan had submitted a list of questions through the press to the President of Wisconsin University, which appeared in the Chicago *Tribune* in July, 1923. My questions were presented in the same month, in reply to Mr. Bryan's. Needless to say, when I ventured those questions two years before I got no answer. The *Tribune* had him interviewed at Winona Lake, Ind., where he was attending a religious convention, and he replied that he had not read my questions; that Mr. Darrow was an agnostic, and that he had no quarrel with agnostics, that his controversy was with men who pretended to be Christians but were not Christians. Even had he read the questions propounded two years before he would have been compelled to choose between his crude beliefs and the common intelligence of modern times.

Now Bryan twisted and dodged and floundered, to the disgust of the thinking element, and even his own people. That night an amount of copy was sent out that the reporters claimed was unprecedented in court trials. My questions and Bryan's answers were printed in full, and the story seems to have reached the whole world.

When court adjourned it became evident that the audience had been thinking, and perhaps felt that they had heard something worth while. Much to my surprise, the great gathering began to surge toward me. They seemed to have changed sides in a single afternoon. A friendly crowd followed me toward my home. Mr. Bryan left the grounds practically alone. The people seemed to feel that he had failed and deserted his cause and his followers when he admitted that the first six days might have been periods of millions of ages long. Mr. Bryan had made himself ridiculous and had contradicted his own faith. I was truly sorry for Mr. Bryan. But I consoled myself by thinking of the years through which he had busied himself tormenting intelligent professors with impudent questions about their faith, and seeking to arouse the ignoramuses and bigots to drive them out of their positions. It is a terrible transgression to intimidate and awe teachers with fear of want.

The next morning I reached court prepared to continue the examination all that day. The judge convened court down in the yard, and another preacher asked the blessing and guidance of the Almighty. After allowing time for taking pictures, the judge arose, rested one hand on the statutes and the other on the Oxford Bible, and said that he had been thinking over the proceedings of the day before AND—in spite of Mr. Bryan's willingness again to take the stand—he believed that the testimony was not relevant, and he had decided to refuse to permit any further examination of Mr. Bryan and should strike the whole of his testimony from the record. Mr. Bryan and his associates forgot to look surprised. It needed no lawyer to grasp that the attorneys for the prosecution could see the effect Mr. Bryan's answers were having on their case and the public in general, and had concluded that something must be done; so it was arranged that the judge should be there in the morning to relieve them of their distress in court. The ruling of the court was by that time extended to forbid the testimony of our scientists as to the meaning of evolution.

The court held that the jury had the statute before them and had heard the testimony of the witnesses proving that Scopes had told his pupils that life began in the sea and had gradually evolved to the various forms of life, including man, that now live upon the earth. The State had offered in evidence the first and second chapters of Genesis, and the jury could judge whether these were in conflict with the teaching of Scopes.

We all agreed that the ruling of the court had made it impossible to introduce any evidence, and useless to make any arguments. The attorneys for Mr. Scopes were satisfied that what we had undertaken, the awakening of the country to what was going on, had succeeded beyond our fondest hopes. Every one had been informed that a body of men and women were seeking to make the schools the servants of the church, and to place bigotry and ignorance on the throne. It was some satisfaction to know that in this organization were very few scholars or men of intelligence, and that the great mass of their following was mostly the illiterate.

We knew that it was hopeless to fight again for a verdict in Tennessee so long as the State remained in its present stage of civilization. All that was left was to take the case to the Supreme Court of Tennessee, and, in the event of defeat, to carry it to the Supreme Court of the United States, if the Fourteenth Amendment was broad enough to give the Federal Court jurisdiction.

The State opened the case with a short address, whereupon we waived our argument and submitted it to the jury. This made it impossible for Mr. Bryan to deliver the speech already prepared so long in advance. This was really a pity, because of all the copies thus withheld from the press. In a short time the jury reported a verdict which was delivered by the foreman, who was by all odds the best looking and most carefully dressed of any member of the twelve, or, for that matter, of any one else in the room. The verdict of course found Scopes "Guilty."

Felix Frankfurter

"Sacco and Vanzetti"

Perhaps the "rapier" way to put what is essential to what you call the "drama of Sacco-Vanzetti" was expressed in a remark made to me by John F. Moors about "two wops." Moors was a Yankee of Yankees, a Bostonian of Bostonians, an intimate, close personal friend; indeed, a Harvard classmate of President Lowell and a member of the Harvard Corporation. His friendship with Lowell survived without strain despite Moors's non-conformist attitude, and indeed he fought hard for the cause of Sacco-Vanzetti. But he said to me after it was all over—this at once shows his breadth and his parochialism, his worthy parochialism—"It was characteristic of Harvard and in a way to the glory of Harvard that two Harvard men were the leaders of the opposing forces in the Sacco-Vanzetti affair. Here was A. Lawrence Lowell, the president of the school, and here was Professor Frankfurter of the Harvard Law School, who were the spearheads of those who expressed conflicting views."

That he should have derived satisfaction from the characteristic broadmindedness of Harvard's non-regimentation of thought illustrates his deep devotion to the law school, but in the course of that talk he said about his friend, Lawrence Lowell, this: "Lawrence Lowell was incapable of seeing that two wops could be right and the Yankee judiciary could be wrong."

That posed a dilemma for Lowell which his mind couldn't overreach, clear and hurdle with ease. His crowd, the Yankees, were right, and the alien immigrants were what they were—pacifists and draft dodgers. He was incapable of doing what men have done, namely, say their crowd was wrong. You have to transcend the warm feeling of familiarity and reject that warm feeling in a spontaneous loyalty that transcends to greater loyalties, abstract virtues, truth and justice. That remark of Moors's for me goes to the root of the difficulty. Just as it was true of Lowell, it was true of many, many people, of lawyers who would suppress their beliefs that maybe something went awry, who would suppress their realization that no matter how disciplined or sterilized, as it were, their biases are through the habit of discipline, nevertheless, judges and courts may go wrong. I wrote in my book on the Sacco-Vanzetti case that, "Perfection may not be demanded of law, but the capacity to correct errors of inevitable frailty is the mark of a civilized legal mechanism."

Now there were any number of lawyers for whom the issue was not should justice be done, but should we weaken the whole structure, namely, respect for our courts. It was the realization that Lowell, a more civilized partisan than Judge Webster Thayer, couldn't transcend his belief in his crowd and entertain the belief that two Italian immigrants might be right, the realization that it was those forces and not merely individuals which saved me from ever seeing the affair in terms of devils.

A very important factor, and one that gnaws at my curiosity all the time, is the fact that men who know do not speak out. Any number of people privately were convinced all was not well, lawyers particularly. A dozen lawyers I can think of who had doubts would have added to the strength of those who did take action. There were a good many people who did take action. Moors was one of the fellows who went up to the governor and got the governor to appoint the Lowell Committee. Then, of course, the simple-

---

In this talk recorded in the 1950s by Columbia University's Dr. Harlan B. Phillips, Supreme Court justice Felix Frankfurter (1882–1965) recalls the case of Nicola Sacco and Bartolomeo Vanzetti, Italian anarchists convicted in 1921 of murder and robbery. After worldwide protests that the two had been falsely convicted because of their radical beliefs, a state-appointed committee including Harvard president A. Lawrence Lowell (1856–1943) reviewed the case; they found the trial fair. Sacco and Vanzetti were executed in 1927.

Sacco and Vanzetti handcuffed together, after five years in prison. 1926.

minded, ingenuous people who don't understand thought that everything was going to be hunkey-dory because the president of Harvard University was appointed. When the Lowell Report came out—it was so vulnerable in so many respects—they didn't say it was a report by Lawrence Lowell. Although it was well known that it was written by him, they did say that it was a report by the highly esteemed president of Harvard University. I remember saying to a dear friend of mine, "Don't talk to me about this report as the report of the president of Harvard University! You must go from the report to Mr. Lowell, not from Mr. Lowell to the report. You must deal with this report as though it was an anonymous report written on parchment, on papyrus, which was discovered way back in some catacomb, and some archeologist who was able to decipher it said, 'This is a report on the conviction of two men. I can't figure out their names—something like Sacco and Vanzetti. This is two thousand-odd years ago, and I'm happy to report that buried with it is the six thousand pages of minutes, so that we can check what was said in this report about these two men against the permanent and controlling facts—the stenographic minutes.'

"You are not thus led to the plausibility of this report by the author of the report, and, if the report is revealed as defective by the minutes of the proceeding, then you don't say that the report must be right because the president of Harvard University wrote it, but what kind of a man was the president of Harvard University to write such a report?"

It is very difficult for people to question authority and very difficult to get people to read documents. I remember being furious, really furious, with a friend of mine, a really intelligent woman, a strong supporter, deeply devoted to the cause of Sacco-Vanzetti. I

COLORPLATE 93

GEORGE CALEB BINGHAM. *The Puzzled Witness*. 1874. Oil on canvas. 23 × 28″ (58.4 × 71.1 cm). Kennedy Galleries, Inc., New York.

COLORPLATE 94

TOMPKINS HARRISON MATTESON. *Justice's Court in the Backwoods.* 1942. Oil on canvas. 31¾ × 44″ (80.6 × 112 cm). New York State Historical Society, Cooperstown.

COLORPLATE 95

GUY PÈNE DU BOIS. *Filibuster.* 1920. Oil on canvas. 20 × 16″ (50.3 × 40.6 cm).
The *Forbes* Magazine Collection, New York.

COLORPLATE 96

THOMAS HART BENTON. *Trial by Jury*. 1964. Oil on canvas. 30 × 40″ (76 × 101.7 cm). The Nelson-Atkins Museum of Art, Kansas City, Missouri. Bequest of the artist.

COLORPLATE 97

NORMAN ROCKWELL. *Marriage License*. 1955. Oil on canvas. 45½ × 42½″ (115.6 × 108 cm). The Norman Rockwell Museum at Stockbridge, Massachusetts. Printed by permission of the Estate of Norman Rockwell. Copyright © 1955 Estate of Norman Rockwell.

COLORPLATE 98

NORMAN ROCKWELL. *The Law Student (Young Lawyer)*. For *Saturday Evening Post* cover, February 19, 1927. Oil on canvas. 36 × 27½" (91.4 × 70 cm). The Norman Rockwell Museum at Stockbridge, Massachusetts. Printed by permission of the Estate of Norman Rockwell. Copyright © 1927 Estate of Norman Rockwell.

COLORPLATE 99

NORMAN ROCKWELL. *The Holdout (The Jury)*. Detail of *Saturday Evening Post* cover, February 14, 1959. Original artwork's whereabouts unknown. Printed by permission of the Estate of Norman Rockwell. Copyright © 1959 Estate of Norman Rockwell.

was furious when I heard that at a private party—of course, the Sacco-Vanzetti case rent families, friendships and associations—people were discussing the case at dinner, and instead of debating with those who asked her questions she answered their questions by saying, "I don't know anything about it. It's enough for me that Felix Frankfurter has taken the position he has."

She hadn't taken the trouble to spend two hours with the little book I'd written in order to qualify herself to talk about the case and to answer the questions of doubters, the skeptics, who also hadn't read the book, who also hadn't familiarized themselves with the facts, but went on generalities about the reliability of Lowell's report. This was true enough in the overwhelming number of cases so that this was a combat in the dark by people who on either side eschewed the responsibility to find out what they were talking about. John Morley says somewhere—I think it's in his important little book *On Compromise*—that the most important thing in a man's life is to say I believe this, or I believe that, on the assumption that when he says that, he has put behind that affirmation the necessary thought and inquiry. Here this woman—I was perfectly outraged—shot off her mouth all over the place, but she couldn't take one evening off to read my little book to find out what the facts were so that she could at least meet people who were honest and groping, if not the ignorant, the set, and the hopeless.

The Sacco-Vanzetti affair has almost every important, really sizable issue that cuts deeply into the feelings and judgments and conduct of the community, implicates factors that transcend the immediate individuals who, in the main, are instruments of forces that affect many, many beyond the immediate actors in the affair. It involves problems that still gnaw at my curiosity. Few questions bother me more from time to time than what is it that makes people cowardly, makes people timid and afraid to say publicly what they say privately. By "people" I mean not those who are economically dependent and who can't call their souls their own because they have to feed their wives and their children, but those who are economically independent, those who have position, those who by speaking out publicly would turn on the currents of reason and check the currents of unreason. What is it that makes so many men timid creatures?

I can give myself some answers. People want to avoid unpleasantness. Life is hard enough even if you've got a bank account. Life is hard enough as it is, Why take on something extra? "Why go out on a limb?" as the phrase runs. "Why stick your neck out?" that other lovable invitation to do nothing! Even people who are economically independent are not socially independent. They may have money in the bank, but that isn't all they want. They want to be asked to dinners at certain houses. They want to run for office. They want to become Grand Masters of the Masonic Order. They want to get a degree from some college or university. They don't want to make trouble for their wives. They have silly wives with social interests or ambitions. Or if they get into public controversies their boy in prep school will be a marked character, "Oh, it's your Dad who says this." There are a thousand and one considerations beyond the immediate enslavement of economic dependence which I know make people hesitant, timid, cowardly, with the result however that those who have no scruples, who are ruthless, who don't give a damn, influence gradually wider and wider circles, and you get Hitler movements in Germany, Huey Long ascendency in Louisiana, McCarthyism cowing most of the Senators of the United States at least to the extent that they didn't speak out, etcetera, etcetera.

So the affair like Sacco-Vanzetti for me was a manifestation of what one might call the human situation. The upshot is that I didn't think that it should be minimized to the trivialities of a few individuals. Oh, sure. If another judge had presided, or if the governor of Massachusetts at that time had been a less crude, illiterate, self-confident, purse-proud creature than was Alvin Fuller, other things might have happened. . . . But these individual effects derived from the fact that there are causes at work on which they can operate.

Hinsdale County Court House, Lake City, Colorado. 1877. Architect: Jonathan Ogden. Photograph by William Clift. Seagram County Court House Archives Collection. © Library of Congress, Washington, D.C.

Ralls County Court House, New London, Missouri. c. 1857–1859. Architect: Henry C. Wellman. Photograph by Harold Allen. Seagram County Court House Archives Collection. © Library of Congress, Washington, D.C.

Starke County Court House, Knox, Indiana. 1897–1898. Architects: Wing and Mahurin. Photograph by Bob Thrall. Seagram County Court House Archives Collection. © Library of Congress, Washington, D.C.

Side elevation, Davis County Court House, Bloomfield, Iowa. 1877–1878. Architects: Thomas J. Tolan and Son. Photograph by Bob Thrall. Seagram County Court House Archives Collection. © Library of Congress, Washington, D.C.

Knott County Court House, Hindman, Kentucky. c. 1930. Architect unknown. Photograph by Jim Dow. Seagram County Court House Archives Collection. © Library of Congress, Washington, D.C.

John M. Woolsey

UNITED STATES v. ONE BOOK CALLED *ULYSSES*

. . . I have read *Ulysses* once in its entirety and I have read those passages of which the Government particularly complains several times. In fact, for many weeks, my spare time has been devoted to the consideration of the decision which my duty would require me to make in this matter.

Ulysses is not an easy book to read or to understand. But there has been much written about it, and in order properly to approach the consideration of it it is advisable to read

---

In his 1933 landmark ruling lifting the ban on James Joyce's Ulysses *(published in Paris in 1922), U.S. District Court Judge Woolsey provided a long-awaited practical definition of obscenity, delivered a "body-blow for the censors," and established himself as a master of juridical prose on the level of Holmes.*

a number of other books which have now become its satellites. The study of *Ulysses* is, therefore, a heavy task.

. . . The reputation of *Ulysses* in the literary world, however, warranted my taking such time as was necessary to enable me to satisfy myself as to the intent with which the book was written, for, of course, in any case where a book is claimed to be obscene it must first be determined, whether the intent with which it was written was what is called, according to the usual phrase, pornographic,—that is, written for the purpose of exploiting obscenity.

If the conclusion is that the book is pornographic that is the end of the inquiry and forfeiture must follow.

But in *Ulysses*, in spite of its unusual frankness, I do not detect anywhere the leer of the sensualist. I hold, therefore, that it is not pornographic.

. . . In writing *Ulysses*, Joyce sought to make a serious experiment in a new, if not wholly novel, literary genre. He takes persons of the lower middle class living in Dublin in 1904 and seeks not only to describe what they did on a certain day early in June of that year as they went about the City bent on their usual occupations, but also to tell what many of them thought about the while.

Joyce has attempted—it seems to me, with astonishing success—to show how the screen of consciousness with its ever-shifting kaleidoscopic impressions carries, as it were on a plastic palimpsest, not only what is in the focus of each man's observation of the actual things about him, but also in a penumbral zone residua of past impressions, some recent and some drawn up by association from the domain of the subsconscious. He shows how each of these impressions affects the life and behavior of the character which he is describing.

What he seeks to get is not unlike the results of a double or, if that is possible, a multiple exposure on a cinema film which would give a clear foreground with a background visible but somewhat blurred and out of focus in varying degrees.

To convey by words an effect which obviously lends itself more appropriately to a graphic technique, accounts, it seems to me, for much of the obscurity which meets a reader of *Ulysses*. And it also explains another aspect of the book, which I have further to consider, namely, Joyce's sincerity and his honest effort to show exactly how the minds of his characters operate.

If Joyce did not attempt to be honest in developing the technique which he has adopted in *Ulysses* the result would be psychologically misleading and thus unfaithful to his chosen technique. Such an attitude would be artistically inexcusable.

It is because Joyce has been loyal to his technique and has not funked its necessary implications, but has honestly attempted to tell fully what his characters think about, that he has been the subject of so many attacks and that his purpose has been so often misunderstood and misrepresented. For his attempt sincerely and honestly to realize his objective has required him incidentally to use certain words which are generally considered dirty words and has led at times to what many think is a too poignant preoccupation with sex in the thoughts of his characters.

The words which are criticized as dirty are old Saxon words known to almost all men and, I venture, to many women, and are such words as would be naturally and habitually used, I believe, by the types of folk whose life, physical and mental, Joyce is seeking to describe. In respect of the recurrent emergence of the theme of sex in the minds of his characters, it must always be remembered that his locale was Celtic and his season Spring.

Whether or not one enjoys such a technique as Joyce uses is a matter of taste on which disagreement or argument is futile, but to subject that technique to the standards of some other technique seems to me be little short of absurd.

Accordingly, I hold that *Ulysses* is a sincere and honest book and I think that the criticisms of it are entirely disposed of by its rationale.

. . . Furthermore, *Ulysses* is an amazing *tour de force* when one considers the success which has been in the main achieved with such a difficult objective as Joyce set for himself. As I have stated, "Ulysses" is not an easy book to read. It is brilliant and dull, intelligible and obscure by turns. In many places it seems to me to be disgusting, but although it contains, as I have mentioned above, many words usually considered dirty, I have not found anything that I consider to be dirt for dirt's sake. Each word of the book contributes like a bit of mosaic to the detail of the picture which Joyce is seeking to construct for his readers.

If one does not wish to associate with such folk as Joyce describes, that is one's own choice. In order to avoid indirect contact with them one may not wish to read *Ulysses*; that is quite understandable. But when such a real artist in words, as Joyce undoubtedly is, seeks to draw a true picture of the lower middle class in a European city, ought it to be impossible for the American public legally to see that picture?

To answer this question it is not sufficient merely to find, as I have found above, that Joyce did not write *Ulysses* with what is commonly called pornographic intent, I must endeavor to apply a more objective standard to his book in order to determine its effect in the result, irrespective of the intent with which it was written.

. . . The statute under which the libel is filed only denounces, in so far as we are here concerned, the importation into the United States from any foreign country of "any obscene book". Section 305 of the Tariff Act of 1930, Title 19 United States Code, Section 1305. It does not marshal against books the spectrum of condemnatory adjectives found, commonly, in laws dealing with matters of this kind. I am, therefore, only required to determine whether *Ulysses* is obscene within the legal definition of that word.

The meaning of the word "obscene" as legally defined by the Courts is: tending to stir the sex impulses or to lead to sexually impure and lustful thoughts. . . .

Whether a particular book would tend to excite such impulses and thoughts must be tested by the Court's opinion as to its effect on a person with average sex instincts—what the French would call *l'homme moyen sensuel*—who plays, in this branch of legal inquiry, the same role of hypothetical reagent as does the "reasonable man" in the law of torts and "the man learned in the art" on questions of invention in patent law.

The risk involved in the use of such a reagent arises from the inherent tendency of the trier of facts, however fair he may intend to be, to make his reagent too much subservient to his own idiosyncrasies. Here, I have attempted to avoid this, if possible, and to make my reagent herein more objective than he might otherwise be, by adopting the following course:

After I had made my decision in regard to the aspect of *Ulysses*, now under consideration, I checked my impressions with two friends of mine who in my opinion answered to the above stated requirement for my reagent.

These literary assessors—as I might properly describe them—were called on separately, and neither knew that I was consulting the other. They are men whose opinion on literature and on life I value most highly. They had both read *Ulysses*, and, of course, were wholly unconnected with this cause.

Without letting either of my assessors know what my decision was, I gave to each of them the legal definition of obscene and asked each whether in his opinion *Ulysses* was obscene within that definition.

I was interested to find that they both agreed with my opinion: that reading "Ulysses" in its entirety, as a book must be read on such a test as this, did not tend to excite sexual impulses or lustful thoughts but that its net effect on them was only that of a somewhat tragic and very powerful commentary on the inner lives of men and women.

It is only with the normal person that the law is concerned. Such a test as I have described, therefore, is the only proper test of obscenity in the case of a book like *Ulysses* which is a sincere and serious attempt to devise a new literary method for the observation and description of mankind.

I am quite aware that owing to some of its scenes *Ulysses* is a rather strong draught to ask some sensitive, though normal, persons to take. But my considered opinion, after long reflection, is that whilst in many places the effect of *Ulysses* on the reader undoubtedly is somewhat emetic, nowhere does it tend to be an aphrodisiac.

Ulysses may, therefore, be admitted into the United States.

Roscoe Pound

"What Constitutes a Good Legal Education"

. . . I should put as the content of a good legal education:

(1) A solid all round cultural training, with a grasp of significant information which such a training involves, but much more with the broadening and deepening of experience and ability to appraise information to which it leads.

(2) A grasp at the ends and technique of the social sciences—this only, for beyond that, what has been taught in their name has been short-lived.

(3) A grasp of the history and system of the common law, of the outline and ends of the legal order, of the theory and ends of the judicial and administrative processes, and of the history, organization, and standards of the legal profession.

(4) A thorough grasp of the organization and content of the authoritative legal materials of the time and place and of the technique of developing and applying them.

If one has these, he has whereon he can build to the exigencies of the many demands of different types of professional activity and of the public need of enlightened judges and wise lawmakers, of law reformers and law teachers, and of legal scholars.

For some years the noted legal educator and jurist Roscoe Pound (1870–1964) divided his career in two; as a botanist, he discovered the rare lichen Roscopoundia. *After 1907, he concentrated on law alone, serving as dean of Harvard Law School from 1916 to 1936. This excerpt is derived from an address he gave to the American Bar Association in 1933.*

George S. Kaufman and Morrie Ryskind

FROM A NIGHT AT THE OPERA

An Opera Star's Contract

Driftwood: Now—uh—here are the contracts. You just put his name at the top and—uh— and you sign at the bottom. There's no need of you reading that because these are duplicates.

Forelo: Yes, duplicates. Duplicates, eh?

Driftwood: I say, they're—they're duplicates.

Forelo: Oh, sure, it's a duplicate. Certainly.

Driftwood: Don't you know what duplicates are?

Forelo: Sure. Those five kids up in Canada.

In this classic take on entertainment law from the Marx Brothers' 1935 movie, Forelo (Chico), the manager of a tenor, and Driftwood (Groucho), who would like to sign the tenor to the New York Opera Company, attempt to seal the deal with a simple contract.

Driftwood: Well, I wouldn't know about that. I haven't been in Canada in years. Well, go ahead and read it.

Forelo: What does it say?

Driftwood: Well, go on and read it.

Forelo: All right—you read it.

Driftwood: All right. I'll read it to you. Can you hear?

Forelo: I haven't heard anything yet. Did you say anything?

Driftwood: Well, I haven't said anything worth hearing.

Forelo: Well, that's why I didn't hear anything.

Driftwood: Well, that's why I didn't say anything.

Forelo: Can you read?

Driftwood: I can read but I can't see it. I don't seem . . . to have it in focus here. If my arms were a little longer, I could read it. You haven't got a baboon in your pocket have you? Here—here—here we are. Now, I've got it. Now, pay particular attention to this first clause because it's most important. Says the—uh—the party of the first part shall be known in this contract as the party of the first part. How do you like that? That's pretty neat, eh?

Forelo: No, that's no good.

Driftwood: What's the matter with it?

Forelo: I don't know. Let's hear it again.

Driftwood: Says the—uh—the party of the first part should be known in this contract as the party of the first part.

Harpo (left) and Groucho in the contract scene from the Marx Brothers' *A Night at the Opera.* 1935.

Forelo: That sounds a little better this time.

Driftwood: Well, it grows on you. Would you like to hear it once more?

Forelo: Uh—just the first part.

Driftwood: What do you mean? The—the party of the first part?

Forelo: No, the first part of the party of the first part.

Driftwood: All right. It says the—uh—the first part of the party of the first part, should be known in this contract as the first part of the party of the first part, should be known in this contract—look. Why should we quarrel about a thing like this? We'll take it right out, eh?

Forelo: Yeah. It's too long anyhow. Now, what have we got left?

Driftwood: Well, I've got about a foot and a half. Now, it says—uh—the party of the second part shall be known in this contract as the party of the second part.

Forelo: Well, I don't know about that.

Driftwood: Now, what's the matter?

Forelo: I no like the second party either.

Driftwood: Well, you should have come to the first party. We didn't get home till around four in the morning. I was blind for three days.

Forelo: Hey, look! Why can't the first part of the second party be the second part of the first party? Then you've got something.

Driftwood: Well, look—uh—rather than go through all that again, what do you say?

Forelo: Fine.

Driftwood: Now—uh—now, I've got something here you're bound to like. You'll be crazy about it.

Forelo: No, I don't like it.

Driftwood: You don't like what?

Forelo: Whatever it is—I don't like it.

Driftwood: Well, don't let's break up an old friendship over a thing like that. Ready?

Forelo: Okay. Now, the next part, I don't think you're going to like.

Driftwood: Well, your word's good enough for me. Now, then, is my word good enough for you?

Forelo: I should say not.

Driftwood: Well, that takes out two more clauses. Now the party of the eighth part—

Forelo: No.

Driftwood: No?

Forelo: No. That's no good. No.

Driftwood: The party of the ninth—

Forelo: No, that's no good too. Hey, how is it my contract is skinnier than yours?

Driftwood: Well, I don't know. You must have been out on a tear last night. But, anyhow, we're all set now, aren't we? Now, just—uh—just you put your name right down there and then the deal is—is—uh—legal.

Forelo: I forgot to tell you. I can't write.

Driftwood: Well, that's all right. There's no ink in the pen anyhow. But, listen, it's a contract, isn't it?

Forelo: Oh, sure.

Driftwood: You've got a contract?

Forelo: You bet—

Driftwood: No matter how small it is.

Forelo: Hey, wait—wait! What does this say here? This thing here?

Driftwood: Oh, that? Oh, that's the usual clause. That's in every contract. That just says—uh—it says—uh—if any of the parties participating in this contract is shown not to be in their right mind, the entire agreement is automatically nullified.

Forelo: Well, I don't know.

Driftwood: It's all right. That's—that's in every contract. That's—that's what they call a sanity clause.

Forelo: Oh, no. You can't fool me. There ain't no Sanity Clause!

Driftwood: Well, you win the white . . . carnation. Sanity Claus.

Benjamin N. Cardozo

FROM THE NATURE OF THE JUDICIAL PROCESS

I have spoken of the forces of which judges avowedly avail to shape the form and content of their judgments. Even these forces are seldom fully in consciousness. They lie so near the surface, however, that their existence and influence are not likely to be disclaimed. But the subject is not exhausted with the recognition of their power. Deep below consciousness are other forces, the likes and the dislikes, the predilections and the prejudices, the complex of instincts and emotions and habits and convictions, which make the man, whether he be litigant or judge. I wish I might have found the time and opportunity to pursue this subject farther. I shall be able, as it is, to do little more than remind you of its existence. There has been a certain lack of candor in much of the discussion of the theme, or rather perhaps in the refusal to discuss it, as if judges must lose respect and confidence by the reminder that they are subject to human limitations. I do not doubt the grandeur of the conception which lifts them into the realm of pure reason, above and beyond the sweep of perturbing and deflecting forces. None the less, if there is anything of reality in my analysis of the judicial process, they do not stand aloof on these chill and distant heights; and we shall not help the cause of truth by acting and speaking as if they do. The great tides and currents which engulf the rest of men do not turn aside in their

---

Benjamin Nathan Cardozo (1870–1938), one of the nation's greatest Supreme Court justices and legal philosophers, writes eloquently of the subconscious forces at work in the judicial process in this excerpt from his classic work, published in 1949.

course and pass the judges by. We like to figure to ourselves the processes of justice as coldly objective and impersonal. The law, conceived of as a real existence, dwelling apart and alone, speaks, through the voices of priests and ministers, the words which they have no choice except to utter. That is an ideal of objective truth toward which every system of jurisprudence tends. It is an ideal of which great publicists and judges have spoken as of something possible to attain. "The judges of the nation," says Montesquieu, "are only the mouths that pronounce the words of the law, inanimate beings, who can moderate neither its force nor its rigor." So Marshall, in Osborne v. Bank of the United States, 9 Wheat. 738,866: The judicial department "has no will in any case. . . . Judicial power is never exercised for the purpose of giving effect to the will of the judge; always for the purpose of giving effect to the will of the legislature; or in other words, to the will of the law." It has a lofty sound; it is well and finely said; but it can never be more than partly true. Marshall's own career is a conspicuous illustration of the fact that the ideal is beyond the reach of human faculties to attain. He gave to the constitution of the United States the impress of his own mind; and the form of our constitutional law is what it is, because he moulded it while it was still plastic and malleable in the fire of his own intense convictions. At the opposite extreme are the words of the French jurist, Saleilles, in his treatise "De la Personnalité Juridique": "One wills at the beginning the result; one finds the principle afterwards; such is the genesis of all juridical construction. Once accepted, the construction presents itself, doubtless, in the ensemble of legal doctrine, under the opposite aspect. The factors are inverted. The principle appears as an initial cause, from which one has drawn the result which is found deduced from it." I would not put the case thus broadly. So sweeping a statement exaggerates the element of free volition. It ignores the factors of determinism which cabin and confine within narrow bounds the range of unfettered choice. None the less, by its very excess of emphasis, it supplies the needed corrective of an ideal of impossible objectivity. Nearer to the truth, and midway between these extremes, are the words of a man who was not a jurist, but whose intuitions and perceptions were deep and brilliant—the words of President Roosevelt in his message of December 8, 1908, to the Congress of the United States: "The chief lawmakers in our country may be, and often are, the judges, because they are the final seat of authority. Every time they interpret contract, property, vested rights, due process of law, liberty, they necessarily enact into law parts of a system of social philosophy; and as such interpretation is fundamental, they give direction to all law-making. The decisions of the courts on economic and social questions depend upon their economic and social philosophy; and for the peaceful progress of our people during the twentieth century we shall owe most to those judges who hold to a twentieth century economic and social philosophy and not to a long outgrown philosophy, which was itself the product of primitive economic conditions."

I remember that this statement when made aroused a storm of criticism. It betrayed ignorance, they said, of the nature of the judicial process. The business of the judge, they told us, was to discover objective truth. His own little individuality, his tiny stock of scattered and unco-ordinated philosophies, these, with all his weaknesses and unconscious prejudices, were to be laid aside and forgotten. What did men care for *his* reading of the eternal verities? It was not worth recording. What the world was seeking was the eternal verities themselves. Far am I from denying that this is, indeed, the goal toward which all of us must strive. Something of Pascal's spirit of self-search and self-reproach must come at moments to the man who finds himself summoned to the duty of shaping the progress of the law. The very breadth and scope of the opportunity to give expression to his finer self seem to point the accusing finger of disparagement and scorn. What am I that in these great movements onward, this rush and sweep of forces, my petty personality should deflect them by a hairbreadth? Why should the pure light of truth be broken up and impregnated and colored with any element of my being? Such doubts and hesitations besiege one now and again. The truth is, however, that all these inward questionings are born of the hope and desire to transcend the limitations which hedge our human nature. Roosevelt, who knew men, had no illusions on this score. He was not positing an ideal.

SERGEI KONENKOV. *Benjamin N. Cardozo.* 1931. Bronze. 21″ high (53.3 cm). Harvard Law Art Collection, Cambridge.

He was not fixing a goal. He was measuring the powers and the endurance of those by whom the race was to be run. My duty as judge may be to objectify in law, not my own aspirations and convictions and philosophies, but the aspirations and convictions and philosophies of the men and women of my time. Hardly shall I do this well if my own sympathies and beliefs and passionate devotions are with a time that is past. "We shall never be able to flatter ourselves, in any system of judicial interpretation, that we have eliminated altogether the personal measure of the interpreter. In the moral sciences, there is no method or procedure which entirely supplants subjective reason." We may figure the task of the judge, if we please, as the task of a translator, the reading of signs and symbols given from without. None the less, we will not set men to such a task, unless they have absorbed the spirit, and have filled themselves with a love, of the language they must read.

I have no quarrel, therefore, with the doctrine that judges ought to be in sympathy with the spirit of their times. Alas! assent to such a generality does not carry us far upon the road to truth. In every court there are likely to be as many estimates of the "Zeitgeist" as there are judges on its bench. Of the power of favor or prejudice in any sordid or vulgar or evil sense, I have found no trace, not even the faintest, among the judges whom I have known. But every day there is borne in on me a new conviction of the inescapable relation between the truth without us and the truth within. The spirit of the age, as it is revealed to each of us, is too often only the spirit of the group in which the accidents of birth or education or occupation or fellowship have given us a place. No effort or revolution of the mind will overthrow utterly and at all times the empire of these subconscious loyalties. "Our beliefs and opinions," says James Harvey Robinson, "like our standards of conduct come to us insensibly as products of our companionship with our fellow men, not as results of our personal experience and the inferences we individually make from our own observations. We are constantly misled by our extraordinary faculty of 'rationalizing'—that is, of devising plausible arguments for accepting what is imposed upon us by the traditions of the group to which we belong. We are abjectly credulous by nature, and instinctively accept the verdicts of the group. We are suggestible not merely when under the spell of an excited mob or a fervent revival, but we are ever and always listening to the still small voice of the herd, and are ever ready to defend and justify its instructions and warnings, and accept them as the mature results of our own reasoning." This was written, not of judges specially, but of men and women of all classes. The training of the judge, if coupled with what is styled the judicial temperament, will help in some degree to emancipate him from the suggestive power of individual dislikes and prepossessions. It will help to broaden the group to which his subconscious loyalties are due. Never will these loyalties be utterly extinguished while human nature is what it is. We may wonder sometimes how from the play of all these forces of individualism, there can come anything coherent, anything but chaos and the void. Those are the moments in which we exaggerate the elements of difference. In the end there emerges something which has a composite shape and truth and order. It has been said that "History, like mathematics, is obliged to assume that eccentricities more or less balance each other, so that something remains constant at last." The like is true of the work of courts. The eccentricities of judges balance one another. One judge looks at problems from the point of view of history, another from that of philosophy, another from that of social utility, one is a formalist, another a latitudinarian, one is timorous of change, another dissatisfied with the present; out of the attrition of diverse minds there is beaten something which has a constancy and uniformity and average value greater than its component elements. The same thing is true of the work of juries. I do not mean to suggest that the product in either case does not betray the flaws inherent in its origin. The flaws are there as in every human institution. Because they are not only there but visible, we have faith that they will be corrected. There is no assurance that the rule of the majority will be the expression of perfect reason when embodied in constitution or in statute. We ought not to expect more of it when embodied in the judgments of the courts. The tide rises and falls, but the sands of error crumble.

Karl N. Llewellyn

"Song of the Law Review"

Oh, I was a bright law student,
My grades were good and high,
They said I'd make the Law Review,
And now I'd like to die.

My eyes they burn, my head is dead,
But still I struggle through;
You aint read half what I have read
To do your work for you.

I have to read advance sheets
And show the faculty
The cases that they ought to read,
The points they ought to see.

Both courts and scholars listen
When I tell them so and thus;
You'll find me cited now as "Notes,"
Now as "Anonymous."

Though most law review editors complain bitterly of long hours, tedious citations, and indifferent faculty advisers, few have seen fit to consign their resentments to the consolations of light verse—as Karl L. Llewellyn has here.

So workers of the Law School world,
While some strength still remains,
Arise, unite, demand a beer,
And slug 'em with your chains.

FROM SPECIAL INVESTIGATION, 83RD CONGRESS

Joseph Welch Cross-Examines Roy Cohn

Mr. Welch: I want to come back, Mr. Cohn, to the item that we were talking about this morning. I gathered, to sum it up a little, that as early as the spring, which must mean March or April, you knew about this situation of possible subversives and security risks, and even spies at Fort Monmouth, is that right?

Mr. Cohn: Yes, sir. . . .

Mr. Welch: Mr. Cohn, if I told you now that we had a bad situation at Monmouth, you would want to cure it by sundown, if you could, wouldn't you?

Mr. Cohn: I am sure I couldn't, sir.

Mr. Welch: But you would like to, if you could?

Mr. Cohn: Sir—

Mr. Welch: Isn't that right?

Mr. Cohn: No, what I want—

Mr. Welch: Answer me. That must be right. It has to be right.

Mr. Cohn: What I would like to do and what can be done are two different things.

Mr. Welch: Well, if you could be God and do anything you wished, you would cure it by sundown, wouldn't you?

Mr. Cohn: Yes, sir.

Mr. Welch: And you were that alarmed about Monmouth?

Mr. Cohn: It doesn't go that way.

Mr. Welch: I am just asking how it does go. When you find there are Communists and possible spies in a place like Monmouth, you must be alarmed, aren't you?

Mr. Cohn: Now you have asked me how it goes, and I am going to tell you.

Mr. Welch: No; I didn't ask you how it goes. I said aren't you alarmed when you find it is there?

In 1954, Roy Cohn, counsel to the leftist-baiting demagogue Senator Joseph McCarthy (1908–1957), made the mistake of threatening the army with an investigation, beginning with Fort Monmouth, if they insisted on inducting a friend of Cohn's. During his cross-examination of Cohn in the subsequent televised Army–McCarthy hearings, the army's attorney, Joseph Welch, provided the climax that permanently damaged McCarthy's career, as seen in this excerpt.

Mr. Cohn: Whenever I hear that people have been failing to act on FBI information about Communists, I do think it is alarming, I would like the Communists out, and I would like to be able to advise this committee of why people who have the responsibility for getting them out haven't carried out their responsibility. . . .

Mr. Welch: Mr. Cohn, tell me once more: Every time you learn of a Communist or a spy anywhere, is it your policy to get them out as fast as possible?

Mr. Cohn: Surely, we want them out as fast as possible, sir.

Mr. Welch: And whenever you learn of one from now on, Mr. Cohn, I beg of you, will you tell somebody about them quick?

Mr. Cohn: Mr. Welch, with great respect, I work for the committee here. They know how we go about handling situations of Communist infiltration and failure to act on FBI information about Communist infiltration. If they are displeased with the speed with which I and the group of men who work with me proceed, if they are displeased with the order in which we move, I am sure they will give me appropriate instructions along those lines, and I will follow any which they give me.

Mr. Welch: May I add my small voice, sir, and say whenever you know about a subversive or a Communist or a spy, please hurry. Will you remember those words?

Senator McCarthy: Mr. Chairman.

Mr. Cohn: Mr. Welch, I can assure you, sir, as far as I am concerned, and certainly as far as the chairman of this committee and the members, and the members of the staff, are concerned, we are a small group, but we proceed as expeditiously as is humanly possible to get out Communists and traitors and to bring to light the mechanism by which they have been permitted to remain where they were for so long a period of time.

Senator McCarthy: Mr. Chairman, in view of that question—

Senator Mundt: Have you a point of order?

Senator McCarthy: Not exactly, Mr. Chairman, but in view of Mr. Welch's request that the information be given once we know of anyone who might be performing any work for the Communist Party, I think we should tell him that he has in his law firm a young man named Fisher whom he recommended, incidentally, to do work on this committee, who has been for a number of years a member of an organization which was named, oh, years and years ago, as the legal bulwark of the Communist Party, an organization which always swings to the defense of anyone who dares to expose Communists. I certainly assume that Mr. Welch did not know of this young man at the time he recommended him as the assistant counsel for this committee, but he has such terror and such a great desire to know where anyone is located who may be serving the Communist cause, Mr. Welch, that I thought we should just call to your attention the fact that your Mr. Fisher, who is still in your law firm today, whom you asked to have down here looking over the secret and classified material, is a member of an organization, not named by me but named by various committees, named by the Attorney General, as I recall, and I think I quote this verbatim, as "the legal bulwark of the Communist Party." He belonged to that for a sizable number of years, according to his own admission, and he belonged to it long after it had been exposed as the legal arm of the Communist Party.

Knowing that, Mr. Welch, I just felt that I had a duty to respond to your urgent request that before sundown, when we know of anyone serving the Communist cause, we let the agency know. We are now letting you know that your man did belong to this organization for either 3 or 4 years, belonged to it long after he was out of law school.

I don't think you can find anyplace, anywhere, an organization which has done more to defend Communists—I am again quoting the report—to defend Communists, to defend espionage agents, and to aid the Communist cause, than the man whom you originally wanted down here at your right hand instead of Mr. St. Clair.

Senator Joseph McCarthy, with the aid of a map, testifies on Communist party organization. Army counsel Joseph Welch (left) sits with head in hand in disgust. June 10, 1954.

I have hesitated bringing that up, but I have been rather bored with your phony requests to Mr. Cohn here that he personally get every Communist out of government before sundown. Therefore, we will give you information about the young man in your own organization.

I am not asking you at this time to explain why you tried to foist him on this committee. Whether you knew he was a member of that Communist organization or not, I don't know. I assume you did not, Mr. Welch, because I get the impression that, while you are quite an actor, you play for a laugh, I don't think you have any conception of the danger of the Communist Party. I don't think you yourself would ever knowingly aid the Communist cause. I think you are unknowingly aiding it when you try to burlesque this hearing in which we are attempting to bring out the facts, however.

Mr. Welch: Mr. Chairman.

Senator Mundt: Mr. Welch, the Chair should say he has no recognition or no memory of Mr. Welch's recommending either Mr. Fisher or anybody else as counsel for this committee.

I will recognize Mr. Welch.

Senator McCarthy: Mr. Chairman, I will give you the news story on that.

Mr. Welch: Mr. Chairman, under these circumstances I must have something approaching a personal privilege.

Senator Mundt: You may have it, sir. It will not be taken out of your time.

Mr. Welch: Senator McCarthy, I did not know—Senator, sometimes you say "May I have your attention?"

Senator McCarthy: I am listening to you. I can listen with one ear.

Mr. Welch: This time I want you to listen with both.

Senator McCarthy: Yes.

Mr. Welch: Senator McCarthy, I think until this moment—

Senator McCarthy: Jim, will you get the news story to the effect that this man belonged to this Communist-front organization? Will you get the citations showing that this was the legal arm of the Communist Party, and the length of time that he belonged, and the fact that he was recommended by Mr. Welch? I think that should be in the record.

Mr. Welch: You won't need anything in the record when I have finished telling you this.

Until this moment, Senator, I think I never really gauged your cruelty or your recklessness. Fred Fisher is a young man who went to the Harvard Law School and came into my firm and is starting what looks to be a brilliant career with us.

When I decided to work for this committee I asked Jim St. Clair, who sits on my right, to be my first assistant. I said to Jim, "Pick somebody in the firm who works under you that you would like." He chose Fred Fisher and they came down on an afternoon plane. That night, when he had taken a little stab at trying to see what the case was about, Fred Fisher and Jim St. Clair and I went to dinner together. I then said to these two young men, "Boys, I don't know anything about you except I have always liked you, but if there is anything funny in the life of either one of you that would hurt anybody in this case you speak up quick."

Fred Fisher said, "Mr. Welch, when I was in law school and for a period of months after, I belonged to the Lawyers Guild," as you have suggested, Senator. He went on to say, "I am secretary of the Young Republicans League in Newton with the son of Massachusetts' Governor, and I have the respect and admiration of my community and I am sure I have the respect and admiration of the 25 lawyers or so in Hale & Dorr."

I said, "Fred, I just don't think I am going to ask you to work on the case. If I do, one of these days that will come out and go over national television and it will just hurt like the dickens."

So, Senator, I asked him to go back to Boston.

Little did I dream you could be so reckless and so cruel as to do an injury to that lad. It is true he is still with Hale & Dorr. It is true that he will continue to be with Hale & Dorr. It is, I regret to say, equally true that I fear he shall always bear a scar needlessly inflicted by you. If it were in my power to forgive you for your reckless cruelty, I will do so. I like to think I am a gentleman, but your forgiveness will have to come from someone other than me.

Senator McCarthy: Mr. Chairman.

Senator Mundt: Senator McCarthy?

Senator McCarthy: May I say that Mr. Welch talks about this being cruel and reckless. He was just baiting; he has been baiting Mr. Cohn here for hours, requesting that Mr. Cohn, before sundown, get out of any department of Government anyone who is serving the Communist cause.

I just give this man's record, and I want to say, Mr. Welch, that it has been labeled long before he became a member, as early as 1944—

Mr. Welch: Senator, may we not drop this? We know he belonged to the Lawyers Guild, and Mr. Cohn nods his head at me. I did you, I think, no personal injury, Mr. Cohn.

Mr. Cohn: No, sir.

Mr. Welch: I meant to do you no personal injury, and if I did, I beg your pardon.

Let us not assassinate this lad further, Senator. You have done enough. Have you no sense of decency, sir, at long last? Have you left no sense of decency?

Senator McCarthy: I know this hurts you, Mr. Welch. But I may say, Mr. Chairman, on a point of personal privilege, and I would like to finish it—

Mr. Welch: Senator, I think it hurts you, too, sir.

Senator McCarthy: I would like to finish this.

Mr. Welch has been filibustering this hearing, he has been talking day after day about how he wants to get anyone tainted with communism out before sundown. I know Mr. Cohn would rather not have me go into this. I intend to, however. Mr. Welch talks about any sense of decency. If I say anything which is not the truth, then I would like to know about it.

> The foremost legal bulwark of the Communist Party, its front organizations, and controlled unions, and which, since its inception, has never failed to rally to the legal defense of the Communist Party, and individual members thereof, including known espionage agents.

Now, that is not the language of Senator McCarthy. That is the language of the Un-American Activities Committee. And I can go on with many more citations. It seems that Mr. Welch is pained so deeply he thinks it is improper for me to give the record, the Communist-front record, of the man whom he wanted to foist upon this committee. But it doesn't pain him at all—there is no pain in his chest about the unfounded charges against Mr. Frank Carr; there is no pain there about the attempt to destroy the reputation and take the jobs away from the young men who were working in my committee.

And, Mr. Welch, if I have said anything here which is untrue, then tell me. I have heard you and everyone else talk so much about laying the truth upon the table that when I hear—and it is completely phony, Mr. Welch, I have listened to you for a long time—when you say "Now, before sundown, you must get these people out of Government," I want to have it very clear, very clear that you were not so serious about that when you tried to recommend this man for this committee.

And may I say, Mr. Welch, in fairness to you, I have reason to believe that you did not know about his Communist-front record at the time you recommended him. I don't think you would have recommended him to the committee if you knew that.

I think it is entirely possible you learned that after you recommended him.

Senator Mundt: The Chair would like to say again that he does not believe that Mr. Welch recommended Mr. Fisher as counsel for this committee, because he has through his office all the recommendations that were made. He does not recall any that came from Mr. Welch, and that would include Mr. Fisher.

Senator McCarthy: Let me ask Mr. Welch. You brought him down, did you not, to act as your assistant?

Mr. Welch: Mr. McCarthy, I will not discuss this with you further. You have sat within 6 feet of me, and could have asked me about Fred Fisher. You have brought it out. If there is a God in heaven, it will do neither you nor your cause any good. I will not discuss it further. I will not ask Mr. Cohn any more questions. You, Mr. Chairman, may, if you will, call the next witness.

Senator Mundt: Are there any questions?

Mr. Jenkins: No further questions, Mr. Chairman.

Erle Stanley Gardner

"Confessions of a Cross-Examiner"

I know that from time to time members of this academy have expressed some concern over cross-examination, particularly in regard to the question of compensation.

When I was practicing law I more or less specialized in cross-examining experts. At times I would be asked by other attorneys to sit in the case for the sole purpose of cross-examining the doctors. I thought you might be interested in hearing something from the other side of the fence—the viewpoint of the cross-examiner himself.

The expert witnesses who befuddled me were the ones who followed certain tactics. Fortunately there weren't too many of them, but these few experts followed a certain general plan of procedure. I was never able to find the answer to tactics of the type they used and I don't think there is any answer.

When a lawyer asks an expert about his compensation it is usually in a case being tried before a jury and the lawyer tries to be as unfair as possible. The question is almost never asked for the purpose of legitimate information, but is asked purely for the purpose of embarrassing the witness and of getting him on the defensive. The general idea is that jurors with average incomes will distrust a man who charges one-hundred-and-fifty or two-hundred-and-fifty dollars a day.

The cross-examiner, trying to be as unfair as possible, looks witheringly at the witness and says, "Doctor, you expect to be paid for your testimony in this case, don't you?"

That's the way I did it.

The witness who shifted his position, cleared his throat and started to explain was my meat.

The question was framed so as to show that the witness expected to be paid for his *testimony*. As above mentioned, the question was deliberately unfair. Most cross-examiners don't want to be fair; they want to discredit the witness.

But every once in a while a smart one would look me in the eyes and say, "No!" and let it go at that.

Then, when I would be trying to recover from the shock and, before I could quite ask the next question, the witness would say, "I expect to be paid for the *time* I have spent in research and for the *time* I am *forced* to put in the courtroom. I *never* take pay for my testimony."

It was then up to me to either ask him about what he expected to charge for his time, or quit. If I asked him about the value of his time, the smart witness would smile at me, turn to the jurors and explain that his time had to include his overhead, the cost of maintaining his office, his books, his telephone, his secretary, the purchase of new machines or instruments, and the purchase of new books.

Then, still facing the jurors, he would say, "For instance, recently I installed a new machine," and then he would go on and start describing the machine, what it would do, the reason for it, how it worked. I was, of course, at liberty to stop him and I had to stop him because with every word he was selling himself to the jury. But when I stopped him the jurors felt as though I had jerked a magazine out of their hands just as they were reading the most interesting installment of a continued story.

Jurors are always interested in gadgets and a good expert witness can describe something as simple as a diathermy machine in terms of what it is expected to accomplish, and how it does it, so that the jurors will be following him with rapt interest.

Besides writing innumerable and best-selling "Perry Mason" books, Erle Stanley Gardner (1889–1970) was, until 1938, a practicing attorney and an acknowledged expert in the cross-examination of expert witnesses, as he demonstrates in this 1957 speech to the American Academy of Forensic Sciences.

If I couched questions in the technical terms I had so painstakingly looked up in the medical dictionary the expert would explain those terms to the jurors before answering the question. If I asked the doctor about a traumatic ecchymosis, he'd turn to the jury, say with an amused smile, "A traumatic ecchymosis is simply a bruise" and then answer the question.

The witness would always be courteous to me, but he'd always explain my technical terminology to the jurors and, while he was about it, explain his opinions and conclusions and his reasons for reaching them. And he'd keep the jurors so interested they hung on his words.

We've heard a lot lately about demonstrative evidence. The lawyer puts things on a blackboard. He draws diagrams. He keeps the jurors interested. The good expert is the one who makes a verbal blackboard to illustrate his testimony. The expert should bear in mind what lawyers have discovered they can do with demonstrative evidence and keep his verbal blackboard in mind whenever a question is answered.

The doctor who would let me question him, using the words I'd so carefully looked up in the medical dictionary, and reply in similar terms, and talking to me instead of the jurors, was my meat.

The jurors would hear the technical terminology going back and forth. They wouldn't know what we were talking about, but they'd say to themselves, "That lawyer knows as much as the doctor."

The doctor who twisted and squirmed and let me get him on the defensive as he tried to justify his expert medical fees for courtroom appearance was duck soup. I would make it appear he was getting such a high fee it amounted to selling his testimony, yet indicate to the jury that he was selling out pretty cheap at that.

The doctor who cheerfully explained what went into his office overhead in terms of specifically describing some new gadget he'd bought and why it was used and what it would accomplish was selling himself all the time he was justifying his fees. He'd already done my side of the case plenty of damage on his direct testimony, so he'd gladly smother my cross-examination beneath a barrage of words about anything he felt would interest the jurors.

In this still from the original "Perry Mason" series, the redoubtable lawyer (Raymond Burr) and his assistant Della Street (Barbara Hale) confer during a case. The popular television show was based on the novels by Erle Stanley Gardner.

Robert O'Neil Bristow

"Beyond Any Doubt"

Tom Howell stubbed his cigarette in the cluttered ash tray on the table. As he did so, he looked thoughtfully from face to face, at the eleven men seated around the table. They were solemn faces. Intense and resentful. The men were tired, some of them growing angry from the exhaustion of deliberation in the jury room. On the wall the second hand of the clock moved silently, relentlessly, in its course. The jury had been out for thirty-one hours, deliberating the Echols case. The vote was eleven for death. One for acquittal. The single dissenting vote had been cast by Tom Howell.

Now, strenuously urged by the judge to reach a decision, the eleven men concentrated their attention on the single vote that stood between Jack Echols and the electric chair.

Tom reached for another cigarette, sighing deeply. He very desperately wished he was back on the job at the drug store he managed. Or better still, at home with Jane, his wife, and Randy their eleven year old son, perhaps sitting comfortably on the lawn with a cool drink in his hand. There his responsibility was limited to his family. He disliked having the power to save or destroy another man's life by a single irrevocable decision.

Tom Howell was a small, very lean man. As the result of a mine explosion on Guadalcanal, he wore thick-lensed glasses which gave him 20/40 vision. While the other men in the jury room were dressed in suits and ties, Tom Howell wore no jacket. His clean white shirt was frayed at the collar, his tie was inexpensive.

The foreman was Doctor McNair, a heavy man of florid complexion, and a man of some standing in the small midwestern city. He was tolerant and diplomatic by nature. His vote had been cast for death. The others, several of them successful businessmen, had also voted for death on the first ballot.

The acknowledged leader for the death penalty group was Carl Purvis, a wealthy man who owned land and had other interests, including the hardware store where Tom Howell had formerly worked. Carl Purvis had fired Tom in a fit of anger over a mixup in a wholesale order. Carl Purvis was fifty-five years old, a political power in the county, an abrupt egocentric. He was impatient and intolerant of opposition of any kind.

Dr. McNair's voice interrupted the uncomfortable silence. "Tom," he said, making an effort to smile. "We want to reach a decision tonight. We've been over and over the case. Now . . . again I'd like to ask you to repeat your stand."

Tom Howell loosened his tie and ran his forefinger around the irritated flesh on his neck where the frayed edge of collar had rubbed. He cleared his throat, and as he began to speak, his voice cracked.

"The judge said that if there was a reasonable doubt of guilt, we should not give the death penalty. That's why I can't vote for death. I think there is a doubt that Echols killed the man."

"Oh, *for God's sake!*" The voice was Carl Purvis's. He slammed a heavy fist against the table and muttered to himself.

"The evidence," Tom went on, ignoring Purvis, "that the State emphasized, was the fact that Echols was apprehended in the middle of a robbery, with the gun that had killed a policeman three months earlier. I'm not arguing that it wasn't the gun at all. The ballistics expert showed that to be true. But Echols said he bought the gun from a man he hardly knew after they met in a bar. He swore he didn't own the gun at the time of the killing. I'm saying there is some doubt whether or not he did have the gun when the police officer was killed."

A "hung" jury is the bane of prosecutors, but in this absorbing fictional account of jury deliberations at a murder trial, the contemporary American author Robert O'Neil Bristow reveals the psychological dilemma presented by the death penalty.

"For God's sake, Howell," Carl Purvis shouted, "do you think Echols would admit he owned the gun at that time? What the hell would *you* do?"

I don't know. I repeat that there is simply no proof that Echols had the gun before the killing. Certainly he had it when he robbed the supermarket, but I can't believe a man who had killed a policeman would *keep* the gun. He'd know if he was caught, the murder would be traced to him. To me that would be stupid."

"It would be stupid!" Purvis said. "It would be damned stupid, but just how smart do you think this Echols is? He's spent half of his life behind bars. He doesn't have the brilliant mind that you have. . . ." Purvis's voice ended with a tone of heavy sarcasm.

"If he was a confirmed criminal," Tom said evenly, his jaws growing tense, "it seems to me that he'd have even more reason to get rid of the gun if he'd used it to kill the policeman. A first offender might not consider that, but a confirmed criminal like Echols would dispose of the gun. I think Echols bought the gun from the killer, with no idea that it had been used to murder a lawman."

Carl Purvis cursed and stood up, moving angrily away from the table.

"I think Mr. Purvis has a point," Dr. McNair said diplomatically. "The defendant wasn't very smart or he'd never have been in prison on so many counts. Do you know he raped a girl when he was seventeen?"

"Doctor!" Tom said suddenly. "We aren't trying this man for rape."

"Of course. Yes. But he had no alibi in this case. Tom, he could not prove. . . . "

"He said he was in his room at the Majestic Hotel."

"He said that," the doctor agreed, "but was he? Surely someone would have seen him enter and leave. The hotel clerk testified that he hadn't seen Echols all day. He said he thought he was gone at the time."

"Did he go look? Did he know for sure?" Tom asked.

"Howell, it's a small hotel. A flop house. If Echols had been there, the clerk would have known."

"Echols said he was drunk. He said he didn't even go out to eat that night."

Carl Purvis wheeled around and paced to the table, standing angrily over Tom Howell.

"You're pretty naive, son. You didn't expect that killer to stand in the box and tell the truth, did you? Don't you know he's been in and out of trouble all his life?"

Tom Howell adjusted his glasses nervously. This was becoming a terrible strain. Several times he had been almost prepared to tell them that if they were so certain, he'd go along with the death penalty. But at the moment, when he might have changed his vote, something had held him back. He was tempted now, but once again he resisted, although less forcefully than before.

"Mr. Purvis," Dr. McNair said, "why don't you come sit down and we'll talk this over some more."

Carl Purvis, casting an angry glance at Tom, returned to his seat, mumbling profanity.

"There was the identification by the other police officer," Dr. McNair said. "He positively identified Echols as the man who wounded him."

"True," Tom admitted. "Officer Tolliver was directing traffic when the killer drove through a light at the intersection. Officer Tolliver fired two shots and the killer fired back, hitting him in the leg. That's the way they said it happened. But the defense attorney showed that the killer's car was doing forty-five miles an hour. Officer Tolliver saw him for just an instant. I think the defense attorney was right when he reasoned that it simply wasn't possible, in a hail of bullets, to positively identify a man while he's traveling that fast in a car. The officer saw only the face, the killer was wearing a hat. I think the officer is honest, but I can't believe that he can make a positive identification." Tom Howell mopped his forehead with his handkerchief. He shook his head. "From all that testimony we heard," he said wearily, "and our discussion . . . I still think there is a doubt."

"That's right," Carl Purvis snapped, "and there's a doubt if the sun will come up tomorrow too. But it's a pretty thin doubt. You're hiding behind it, Howell."

"Gentlemen, please," Dr. McNair said.

"He should have disqualified himself for jury duty," Purvis shouted. "He isn't holding out because he thinks the man is innocent. He's holding out because he hasn't got the guts to give death. He's never had any guts. I ought to know."

"Sit down, please, Mr. Purvis," Dr. McNair said.

Carl Purvis glared and remained standing.

How often Tom had asked himself if he could serve on a jury when a death penalty was possible. He let his mind slip back to the morning after he had been subpoenaed. Jane had put his toast and eggs on the table, but he had left them untouched, uneaten and cold.

"You're worrying about it too much, Tom," she said.

"Ummmmm . . . it's not just the jury duty. I can spare the time for that. It's the death penalty. They'll ask me and I'm not sure what to say. Who wants to have that responsibility. . . . I mean really *wants* it? And yet *somebody* is going to qualify. Maybe several of those self-righteous zealots. Can't you hear them after they've given him death, describing how troubled they were, how tremendous a decision it was? I can see it. In fact, I could name a dozen right off hand."

"But that doesn't answer your question, does it, Tom?"

He had smiled. "No . . . that doesn't make me any more certain whether or not I should disqualify myself." He pushed the eggs away. "I'm sorry," he said. He lighted a cigarette and smoked thoughtfully. "I *could* give death. I would. But I'd have to be sure. I'd have to be so damned sure I could turn over and fall asleep every night without thinking back and wondering. Does that qualify me?"

Jane had taken the cigarette from his fingers and drawn on it, returning it to him. "It's your decision," she said. "*You* know."

Tom coughed and was aware of the gnawing fear, the uncertainty in his mind. Could he change now? Should he change? Let them have it the way they saw it . . . could he hold out? He looked around the jury room.

"Look . . . I'm not eager to send a man to death. I admit that. But maybe that's because I saw too much of it. I saw hundreds of men die and I had a hand in it. No, I'm going to be very careful before I send a man to the electric chair."

He noticed several eyebrows raise. Had he admitted that he thought they might be right after all? Was this the first sign of surrender?

"Maybe I shouldn't be on this jury," he said. "I don't know. I wish now that I hadn't been called. But let me say this. If I'm not eager to give death and should not be here for that reason, I think that there are some of us here who are just a little bit too *eager* to give him death, and they don't belong on this jury any more than I do. This is supposed to be a group of impartial men . . . and I wonder if, after all the newspaper publicity, the pictures of the policeman's widow and all. . . . I wonder if any of us came here with completely impartial minds."

"See there!" Carl Purvis shouted, "he's admitting he doesn't belong on this jury."

Dr. McNair was showing frustration. "Please, gentlemen," he said. "Let's be sensible."

And for several moments the terrible silence again returned and the second hand of the clock moved, and moved.

Somewhat more restrained in tone, Carl Purvis spoke. "Howell, you used to work for me. You didn't like me and I never cared much for you. I want to say this. I think you're holding out because I fired you, and I'm on the other side. I think it has nothing to do with this case at all. You're just trying to take out your resentment against me, in this cheap, filthy way."

For the first time, Tom stood to speak, and if he had ever felt hate, he felt it then.

"You couldn't be more right," he said loudly. "I don't like you. I think you're a bigoted, egotistical slob." He was breathing hard now and he was surprised to find it so difficult to draw air into his lungs. "But I wouldn't pardon a guilty man just because I resent you. You, Mr. Purvis, are the *least* important part of this whole rotten mess. I wouldn't like you even if you were voting for acquittal. Not one damned bit. But . . . " he paused to get his breath, "I'm voting this way because I feel there is a doubt. I see that

Daniel Celentano.
Jury Dead Lock. 1930s.
Ink on paper.
8 × 7″ (20.3 × 17.8 cm).
Courtesy Janet Marqusee
Fine Arts, New York.

man out there waiting for a decision whether we kill him or let him live. I couldn't care less about your personal feelings for me or mine for you."

"This discussion has gotten out of hand," Dr. McNair said. "This is neither the time nor the place for personality conflicts, and I ask you not to let personal antagonism enter into this deliberation."

Tom sat and buried his face in his hands, emotionally exhausted. He remembered Carl Purvis's fit of rage, that day in the hardware store, his face growing dark, menacing, his voice loud, uncontrolled.

In the presence of the other clerks, Carl Purvis had fired him, not even learning all the facts about the mistake in the wholesale order. Not caring.

It had not been easy for Tom to get another job because the whispering that followed his dismissal hinted vaguely at dishonesty. He refused to leave town to take another position, with another hardware firm.

"No," he argued, "if I run, they'll believe I did something wrong. I'll make out and eventually people will know that Carl Purvis made an impulsive, hot-headed decision."

Tom had stuck. In two years he had added another thousand dollars to his savings. He was all right now. He had recently talked to the banker, and if his loan came through as he expected, he would soon open his own store, a fishing and hardware specialty house, on a small scale at first. But it would grow, Tom felt sure.

Tom glanced up from the table. The room had been silent for some time. It seemed uncomfortably crowded, all of them watching him wearily, impatiently.

Tom recognized the deep resentment he felt against Carl Purvis. With studied honesty, he asked himself if it *was* possible that he was holding out because of his hatred for Purvis. Did he really doubt that Echols was guilty? Again the wave of uncertainty swept over him. It would be easy to stop now, to go along with the other eleven. He considered it very seriously.

"Tom," Dr. McNair said, "look at it the other way. If you can, just look at the evidence. We are dealing with a known criminal. He's been in jail for years. He never got past the third grade. He raped a girl when he was seventeen. He beat her. He showed that he could be cruel, even kill perhaps, if necessary. He went into a liquor store with a mask and held the place up. Then he got in the car and started off. The policeman reached the scene, and when he tried to stop the criminal, he was shot down. The killer then made an escape, wounding the traffic officer as he fled. Later . . . Echols was arrested in possession of the gun that had killed the officer. He was checked out carefully and he could give no alibi at all. Echols didn't deny owning the gun. He said he bought it from a man and described that man vaguely. He couldn't even give the man's first name. The traffic officer who tried to stop him identified Echols as the man who shot him in the leg. Now, our point is this . . . if Echols could prove that he had been in his room . . . or if he could prove that he had bought the gun from someone, and provided a name, it might be different. If the police officer had even said that he was *almost* sure that Echols was the killer . . . then Tom, we feel there would be doubt. As it is, Echols has failed to clear himself, on any single point. Nobody really wants to send a man to his execution. It would take a neurotic sadist to enjoy that.

"And yet . . . can we turn men like Echols free? Are our police officers to go out and patrol, knowing that they may be killed, if the people they are protecting do not in turn protect the officers? Tom, please . . . we have a responsibility here. Eleven of us are deeply convinced that Echols was the killer. We have no doubt. Don't you think, as a medical man dedicated to saving lives, that if there was any doubt, I'd be the first to vote against the death penalty?"

"I think you would," Tom agreed.

"Very well. As foreman, I'm calling a coffee break. Let's all relax and reconsider the facts. After the break, we will take another ballot. Someone rap on the door and send out for coffee."

One of the jurymen went to the door and ordered. Then, splitting up into groups, the jurymen talked softly to one another, leaving Tom alone at the end of the table.

Tom overheard the high-pitched tenor of the music teacher as he discussed the case, the talented hands gesturing in jerky movements.

"Well . . . if you want to know what I think . . . I think this criminal is not *worth* salvaging. I frankly don't have any doubt, but if I did, I think I'd just take into consideration that he isn't worth the risk he poses to good decent people. Now, I mean that's just my idea, but he's simply *nothing*. Nothing!"

Tom removed his glasses and wiped them clean with his handkerchief. He discounted what the music teacher said. It was only to be expected from an overly emotional man. But Dr. McNair, he thought, was an honest, level-headed, decent man. He *was* committed to the saving of lives. Certainly he would be the last to condemn a man to death if there was any doubt. The concise, simple way he had presented the argument left Tom with less conviction that Echols was innocent. If only he could remove that lingering uncertainty. Could he be right, when all the others were so thoroughly convinced? He wondered if perhaps, in his feeling for the underdog, he had given too much credence to the presentation by the defense. He didn't want to send a man to death, and yet, if Echols was guilty, he knew that he had to make the decision.

The gun, the lack of an alibi, the identification of the police officer . . . it was damning enough. Yet, somehow he couldn't find it conclusive.

He remembered the looks on the faces of the townspeople after he had been fired at the hardware store. Some of them, on the basis of circumstances, were ready to believe that he had been dishonest, that he had been fired for that reason.

There had been no way to defend himself against these unspoken accusations. There were the long nights, lying awake, projecting their faces on the shadowy ceiling, mentally gauging their distrust of him.

Tom wondered if he was unwilling to believe that Echols was guilty because of his own experience. *Was he in reality only defending himself now? Or was there a genuine doubt?* He wondered.

None of the other men were in question. The music teacher. The football coach. The businessmen. They all knew. They found no agony, no doubt, in rendering a decision. Tom lighted a cigarette, and while it tasted raw in his mouth, he smoked it thoughtfully. If *they* were so certain, he reasoned that he must be wrong. If only one of them had been in doubt, it would have made a difference.

But they had not shown such doubt. He was alone. He had never been so thoroughly alone in his life. He considered how easy it would be on the next ballot to write *guilty*. A word. A single word that would relieve him of all responsibility. He took a slip of paper and wrote the word, speculatively. He studied his writing. It was not as difficult as he had imagined. If he put his faith in the other eleven men, it would not be hard. If he did not, he was again very much alone. He told himself to stop the fight now. *Vote guilty. Vote for death.*

It would be easy. Or would it? Maybe it didn't stop there. It was just possible that if he appeased these men here, he might appease them outside the courtroom. *Go along with the crowd. Don't be a dissenter. The way to get ahead is to go along. Sell out.*

He glanced up as Carl Purvis drew a chair beside him. "Tom . . . I'm a blunt man," he said levelly, without anger, "and I know you've been to the bank to borrow money to start a hardware store in competition with me. That doesn't bother me. I can take competition. There's room enough for both of us. I said I was blunt, and I am. I have a strong vote on the board of directors at the bank. It comes down to this. If you vote with us, you get the loan. If you don't, I'll stop it. The rest of us are convinced. Now just face the truth and go along. You'll have your loan and a lousy rapist criminal will go to the chair. If we don't give it to him, he'll kill somebody else before it's over. He'll go there one way or another. All you do is ease off and go along. That shouldn't be too hard."

"You mean that?" Tom asked. "About the loan? You really do?"

Carl Purvis spoke softly, but with strength. "I mean it. You can yell your head off and I'll deny ever saying it, but, boy, you'll know!"

Carl Purvis pushed his chair away and joined the others as coffee was brought into the room.

Tom drank slowly, very thoughtfully. He refused to allow himself to grow angry. Not now. What Purvis had said was undeniably true. He was in a position to block the loan. And yet, perhaps, considering the testimony, Echols *was* guilty. If so, he should face the death penalty. Then there was also Dr. McNair's studied decision. Tom respected that. There were the facts as they had seen them. Echols was a confirmed criminal. Freed of this crime, he might go on to commit another that would inevitably lead him to the electric chair. Eleven against one. Were they right? He considered his long-cherished hope for a business of his own. This too was in the balance. Was he so certain that Echols was innocent that he would sacrifice his own future?

Dr. McNair hesitated as he reached Tom's chair. Tom felt the doctor's hand on his shoulder. "Tell me, Tom," McNair said, "do you really have a doubt? Or is it too difficult to back down?"

Tom looked up into the doctor's face. He was very tired. "Have you asked yourself the same thing?" he said.

"What do you mean?"

"With the comfort of ten others, it might be hard for you to change too."

Dr. McNair did not reply.

"I know how I *feel*. I feel like he's guilty," Tom said.

Dr. McNair raised an eyebrow and leaned closer. "Go on," he said.

"But . . . they didn't prove that in court. They left some doubts. Not for the others, but for me."

"Yet, you feel . . . "

"Yes, I feel he's guilty. Do you want me to vote what I feel or what I know?"

Dr. McNair shook his head slowly.

"Maybe sometime—I don't really know—but maybe you had a patient and you felt certain that you had diagnosed the trouble. Maybe you treated it and later, when the patient died, you found that it was something else. Maybe some of these men just don't want to doubt. You probably don't even understand . . . "

Dr. McNair looked about the room thoughtfully. "We'd better start," he said softly. He took his place at the head of the table. The others followed quickly. "Gentlemen, in a spirit of deep sincerity, I ask you to draw a paper and pencil and cast a ballot."

The men wrote quickly and folded the one-word messages as Dr. McNair passed the plate. Tom studied them before writing. He considered the prisoner waiting below. He considered his wife and Randy. The small business he wanted so badly. And before he wrote, he considered the facts in the case—those controversial facts that were so strangely elastic in interpretation. Was there really any doubt? The key word. *Doubt.*

Tom was the last to drop his paper in the plate. He had written thoughtfully. The plate was then handed to the foreman.

The doctor announced seven guilty votes before he paused. "Not guilty," Dr. McNair read, and dropped the paper on the table.

Tom Howell stood slowly. His voice was so subdued that the others leaned toward him to hear him.

"Once and for all," he said, his eyes growing damp behind his thick glasses, "I vote for acquittal. As I do so, I know the very great responsibility I have taken. I can tell you now that if we sit here and deliberate until the world ends, I will not change my vote. I will under no circumstances change my vote. Not to please you, . . . nor help you get this over with."

Tom sat down. Dr. McNair shuffled through the ballots. Tom glanced quickly at Carl Purvis. Perhaps what hopes he had had for the bank loan were destroyed by his brief announcement. He suspected that it was just possible that the board of directors would ask Purvis not to cast a vote, since the loan involved a business competitive to his. It did not matter. Tom would get the money somehow, someday.

He knew also that if he was deeply disappointed in this, still he had acted in good faith. He would not have to live without respect for himself.

"That wasn't really necessary, Tom," Dr. McNair said gently. He gestured with the ballots. "I had not finished counting." The men sat silently. Dr. McNair lighted a cigarette. "The vote has changed," he said. "It is now two for acquittal, ten guilty."

Tom let his eyes move quickly from man to man. He saw the surprise register in the face of the music teacher. It was not so comfortable now with two votes opposing him. His narrow face was troubled. Tom saw indecision there, a weakening. He glanced at the coach. He looked as though he might be ready to call another play before it was too late.

And Tom heard Dr. McNair's voice, coaxing, and sensed that it was he who had changed his vote.

". . . not what we feel, but what we know for fact. This is the basis, and if there is doubt—as two of us believe now—"

Tom detected the change that had taken place in the room. Even Purvis was nodding with McNair.

Tom Howell adjusted his glasses as the weariness began to leave him. He was feeling better. When the time came, he had rewarded himself with human dignity by standing alone. This was enough.

The music teacher raised his hand, like a schoolboy, and asked for another vote. Tom smiled and reached for his pencil. It would be over soon.

Martin Luther King, Jr.
John F. Kennedy
Lyndon B. Johnson
On Enactment of the Civil Rights Act of 1964

DR. KING:

For years now I have heard the word "wait." It rings in the ear of every Negro with piercing familiarity. This "wait" has almost always meant "Never." We have waited for more than 340 years for our constitutional and God-given rights. The nations of Asia and Africa are moving with jet-like speed toward gaining political independence, but we still creep at a horse-and buggy pace toward gaining a cup of coffee at a lunch counter; when you take a cross-country drive and find it necessary to sleep night after night in the uncomfortable corners of your automobile because no motel will accept you; when you are humiliated day in and day out by nagging signs reading "white" and "colored"; when your first name becomes "nigger," your middle name becomes "boy" (however old you are) and your last name becomes "John," and your wife and mother are never given the respected title "Mrs."; when you are harried by day and haunted by night by the fact that you are a Negro, living constantly at tiptoe stance, never quite knowing what to expect next, and are plagued with inner fears and outer resentments; when you are forever fighting a degenerating sense of "nobodiness"—then you will understand why we find it difficult to wait.

PRESIDENT KENNEDY:

We are confronted primarily with a moral issue. It is as old as the Scriptures and it is as clear as the American Constitution. The heart of the question is whether all Americans are to be afforded equal rights and equal opportunities, whether we are going to treat our fellow Americans as we want to be treated. . . .

One hundred years of delay have passed since President Lincoln freed the slaves, yet their heirs, their grandsons, are not fully free. They are not yet freed from the bonds of injustice. They are not yet freed from social and economic oppression. And this Nation, for all its hopes and all its boasts, will not be fully free until all its citizens are free.

Now the time has come for this Nation to fulfill its promise. The events in Birmingham and elsewhere have so increased the cries for equality that no city or state or legislative body can prudently choose to ignore them.

We face, therefore, a moral crisis as a country and as a people. It cannot be met by repressive police action. It cannot be left to increased demonstrations in the streets. It cannot be quieted by token moves or talk. It is a time to act in Congress, in your state and local legislative body and, above all, in all of our daily lives.

In April 1963, from his Birmingham jail cell, Dr. Martin Luther King, Jr. (1929–1968), wrote this famous reply to the clergymen who denounced him for marching in protest of segregated lunch counters. Two months later, following the violent submission of marchers in that same Alabama city, President John Fitzgerald Kennedy (1917–1963) gave one of his greatest speeches, his televised introduction of a politically dangerous civil rights bill. It was a long road to the signing into law of the Civil Rights Bill of 1964 by President Lyndon Baines Johnson (1908–1973).

Next week I shall ask the Congress of the United States to act, to make a commitment it has not fully made in this century to the proposition that race has no place in American life or law.

PRESIDENT JOHNSON:

I am about to sign into law the Civil Rights Act of 1964. I want to take this occasion to talk to you about what the law means to every American. We believe that all men are created equal. Yet many are denied equal treatment. We believe that all men have certain unalienable rights. Yet many Americans do not enjoy these rights. We believe that all men are entitled to the blessings of liberty. Yet millions are being deprived of those blessings—not because of their own failures, but because of the color of their skin. . . . But it cannot continue. Our Constitution, the foundation of our Republic, forbids it. Morality forbids it. And the law I will sign tonight forbids it. Its purpose is not to punish. Its purpose is not to divide, but to end divisions—divisions which have lasted too long. Its purpose is national, not regional. Its purpose is to promote a more abiding commitment to freedom, a more constant pursuit of justice, and a deeper respect for human dignity. We will achieve these goals because most Americans are law-abiding citizens who want to do what is right.

Elizabeth Eckford passes through lines of National Guardsmen as she enters segregated Central High School in Little Rock, Arkansas. September 1957.

George W. Crockett, Jr.

"Racism in the Courts"

I refuse to allow myself to forget the fact that I am a black judge. Once I do that, I think I'm lost. I recognize that I wouldn't be a judge on Recorder's Court today if I were not a black man. It just would not happen. And so, I must be on the court for some special purposes. I think the first special purpose the black judge serves is that he is a symbol, a symbol of hope, a symbol of belief on the part of America's black people that they also are included in the Constitution's "We the people." It does me good when classes from high schools come to visit Recorder's Court—they may be integrated classes—and I see the eyes of the little black boys and girls just open up. It never occurred to them that they were coming to a court where there would be a black man sitting on the bench as a judge. That's what I mean when I say the Negro judge is a symbol of hope that eventually America will come to its senses, that eventually justice will be the same for all, regardless of race, creed, color, or economic status. As long as there is that hope, that black child can aspire to be anything that any other American can be.

The second thing I like to remember is that a black judge must be a special guardian of the rights of minority groups. We live in a country that spends a lot of time talking about majority rule, and forgetting or ignoring minority rights. As a black judge, I am the product of a history that compels me to be concerned with minority rights, the rights of the poor, and of the underprivileged. So I go behind whatever is presented to me. I don't take the policeman's version at face value, and I persist in asking "Why." I want the full story in the record. I know from my own experience as a black man and as a black lawyer what has been going on, and still goes on under the guise of "discretion." It is an important part of my job to lay bare the actual happening, not to cover it over.

This brings me to the third special function of the Negro judge, and that is to serve as the conscience of the court in racial matters. During the riot last summer, when I found that my fellow judges were literally tearing up the Eighth Amendment to the Constitution, I sent each one a letter reminding him that the law of Michigan as well as the law of the United States forbids a judge fixing high bail just for the purpose of holding people in jail. Then I went on the bench and said the same thing in a loud, clear voice for the benefit of the press. I then proceeded to release people on what you call OR (personal bond), if my own questioning of them satisfied me that their community or family ties were such that they could be expected to return to court voluntarily when wanted. And partly because I took that position, my fellow judges, after about two days of fixing high bail of $10,000 for everyone, came in line and started also fixing bail that was more in accord with reason and the circumstances of the individual defendant. It is because a Negro, who has himself been a victim of these experiences, is on the court to serve as the conscience of the court, that eventually his fellow judges can be counted on to lay aside their prejudices and do what is required to be done under the law.

* * *

It is a fact that the image of the Negro lawyer nationally is not a good one intellectually or economically. What is so little understood, however, by our white brothers in the profession, is the degree to which their own racial discriminations and prejudices have contributed to the Negro lawyer's poor national image. Past discriminatory practices by white law schools have resulted in a national Negro bar composed in the main of products

---

With the onset of the Civil Rights movement in the early sixties, the emerging role of blacks in the legal profession became a major issue. In this excerpt from an article written in 1969, George W. Crockett, Jr., reflects on his role as a black judge and on the progress of African-Americans in general.

of Jim Crow law schools—schools which offered an admittedly inferior legal education.

Past exclusion of black lawyers from the American Bar Association and from various state and local legal societies have denied them access to continuing legal education institutes, to adequate law libraries, and to a working acquaintanceship with current legal periodicals. The geographic exclusion of the black lawyer from the downtown areas of our cities; his exclusion from membership in country clubs and business clubs, where important contacts are often made and maintained; the grudging respect accorded him by some judges; and the withholding from him of that spirit of mutual professionalism which invites comradely exchange of views on difficult or involved legal questions—are just a few of the practices which account for the poor national image of the black lawyer.

Because of these practices, the Negro lawyer is limited for the most part to black clients and usually to the less affluent black client. Because of these practices, he is required to represent a disproportionate number of impoverished clients. Because of these practices, he must be content with court assignments refused by others. Because of these practices, he must devote an inordinate amount of his time to Civil Rights and other areas where there are only nominal or no monetary awards. And he must do it all with grossly inadequate equipment, personnel, and physical surroundings. No wonder the average net income of full-time Negro lawyers in 1965 was $11,300. There are a few hopeful signs on the horizon: the appointment of a Negro Solicitor General, a Negro U.S. Supreme Court Justice, several United States District Attorneys, and 15 out of more than 300 Federal Judges. These appointments, and the existence of about 65 Negro state judges of courts of record in the United States, help improve the image of the Negro lawyer. But none of these legal positions is in the deep south where the bulk of the black people live, where a Negro judge could spell the difference between justice and injustice, and where the presence of a Negro judge would give concrete meaning to the ideal of equal justice and would serve as a stimulus to Negro youth.

Some progress also has been made in the employment of Negro lawyers in government, in industry, and as partners or associates in predominantly white law firms. But, in the main, these appointments are appointments as house counsel, positions which permit very little courtroom exposure. Moreover, all too frequently, these appointments are made for purposes of show or to comply with the no-discrimination clauses in government contracts or they are made purely for political reasons. There is minimal opportunity for advancement and virtually no out-of-office association. Because of these limitations, the better trained, the more aggressive black lawyers are refusing governmental and house counsel appointments.

The truth of the matter is that the Negro lawyer who, despite his poor pre-law training, and his economic and social deprivations, has managed to successfully compete with his white classmates and to graduate from one of our top white law schools is far superior to most white lawyers usually found in government service or on the house counsel staffs of large corporations. The black lawyer has to be superior to be noticed. I share the view that the future of the Negro lawyer will become brighter and brighter, and this irrespective of the rate at which the legal profession voluntarily integrates. Three reasons support this view. First, because most of the Jim Crow law schools have closed or are closing. The two or three remaining predominately Negro law schools are becoming integrated and are receiving substantial money to upgrade their curriculums and improve their faculties. This development, together with the increased admission of black students to northern white law schools, is bound to produce a higher caliber of black lawyer who will be able to attract to his office the large number of affluent Negro patrons who until now, and with some justification, doubted the ability of the black lawyer to compete in a "white" court and against a white lawyer.

The second reason why I look for continued improvement is the growing political power of the Negro voter. This growing political power will guarantee more elected and more appointed Negro officials, more integrated courtroom staffs, and hence more confidence by Negro litigants in the ability of black lawyers to get an impartial hearing in courts that are no longer all white. The third reason why I look for continued improvements in the economic status of the black lawyer is the greatly increased consciousness that Negroes have today of their racial identity. This is causing, and it will continue to cause, more Negroes to seek out and employ black counsel and to boycott industrial firms and law partnerships that do not utilize the services of black lawyers.

Already, the formation of interracial law firms is on the increase in many of our major cities. Many white law firms, and the corporations they represent, are suddenly awakening to find that they are located in the core city, and are now surrounded by Negroes as their white clientele continues to flee to suburbia. More and more blacks are being called to jury duty. If this trend continues, and all predictions are that it will, the day is not far distant when these corporations and white law firms in any of fifty of our largest cities will welcome a black lawyer to represent them before these predominantly black juries.

Leon Jaworski

FROM THE RIGHT AND THE POWER

"We Affirm the Order . . ."

We had subpoenaed the sixty-four conversations because we needed them to round out the evidence in the cover-up case before it went to trial—and to provide the defendants with any exculpatory information they might find in them.

Strong in my mind was the President's refusal to supply us with the eighteen conversations I considered most vital to our case after he had reviewed them—electing instead to be exposed as an unindicted co-conspirator in the bill of particulars. Somewhere in those conversations, I was sure, was evidence even more damaging than that we had compiled, but it would never be made public if we lost our case before the Supreme Court.

* * *

I was to take the laboring oar and open our argument for an hour. [James] St. Clair then was to argue some seventy-five minutes. My counsel, Philip Lacovara, was to have thirty minutes to close, then St. Clair would have fifteen minutes more. Lacovara and I seated ourselves at the counsel table facing the bench. Nine empty chairs behind the bench awaited the Justices. I looked around me. There are larger rooms than this, I thought, but it seems as massive as a great cathedral. Even the dark rows of seats emitted strength, as if they had been carved from an imperishable wood. I had argued several cases before this Court and I was struck as always by the vast dignity this room imposed on one. It seemed that every face around me reflected the sudden knowledge that this was a *special* place where the honor of the Republic reposed. The double row of pillars on each side of the room appeared capable of holding up every good intention every Administration had entertained.

"Oyez! Oyez! Oyez!" The marshal was calling the Court into session—and my ner-

---

In 1973, Americans were shocked to learn that their president, Richard Milhous Nixon (1913–), had been bugging his own Oval Office and would not release what were believed to be incriminating tapes for use as evidence against the Watergate conspirators. In this excerpt from his 1976 book, Special Prosecutor Leon Jaworski (1905–1982) recounts his argument before the Supreme Court, the final step in his struggle to obtain the tapes.

vousness disappeared. Behind the bench, from behind heavy burgundy drapes, emerged the eight black-robed Justices who would hear the case. All of these months, I thought suddenly, it has been like walking on a tightrope, hoping I wouldn't slip, hoping someone else wouldn't make me slip, knowing always that a slip would be pounced on, knowing that a slip could cost it all. The timing had been everything, I thought. An unseen hand had arranged the timetable so that even the grinding frustrations had played their part in delaying or hastening the action so that all of us, at this precise moment in time, had reached this rendezvous with history.

The preliminaries were over and I was on my feet facing the Justices. To my far left was Justice Powell. Then Justice Marshall. Justice Stewart. Justice Douglas. Chief Justice Burger in the center. Then Justice Brennan, Justice White, Justice Blackmun. Justice Rehnquist's chair was empty.

From the beginning it was obvious the Justices were not in the frame of mind for oratory. They wanted facts and the truths on which they rested. In my allotted hour I was interrupted 115 times. There was no opportunity for a sustained, orderly presentation. Despite the lack of continuity in my argument, I was grateful for the interruptions; they enabled me to explain more fully salient points, and they allowed the Justices to get a better grasp on the ramifications of the issues.

I began by referring to the cover-up indictment, the grand jury's vote that the President should be named as an unindicted co-conspirator, our subpoena for the tapes, St. Clair's motion to quash it, and the subsequent revelation of the President's unindicted co-conspirator status.

A Justice broke in. "I don't see the relevancy of the fact that the grand jury indicted the President as a co-conspirator to the legal issue as to the duty to deliver pursuant to the subpoena that you are asking for."

While I was explaining the relevancy, Justice Stewart broke in, and he was followed by Justices White, Brennan, and Powell. We thrashed out the question, and I made my point that the President's status made evidence admissible for trial that otherwise would not be, that his being named a co-conspirator made absolute our right to the tapes. In the process I also was striking a blow at executive privilege since in this instance it was a shield for wrongdoing in the White House, and not a safeguard for military or diplomatic secrets.

I made my way through the questions to bear down on what I considered to be the heart of our argument:

> Now enmeshed in almost 500 pages of briefs, when boiled down, this case really presents one fundamental issue—who is to be the arbiter of what the Constitution says? Basically this is not a novel question—although the factual situation involved is, of course, unprecedented.
>
> There are corollary questions, to be sure. But in the end, after the rounds have been made, we return to face these glaring facts that I want to review briefly for a final answer.
>
> In refusing to produce the evidence sought by a subpoena *duces tecum* in the criminal trial of the seven defendants—among them former chief aides and devotees—the President invokes the provisions of the Constitution. His counsel's brief is replete with references to the Constitution as justifying his position. And in his public statements, as we all know, the President has embraced the Constitution as offering him support for his refusal to supply the subpoenaed tapes.
>
> Now, the President may be right in how he reads the Constitution. But he may also be wrong. And if he is wrong, who is there to tell him so? And if there is no one, then the President, of course, is free to pursue his course of erroneous interpretations. What then becomes of our constitutional form of government?
>
> So when counsel for the President in his brief states that this case goes to the heart of our basic constitutional system, we agree. Because in our view, this

COLORPLATE 103

BEN SHAHN. *Integration, Supreme Court.* 1963. Tempera on paper on masonite. 36 × 48″ (91.4 × 121.9 cm). Des Moines Art Center. Purchased with funds of the Edmundson Art Foundation, Inc.

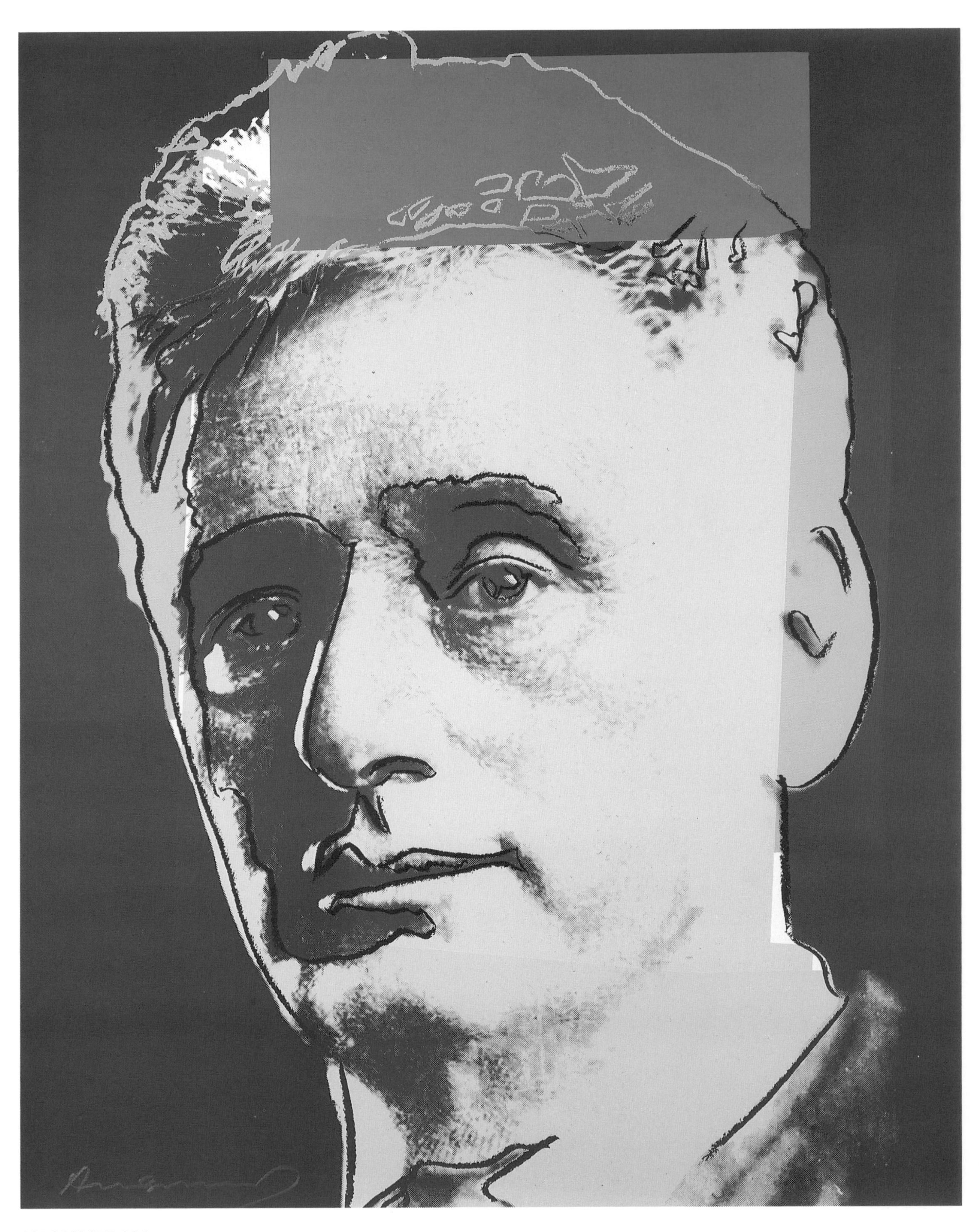

COLORPLATE 104

ANDY WARHOL. *Louis Brandeis.* 1980. Silkscreen print, edition of 200. 40 × 32″ (101.6 × 81.3 cm). Courtesy Ronald Feldman Fine Arts, New York. Copyright 1990 The Estate and Foundation of Andy Warhol / ARS, New York. *Graduating at the head of his class at Harvard Law School in 1877, Louis Dembitz Brandeis (1856–1941) became an often unpaid "people's attorney," breaking legal ground in areas affecting the welfare of working people, such as affordable life insurance and labor-management relations. Despite opposition due to his reputation as a radical, he was appointed U.S. Supreme Court justice in 1916.*

COLORPLATE 105

JACK LEVINE. *The Trial.* 1953–1954. Oil on canvas. 72 × 63" (182.9 × 160 cm). Art Institute of Chicago. Friends of American Art.

COLORPLATE 106

HANK VIRGONA. *The Defense Sums Up*. c. 1970. Watercolor and oil on paper. 11 × 13⅛″ (27.9 × 33 cm). Courtesy of the artist.

Leon Jaworski, special prosecutor in the Watergate investigation, arrives at the U.S. Supreme Court. July 8, 1974.

> nation's constitutional form of government is in serious jeopardy if the President, any President, is to say that the Constitution means what he says it does, and that there is no one, not even the Supreme Court, to tell him otherwise. . . .

St. Clair argued that the Court had no right to rule on the case because, he said, it was a political procedure from which the Court was excluded. The House Judiciary Committee's impeachment inquiry was political, he said, and because the Special Prosecutor would give the tapes to the Committee, the entire process was political.

Justice Marshall said, "The only thing before us is as to whether or not the subpoena should issue. That's not political . . . you are still saying the absolute privilege to decide what shall be released and what shall not be released is vested in one person and nobody can question it. . . . "

St. Clair replied, "Insofar as it relates to the presidential conversations, that is correct, sir. . . . "

In his rebuttal argument, Lacovara said, "This is a criminal proceeding, a federal criminal case against six defendants. A subpoena has been issued to obtain evidence for use at the trial. . . .

"The Court cannot escape the fact that this is a trial of tremendous national importance, but a trial that was brought to a head without regard to the impeachment inquiry. . . ."

St. Clair wound up by saying that the Court should stay its hand until after the impeachment hearing had run its course. "Because those are political decisions being made, they should not bear the burden, either way, of a judicial decision."

Said Justice Douglas: "Well, under that theory, all the criminal trials that are going on should stop, then."

Said St. Clair: "That would not be the first time, Mr. Justice Douglas, that a criminal trial was delayed. And in balancing the importance to this nation, I would suggest that this is clearly indicated."

Time was up. As I made my way out of the Court I recalled a pointed statement by Justice Douglas. I had been emphasizing that St. Clair's briefs time and time again insisted that only the President was the proper one to interpret the Constitution on executive privilege.

Justice Douglas had leaned forward and said, "Well, we start with a Constitution that does not contain the words 'executive privilege'—is that right?"

"That is right, sir," I had said.

And Justice Douglas had said, "So why don't we go on from there. . . ."

As I neared the sunlight I didn't feel exhilarated, but I did feel that we would prevail, and by a one-sided margin. I was preoccupied with my thoughts, and some of the reporters who greeted me outside later said that I appeared unhappy. St. Clair, some wrote, appeared triumphant. I may have been a bit brusque when the press questioned me.

Suddenly a crowd was around me at the top of the steps. The applause was loud, and someone shouted, "Way to go, Leon!" I had to push my way through, and then the crowd followed me. A few people were knocked down in the crush, and one man tumbled into a flowerbed. Finally I made it to my car. "Law students," said one of the staff. "Ninety percent of those people are law students."

* * *

Outside the Supreme Court, the crowd had seemed larger than when we had tried the case—and louder. Inside the packed hall the tension was palpable. Neal and Lacovara were with me at our table. St. Clair was not at his table; others were there to take the decision. St. Clair was with [Alexander] Haig and other presidential aides in San Clemente. The President, I had strong reason to believe, was waiting confidently for news of victory, though I had no idea of what St. Clair had been telling him. Further, I had reason to believe that Nixon, from the time he first concluded not to surrender the tapes, was confident that his assertion of executive privilege would prevail. We would soon know.

The marshal cried out his ancient command. The drapes parted and the eight Justices took their seats. At that moment my body relaxed. I felt relieved of a burden. All will be well, I thought. I waited for Chief Justice Burger to read the Court's opinion, which he had written.

But he spoke first in memory of former Chief Justice Earl Warren, who had just died in California. It was fitting, I thought, that he should speak of Warren on this day, in this Court. Warren had been both praised and demeaned because he stretched and broadened the power of the Court. Today Chief Justice Burger and his associates would plow virgin land.

He began reading the opinion in a clear and expressive manner, speaking with an assurance, it appeared, that the holding he was revealing was sound and just. The case, he said, had satisfied all the legal requirements to be properly before the Court; and then he launched into the Court's opinion on the question of the Special Prosecutor's right to sue the President.

In the District Court [he said] the President's counsel argued that the court lacked jurisdiction to issue the subpoena because the matter was an intra-branch dispute between a subordinate and superior officer of the Executive Branch and hence not subject to judicial resolution. That argument has been renewed in this Court. . . .

The President's counsel argues that the federal courts should not intrude into areas committed to the other branches of Government. He views the present dispute as essentially a "jurisdictional" dispute between two congressional committees. Since the Executive Branch has exclusive authority and absolute discretion to decide whether to prosecute a case, it is contended that a President's decision is final in determining what evidence is to be used in a given criminal case. . . .

Our subpoena was justified!

While the Chief Justice had been reading smoothly, placing emphasis where emphasis was needed, it seemed to me that now he took a longer pause than usual, as if he were preparing to explain the heart of the matter.

We turn to the claim that the subpoena should be quashed because it demands "confidential conversations between a President and his close advisors that it would be inconsistent with the public interest to produce." The first contention is a broad claim that the separation of powers doctrine precludes judicial review of a President's claim of privilege. The second contention is that if he does not prevail on the claim of absolute privilege, the court should hold as a matter of constitutional law that the privilege prevails over the subpoena *duces tecum*.

In the performance of assigned constitutional duties each branch of the Government must initially interpret the Constitution, and the interpretation of its powers by any branch is due great respect from the others. The President's counsel, as we have noted, reads the Constitution as providing an absolute privilege of confidentiality for all presidential communications. Many decisions of this Court, however, have unequivocally reaffirmed the holding of *Marbury* v. *Madison* . . . that "it is emphatically the province and duty of the judicial department to say what the law is."

No holding of the Court has defined the scope of judicial power specifically relating to the enforcement of a subpoena for confidential presidential communications for use in a criminal prosecution, but other exercises of powers by the Executive Branch and the Legislative Branch have been found invalid as in conflict with the Constitution. . . .

Since this Court has consistently exercised the power to construe and delineate claims arising under express powers, it must follow that the Court has authority to interpret claims with respect to powers alleged to derive from enumerated powers. . . .

Notwithstanding the deference each branch must accord the others, the "judicial power of the United States" vested in the federal courts . . . by the Constitution can no more be shared with the Executive Branch than the Chief Executive, for example, can share with the Judiciary the veto power, or the Congress share with the Judiciary the power to override a presidential veto. Any other conclusion would be contrary to the basic concept of separation of powers and the checks and balances that flow from the scheme of a tripartite government. . . .

We therefore reaffirm that it is "emphatically the province and the duty" of this Court "to say what the law is" with respect to the claim of privilege presented in this case. . . .

I had said, "Now the President may be right in how he reads the Constitution. But he may also be wrong. And if he is wrong, who is there to tell him so?" The Chief Justice had just answered that question—the Court would tell him so.

Chief Justice Burger read on. His voice, reaching every corner of the hall, was the only sound to be heard. His listeners were rapt. What was the law with respect to the claim of privilege presented in this case?

> We conclude that when the ground for asserting privilege as to subpoenaed materials sought for use in a criminal trial is based only on the generalized interest in confidentiality, it cannot prevail over the fundamental demands of due process of law in the fair administration of criminal justice. The generalized assertion of privilege must yield to the demonstrated, specific need for evidence in a pending criminal trial. . . .
>
> On the basis of our examination of the record we are unable to conclude that the District Court erred . . . accordingly we affirm the order of the District Court that subpoenaed materials be transmitted to that court. . . .

We had won.

Chief Justice Burger continued, explaining the District Court's heavy responsibility in seeing that presidential conversations which were not relevant to the case were "accorded that high degree of respect due the President of the United States." He concluded: "Since this matter came before the Court during the pendency of a criminal prosecution, and on representation that time is of the essence, the mandate shall issue forthwith. . . ."

We had won. And then came the information I had so much wanted to hear: the holding of the Court was unanimous!

Scott Turow

FROM ONE L

3/29/76

Spring vacation. Lord, how often I wondered if I'd ever make it this far.

In the past two weeks, the weather, after sporadic temptings, has lolled into spring. The gray is out of the sky and the feeling is pure liberty.

A week away from the Mighty H: Harvard, Harvard, Harvard—I cannot describe how sick I am of hearing that name. The whole university is suffused in such crazy pretense, a kind of puritan faith in the divine specialness of the place and its inhabitants. It's upper-class parochialism. I was told a story recently about a secretary who was fired after her first day on the job because she did not know how to spell the name of the university's president.

The law school is hardly immune from that kind of snobbism. It is an education in itself, learning to worship HLS. A few years ago the man then dean would instruct each student entering to refer to it as "*The* Law School." Much of that attitude seems to carry over to the present faculty. Fowler recently presented a problem in mortgage law which, he said, "you won't find troublesome when you encounter it in practice, unless, of course, the other side is represented by a graduate of the Harvard Law School, or perhaps Yale."

Former English teacher Scott Turow (1950–), author of the best-selling and critically acclaimed novel Presumed Innocent *(1987), entered Harvard Law School at the advanced age of twenty-six. This excerpt is from his 1977 autobiographical work, which comprises journal entries made during his first year at* The *Law School.*

Harvard-love at HLS even goes so far as to amount to a kind of prejudice in favor of the law made by Harvard jurists. Perini never fails to mention it when an opinion he likes was authored by a judge who is a graduate of HLS. Most revered is the late Justice Felix Frankfurter, now a sort of Harvard Law School idol. Frankfurter was an HLS professor when he was elevated to the U.S. Supreme Court, and I guess he is the embodiment of half of the faculty's lushest fantasy. In addition, many profs were his students; a number—including Fowler—were his clerks. Frankfurter, in truth, was a giant, but his opinions are all treated like biblical texts and his style of jurisprudence, now probably dated, is uncritically endorsed in most classrooms.

Amid the adversities of the first year, we have all been particularly susceptible to this kind of thinking about HLS. It must be special, you tell yourself; why else, in God's name, am I going through this? Our presence at Harvard Law School is for many of us the only thing left on which to rest our self-esteem and we have all at one time or another gone around assuring ourselves how fortunate we are to be here, how smart we must be. The standard of excellence stuff feeds on all of that—makes us run harder to prove that we are worthy, really are the best.

Of course all the HLS chauvinism would be silly, as well as offensive, were it not for the fact that over time people at Harvard Law School have made believers of so many others. It might all be a snow job, but there is still that aura which draws the firms and the politicians, and even the tour buses on the weekends. (In the latter case, it may be nothing relating to the law which is the attraction. I was standing in front of the law school recently when three young women piled off one of the buses and begged me to point out the dormitory where the young hero lived in *Love Story*.) In the legal world, with its formalities and stratifications, people cannot resist thinking of a top layer of law schools, and Harvard and Yale are pretty much it.

As a result, it is simply assumed at HLS that a Harvard J.D. is a stepping stone to big things. Mann often told us he was addressing us as a group of future judges and law profs. Guy Sternlieb goes even further. We are now doing a section on what Guy calls "political analysis." We dissect political environments and evaluate options for actors within them. Sternlieb will often issue challenges to the class. "Damn it, there's a reason I teach this course. You people are going to be congressmen and mayors and State Department officials in twenty years. What will you do in these situations? What will you say?"

I am glad Guy asks those questions, but I am still a little discomfited by a place which is so cheerfully assumed to be the training ground for the power elite. That peculiar pride represents an incredible, if tacit, stake in the status quo, and also amounts to a quiet message to students that their place in the legal world should always be among the mighty. It produces the kind of advocate who is uncommitted to ultimate personal values and who will represent anyone—ITT, Hitler, Attila the Hun—as long as the case seems important.

Am I saying, then, that I'm sorry I'm at Harvard Law School? I don't think so (although looking ahead to spring exams, which are always thought of as the pit of the first year, I reserve judgment). None of my observations on the law school are meant to be wholeheartedly damning. It's just that three quarters of the way through the year, I have realized that HLS, with its great size and wealth of resources, is a place where you must always pick and choose. I see myself in these last few months making an effort to regard the place more realistically, to keep myself from looping into either ecstasy or despair as I meet up with the diverse range of what is offered. And the arrogance of HLS is one of the things I am most eager to escape. It makes the environment even more claustrophobic and consuming and leaves me grateful for whatever few reminders I get that Harvard and the law school are not really the center of the universe. I had a nice one last week, a letter from a poet friend, a professor at a southern university, to whom I'm sure the Ivy League has always been a kind of distant mystery. The letter was long delayed in reaching me because it had been addressed care of Harvard Law School, Harvard University, New Haven, Connecticut.

Jurors' chairs in Grady County Courthouse, Cairo, Georgia. 1976–1978. Photograph by Jim Dow. Seagram County Court House Archives Collection. © Library of Congress, Washington, D.C. Photograph courtesy Jim Dow.

Melvin Belli

FROM MY LIFE ON TRIAL

When I stand up to argue a case, heaven knows what knowledge and what experience I will call upon to make a point. It may have been something that happened at sea years ago while I was standing watch on the foc'sle head. It may have been something I learned while riding the rods during the Depression. In the middle of a prepared argument I may see something in an exhibit I'd never really noticed. If I can relate that to an event in my own life years before, I might help a jury to better see the central issue in a case. See it my way.

Sometimes a single word or a phrase can win—or lose—a case. Once I had a doctor on the stand (my witness in a medical malpractice case) who was attempting to explain to my jury what had happened wnen a young man bled to death after a simple tonsillectomy. The doctor reconstructed the operation and its aftermath. "And then," he said, "the patient exsanguinated."

"Doctor," I said, "what is that?"

" 'Exsanguinated,' " he said, "is when you seize a chicken by the legs, turn it upside-down and cut its throat. When all the blood has drained out of the chicken, it's 'exsanguinated.' "

In my final argument to the jury, I didn't have to go into any lengthy description of what had happened to my young man. The word *exsanguinated* was enough.

The flamboyant "King of Torts," Melvin Belli (1907–), relates some spectacularly successful courtroom tactics and reflects on the role of the lawyer in America today in these excerpts from his 1976 memoirs.

Another time, trying a wrongful death case in federal court in Portland, Maine, I think I won with four little words. My client was a famous little Chinese boy who had lost his mother. In my second day of trial, when it was my turn to speak, I bowed to the jury and said, *"Gung hoy fat choy."* Judge, jury and the other side's counsel were equally astounded. So I said it again. *"Gung hoy fat choy."* Opposing counsel stuttered an objection. The judge said, "What is that, Mr. Belli?"

"It is Chinese New Year's today," I explained. "My little client simply wants to wish a Happy New Year to the jury and to Your Honor. It is an ancient Chinese custom."

The judge could only beam. So did most of the jury. But during recess my adversary hustled out to the nearest phone booth in the hall. I followed, entered the phone booth next to his and heard him telling someone, obviously the "home office" of his insurance company, "Yeah, no, I'm not drunk, that's what he said, something like *'gung hoy fat choy.'* He said it meant 'Happy New Year' but whatever it was, the son-of-a-bitch has won over the jury. We'd better bail out." His company authorized him to settle for $250,000—which was an extremely high award for New England in the late fifties. I think it was mostly my *"gung hoy fat choy"* that did it.

Of course, *gung hoy fat choy* is not so very arcane to me. My office is only a block away from San Francisco's Chinatown. I frequently lunch there and enjoy the celebration each year of the Chinese New Year. Knowledge is where you find it. And I find it everywhere, near and far.

★ ★ ★

Anyone who takes an overall look at two hundred years of American history must conclude that this is a great nation, holding for the most part on course. Our friends and enemies abroad might judge from their observation of all the bickering on the bridge that the U.S. ship of state is going nowhere in particular. But they would be wrong. We are a contentious people, and as de Tocqueville observed way back in 1834, a litigious people as well. "Don't tread on me" was the legend under a coiled rattlesnake on more than one of our original state flags. But we are great precisely because we are contentious. All the arguing and litigation only make us stronger. Macaulay wasn't too far wrong when he said we obtain the best decision "when two men argue, as unfairly as possible, on opposite sides." Good ideas only get better when they have to meet a challenge in a public forum, whether that forum be in the news media or in a courtroom.

Our system is great, I believe, because it puts the highest value on open advocacy. No one has exclusive possession of "the public interest." We need an effective urging of opposing views to sharpen every issue and help identify where the public interest really lies. And for this we need lawyers, too. In the wake of Watergate (whose horrors were perpetrated by some who were, in fact, lawyers) critics are proposing the elimination of attorneys from public councils. But Richard Nixon and his gang weren't removed from office by a bloody coup. They were eased out by due process of law—in part by other lawyers who weren't politicians.

And I am encouraged by many other signs of the times. Increasingly, I see good law and good lawyering working to the benefit of all the people, thus protecting the people from the lawlessness of big business and big government. I realize businessmen and bureaucrats don't think of themselves as outlaws. Businessmen say all they want to do is make a profit. All bureaucrats want is the power to get us in line and make us march to the beat of their drums. And I'll be the first to admit I'm a capitalist and I carry insurance and use banks, the telephone and buy products from Standard Oil.

When the people at large see official lawlessness (and they do, thanks to a press which gets more vigilant every year), they do not turn to revolution and armed insurrection, they turn to the law. For every injury and injustice, there is a remedy in the law. Or ought to be. In the past, this ancient axiom worked only for those who had the money to hire a good lawyer—which hardly made for any kind of equality under the law. That's changing in America. Now, everyone who is criminally accused gets an attorney (and generally a damn good one) whether he can afford one or not. Now, every person who is civilly wronged is increasingly able to obtain counsel who will take a case for a share of the award or for a surprisingly realistic fee. Access to a good lawyer gets easier every day.

Our numbers are increasing; the law schools are jammed with smarter, more socially oriented men and women, and the last restrictions against a lawyer's advertising his availability are crumbling. And that . . . I had something to do with. The canons of the Bar have banned advertising up to now; it was unseemly and unethical to "stir up litigation." As far as I am concerned, it still is. I think there is entirely too much litigation in America today, too many people filing lawsuits against a neighbor with a barking dog, too many Redskin fans raising a legal question about a referee's decision that cost their team a victory. Twenty-eight of every thirty people who phone me on a given day don't really have a case. And I tell them so.

But advertising need not "stir up litigation." There are many, many people with good causes for legal action who never contact any lawyer. They don't know how—or whom—to call, and for that reason they are not *equal before the law*. The law and the Constitution are not self-executing. Due process is a sham unless you can get a lawyer to drive the due-process vehicle—and I think the right kind of advertising will help people find attorneys who will do that for them.

The Federal Trade Commission and the U.S. Justice Department and the courts have now come to see the logic of all this; they have reevaluated the old strictures on advertising by lawyers. Now, if I interpret the Goldfarb case correctly, lawyers *can* advertise. And so, in the past few months, I have planned a display ad in the Yellow Pages:

CONSULTATIONS
3–5 P.M.
Monday, Wednesday, Friday
Melvin M. Belli
The Belli Building
722 Montgomery Street
San Francisco

Our aim: to make due process available to *everyone*. The rich have always had legal care, and in the past ten or fifteen years so have many of the poor. But we ignore the majority of middle-class Americans. Our consultation may help change this situation. (And so will a newly emerging form of prepaid legal care, an idea Danny Jones and I espoused fifteen years ago, fifteen years ahead of time.) I have each of the lawyers in my office take turns on consultation duty and I take my turn, too. What do we get out of it? A sense of satisfaction in the thought that we are helping people. For the most part, we refer people to another public or private agency, but we are always on the lookout for something interesting—not a big, obvious money-maker (because those cases will have been chased and lined up by others long before they come walking in my door) but a situation, perhaps, which cries out for some creative imagination and may help us pioneer a new trail in the law. As I've said in lectures to attorneys all over the land, no one ever walked into a lawyer's office and announced, "I have a case that will make legal history." A good legal mind has to see through to the core of a case, explore its ongoing legal ramifications and its social importance—and then work with all his ingenuity to make the wheels of justice turn in a new way.

This is the challenge of the law for me and the lawyers in my office. We are trying to help make a good system better, trying to help make the promises of the Constitution a reality for all.

We are not the only ones who do this. There are hundreds (I hope thousands) of lawyers in America engaged in a similar struggle, particularly the younger ones: providing counsel for those who have none, harmonizing relations between the races, assisting the consumer, protecting the environment, advancing individual rights. I am thinking of the members of my trial bar, the Association of Trial Lawyers of America, of Ralph Nader and his lawyer teams around the country, various public-interest law firms and of Morris

Dees and Julian Bond of Alabama, who have involved me in their lawsuit against a family planning clinic in Montgomery and various federal agencies for sterilizing two poor, ignorant, black teenage girls without adequate consent. I was happy to get into their Relf case; it seemed like a clear-cut way to strike another blow for the rights of the individual against the potentially untrammeled power of big government. And I was happiest to think that these younger lawyers wanted to include me in their community of concern.

No matter where I go in America, no matter what accents I hear, I find that these younger lawyers and I are speaking the same language, and that our brainstorming sessions are informed by the same understanding of the Constitution. These lawyers keep me young, they teach me new applications of the law (often enough, those who teach me are the youngest, freshest faces around the table) and they make me proud to be a lawyer.

Justice Oliver Wendell Holmes once said that a man must share the passion and the action of his times—or run the risk of not having lived. I have shared. I have lived. And I expect to keep on doing so for some years to come.

Louis Nizer

FROM REFLECTIONS WITHOUT MIRRORS

I enjoyed the practice of law more when we were a small firm with one clerk. Each client received personal attention at all times. There were no departments to which he was sent for specialized advice to be ushered back to the senior for final decision. But the complexity of society has revolutionized law offices, just as it has the medical profession and business.

Today there is barely a legal service that may not be affected by tax consequences. So there is a tax department—lawyers who have made a life study of the tax laws and their kaleidoscopic changes from year to year.

Modern business is not content with internal growth. Acquisitions and mergers are resorted to for accelerated advancement. So there is an acquisitions department—manned by lawyers who understand the applicable regulations and procedures of the Securities and Exchange Commission.

On the other hand, growth can run afoul of the antitrust laws. So there is a department knowledgeable in the law of monopoly.

The public is now the largest of all corporate investors. So stockholder minority suits and proxy battles for control abound. There is a department trained to defend or conduct such contests.

So it is with wills and trusts, copyrights, divorce, real estate, libel, international law, and myriad other problems a law firm must solve to give a client a full rounded professional service. That is why, unfortunately, the individual practitioner or small law firm is at a great disadvantage. That is why law firms today are composed of fifty, a hundred, and even several hundred lawyers under one firm name and under one roof.

The process is not dissimilar to that which has occurred in business, where the small entrepreneur is at an ever-increasing disadvantage against the chain or huge competitor.

As an entertainment lawyer, the London-born Louis Nizer (1902–) has represented such luminaries as Charlie Chaplin and Mae West in dramatic cases. Nizer is the author of several books, including My Life in Court *and* The Jury Returns. *This excerpt is from his 1978 book, subtitled* An Autobiography of the Mind.

Even in medicine scientific advances make medical complexes with available laboratory services, and specialists in various branches, superior to the individual practitioner. How is one doctor to keep abreast of all the progress daily recorded?

Sometimes people introduce themselves and tell me they are clients of my office. I am always humiliated by such an incident, because I consider the role of adviser and counsel uniquely personal. But a complex society separates us from intimacy. There was a time when if your neighbor was ill, you would bring him soup, a hot-water bottle, and your personal solicitude. Today we live in huge cement cubicles and we do not even know who our neighbor is, though he may reside a few feet away.

I cherish the anecdote of the family doctor in a little town who has delivered children, treated them during infancy and maturity, and brought their children into the world. He has taken care of all ills from surgery to mental disease, and his intimate knowledge of the patient and his forebears have given him insights which no contemporary analyses alone could provide. Having grown old and tired from caring for an ever-increasing flock, he heartily welcomes a new graduate who has come into town to practice medicine. He hopes the young doctor, superbly trained, will relieve him ultimately of his responsibilities, but he soon learns that the newcomer does not intend to be a general practitioner. He will be a specialist. "Of the stomach?" the old doctor asks. "Oh no, that is too large a field for one man to master."

"Of the ears, nose, and throat?"

Of course not, there has been such an accumulation of knowledge in these areas that he cannot hope to absorb it all.

The old practitioner can contain himself no longer.

"What nostril do you intend to specialize in?" he asks.

Despite the growth of legal domains, I have striven with might and main to keep direct contact with each client. For I firmly believe that the psychological comfort which a client derives from his lawyer or doctor is of immense importance. A man or woman in trouble needs more than advice or even ultimate relief. There is the intervening period of deep anxiety which must be bridged. It is unnecessary torment, because it contributes nothing to solution, and enervates the victim, whose cooperation is necessary. I consider it the lawyer's duty to address himself to this problem as much as to the pure legal problem presented.

The client, like a patient, who is in trouble is highly sensitive to the demeanor of his adviser: a smile and confident manner are great therapy. A furrowed brow or pursed lips strike terror in the heart of the troubled. The attorney or doctor may only be gesturing unconsciously about a minor aspect of the difficulty, but to the overwrought, disaster is being registered. Scowls should be reserved exclusively for the adversary. Whether the condition is physical or mental, the body does wonders to ease the suffering, if given a chance.

Of course, the truth cannot be tampered with even to assuage suffering. But what is the truth and how is it to be presented? I tell the client that the problem is serious, and that I do not take a Polyanaish view of it, but I am confident that it can be solved, that far worse has been overcome, and that he may be sure all our energy and resourcefulness will be applied to correct the situation. This is combined with a direct appeal to leave his worries on our doorstep. If he will realize that the ogres he dreams about are exaggerated shadows cast by him standing in his own light, he will understand that they are not real. Some peace of mind then becomes possible.

There is also the matter of "client relationship." Often lawyers are too busy and harassed taking care of the client's battles to worry about informing him or her of developments. What is more cruel than such suspension? Even adverse news is preferable to the imagined disasters conjured up by silence. Frequently there is no news, nothing but delay, but this is no excuse for not reporting—not if the attorney is sensitive to the client's fears. A telephone call or personal report of developments, even if they are thin or nonexistent, is tonic for the client's nervous system.

In short the lawyer or doctor who ignores the psychological areas of his professional duty is as unfaithful to it as if he were guilty of malpractice. Indeed it is humanistic malpractice to be unaware of the client's or patient's suffering when it is possible to alleviate it.

To overcome the impersonal aspect of a large law office, and mindful of the importance of knowing the client profoundly, I adopt what may be considered an inefficient procedure of inviting the most junior associate who may assist in a case to sit in at the very first conference with the client. The young lawyer is not assigned to a cubbyhole to prepare pleadings or bills of particular, or to research in the library, on the basis of an abstract presentation of the problem. He is introduced to the human side of the law, literally and in person. He hears the original, perhaps disjointed, and self-conscious description by the client, with all its telltale emphasis, evasions, or irrelevant excursions. He observes the client's candor, sometimes significantly burned at both ends. If he is perceptive, avenues for further factual research may open up, and may lead to resourceful legal ideas.

Also, empathy for the client is likely to be created (if it is distasteful, he should be taken off the case quickly), and this stimulates the effort, just as hostility dampens it.

I recall a matrimony case in which my associate dedicated himself at all hours on behalf of our client. However, when we discussed developments privately, he laughingly doubted her protestations of virtue.

The client repeatedly pleaded with me to have a junior, who was assisting in the case, assigned to her. She paid tribute to the talents and devotion of the associate, but she was enamored with the talents of the junior, not half as able.

The associate was flabbergasted by her ingratitude. I suggested that his private opinion of her had come through to her. He remonstrated that this could not be, he was fond of her and had never indicated his skepticism. It was difficult for him to realize that there are emanations which cannot be disguised.

Seymour Wishman

FROM CONFESSIONS OF A CRIMINAL LAWYER

My mind drifted to my preoccupations of the last months—I wondered how many times I had been asked what I got out of being a criminal lawyer. "You spend most of your time with monsters," "You're in and out of depressing places like prisons all day long," "The pay isn't extraordinary," "You're looked down upon by judges, other lawyers, and the public." It wasn't hard to explain why very few lawyers did criminal work and even fewer went on doing it for any length of time. I struggled to understand why I had remained in this work for more than fifteen years.

Most criminal lawyers I had met over the years were extraordinarily perceptive about the personalities of others. They could impressively predict how a person would respond to certain kinds of pressures or questions. But in their personal lives these same lawyers, with their enormous egos, fed by the "power" available to them in the courtroom, and reinforced by their "victories," often had little understanding of their own behavior. And

---

Criminal attorney Seymour Wishman (1950–) analyzes the complex relationship between his courtroom work as a defender of accused criminals and his personal life in this excerpt from his soul-searching account of his life.

William Gropper. *Cross Examination.* Before 1971.
Lithograph. 12 × 7⅜″ (30.5 × 18.7 cm).
Harvard Law Art Collection, Cambridge.

William Gropper. *Conference at the Bench.* Before 1971.
Lithograph. 12 × 7⅜″ (30.5 × 18.7 cm).
Harvard Law Art Collection, Cambridge.

as a psychological defense mechanism, they concealed even from themselves their failure to understand their own motivation by claiming to have little interest in it.

The courtroom was a forum in which the lawyer could act out a whole range of intense emotions. Half joking, a colleague once told me, "It's better than going home and beating up my wife." I looked at him and wondered how much this was actually a joke.

Over the past years I had often expressed rage, or indignation, or joy, or sadness in a courtroom. At one level these displays had been fake or, at least, suspect: they were controlled and purposeful. I'm sure I wasn't the only trial lawyer who knew exactly when he was going to "lose his temper," what he would say or do while his temper was "lost," and how long it would be before he recovered.

The Supreme Court of Tennessee once said in a written opinion that the use of tears is "one of the natural rights of counsel which no court or constitution can take away," and that "indeed, if counsel has them at his command, it may be seriously questioned whether it is not his professional duty to shed them whenever proper occasion arises. . . . "

At another level, I realized, this display of contrived emotions had been as real as anything else in my life. I had felt genuine rage during an outburst when I had trapped a cop lying; I'd had real tears in my eyes when describing a horrible wound.

For years I had been troubled by my difficulty in expressing the same range and depth of feeling outside the courtroom. A personal relationship seemed infinitely more threatening than a packed courtroom. Frequently, the problem wasn't just in the expression of feeling but in a failure to experience those feelings, or to experience them with sufficient intensity to recognize them.

What was there about the courtroom that made the expression of emotions possible? The lawyers knew the rules and the acceptable limits of any emotional outburst. We were given license to be demonstrative, in fact, we were encouraged to be, because that was the way the system operated; that was the way lawyers had always acted; it was only a performance anyway, and everybody knew it; and it was all done on behalf of someone else—the client.

But getting angry in a personal confrontation could mean actually losing control and becoming vulnerable, and that could be terrifying. We never lost control in the courtroom. Quite the opposite, we showed virtuoso skill at appearing transported by emotion, while every moment keeping it all on a tether.

All the emotions and skills on that tether were supposed to be deployed for one purpose—winning. During the cross-examination, all available energy was spent on beating the witness. With a tough witness, the duel could be dramatic. Only rarely, and with great reluctance, would a lawyer admit that more than the pleasure of good craftsmanship had been involved in his subduing of a witness, but I had seen lawyers work a witness over, control him, dominate and humiliate him, then torment him. Deriving enjoyment from inflicting that unnecessary measure of pain might be rare, but not that rare. If the witness was a woman, there might even be sexual overtones to the encounter. With some lawyers, perhaps sometimes with me, similar patterns could be played out in personal relationships.

* * *

About a month earlier, an acquaintance had come to see me, filled with enthusiasm about a rehabilitation project he wanted to launch. As he excitedly explained his plan to set up a center to help drug addicts, I found myself pulling away physically, leaning back in my chair. Here was someone I had known for several years, someone who should have been an intimate friend, speaking with concern and insight about a subject I knew well and should have cared more about. Coldly I marshaled statistics and logic and, with lawyerly skills developed over the years, demolished his plan—never considering with generosity whether the plan had any merit. After my acquaintance left my office deflated, as perhaps others had done before him, I realized I envied his optimism, admired his eagerness to do something about an outrageous problem. My own capacity for outrage, genuine outrage, had long ago been traded for cynicism. What had once been a shield of self-protection separating me from a psychologically threatening criminal world had assumed the pretension of a personal philosophy. The chances for intimacy with new friends or new ideas had diminished slowly over the years without my noticing it. With lower expectations of people and ideas, I could no longer be disappointed easily. Aside from the self-defeating limits this attitude imposed on my relationships, it was a depressing world view to be alone with.

Charles R. Maher

*"The [1] *[1]Infernal Footnote[2]"*

*[4]COUNTLESS[3] *[5]law students and legal researchers have been afflicted with Ping-Pong Ocular Syndrome,[4] *[6]and several with Brightoncliffe's Phenomenon,[5] *[7]because of the apparently incurable addiction of legal writers to the footnote.[6]

Legal footnotes are the bane of law scholars; this rule applies to both readers and authors. But the "footnote menace" described in this article, once properly dissected, can also give rise to a few laughs.

[*8]You've doubtless seen scores[7] [*9]of illustrations of this addiction in *Corpus Juris Secundum,*[8] [*10]Kluptpfester's *Negligence in the Operation of Funicular Railways*[9] [*11]and other celebrated works. At the top of a page will be two or three lines of text, the balance of the page being covered by a Himalayan heap of footnotes, some of which have probably spilled over from the previous page, at the top of which was one line of text. Assuming, arguendo,[10] [*12]that people who do things like that should not be publicly flogged, the question arises: How otherwise to combat the footnote menace?[11] [*13]The answer, of course, is to expose it, and this article has been prepared in easy-to-read fashion to do precisely that.[12]

[*14]In the case of encyclopedic works, perhaps, authors may be excused if their footnotes happen to occupy only slightly less space than the surface of Saturn. It must be admitted that case citations are at least occasionally useful to the legal practitioner.[13] [*15]Similarly, authors of law review articles may be pardoned for their footnotational extravagances. When you've got too much junk to fit in the house, the cellar may be about the only place to put it.

Not to be forgiven, however, are three other breeds of footnote artists: the Exhibitionist,[14] [*16]the Obsessive Annotator[15] [*18]and the Midsentence Dislocationist.[16] [*20]All such footnotefeasors are guilty (as the jury will be instructed to find before their trial begins) of an unspeakable offense.[17]

FOOTNOTES

1. Warning to reader: This article contains compound footnotes and reciprocal reference marks, either of which may cause dizziness or split vision unless handled according to directions. Reciprocal reference marks are asterisks followed by numbers (*e.g.:* ***10**). These symbols, revolutionary in concept, are found in the footnotes and direct the reader to *preceding* rather than to subsequent points in the article. They are introduced by an arrow symbol, →, meaning "Kindly go back to the point indicated by the reciprocal reference mark, and be quick about it." You will encounter the first such symbol at the end of this paragraph and will be directed to the reciprocal mark ***1**, suspended just before the second word in the title of the article. Once there, begin reading at that word and continue until you encounter a conventional, asterisk-free footnote mark directing you elsewhere. Repeat this procedure each time you arrive at a raised reciprocal mark in response to an arrow command. Caution: When finished reading, do not operate forklifts or heavy machinery for at least three or four hours, whichever occurs sooner.**→*1, title.**

2. Welcome back. A footnote is "a note of reference, explanation or comment placed below the text on a printed page or underneath a table or chart. . . ."[a] [*2]Abbrev.: fn.[b] [*3]*Webster's Third New International Dictionary of the English Language,* at 885 (abbrev. at 880).[c]

3. countless: of such great number as to defy counting. . . ." *Ibid.,* at 521. Sometimes also used to describe the status of a widowed countess, as in "The countess is countless."

(You are approaching another reciprocal reference mark and are entitled to know that for purposes of brevity, as well as confusion, the abbreviation **t** will be used hereinafter for **text.**) **→*5, t.**

4. So called because the reader's eye, jumping from text to footnote and back to text, resembles that of a spectator at a Ping-Pong match. The difference being that the spectator at least knows what the score is. **→*6, t.**

5. Named for the renowned Lord Justice Percival Brightoncliffe, whose practice it was to keep his left forefinger pointed at footnote numbers in the text while tracing the footnotes themselves with his right forefinger. Alas, he panicked one day while trying to follow a particularly treacherous footfootnote. This triggered a convulsive reaction known as "forefinger recoil," the lamentable result of which was that the good justice poked out both of his eyes. And thus was born the expression "justice is blind."**→*7, t.**

6. See **fn 2** and its progeny. Then **→*8, t.**

7. Of which the following are merely a few examples:

Green Bay 17, Chicago 16

St. Louis 14, Philadelphia 10
Houston 3

(Because of an oversight by the schedule makers, Houston played this particular week without an opponent. After failing to cross midfield for more than three periods, the Oilers finally won the game when one of their backs muffed a pitchout, swung his foot at the ball in disgust and inadvertently kicked a field goal.) **→*9, t.**

8. West Publishing Co. (St. Paul: 1963). Watch for the gripping sequel, *Corpus Juris Thirdum.* Sorry, but we're sworn not to reveal the electrifying ending. **→*10, t.**

9. Symon & Shyster (Ober Grafendorf: 1839). Translated from the Tyrolean by O. d'Laeheehu. **→*11, t.**

10. This word is a corruption of R. Guendeaux, the name of an infamous 16th century Transylvanian war minister known for his disputatious manner and loud neckties. **→*12, t.**

11. The runaway growth of the footnote industry is thought by many to rank right up there with the skateboard craze among the great perils faced by Western society since World War II.[d]

12. To be sure, easy reading like this can wear you out. You may feel free at this point to take a break, the time for which has just expired. And now, as a reward for having come this far, you may proceed to any footnote or footfootnote of your choice.[e]

13. See Dimwitty's *Advanced Legal Research and Other Parlor Tricks.* Tragically, the author died at a rather early age (11) and left only one copy of this masterpiece, in handwritten manuscript form done entirely in crayon. But legal scholars will find it readily available at his mother's house, just up the street from the 7-Eleven. **→*15, t.**

14. His byword. "If you don't think that was a great article I wrote, just count the footnotes." **→*16, t.**

15. Some writers annotate excessively not to show off but simply because they can't help it.[f] [*17]Perhaps the most irredeemable of this class was Prof. S. Llewellyn Screed, author of an unpublished treatise (*The Dry Well and Its Place in Riparian Law*) containing 39 words of text and 78,853 words of footnotes, some of which were so extended they had to be broken into chapters. **→*18, t.**

16. This is the writer who plants a footnote number in a long sentence, sending the reader scurrying to a note the length of the Palsgraf case.[g] [*19]Having returned from that note after hacking through a half acre of typographical underbrush, the reader apparently is expected to resume reading the text at midsentence as though not the slightest distraction had intervened.[h]

17. Gross abuse of footnation, for which the minimum penalty is amputation of both feet, above the wrists. Although footnotes are at best rather hard-to-reach subterranean storage vaults that should be used as little as possible, if that often, they have been used by these defendants knowingly, wilfully, intentionally, consciously, deliberately and more or less on purpose for misplacement of two common types of material: (1) that which properly belongs only in the custody of a licensed trash collector, and (2) that which is worth preserving but which could just as easily be worked into the text.[i]

FOOTFOOTNOTES

a. Hi. The origin of the footnote is lost in antiquity. One legend is that it was introduced circa 3777 B.C. by the Abalonian writer Hammerknocker. Composing a love verse in stone one day, Hammerknocker committed a transpositional blunder, chiseling out "moon harvest" instead of "harvest moon." This, of course, was before the development of erasable stone. Not wishing to discard an otherwise flawless work, Hammerknocker invented the asterisk, inserted a specimen of his invention after "moon harvest" and, in history's first footnote, chiseled at the bottom of the stone: "*Sometimes also called 'harvest moon.' "

What you are reading now, by the way, is called a footfootnote (ffn) or footnotenote (fnn). For a penetrating study of this device, see Fleishbender's *The Pathology of the Foot-*

footnote and Related Disorders of the Lower Extremities. Pathological Press (Skittsafrenia, N.Y.: 1937). **→*2, footnote 2** (and, in case you still haven't got the hang of it, begin reading at "Abbrev.," the word following the raised symbol *2).

b. The abbreviation **n** is more common in legal texts and other whimsical works. But the more formal **fn** is better suited to serious writing and accordingly will be used hereinafter. **→*3, fn. 2.**

c. G. & C. Merriam Co. (Springfield, Mass.: 1966). This volume also contains an excellent full-page color illustration of butterflies and moths (facing page 297). Note particularly the sinister Pipevine Swallowtail butterfly. How'd you like to meet one of these in a dark meadow?

(You are about to receive an arrow command directing you to the first raised reciprocal mark in the text. Remember, whenever sent in search of such a mark, to look first for an asterisk, so as to avoid confusing a reciprocal mark with a like-numbered footnote mark that may be hovering nearby.) **→*4, text.**

d. For the benefit of younger readers, World War II was a rather drawn-out and at times impolite confrontation in which the Allies finally prevailed after the intervention of John Wayne. **→*13, t.**

e. Except this one, which is none of your business. **→*14, t.**

f. Their inability to restrain themselves makes them no less detestable. **→*17, fn 15.**

g. *Palsgraf v. Long Island R.R. Co.*, 162 N.E. 99 (1928). By the way, while this overrated case is fresh in mind, can anyone explain how on earth the explosion of a small package of firecrackers at one end of a railway platform "threw down some scales" clear at the other end, causing injury to the estimable Mrs. Palsgraf? After 55 years, it's high time we got an answer to this question—and it better be good. **→*19, fn 16.**

h. California's best-known legal writer, Bernard E. Witkin, touches on the problem of reader dislocation in his *Manual on Appellate Court Opinions*. West Publishing Co. (St. Paul: 1977), at 78–80:

" 'If judicial opinions had Blue Cross, they could go to the hospital and have their footnotes removed.' (Gordon, August 1974 *ABA Journal*, page 952). A converted former 'ardent footnoter,' Justice Gordon directs his main attack at the placement in footnotes of holdings on points of law, but he also complains of the difficulties facing 'the reader of the footnote-bedecked decision,' *who must deal with the physically separated pieces of the opinion*. [Emphasis supplied.]

" . . . [E]ven where footnoting is appropriate, it ought to be reasonable in size and scope. . . .

"One commentator (Simonett, December 1969 *ABA Journal*, page 1141) has a few words of tongue-in-cheek praise for '[t]he essay footnote, the commentary that competes with the main text, where the author undertakes an excursion on some tangential point, interesting in itself if not essential to the text. . . .' "

Simonett (as quoted by Witkin) then excavates an abyss into which to hurl himself: "Legal writing is reasoned writing and tends to be taut."

One could readily argue, in response, that legal writing not only doesn't tend to be taut but often doesn't even tend to be taught.

Simonett continues: "[A]nd yet there must be some flexibility, some room. The excursionary footnote provides this extra space, a kind of necessary extravagance. Tea need not be served in a cup with a saucer, but the saucer does add a touch of elegance and catches the spillage."

Which spillage is poured down the sink, where it belongs. **→*20, t.**

i. Where it could be read with less irritation and more comprehension. Reason: Continuity is to understanding what Simon was to Garfunkel, and footnotes are the enemies of continuity. In fact, when used indiscriminately, rather than in the judicious manner employed here, footnotes may leave readers hopelessly disoriented, so that they will never get to the point you will have reached with no difficulty in just two more words.(1)

---

(1) The end.

COLORPLATE 107

GEORGES ROUAULT.
Justiciers
(Men of Justice).
c. 1913.
Crayon, ink,
and watercolor
on paper.
$11\frac{13}{16} \times 7\frac{1}{2}''$
(30 × 19 cm).
Musée d'Arte
Moderne de la Ville
de Paris.

COLORPLATE 108

BEN SHAHN. *The Passion of Sacco and Vanzetti.* 1931–1932. Tempera on canvas. 84½ × 48″ (214.6 × 121.9 cm). Whitney Museum of American Art, New York. Gift of Mr. and Mrs. Milton Lowenthal in memory of Juliana Force. *Despite the circumstantiality of the evidence, Nicola Sacco (1891–1927) and Bartolomeo Vanzetti (1888–1927) were arrested on May 5, 1920, for robbery and murder, at least partly because of their reputation as revolutionaries, anarchists, and draft evaders during the "Red Scare" of 1919–1920, and because of their being Italian. Condemned to death after a patently unfair trial and denied an appeal for a new trial, despite worldwide protest and a confession to the crime by another convict, they were executed in August 1927.*

COLORPLATE 109

BEN SHAHN. *Voting Booths.* From the series *Great Ideas of Western Man.* 1950. Gouache on canvas. 15⅞ × 12″ (40.2 × 30.4 cm). National Museum of American Art. Smithsonian Institution, Washington, D.C. Gift of the Container Corporation of America.

COLORPLATE 110

NORMAN ROCKWELL. *The Problem We All Live With.* 1963. For *Look* magazine, January 4, 1964. Oil on canvas. 36 × 58" (91.4 × 147.3 cm). The Norman Rockwell Museum at Stockbridge, Massachusetts. Printed by permission of the Estate of Norman Rockwell. Copyright © *Look* 1963 Estate of Norman Rockwell.

DEPUTY
U.S.
rockwell

COLORPLATE III

JACOB LAWRENCE. *To the Defense*. 1989. Gouache on paper. 31⅝ × 24″ (80.3 × 61 cm). Courtesy of Francine Seders Gallery, Seattle, and the artist.

COLORPLATE 112

JAUNE QUICK-TO-SEE-SMITH. *Courthouse Steps.* 1987. Oil on canvas. 72 × 60″ (182.8 × 152.4 cm). Courtesy of Bernice Steinbaum Gallery, New York. *When a land developer intended to turn a New Mexican petroglyph park (in which there were rocks with ancient Indian pictograms and others with early Spanish markings) into a golf range, a court order was obtained against him. In the middle of the night, consequently, the developer removed a two-ton stone from the park and laid it on the courthouse steps (shown in the middle of the painting).*

COLORPLATE 113

ANDY WARHOL. *Red Disaster*. 1963. Silkscreen on linen. 93 × 80¼" (236.2 × 203.8 cm). Museum of Fine Arts, Boston. Charles H. Bayley Picture and Painting Fund. Copyright 1990 The Estate and Foundation of Andy Warhol / ARS, New York.

Donald J. Evans

"Forgotten Trial Techniques: The Wager of Battle"

It looked like a straightforward property controversy. Two neighbors, Killscheimer and Zagortz, had not spoken to each other for 15 years. When Killscheimer went on vacation, Zagortz put up a fence that ran through some long-disputed territory on the border of their lots. When he returned, Killscheimer insisted that the fence encroached on his property. Zagortz claimed the land was his.

One of our partners had advised Killscheimer successfully on a complex capital gains problem, so Killscheimer paid him a visit when he received a menacing-looking document from Zagortz. The tax partner sniffed at it suspiciously and finally identified it as a summons and complaint. Suggesting that a second opinion would be prudent, he hastily ushered Killscheimer down to my office, introduced us and fled.

Zagortz, it developed, was represented by a certain Abner Bailey, Esq., a moth-eaten but wily old lawyer who knew every trick in the book—and had devised many of them. Shortly before the trial date, Bailey sent me an envelope containing an old glove stapled to a legal-size piece of paper. Under the caption of the case, it read:

> WAGER OF BATTLE
>
> By ancient right of the Common Law of this State, Claimant Zagortz does hereby require that Demandant Killscheimer appear on the date appointed in his proper person or by champion on the field of battle, there and then to wage battle and so prove by his body the truth of the matter hereinabove captioned.
>
> Yours very truly,
> Abner Bailey, Esq.

Bailey had neatly attached our state's newly revised rules of civil procedure to the forms of medieval trail by combat. It looked as if he had finally gone off the deep end.

DUFFY'S RESEARCH

That afternoon I told one of our first-year associates, a bright kid named Duffy, to prepare a motion to dismiss Bailey's gambit. About a week later I asked Duffy how he was doing.

"Well, sir," Duffy spluttered, "it's not exactly a simple matter."

"What do you mean?" I said, a sinking feeling welling up in my chest.

"The wager of battle. My research indicates that it probably remains a legally available form of trial in this state."

The sinking feeling moved to my stomach.

"The wager of battle was a valid, though little-used, part of the common law of England as late as the 19th century. It was invoked so infrequently that I guess Parliament never got around to abolishing it until 1819. In the meantime, of course, the American colonies had declared independence and were not affected by the 1819 English reform statute. The problem is that our state constitution provides that the inhabitants of this state"—he picked up a book and read—" 'are entitled to the Common Law of England . . . and to the benefits of such of the English statutes as existed on the Fourth day of

---

In this parody of hard-boiled pulp fiction, Raymond Chandler is mixed with old English common law to produce a wry tale of legal and lethal battle.

July, seventeen hundred and seventy-six.' Because our legislature has never passed a bill abolishing this particular common law right, it looks like Zagortz is legally entitled to demand a battle. Interesting, isn't it?"

Duffy was just warming up. "It turns out that in criminal trials by battle, the challenged party had to fight the battle himself—'in his proper person.' But in civil cases, a person could have a champion fight his trial for him. Killscheimer won't have to fight the battle himself."

"Killscheimer will be thrilled." I perked up a little. "Come to think of it, I know a couple of big ex-cons—former clients as a matter of fact—who could probably handle themselves pretty well in a trial by combat."

"Er, there's a problem with that," Duffy said. "I checked informally with a buddy of mine at the state board of legal ethics. He feels that a hired champion in a trial by combat would actually be representing a client in a court of law. To avoid a charge of unauthorized practice of law, the hired champion would have to be an attorney."

I had never knowingly glowered at anyone in my life, but I was doing it now.

GOLDSTEIN'S ASSESSMENT

That night I was brooding over a drink at the darkest end of a bar when Goldstein, one of our partners and a sometime friend, plopped down next to me. "Why so glum?" Goldstein said, ordering drinks for both of us.

"Did you hear about old Bailey?" he asked. "He's always been a solo but they say he just hired a young associate who goes about six-foot-four, 220 pounds. They say he's the orneriest son-of-a-gun ever to graduate from State Law. They call him Grunt Malone."

"When exactly did Bailey hire him?"

"About two weeks ago."

"Just before Bailey demanded a trial by battle in the Killscheimer case?"

"Come to think of it, yeah."

All began to come clear. Under the procedures applicable to trials by combat, the defendant's champion had either to defeat the claimant in battle or maintain the battle from dawn until the first star appeared in the sky. Goldstein cooed comfortingly while I explained that a member of our firm was apparently going to have to go *mano-a-mano* with a gentleman by the name of Grunt, with permanent maiming a distinct possibility. Goldstein patted my hand and departed, leaving me with the tab.

A SEARCH FOR REINFORCEMENTS

The next morning I asked our office manager for the résumés of recent applicants to our firm. Perhaps I could beat Bailey at his own game. I told her to throw out all the Ivy Leaguers and put anyone from the Big 10 on the top of the pile. Unfortunately, very few law school graduates are also sumo wrestlers or international terrorists. One applicant's résumé indicated that he had been on his college crew team, and I summoned him for an interview. He turned out to have been a coxswain. I fairly booted him from my office.

We had filed a thick motion with the court pointing out 18 different reasons why Bailey's maneuver should be rejected. But the court felt itself bound by Zagortz's undeniable rights under the common law as it had existed in 1776.

THE TRIAL DATE

Dawn on the appointed day arrived. The sky was just brightening when Duffy picked me up and drove me to the park in front of the courthouse.

I had tried to borrow an impressive-looking suit of armor from the museum in town, but the curator was worried that it would get dented and scuffed. Fortunately, my brother-in-law is the coach of our high school football team. He lent me a uniform complete with an oversized set of shoulder pads. A ragged orange life jacket completed my ensemble.

The sun was almost up and a sizable crowd had begun to form. Killscheimer and Zagortz were there, glaring at each other from opposite sides of the clearing. Killscheimer, my client, expressed his confidence in me by asking whether we could appeal the outcome.

Malone, Bailey and Zagortz were standing on the opposite side of the clearing, joking and laughing with the museum curator, who was counting a fistful of bills. Malone looked like a cross between a bull and one of the larger primates. He was garbed in a sartorially perfect suit of 16th century armor.

Judge Aubery Bennington had drawn the unhappy lot of presiding over the proceedings. He was obviously cross at having to get up at sunrise. Judge Bennington asked if the parties were present. Malone and I clanked and lumbered forward. The judge's law clerk held up a dusty old book from which he read the prescribed ritual. Malone was obliged to swear that the tenements in dispute did not belong to Killscheimer. Whereupon I swore that the tenements in dispute did not belong to Zagortz. Each of us then swore the required oath against enhancement:

"Here ye, ye justice, that I have this day neither eat, drank, nor have upon me, neither bone, stone, or grass; nor any enchantment, sorcery or witchcraft, whereby the law of God may be abased, or the law of the devil exalted. So help me God and his saints."

With that, Judge Bennington retired to a chair set up at one end of the clearing and made himself comfortable.

ON TO BATTLE

There had been a few points that Bailey and I had worked out at the pretrial conference. The rules of battle permitted each champion a stave "an ell long," but the size and character of this item was in dispute. We compromised on baseball bats. Thus armed, Malone and I carried our weapons to the center of the clearing.

As Malone and I approached each other in the middle of the clearing, he began to loom a lot bigger than six-foot-four. I began to think of the ancient rule of battle by which either combatant could at any time cry out "Craven!" thereby conceding the fight and at the same time dooming himself to lifelong ignominy. Suddenly lifelong ignominy didn't seem all that bad.

All I had to do was stay clear of him until the first star appeared in the sky, and victory would be mine. I was starting to show Malone my Ali shuffle when he landed a murderous

Engraving of knights engaged in a trial by wager of battel. Fifteenth century. Library of Congress, Washington, D.C.

blow to my rib cage. I could hardly move without excruciating pain, much less dance nimbly around the clearing for 12 hours. We circled each other, dealing and warding off blows with an enormous clatter.

After an hour and a half of combat, I had become a primitive man. I found myself adopting the classic aggressive postures of a mature primate I had seen on a *National Geographic* TV special. But, at age 37, even a mature primate who jogs a few miles a week and eats French yogurt will tire rapidly. Malone looked like he was just getting warmed up. I figured that Malone's head was his least sensitive organ, so I went for his body. With a lucky swing of my bat, I caught him in the groin and left him on the ground making noises like a dying boar.

But he got up and came on like a madman, wielding his bat with a fury that would have impressed Attila. One of his blows broke my bat, another ripped my shield away, a third tore the helmet off my head. Malone kicked me in the stomach, and I fell backwards.

I looked up and saw stars. Could they be the first stars of the evening? I shook my head and the stars disappeared. Instead, I saw Malone lifting his giant bat high over his head in preparation for the coup de grace.

QUICK THINKING

At that instant I spotted a small furry thing hanging from Malone's armor. "Your honor!" I cried, raising myself on one arm. "The plaintiff's champion has upon his person an enchantment of bone, to wit, that rabbit's foot hanging from his armor. He has therefore foresworn his oath against the use of amulets of sorcery. I move for a directed verdict." Then I blacked out.

Later, at the hospital, I was told that Judge Bennington had examined the lucky rabbit's foot, referred back to the proscription on articles of sorcery and enchantment and pronounced immediate judgment for Killscheimer. There was jubilation, I was told, among the small group of fools who had laid wagers on my victory. On Zagortz's side there was much weeping and gnashing of teeth. The fence would be removed.

A couple of weeks later I limped gingerly into the office. "Hey," Goldstein called as I made my way slowly past his office. "I've got a client who'd like you to represent her in a trial by combat against her ex-husband. How about it?"

I bopped him expertly with my cane.

Jerry Phillips

"Thirteen Rules for Taking Law Exams"

After grading nearly 200 3-hour law exams over a 10-day period of approximately 10 hours a day, I began to observe certain elementary rules of examination-taking which I will describe for the benefit of present and future students.

I

1. The first rule is: never spell correctly any word which is central to the content of the course. For example, if the course has had the law of libel as a central theme, and the

---

For most would-be attorneys, taking legal exams is a patently serious matter. But there are ways to circumvent the drudgery element and still succeed, as this risible self-help essay points out.

word is in the examination question, spell it "lible," or—more commonly—"liable." If the course has dealt almost exclusively with the hearsay doctrine, and the word is in the exam, spell it "heresay," or better yet, "heresy."

Such misspellings serve several purposes. For one thing, they establish your independence of thought. They also allow you to reaffirm the principle that you are studying law and not English. But perhaps most importantly, they weaken the teacher's resistance so that he will more readily accept greater errors to come.

2. The second rule is a corollary of the first: be ungrammatical. This rule not only allows you to reaffirm the principle that you are studying law and not English, but it also allows you to becloud your thinking so that the teacher is unable to tell whether you know what your are talking about or not. The importance of being able to do this is obvious.

3. A rule that is very similar to the rule of ungrammatical construction is that of internal errors. This handy rule may take a variety of forms. For example, you can write "plaintiff" when you mean "defendant," or "do" when you mean "do not," or "three" when you mean "two," or vice versa, *ad infinitum*. This rule also serves the dual purpose of confusing the professor and of concealing your lack of knowledge.

An important variation on the internal-error rule is to fail to number your answers. In this situation the teacher will usually be unable to tell one answer from another, based simply on their content, with the result that he will hopefully assume that you have written a minimally passing answer to all questions. Also, if the answers are weighted you can cancel out any adverse effect that might otherwise accrue as a result of this factor.

A variation on the variation is to spread your answer to a single question intermittently throughout one or more answer booklets. You may state, "See first page in next booklet," in which event be sure to use the last page of the present booklet, or vice versa. But you need not give any direction at all. The teacher is expected to read everything that you write, no matter what the order. Or, you may tear out a page of an answer from one booklet and insert it in another, with no indication as to where it belongs in the examination sequence.

You may vary this routine by writing marginal explanations and qualifications that curl around, convolute and crowd in upon the main body of the answer in such a way that neither is decipherable.

4. Rule 3 brings us inevitably to Rule 4, which is one of the most basic rules of all: write illegibly. You may write your entire examination illegibly, but if you do that you run some risk of alienating the teacher to such an extent that he may fail you out of exasperation. The better practice seems to be to write most of the exam semi-legibly, so as to tire the teacher, and then sneak in total illegibility at various critical points where you are unsure of yourself. The teacher may then conclude that your brain is working faster than your hand and thus give you an acceptable grade, or in all events his resistance or eyes will be so weakened by the time he reaches the critical portions that he will knuckle under and assume that the illegible portions are no worse than the semi-legible ones.

Thus the advantages of illegibility are clear. Moreover, you can always justify your illegibility on the ground that you are studying law and not penmanship.

5. One of the most important basic rules is to repeat yourself *ad nauseam* throughout your answers. Possibly the teacher will not recognize the repetition for what it is if you vary the language sufficiently, and you may thereby gain additional points. Also, such repetition serves to camouflage the fact that you can't think of anything else to say.

Perhaps the best way of starting an answer is by restating the facts and issues of the question. If you are sufficiently verbose, you can usually take up at least one page of a three-page answer in this way, and thus decrease the amount of independent writing that you would otherwise have to do. You can also restate portions of the facts farther along in the answer when you can't think of anything else to say.

Repetition has numerous advantages. Besides helping to fill your booklet, it permits you to tread on sure, firm ground. What can be more acceptable than the words of the teacher himself? One of the cardinal virtues in answering a law school examination is to deal with the facts, and Rule 5 permits you to do just that.

II

Thus far, this primer has dealt with what might be termed elementary or mechanical rules of examination-taking. There are also more advanced rules that require significantly more skill to apply. However, based on extensive first-hand experience, I have implicit faith that the average student with a reasonable expenditure of effort is capable of adapting these more advanced rules to his own needs and abilities.

6. The first more advanced rule—and the sixth in your development—is never to answer all of the issues raised by the question. If the teacher does not expressly state the issues to be discussed, it may be comparatively easy to apply this rule. But an express statement of the issues should never deter you. Although you may find it difficult to do so, just pick one or two of the issues at random and leave them out of your answer.

The advantages of this rule are almost unlimited. The teacher usually has four or five issues in a question he considers basic to the answer. He thinks these issues are fairly obvious, and occasionally if he has any doubt he will leave red flags lying in the hypothetical so that the student will be sure to see them. Acting on this assumption, he will compute his grading scale based on the simplistic idea that the student will at least touch on all the issues.

Imagine, then, the havoc you can create in his grading scale by leaving out one or more of the issues! You can be fairly certain that by the law of averages different groups of students will leave out different issues so that the process of making any meaningful comparison of answers will be rendered virtually impossible. The choices available to the teacher are essentially three: (1) to fail substantially all of the class, which is politically infeasible; (2) to pass substantially all of the class, which is totally unrealistic; or (3) to grade arbitrarily, which enables you to shift all blame to the teacher and to conclude that the whole system is a hoax. The psychological advantages alone are worth it.

One may conclude that all of the more advanced rules of examination-taking are merely corollaries of Rule 6. Nevertheless, it is worth your while to consider some of these corollaries in detail.

7. A most useful rule is to misread the question, or else to fail to read it fully. Thus you can in effect rewrite the question more to your own preconceptions and abilities. Alternatively, you may make assumptions or inferences that are unsupported by the question, and then base your answer in whole or in part upon such asssumptions and inferences.

The teacher has already been properly softened by your orthographic and grammatical errors. If he has an ounce of humanity he will hopefully conclude that a misreading differs from a misspelling in degree only. Thus, you accomplish your primary purpose of foisting mediocrity on the teacher, and hopefully ultimately of doing the same to the unsuspecting public as well.

8. Never follow through on an issue. If there is an applicable general rule, it is all right to state it, but never state its critical qualifications to which the question is actually directed.

Another way of applying this rule is by referring to some case in the text that dealt with a similar situation without pointing out the important differences between the case in the text and the hypothetical at hand. Surely the humane teacher will give you at least a minimally passing grade for remembering that there were similar cases.

If you follow through on an issue, you may become confused. You may find that certain issues on an examination are bottomless, and if you get too involved you may blow it completely. Of course it is possible to map out the alternatives and a plan of attack for an answer before beginning to write, but this approach is unnatural and furthermore, it wastes valuable examination time.

9. Stick to generalities since this always provides an avenue of safety. If you have read or at least skimmed substantial portions of the text for the course, and/or if you have attended an average number of classes, then in all likelihood the material on the exam will bear some resemblance to a number of matters to which you have been exposed during the course. By regurgitating generalities you can kill two birds with one stone: first, you can demonstrate your breadth of knowledge; second, you can avoid the thorny, nitty-gritty issues of the actual question. What could possibly provide a happier compromise?

10. Reach a conclusion, and assume categorically that the contrary position is untenable. Thus you can avoid discussing the contrary position, about which you know little or nothing.

11. Under no circumstances should you give any semblance of order to your answer. No less an authority than Emerson said that consistency is the hobgoblin of little minds. Furthermore, order and development of presentation are liable (libel?) to reveal the extent of your knowledge of the course. In any event, you are taking a law exam and not writing an English essay.

12. Never state an issue concisely (or better yet, never state an issue). Thus you keep the teacher guessing as to whether you know what he is talking about, or what you are talking about. This rule is particularly helpful if you don't know what either you or he is talking about.

13. The last rule, and the most critical of all, is always to avoid using any imagination in answering a question. Imagination is one of the most dangerous attributes of the human mind. From the first grade, if not before, you have been taught to conform, so that by the time you reach graduate school non-conformity is generally recognized to be irrelevant. The result is that any imaginative effort you may undertake you assume will be ludicrous—with the self-fulfilling result that it usually is. Therefore, stick to stating generalities, or to repeating the facts, or, if you are an above-average student, to stating generalities and applying them precisely to the facts. But in no event and under no circumstances should you ever attempt to burst any boundaries or rearrange any chaos. The teacher does not deserve to be stimulated when grading papers.

Or, if you choose to burst some boundaries, then go completely wild. Forget the law, forget the fine distinctions of judgment that have been suggested by the text and (hopefully) by your teacher, and talk instead about God, man, and the universe. Surely the teacher will recognize unharnessed genius!

III

The application of these 13 simple rules of course will not enable you to write an excellent examination, since they are not designed for that purpose. Their purpose is rather to enable you to write a minimally acceptable examination in order to get by. They are designed for those who feel that getting by is all that is necessary or desirable.

For the student who may sometime want to try his hand at writing an outstanding examination, a good starting place is to apply each of the 13 rules in reverse. Spell correctly, write grammatically, consistently, legibly and economically, answer the questions fully and accurately, follow through on your reasoning, be specific, be sparing in your assumptions and liberal in your qualifications, be orderly in your presentation, state the issues precisely and then stick with them, and use a disciplined imagination throughout.

Such a reverse application of the rules has its attendant difficulties. In the first place, it requires bringing to bear all of the skills that you have learned throughout your entire education, and not just a few simple principles.

Members of the U.S. Supreme Court, April 15, 1988. Front row, from left to right: Thurgood Marshall, William J. Brennan, Jr., Chief Justice William H. Rehnquist, Byron R. White, and Harry A. Blackmun. Standing, from left to right: Antonin Scalia, John Paul Stevens, Sandra Day O'Connor, and Anthony M. Kennedy.

Louis Auchincloss

FROM DIARY OF A YUPPIE

"I" am Robert Service, aged thirty-two, an associate in the law firm of Hoyt, Welles & Andrew (thirty-six partners, a hundred clerks), and I have been privately assured (not guaranteed—they never do that) of my ultimate promotion on the first day of this coming January, 1980. Partnership has been my sole ambition—you might even call it my obsession—throughout eight years of driving work, including most weekday nights and many weekends. And what do I feel, now that triumph is nigh? Very little.

I have become a specialist in corporate takeovers. The one I am working on now, under Branders Blakelock, is the bitterly contested bid of Atlantic Rylands to take control of Shaughnessy Products. We represent the aggressor (I use the word advisedly), and the "target" is engaging in every defense of the game, including the "scorched earth" policy of encumbering its properties with debts and long-term leases to discourage the predator. It is also starting up new lines of business, closely allied to Atlantic's, so that the latter may be faced with the menace of an antitrust suit in the event of victory. In such warfare all is fair.

Or should be. Mr. Blakelock is my problem. It has come about this way. A routine procedure is the search, sometimes through paid informers, for evidence of improper conduct of the officers of a target company. Armed with such a find, one can sometimes blackmail the target into a compromise or at least, by means of a derivative stockholders' suit, get rid of a troublesome officer. Examination of "abandoned property," a euphemism for the contents of the target's trash baskets, is often rewarding. Mr. Blakelock finds these tactics offensive, and I try to shield him from awareness of them, but I had to

---

Attorney and author Louis Auchincloss (1917–   ), scion of a prominent New York family, is a partner at New York's Hawkins, Delafield, and Wood. This excerpt is from his best-selling 1987 novel about an upwardly mobile young lawyer.

tell him about one shredded document, which we had pieced together, to get his permission to bring a suit against Albert Lamb, Shaughnessy's president.

It was a memorandum from an accountant to the company treasurer about Hendrickson Lamb, Albert's younger brother, an alcoholic with a sinecure job and a salary paid by Albert personally. The interesting part of the memorandum dealt with what appeared to be an embezzlement of company cash by the brother. The memo read: "As you know, it is Mr. Lamb's practice to refund such defalcations promptly from his own account."

So there it was. Perhaps not much, but enough to start a stockholders' suit seeking the removal of Albert Lamb from Shaughnessy. And Albert was causing Atlantic's biggest headache in the attempted takeover.

I knew that I should have trouble with Mr. Blakelock, and I waited for some time this morning for the right moment to break it to him. He had called me to his office to discuss a motion in the federal District Court that I am to argue next Monday. He has great confidence in himself as a coach and likes to imagine himself as an impresario, a kind of Svengali who can inspire or even hypnotize a disciple into a brilliant performance. I always sit patiently and silently through these sessions.

Indeed, I hardly look up at him. It is enough to sense him towering above me, standing tall and bony in one of those baggy black suits that he has worn throughout the eight years I have known him, booming or shrilling alternately down at me from the mahogany lectern at which he likes to stand as if he were some Abelard of old preaching to students.

"And remember, Robert, when you have finished your oral argument, don't trail off, or glance at your notes for some afterthought or final emphasis, but obey the immortal command of the late John W. Davis, the greatest pleader it was ever my privilege to hear"—here the reedy voice becomes suddenly stentorian—"and *sit down*!"

But this morning I am tired of it. The job has been too long and grinding, and it is not half done. The knowledge that I should soon be a partner has not brought the anticipated ecstasy but instead a quickening anxiety as to whether I have chosen the right firm. Of course, I have always been like that; foretasting is so much of my satisfaction that I rarely enjoy even a brief elation upon fruition. It seems to me that I am weary at last of Blakelock's paternalism. He has liked me, preferred me, per-Antinous? What is he, poor Bithynian lad, if not the beloved of Hadrian? I do not suggest that Blakelock has lascivious designs on me—nothing, I am sure, would shock him more, even in his most secret thoughts—but I do note that his protégés have all been handsome, and we know what a cesspool the subconscious can be. Or, to put it more innocently, perhaps he conceives of me as a kind of faithful wolfhound, crouched submissively at his side but ready at a signal to leap, to rush, to kill.

"Remember, also, Robert, that Judge Axeman, like so many of our federal bench, thinks of himself as a man who can change the world. While the president and Congress are paralyzed by party faction, *he* will ensure that discrimination shall be abolished, if he has to bus our youth a million miles a day; that votes shall be equal, if he has to redistrict all our states; and that the environment shall be preserved, if he must bring industry to a grinding halt! God bless him—I'm half on his side. But what, you will ask, can a reforming judge expect to accomplish in a corporate takeover? Is it not a case of two scorpions in a bottle? Perhaps. But remember that behind every judicial idealist there lurks a lover of power. Axeman likes to play with our big companies as a boy with an electric train. And that is where your role comes in. You must make him feel that the takeover of Shaughnessy Products is a more efficient way of distributing the loaves and fishes to the multitude! You must help him to don the toga of the public servant. Precedent must bow to the general welfare—that is, when precedent is against us!"

But I have heard it all before. Looking down the long oblong sparsely furnished chamber—two rather fine English cabinets, a Colonial bench and some wooden uncushioned armchairs, signed photographs of judges on the walls and "spy" cartoons of British lawyers—it strikes me that litigation has survived in a world of computers like a Toonerville trolley on the track of a Metroliner. Yet its very survival has made it curiously revered. The tricks and winks and chuckles of the courtroom technique, the voice of thunder, the sly insinuations, the throat clearings, the whispered conferences, the whole hammy vaudeville adored by judge and jury—and by television audiences—has become too sacred to be touched, has even in some crazy way taken the place of our empty churches as the shrine of the oldest American virtue.

It is now that I choose to blurt out my discovery about Lamb. It is not the right moment—it is never the right moment—but at least I have his attention.

"Where the hell did you dig that up?"

I hesitate. "Do you have to know?"

"I suppose it was an 'abandoned property' search? Very well, don't tell me. I don't want to know. You're surely not planning to use it?"

"Of course I am. I plan to use it as the basis of a suit to remove Lamb as c.e.o. of Shaughnessy."

"You've got to be crazy, Bob. I knew about Al's brother. He's a kind of kleptomaniac. Al has always looked after the poor nut."

"Nut? Has he been judicially declared incompetent?"

"Of course not. Al was much too proud. He handles his family problems himself. He's supported that brother all his life and put his son and daughter through college. He even manufactured a kind of career for him in Shaughnessy, at his own considerable expense. I never heard of anyone who did more for a sibling."

"But a brother's hand in the till is still a crime, isn't it? And isn't Albert's covering it up another?"

"I suppose, technically. But it can all be explained."

"Can it? And even if it can, would Albert Lamb like the exposure?"

"Hell, no! It would probably kill the poor loon of a brother."

"Then there you are. Albert will have another inducement to settle. Isn't that what we're after?"

"Robert, I can hardly believe my ears. Is it really you talking?"

"Do you suppose Albert Lamb would think twice before using a weapon like this against any officer of Atlantic?"

Blakelock has to pause at this. "Well, you have to remember that Albert feels that Atlantic is trying to destroy his very lifework in Shaughnessy. A man in that position gets pretty desperate. But you and I are not in that position, Bob."

"Our client is. Atlantic has very high stakes in this case. What can we lose, Mr. B, by taking the chance?"

"Nothing, I suppose, but honor."

"Where is that? Didn't we check it when we went into the takeover business? Why don't you let me try it, anyway? There's nothing like one bit of dirt to start up another. People hearing about the case may suddenly remember more. We may dig up enough dirt about Lamb to blow up his whole board of directors!"

"No! Never! I won't have it!"

His indignation makes me bold. "You talk about honor. What about duty to a client?"

"Can you really believe that it obliges me to pick up a tarnished piece of family gossip and puff it into a scandal that may destroy Albert's peace of mind and perhaps his brother's very life?"

"Why is that relevant? It's a fact, isn't it, that Albert Lamb covered up the crime of a junior officer? And isn't it our duty to use every fact at our disposal? Lamb knows that as well as we do. When he got into this fight he knew that everything in his past would be pored over and used. That's how the game is played, Mr. B, and what's more, I think it's basically how it was always played. Only today we're franker about it. And I think that's better."

"I think it's worse. Much worse. I think it's obscene, and there's no place in my law practice for obscenity."

In the silence following this I look up at last, intending defiantly to meet my boss's eyes. But he has turned his back to me, and his shoulders are stooped with what strikes me as a rather melodramatic expression of dismay and grief.

"You'd really sling that kind of mud, Robert?" the sad, now deep voice rumbles at me.

"I'd sling any mud I could make stick. Albert Lamb is the key to the whole defense."

"Even admitting it's mud?"

"But legal mud, Mr. B!"

"I had not been aware that mud observed these distinctions."

"Why shouldn't it?"

"Robert, you appall me. You would really, for a dubious advantage to a client, so bespatter your adversary?"

"You mean it would be all right if the advantage were less dubious?"

After another solemn silence Mr. Blakelock speaks with a faint note of weariness. "Let me put it very simply, then. This material will *not* be used."

"Can't we think it over for a day or so? Give me a little time to convince you."

"I'm not going to change my mind, Robert. The material on Lamb's brother will not be used by this firm in a derivative stockholders' suit or in any other way. I am no longer concerned about that. What concerns me much more is your amorality. It comes as a sad surprise to me. I feel almost as if I did not know you."

"Have you ever wanted to know me?"

"Go home, Robert! Go home before I lose my temper! Take the weekend off; stay away from the office. Tell you darling wife what you have told me and listen carefully to what she says. I miss my guess if she will not agree with me. Let her help you, my boy. Let her guide you! I fear I must have been a false leader."

"Mr. Blakelock—"

"Go home, son, go home! I've had enough of you for one day."

George Willoughby Maynard. *Justice*. Before 1898.
Mural. One of eight female figures, each 66″ high (167.6 cm).
Library of Congress, Washington, D.C.

INDEX

Page numbers in italic denote illustrations. Colorplate numbers are given in parentheses.

PHOTOGRAPHY CREDITS

p. 28: Scala/Art Resource, NY
p. 32: Alinari/Art Resource, NY
Colorplate 1: Scala/Art Resource, NY
Colorplate 3: Photo, Jörg P. Anders
Colorplate 5: Scala/Art Resource, NY
Colorplate 6: Scala/Art Resource, NY
Colorplate 9: Photo, H. Maertens
Colorplate 10: Photo, H. Maertens
Colorplate 11: Scala/Art Resource, NY
Colorplate 12: Scala/Art Resource, NY
Colorplate 13: Scala/Art Resource, NY
p. 50: Alinari/Art Resource, NY
p. 54: Scala/Art Resource, NY
p. 60: The Bettmann Archive
Colorplate 15: Oronoz, Madrid
Colorplate 18: Oronoz, Madrid
Colorplate 19: Scala/Art Resource, NY
Colorplate 21: Archiv für Kunst und Geschichte, Berlin
p. 80: Archiv für Kunst und Geschichte, Berlin
Colorplate 23: Giraudon/Art Resource, NY
Colorplate 24: Giraudon/Art Resource, NY
Colorplate 25: Photo, Alan Greeley
Colorplate 28: Scala/Art Resource, NY
Colorplate 29: Explorer-Archive, Paris
Colorplate 31: Giraudon/Art Resource, NY
Colorplate 34: Photo, Witkam en Zweerts
Colorplate 35: Photo, Alan Greeley
Colorplate 37: La Réunion des Musées Nationaux, Paris
p. 106: Ancient Art and Architecture Collection (Ronald Sheridan's Photo-Library), London
p. 108: Marburg/Art Resource, NY
Colorplate 43: Scala/Art Resource, NY
Colorplate 44: Giraudon/Art Resource, NY
Colorplate 48: Scala/Art Resource, NY
Colorplate 51: Archiv für Kunst und Geschichte, Berlin
Colorplate 52: Bridgeman/Art Resource, NY
p. 139: Giraudon/Art Resource, NY
p. 140: Photo, Joan Broderick
p. 149: Bettmann/Hulton
Colorplate 53: Scala/Art Resource, NY
Colorplate 54: Scala/Art Resource, NY
Colorplate 55: Scala/Art Resource, NY
Colorplate 56: Scala/Art Resource, NY
Colorplate 57: Scala/Art Resource, NY
Colorplate 58: Photo, Nicholas Whitman
Colorplate 59: Photo, Nicholas Whitman
p. 196: The Bettmann Archive
Colorplate 69: Giraudon/Art Resource, NY
Colorplate 70: Stein-Mason Studios
Colorplate 71: Stein-Mason Studios
Colorplate 73: Giraudon/Art Resource, NY
Colorplate 77: Giraudon/Art Resource, NY
p. 218: The Bettmann Archive
p. 219: Snark/Art Resource, NY
p. 226: Culver Pictures
p. 251: Courtesy, United States Air Force Art Collection
p. 252: Culver Pictures
p. 275: Culver Pictures
p. 277: The Bettmann Archive
p. 279: The Bettmann Archive
p. 282: The Bettmann Archive
p. 288: Brown Brothers
p. 303: The Bettmann Archive
p. 311: UPI/Bettmann Newsphotos
p. 315: Kobal Collection
p. 324: UPI/Bettmann Newsphotos
p. 337: UPI/Bettmann Newsphotos
Colorplate 108: Photo, Geoffrey Clements
Colorplate 111: Photo, Chris Eden
p. 368: UPI/Bettmann Newsphotos